★
A CIVILIAN'S
GUIDE TO THE
U.S. MILITARY

A Comprehensive Reference to the Customs, Language, & Structure of the Armed Forces

BARBARA SCHADING, PH.D.

with Richard Schading, U.S. Marine Corps
& Major Virginia Slayton, U.S. Army, (RET)

WRITER'S DIGEST BOOKS

writersdigest.com
Cincinnati, Ohio

Visit our Web sites at www.writersdigest.com and www.wdeditors.com for information on more resources for writers.

To receive a free weekly e-mail newsletter delivering tips and updates about writing and about Writer's Digest products, register directly at our Web site at http://newsletters.fwpublica tions.com.

15 14 13   9 8 7

Distributed in Canada by Fraser Direct, 100 Armstrong Avenue, Georgetown, ON, Canada L7G 5S4, Tel: (905) 877-4411; Distributed in the U.K. and Europe by David & Charles, Brunel House, Newton Abbot, Devon, TQ12 4PU, England, Tel: (+44) 1626 323200, Fax: (+44) 1626 323319, E-mail: postmaster@davidandcharles.co.uk; Distributed in Australia by Capricorn Link, P.O. Box 704, Windsor, NSW 2756 Australia, Tel: (02) 4577-3555

Library of Congress Cataloging-in-Publication Data

Schading, Barbara.

 The civilian's guide to the U.S. military / A comprehensive reference to the customs, language, and structure of the Armed Forces / by Barbara Schading, Ph.D. With Richard Schading, former Sergeant, U.S. Marine Corps And Virginia R. Slayton, Major, U.S. Army (RET). -- 1st edition.

    p. cm.

 Includes index.

  ISBN-13: 978-1-58297-408-8 (pbk. : alk. paper)

  ISBN-10: 1-58297-408-X (pbk. : alk. paper)

 1. United States--Armed Forces--Handbooks, manuals, etc. I. Schading, Richard. II. Slayton, Virginia R. III. Title.

 UA23.S298 2007

 355.00973--dc22

                    2006025881

Edited by Michelle Ehrhard

Designed by Claudean Wheeler

Production coordinated by Mark Griffin

F+W PUBLICATIONS, INC.

AUTHOR'S NOTE AND ACKNOWLEDGMENTS

The idea for this book came about as I sought useful information about the American military, but found it wasn't available in a simplified, cohesive source. Information was spotty and varied from tomes of dry statistics to in-depth descriptions of equipment to fictionalized "war stories" difficult to relate to. Vast quantities of details ever-present on the Internet and elsewhere often failed to cut to the nitty-gritty and present the basic facts cleanly and clearly. Incomprehensible acronyms and "Operation-This-or-That" left me feeling out of touch with what was going on with our military, and more importantly, why it was going on.

I believe that engaging in an academic discussion of, for example, whether the military should participate in a particular operation or another is meaningless unless one has a basic understanding of the military's function, its modes of operations, and its capabilities, at the very least. To the outsider, our military might seem to be merely flexing its muscles. Documentaries and war movies are often overdramatized with confusing terminology, equipment, and situations that are beyond the average civilian's experience. Even nightly newscasts from war zones have a surreal quality; how can these strange people in bizarre costumes be fighting for our freedom? Even with family members in or retired from the military, a full understanding of the total "package" is hard to obtain for many people. Likewise, while most military personnel are highly knowledgeable about their branch of service and are fiercely loyal to it, they often have a limited knowledge of the other branches. Family members of a new recruit would benefit greatly from a clear, concise explanation of what each branch does, what it represents, and what the fledgling member can expect to gain from his or her service commitments.

As a reader and writer, odd details of military life have always intrigued me. Mysterious things like the distinction between "special forces" and "Special Forces," and why the Navy "SEALs" never capitalize that last letter are puzzling. This was a wonderful opportunity for me to become knowledgeable about an important component of today's world, both within our country and outside of it.

Along the way, I've gained an immense appreciation for our men and women in the armed forces, and for their sacrifices, sometimes the supreme sacrifice, for our nation. All branches of the service have played an important role in our history and continue to be valuable today. All the components work together for the same purpose, like a massive body of water flowing in the same direction, and together, their strength is unsurpassed.

I truly believe that a good understanding of the subjects covered here is important for today's citizens of the world. Not only is it interesting, but we need to know the purpose of our military and how it evolved if we are to understand what it is doing around the world and at home. We must understand fundamentals like the difference between ranks to comprehend significant current events in which various levels of the military play a part. Understanding the significance of the Medal of Honor or why the flag is such a revered part of our nation's tradition are life lessons we all should learn. Comprehending the essence of the Missing Man Formation or learning the lyrics to the "Marine's Hymn" will bring understanding to why viewers weep or get goose bumps when they encounter these evocative symbols. We must never forget the rationale for the Geneva Convention if we are to evaluate our leaders and judge their actions in these arenas with good conscience and our own integrity.

The meanings of military traditions are often difficult for civilians to grasp. Customs may appear complex yet are sometimes painfully simple; many represent visceral and overpowering images that are fundamental to each branch. It is crucial to realize that nearly all military traditions stem from one simple concept: The men and women of the American military are willing to lay down their lives so that this nation can live in peace and freedom. There is nothing more honorable than that.

I wish to express my deep gratitude to each branch of our nation's military: the United States Army, Navy, Marine Corps, Air Force, and the Coast Guard, and all of the associated Reserves and National Guards for the assistance they provided in producing this book.

Military contacts providing assistance at varying levels included: former Sergeant Richard L. Schading, U.S. Marine Corps; Major Virginia R. Slayton, U.S. Army (RET); former Captain Herbert S. Harvis, U.S. Army; Colonel Bob Boswell, U.S. Air Force (RET); First Sgt. Donna Ferguson, U.S. Air Force, (RET); Chief Petty Officer Mike Setzer, U.S. Navy (RET); MKC Chief Bromley Ball, U.S. Coast Guard; MK1 Mark Carstens, U.S. Coast Guard; Steve Blando, Deputy Chief, Community Relations Branch, U.S. Coast Guard; Kelly A. Sherman, Office of the Chief of Public Affairs, U.S. Army-Pentagon; Dr. Betty D. Maxfield, Chief, Army Demographics Office, Office of the Deputy Chief of Staff for Personnel, U.S. Army; Captain Maureen Schumann, Air Force Branding and Trademark Licensing, U.S. Air Force; Jay Godwin, Heraldry Archivist, Air Force Historical

AUTHOR'S NOTE AND ACKNOWLEDGMENTS

Research Agency, U.S. Air Force; Kenneth E. Warren, Patrick AFB, U.S. Air Force; Dr. Buddy Coard, Defense Equal Opportunity Management, U.S. Army.

Other kind assistance was rendered by Desiree Day, USO Corporate Communications; Maria Trombly, Asia Bureau Chief, Securities Industry News; Rod Powers, www.military.com; Amy Lerner, Stackpole Books; Michael Leventhal, Greenhill Books; Jeff Block, www.GruntsMilitary.com; Veteran Sergeant of U.S. Marine Corps and Master Sgt. Glenn B. Knight, U.S. Air Force (RET); http://4mermarine.com/USMC/dictionary.html; Stanley Haas and the Institute of Heraldry for photos of medals; and a host of others I may have neglected to mention personally.

Editorial thanks go to Writer's Digest's executive editor, Jane Friedman, for believing in this project, and to my tireless managing editor, Michelle Ehrhard, for her constant assistance.

Special thanks to my husband, Dick Schading, for his collaboration and intensive efforts on my behalf, and always for his belief in me. Thanks also to my sister, Virginia R. Slayton, Major, U.S. ARMY (RET) for her collaboration and efforts on my behalf.

Any technical errors, either factual or by way of omission, are my fault alone.

A final heartfelt thank you to all the men and women of the American military. I am truly grateful for, and humbled by, your contributions.

I salute you all.

BARBARA SCHADING, PH.D., July, 2006

CONTENTS

FOREWORD

Today's military is comprised of men and women of all ranks, from all branches of service in the Active Duty, Reserve, and Guard. An understanding of the roles these members play in the world today starts with a broad knowledge of the responsibilities of each Service Department to which they are assigned. Each service is unique with a different mission, force structure, and capability. None can completely fulfill the mission of the other. No one service does it all.

To further comprehend today's American military personnel, one must look at the location and specific organization to which the member is assigned and the position the member occupies. Being able to recognize insignia representing the ranks of the members will help identify their individual duties and responsibilities. With a little practice, one can identity a Department of the Air Force member by his uniform, a captain by his insignia, and an F-15 pilot by his Silver Wings and unit patch.

The next challenge is understanding what the captain is talking about. Most military organizations have their own special set of behaviors, with unique dialogue and expressions. Based primarily on the English language, the daily rhetoric is rich in shortcut abbreviations, jargon, and slang terms. This tradition has evolved from the earliest recorded history, and these unique expressions and nicknames give the military a special character of its own. The reason for this complex jargon is that specific goals and objectives require immediate responses to both preplanned and unplanned events. Abbreviations necessarily simplify complex situations, equipment, operations, and actions; there is no room on the battlefield for long-winded terminology.

Interestingly, as these shortcut terms have developed, they often take on a life of their own. For example, terms that refer to an awkward official title may be reduced to a simplified acronym. Thus, an operational readiness inspection becomes the "ORI." As the daily use of the English language continues to evolve, so will the jargon of the military as it reflects the uniqueness of their character. An appreciation of this special language is helpful in identifying the roles and mission of our military forces, and understanding the integral part they play in supporting the United States at home and abroad.

In these times of active American military involvement around the world, citizen readers and writers alike will benefit from an overall understanding of the armed forces of the United States as a tool to understand the entire picture of America's role in the world. This guide provides concise insight into our military and its organization, members, and unique language.

COLONEL BOB BOSWELL, U.S. Air Force (RET)
The Retreat at Sun Tree

CHAPTER 1

MILITARY RANK AND PROTOCOL

★ INTRODUCTION ★

What would you think if you encountered the following paragraph in a novel?

> *When their car arrived at the port, the nuclear submarine was already docked, the stench of its diesel engines choking the air. The four conspirators flashed their faked credentials to the officer of the day with more bravado than any of them felt, but the officer merely nodded and led them to the front of the ship. Craning his neck to catch a glimpse of the fly-by of Navy F-15s that screamed overhead, the solitary Marine guard grinned at the officer and motioned with his M-1 rifle to let them pass. At the top of the gangplank, they were greeted by the officer of the deck, whom they'd been drilled to ask for permission to come aboard the ship. Their credentials were briefly inspected, accepted, and before their hearts began beating again, they found themselves ushered through the door to the captain's cabin and offered a stiff drink.*

If you have military training, you may spot at least ten fatal flaws in the five sentences above (see pages 24–25 for the mistakes). A writer committing these gaffes would instantly be branded with no credibility. Yet, many writers without military backgrounds still desire to create characters who have varying levels of military experience. Likewise, civilians who want to understand the guts and glory of our U.S. military may need to search dozens of Web sites to find a simple explanation. New recruits, their families, and those considering a military career would benefit from a single source of information clarifying the structure, mission, and terminology of each of the services.

That is the purpose of this book. *The Civilian's Guide to the U.S. Military* is a basic explanation of our armed forces, their organization and structure, and much more. For the writer or other civilian needing to understand the history and traditions within each branch of the military, it's all here in one location. We've included special sections listing common military abbreviations, acronyms, and expressions broken down by branch; rules for saluting and other aspects of protocol; and images of insignias worn by military personnel. Chapters describe the different special operations forces and the basic equipment used by each branch. The Geneva Conventions, which outline the "laws of war," are demystified. Details like the words to the hymns of each branch as well as the individual codes of conduct are spelled out. For the writer—or reader—who wishes to understand how the military has—or has not—changed over the years, an essay on this subject is included. We've also provided resources of interest including addresses, books, and Web sites.

This book does not attempt to compete with the volume of available material about the military. A recent Internet search on www.msn.com for the key words "U.S. military" yielded 14,352,638 hits; www.yahoo.com revealed even more: 86,500,000 hits. The intention of this work is to provide essential information in a concise and easy-to-read form.

★ GENDER IN THIS BOOK ★ AND WOMEN'S ROLE IN THE MILITARY

Strictly for linguistic convenience, the masculine pronoun is generally used here. We often simply use the term "men" as plural for soldiers and others. By no means does this imply that the female contribution to today's military is unnoticed or unappreciated. The American military asserts "today's military has no gender." That statement is *almost* true. Women are employed in nearly every branch, including most ranking positions. Opportunities for training in many areas formerly available only to men are now open to women. An exception is service in active fighting units such as infantry, artillery, armor, or special operations forces. Arguments for keeping women out of these units include: the possibility of inappropriate interactions ranging from distraction to romance to rape between men and women in both friendly and enemy forces; risk-taking by men on behalf of female soldiers; sexual harassment; the inherent "weaker" physical nature of women; and religious objections. Although these "justifications" can be strongly argued against, tradition in the American military and most other military programs maintains some limitations for women. Overall, in today's armed forces, women are effective and valuable members, and many find challenging and rewarding careers as leaders.

★ MILITARY RANK ★

The structure of military rank is probably the most confusing aspect of military life for civilians. This system for naming, numbering, and distinguishing the "pecking order" is what drives nearly all interactions in the military. It is a multi-tiered division of personnel that signifies who answers to whom and who has what responsibilities—an arrangement complicated by minor variations in each branch of the military. Civilian readers, take heart. It's just as confounding to new recruits, who must memorize and respond to ranks and associated insignia very early in their training.

All American military services follow the same general command structure with three military rank categories of enlisted personnel, noncommissioned officers, and commissioned officers. See appendix B for a description of the rank series for each service. Note the distinction between rank (e.g., private first class, sergeant, major) and pay grade (e.g., E-2, E-5, O-4). Pay grades are designated levels of salary. For example, "E" stands for "enlisted," and "O" refers to "officer." The lowest pay grades are E-1 and O-1; they rise in sequence to E-9 and O-10, indicating the top of the service. Service members often refer to each other by pay grade, which can identify rank to another military person.

ENLISTED. Enlisted personnel make up the bulk of military manpower. They are just beginning their careers in the military and are in pay grades E-1 to E-4 (E-3 for the Navy and the Marine Corps). They are often young and experiencing their first time away from home after high school. Some have college credits or two-year degrees, and a few may have four-year college degrees. Some enter the service to learn a trade for use after their enlistment is completed; others may wish to take advantage of military benefits such as college funds. Many have a sense of patriotism and are looking for the adventure, travel, and new experiences offered by military service.

Pay grade E-1 personnel are called privates in the Army and Marines, and seaman apprentices in the Navy and Coast Guard. Air Force enlistees are airmen basic at pay grade E-1 during basic training. After graduation they may advance to pay grades E-2 and E-3.

NONCOMMISSIONED OFFICERS. The second level of the command structure includes noncommissioned officers, often called "NCOs," who provide direct tactical leadership in combat units, technical skills, and direction in support commands. Generally, noncommissioned officers provide direct supervision and leadership of enlisted personnel. Noncommissioned officers are in pay grades E-5 to E-9; the Marines and Navy also include pay grade E-4 (Marine corporals and Navy petty officers 3rd class) because they have small unit leadership responsibilities. NCOs are well-educated. All must be high school graduates, and many have two- or four-year college degrees or additional advanced training pertaining to their specific military occupational specialties.

Promotion to noncommissioned officer is always by advancement through the ranks. Promotion criteria differ between services but are usually based on time in present grade and overall time in service, on performance reviews, and on recommendations by superiors. Several branches of the military use standardized tests, particularly in more technical fields.

The command structure for noncommissioned officers is separated into two categories: junior NCO and staff NCO. *Junior NCOs* (in pay grades E-4 and E-5 in the Navy and Marines, and E-5 in the Army, Air Force, and Coast Guard) have leadership responsibility for small units such as a machine gun section of four to five men or a small section in a technical unit. S*taff NCOs* (in pay grades E-6 to E-9) are committed to careers in the military. They are used as platoon leaders in the Army and Marines or as section chiefs in the Navy, with command of forty to fifty personnel. Staff NCOs provide hands-on leadership to progressively larger units and may also hold administrative positions and work as senior advisors to commanders regarding enlisted personnel.

The pinnacle of achievement for an enlisted person is to serve as the senior enlisted member for their respective service. This individual (designated by pay grade E-9) is the sergeant major of the Army, master chief petty officer of the Navy, sergeant major of the Marine Corps, chief master sergeant of the Air Force, or master chief petty officer of the Coast Guard. In this position, they are the spokespersons for the enlisted forces at the very highest level.

It is important to note that NCOs at equal pay grades do not necessarily hold the same rank. For example, an E-4 specialist and an E-4 corporal in the Army have the same pay grade, but because the corporal is trained in combat arms and has leadership responsibilities, he outranks the technical specialist. In the Marine Corps, a master gunnery sergeant and a sergeant major are both at pay grade E-9, but the sergeant major has the higher rank. He or she has command responsibilities, while the master gunnery sergeant has primarily technical duties.

COMMISSIONED OFFICERS. In the armed forces, commissioned officers have the most responsibility for personnel and materials. As one advances through the ranks, responsibilities increase. Officers hold presidential commissions and are confirmed in their ranks by the U.S. Senate. The lowest-ranking officer is a second lieutenant in the Army, Air Force, and Marines, or an ensign in the Navy and Coast Guard (at the pay rate O-1). The highest rank is a four-star general or admiral (an O-10).

The *warrant officer* is a special classification of commissioned officer. Warrant officers do not typically serve in command situations, but are commissioned for their technical skills and expertise; e.g., helicopter pilots in the Army. (The Air Force, incidentally, does not have warrant officers.) Technically, the lowest-ranking commissioned officer in any service is superior in rank to the most senior NCO. In reality, the noncommissioned officer's responsibilities are usually much greater than those of a junior commissioned officer. Warrant officers are in separate pay grades of W-1 to W-5; chief warrant officers are in pay grades WO-1 to CWO-5.

Commissioned officers are typically college educated and are often members of Reserve Officer Training Corps (ROTC) while in college. Or they may be commissioned from the enlisted ranks after serving with exemplary performance and attending officer training school. Many career officers receive advanced degrees from the specialized military college for their branch of the armed forces.

The officer corps is divided roughly into three basic categories: junior or company grade, field or mid grade, and general or flag grade officers.

Newly commissioned officers in pay grades O-1 to O-3 are termed *company grade* officers in the Army, Marines, and Air Force, or *junior officers* in the Navy and Coast Guard. They typically have advanced training in their specialties and are in command of small units, albeit under close supervision. More experienced O-3 officers may command several hundred men and have more independence of command. Company grade ranks in the Army, Marines, and Air Force are second lieutenant, first lieutenant, and captain. Junior grade ranks in the Navy and Coast Guard are ensign, lieutenant junior grade, and lieutenant.

Field grade or *mid grade* officers are in pay grades O-4 to O-6. The ranks include major, lieutenant colonel, and colonel. These officers typically have between ten and twenty-five years of service. They are well-educated, and many hold master's and doctoral degrees. They are in command of entire operational units such as Marine Corps regiments, Air Force wings, or large Navy ships.

General or flag grade officers are in pay grades O-7 and higher. The ranks start with one-star brigadier general in the Army, Marines, and Air Force, or rear admiral (lower half) in the Navy and Coast Guard, and end at four-star general and admiral. These officers are seldom in direct command of troops. Instead, they command very large units such as divisions, fleets, and Army groups. Very senior general officers often hold senior staff positions in their services' headquarters at the Pentagon.

★ PROTOCOL ★

Military life is full of tradition, formality, and custom. Protocol is inherent to tradition and is fundamental to any military operation. These "rules" are essential for a large organization to function over wide distances or in isolation as may happen in war. Order and accountability are maintained through the traditions of protocol—it's one of the components that makes the military "work" so successfully. Some matters of protocol discussed here include titles of address, respect to the flag, saluting, military occasions, and precedence among the branches of the military.

Titles of Address

Military personnel must use certain forms of address. If they do not, their military career will be short-lived at best. Civilians interacting with military personnel in an official capacity are also expected to show respect by using the proper address. Within the military, proper address is by title or grade. A junior ranking individual may address a senior officer by his or her rank and last name, or merely as "Sir" or "Ma'am." But they may never use the first name. One must not assume a ranking officer is a "he": Rank has no gender.

EXAMPLES OF PROPER ADDRESS. The following are some examples of how to properly address military personnel. Note that the traditions of address are idiosyncratic.

- Lieutenant Colonel Smith is addressed as "Colonel Smith." Likewise, lieutenant generals, brigadier generals, and major generals are all addressed as "General."

- Lieutenants are addressed as "Lieutenant." "First" and "Second" are used in written form only.

- Master Sergeant Parker is called "Master Sergeant Parker" or merely "Sergeant Parker."

- Chief Master Sergeant Spencer is called "Chief Spencer," never "Sergeant Spencer."

- Senior officers may refer to junior officers by their last name, but the informality is not reciprocated.

- Since warrant officers formally rank below second lieutenant and above cadet, they are extended the same privileges and respect as commissioned officers. Essentially, warrant officers are top-grade specialists, with regulated restrictions on command functions. They are addressed as "Mr.," "Miss," or "Mrs.," and sometimes informally as "Chief."

- All chaplains are addressed as "Chaplain" regardless of military grade or official title.

- Cadets of the U.S. Military Academy are addressed as "Cadet," or informally as "Mr.," or "Miss."

- Sergeants major are addressed as "Sergeant Major," and a first sergeant is addressed as "First Sergeant." Other sergeants are addressed as "Sergeant," and a corporal is addressed as "Corporal." Specialists are addressed as "Specialist," and privates are generally orally addressed by their last name only, though the full title "Private _____" is used in written communications.

General Etiquette

Courtesy is a fundamental element of military life. The basics include:

- Phrases like "please" and "thank you" are expected whenever appropriate.
- Formal address for civilian employees is expected. Thus, use "Mr.," "Mrs.," or "Ms." together with a last name.
- Gossip is minimized.
- Being on time is expected.
- Telephone etiquette is formal.
- The senior person receives the position of honor. The junior takes the position to the senior's left.
- Personnel should exit a vehicle when replying to a senior member who is not in the vehicle.
- Vehicles or small boats are entered in order of reverse rank, with lowest rank entering first.
- Respect for authority is both expected and demanded. (Personal admiration, however, is not demanded—you don't have to like your superior officers, just obey them.)
- All service members extend the same courtesies to all members of other services, and likewise, courtesies extend to friendly armed forces of the United Nations.
- When in doubt, follow the lead of other military personnel in the immediate vicinity.

Respect for the American Flag

The American flag is the principal symbol of our country and represents the men and women who died for it and who gave us the freedoms we enjoy today. As such, it must never be abused or mistreated. To the men and women of the American military who risk their lives for what this flag symbolizes, "freedom of expression" never includes any form of disrespect for the flag.

Respect for the flag is integral to the military tradition. "Respect" in this usage has specific meaning and is not a trifling matter or optional consideration. The following describes how this respect is carried out.

Military personnel in uniform outdoors face the flag and salute during the raising and lowering of the flag. Upon hearing the National Anthem or reveille (the bugle call to wake personnel at sunrise), personnel in uniform (but not in formation), stand and face the flag (or the sound of the music if the flag is not visible), and salute. The salute is held until the music has ended. Vehicles in motion stop at the first note of the music and occupants sit quietly for the duration.

If in civilian clothes, face the flag or the source of the music if no flag is visible, and stand at attention with the right hand over the heart for the duration of the music.

If indoors during retreat or reveille, there's no need to stand or salute. Everyone stands during the playing of the National Anthem before the showing of a movie while in a base theater. While listening to the Anthem on the radio or on television, no action is necessary.

Basic Flag Etiquette

SALUTING THE FLAG. When the flag approaches to approximately six paces from the viewer, the viewer salutes and holds the salute until the flag has passed six paces beyond. If outdoors during the raising and lowering of the flag, military personnel in uniform face the flag and salute. One should salute the flag at the first note of the National Anthem (or the first note of reveille) and hold the salute until the last note is played. A folded flag is considered cased and does not require a salute.

WHEN IN CIVILIAN ATTIRE. Instead of saluting, personnel come to attention, remove their hat, and place their hand over their heart for the six-pace duration. Women do not remove their hats, but should place their right hand, palm open, over their heart. When in athletic clothing, individuals face the flag or music, remove their hat or cap, and stand at attention; a hand salute is not given.

Carrying the Flag

WHEN MARCHING. The flag is carried on the right in any procession or parade. If there are other flags, the American flag is carried in the front center position.

WHEN CARRYING A FLAG. The flag is held at a slight angle from the carrier's body. It may also be carried with one hand, resting the staff on the right shoulder.

Displaying the Flag Outdoors

ON A VEHICLE. The flag is attached to the antenna or the flagstaff is clamped to the right fender. Never lay the flag over the vehicle.

ON A BUILDING. The flag is hung on a staff or on a rope over the sidewalk with the stars away from the building. A flag is never used as decoration; bunting should be used instead.

OVER THE STREET. The flag is hung with the stars to the east on a north-south street or north on an east-west street.

WITH OTHER FLAGS ON THE SAME POLE. The flag is hung above any other flag on the same pole.

WITH OTHER FLAGS ON SEPARATE POLES. All flags are hung on equal poles. The American flag is hung so that it is on its own, right of the other flags, and is always hoisted first and lowered last. *Note:* International usage forbids that any one nation's flag be displayed above another nation's flag during times of peace.

WITH ANOTHER FLAG ON CROSSED STAFFS. The American flag should be on the right and its staff should be in front of the staff of the other flag.

IN A WINDOW. The flag is hung vertically with the stars to the left of anyone looking at it from the street.

HALF-MAST. This is a sign of mourning. The flag is raised to the top of the pole then lowered to the half-mast point. Before it is lowered again at the end of the day, it is raised to the top first.

UPSIDE DOWN. An upside-down flag signals distress or a call for help.

Displaying the Flag Indoors

MULTIPLE STAFFS. If the flag is displayed on a staff with other non-national flags around it, the American flag should appear at the center and highest point. For crossed staffs, the American flag should be higher and on the right.

BEHIND A SPEAKER. The flag is hung flat on the wall, with the stars to the left. Never decorate the podium or table with the flag. Use bunting instead.

NEXT TO A SPEAKER. The flag is placed in a stand on the speaker's right. The same placement is used for a religious service.

IN A HALL OR LOBBY. The flag is hung vertically across from the main entrance with the stars to the left of anyone coming through the door.

ON A CASKET. The flag is draped with the stars at the head and over the left shoulder of the body. The flag is not lowered into the grave.

Disposing of a Worn American Flag

As the predominant symbol of American freedom, American flags should never be thrown in the trash or treated with disrespect. Worn or faded flags should not be left on display or left out in the elements. The exception for display of worn flags is if the particular flag is highly symbolic (e.g., the flag from the ruins of the World Trade Center after September 11, 2001). Old, worn or tattered flags should be taken to the local American Legion or VFW post for proper and respectful disposal. Alternately, they may be disposed of in the following formal manner:

1. The flag should be folded in its customary manner.
2. A fire should be large enough and hot enough to ensure complete burning of the flag.
3. Place the flag on the fire.
4. Individuals come to attention, salute the flag, recite the Pledge of Allegiance, and observe a brief period of silent reflection.
5. After the flag is completely consumed, the fire should then be safely extinguished and the ashes buried.

Saluting

BACKGROUND. The custom of the hand salute dates to Roman times when citizens wanting to meet with a public official were required to raise their hand to show they held no weapons. It has become a common practice to indicate respect and formerly included removing the hat. Inconvenience—and wear and tear on the hat—reduced the motion to a mere touch of the hat by the early 1800s. By midcentury, the salute was again reduced, to an open hand, palm to the front. The U.S. military salute was influenced by the British Navy, which presents the hand turned 90 degrees to prevent the customary white gloves from being presented if dirty. This is the hand salute used today. It is a respectful tradition that binds military personnel together.

★ SALUTES ★

The Hand Salute

The hand salute consists of two parts, performed in two counts. On count one, the individual raises the right hand smartly and as directly as possible while extending and joining the fingers. The palm is flat and faces the body. The thumb is aligned with the forefingers, with the palm flat and forming a straight line between the fingertips and elbows. Tilt the palm slightly toward the face. Hold the upper arm horizontal, slightly forward of the body, parallel to the ground. Ensure the tip of the middle finger touches the right front corner of the headdress. If wearing a nonbilled hat, ensure the middle finger touches the outside corner of the right eyebrow or the front corner of glasses. The rest of the body remains at a position of attention. On count two, bring the arm smoothly and smartly downward, retracing the path used to raise the arm. Cup the hand as it passes the waist and return to the position of attention. When returning an individual salute, the head and eyes are always turned toward the person saluted. When in formation, the position of attention is always maintained unless otherwise directed.

The Heart Salute

The heart salute (placing the hand over the heart) is used at a military funeral, all personnel dressed in civilian clothes salute the deceased; males in civilian clothes and uncovered (i.e., not wearing a hat), and females in civilian clothes and covered or uncovered, use the heart salute during the playing of the National Anthem, *To the Color,* or *Hail to the Chief.* It is also used as described previously as a courtesy to the National Anthem.

SALUTE TO HIGHER RANKS. Military personnel salute a higher-ranking individual and receive a salute in return. Enlisted members do not customarily salute among themselves. Generally:

• Enlisted members salute officers or warrant officers.

- Warrant officers salute senior warrant officers and commissioned officers.

- Commissioned officers salute senior commissioned officers.

WHO GETS SALUTED. As commander-in-chief of the military, the president of the United States is always saluted. Commissioned officers, warrant officers, and Medal of Honor recipients are saluted. Officers of friendly foreign nations are saluted as well. On military bases, staff cars are saluted when occupied. The Colors (i.e., the American flag) is saluted.

OCCASIONS FOR SALUTES. Salutes are expected when the National Anthem, *To the Color, Hail to the Chief,* or foreign national anthems are played. Salutes are rendered on ceremonial occasions (e.g., military parades), and at reveille and retreat ceremonies during raising and lowering of the flag. Salutes are also rendered when the Pledge of Allegiance is recited outdoors, during sounding of honors, when turning over control of formations, and when rendering reports.

SALUTING SPECIFICS. The "rules" of saluting include the following, assuming you are the lesser ranking individual:

- You salute the superior-ranking individual first, and he returns your salute in acknowledgment.

- You salute superior-ranking individuals of all branches of the military.

- If you approach a group of superior-ranking individuals, you salute to the group, not to each individual. The salute is intended for the group as a whole and is not specific to the highest-ranking individual.

- A salute is rendered quickly, within approximately six paces of the higher-ranking individual.

- The senior person generally approaches on the right for ease of saluting.

- If you are running, come to a walk before saluting.

- You face toward the person or colors you are saluting if not already facing them.

- The smartness of your salute indicates your pride in your military responsibilities; careless or half-hearted salutes are discourteous.

WHEN SALUTES ARE *NOT* REQUIRED. Salutes are not required under certain situations. These may include:

- When indoors, do not salute except when reporting for duty to an officer.

- No salutes are rendered to persons on guard if the specific duty they are engaged in prevents saluting. Sentinels armed with a pistol do not salute after challenging. They stand at Raise Pistol until the challenged party has passed.

- If you are under arms (e.g., a guard on duty) you do not generally salute anyone regardless of rank or situation as it might compromise your responsibility. In some instances, there are salutes prescribed for the weapon with which they are armed.

- If you are "in-country," that is, in a combat situation, you never salute your superiors. Enemy snipers seek out superior ranking individuals as targets. A superior officer who believes that you are about to salute him may even salute you first to avoid being targeted by a sniper.

- When addressing a prisoner, do not salute.

- When driving a vehicle, while the vehicle is in motion, do not salute.

- When saluting is inappropriate, impractical, or dangerous, it is not necessary to do so. For example, if your hands are full, you are not expected to salute (although a verbal greeting is expected).

- When in formation, e.g., on a march, do not salute.

- In public (i.e., nonmilitary) places or situations, saluting is not necessary. You don't need to salute a senior officer while at a football game or at the grocery store.

- Civilians do not salute military personnel or other civilians.

- When actively working as a group, for example, an officer or a noncommissioned officer in charge will salute or acknowledge salutes for the entire group, as long as he is not actively engaged at the time.

GROUP SALUTES. *In the Mess Room:* When an officer enters a mess room or mess tent, enlisted personnel seated at meals remain seated at ease and continue eating unless the officer directs otherwise. An individual addressed by the officer ceases eating and sits at attention until the conversation is completed. *In the Squad Room:* When an officer enters a squad room or tent, individuals rise and uncover (i.e., remove their hats), and stand at attention. If more than one person is present, the first to see the officer calls, "Attention," to alert the others. In officers' quarters, this courtesy is not observed.

COVERING AND UNCOVERING. Removing the head cover is traditional in many circumstances. *Note:* Sentinels over prisoners *never* uncover. Officers and enlisted personnel should uncover when:

- seated as a member of, or in attendance on, a court or board
- entering places of divine worship
- indoors when not on duty and it is desired to remain informal
- in attendance at official receptions

★ SALUTES AND HONORS RENDERED TO ★ DISTINGUISHED MILITARY AND CIVIL OFFICIALS

Certain military and civil officials in high positions, including foreign officials, are accorded personal honors, which include canon salutes, ruffles, and flourishes played by field music, the National Anthem of our country or of the foreign country, or the General's March, or another march played by the band. These honors are extended upon presentation of the escort and as part of the parade or review of troops. "Ruffles" are notes played on drums; "flourishes" are notes played on bugles. The notes are sounded together: once for each star of the general officer being honored. They are followed by the appropriate music according to the table below (reproduced from *The Army Officer's Guide*, 43rd Edition, Lt. Col. Lawrence P. Crocker, U.S. Army (RET), Stackpole Books).

The music indicated follows the ruffles and flourishes immediately. Unless otherwise directed, civilian officials of the Department of Defense and military department officials will receive the "march:" the 32-bar medley in the trio of "The Stars and Stripes Forever." Foreign military receive the same honors due the American official of equivalent rank. Note that a designated representative of an official entitled to honors is given the honors due the representative, not the person he is representing. The person being honored salutes at first note of the ruffles and flourishes, and remains at the salute until the last note of the music. Persons in civilian clothes salute by uncovering. Military personnel witnessing salutes and honors give the hand salute; individuals in civilian clothes uncover.

ENTITLEMENT TO HONORS	NUMBER OF GUNS			MUSIC	
GRADE, TITLE, OR OFFICE	Arrival	Departure	Ruffles & Flourishes	SONG PERFORMED	
President	21	21	4	National Anthem or "Hail to the Chief"	
Ex-President or President-Elect	21	21	4	National Anthem	
Sovereign, Chief of a State of a foreign country, or member of a reigning royal family	21	21	4	Foreign country's national anthem	
Vice President	19	x	4	"Hail Columbia"	
Speaker of the House of Representatives	19	x	4	March	
American or foreign ambassador or high commissioner	19	x	4	National anthem of official's country	
Premier or Prime Minister	19	x	4	National anthem of United States or official's country	
Secretary of Defense	19	19	4	March	
Cabinet Member, President Protempore of Senate, State Governor, or Chief Justice of the U.S.	19	x	4	March	
Deputy Secretary of Defense	19	19	4	March	
Secretary of the Army, Navy, or Air Force	19	19	4	March	

Directory of Defense Research and Engineering	19	19	4	March
Chairman, Joint Chiefs of Staff	19	19	4	General's or Admiral's March
Chief of Staff, U.S. Army; Chief of Naval Operations; Chief of Staff, U.S. Air Force; or Commandant of the Marine Corps	19	19	4	General's or Admiral's March
General of the Army, Fleet Admiral or General of the Air Force	19	19	4	General's or Admiral's March
Assistant Secretaries of Defense and General Counsel of the Department of Defense	17	17	4	March
General or Admiral	17	17	4	General's or Admiral's March
Governor of a Territory or foreign possession	17	x	4	March
Chairman of a Congressional Committee	17	x	4	March
Under Secretary of the Army, Navy, or Air Force	17	17	4	March
Assistant Secretaries of the Army, Navy, or Air Force	17	17	4	March
American and foreign envoys or ministers	15	x	3	March
Lieutenant general or vice admiral	15	x	3	General's or Admiral's march.

Major general or rear admiral (upper half)	13	x	2	General's or Admiral's march
American ministers resident and ministers resident	13	x	2	March
American charges d'affaires and charges d'affaires	11	x	1	March
Brigadier general or rear admiral (lower half)	11	x	1	General's or Admiral's march
Consuls general	11	x	x	March

Precedence of Military Organizations in Formation

Whenever different components of the armed forces appear in the same formation, such as marching in a parade, they take precedence among themselves in a certain order. Thus, cadets march first, followed by each branch in the order that it was officially recognized as a distinct part of the U.S. military. The full breakdown of "who goes first" is as follows:

1. Cadets, U.S. Military Academy
2. Midshipmen, U.S. Naval Academy
3. Cadets, U.S. Air Force Academy
4. Cadets, U.S. Coast Guard Academy
5. U.S. Army
6. U.S. Marine Corps
7. U.S. Navy
8. U.S. Air Force
9. U.S. Coast Guard
10. Army National Guard
11. Army Reserve
12. Marine Reserve

13. Naval Reserve

14. Air National Guard

15. Air Force Reserve

16. Coast Guard Reserve

17. Other Reserve training organizations of the Army, Marine Corps, Navy, Air Force, and Coast Guard (in that order).

Note: During any time when the Coast Guard operates as part of the Navy (during wartime only), the cadets of the U.S. Coast Guard Academy, the U.S. Coast Guard, and the Coast Guard Reserve will take precedence, respectively, next after the midshipmen, U.S. Naval Academy, the U.S. Navy, and the Naval Reserve.

Military Funerals

CEREMONIAL CUSTOM OF MILITARY FUNERALS. Elements of contemporary military funerals are derived from ancient military usage and sometimes from the conveniences taken on battlefields long ago. Covering the casket with a flag originated with the custom of wrapping the bodies of dead infantrymen in the field, using the flag as a pall to carry the soldier. The laying of an American flag across the casket symbolizes that the soldier served in the Armed Forces and that the United States now bears the sacred and solemn responsibility of burying the soldier. The sounding of "Taps" over the grave recalls the last bugle call the soldier hears at night and signifies the beginning of a long sleep with hopes for reveille (signifying life in the hereafter) to come.

COURTESIES AT A MILITARY FUNERAL. All uniformed personnel attending military funerals face the casket and execute the hand salute when the casket is being moved, while the casket is being lowered into the grave, during the firing of the volley, and while "Taps" is being sounded. Honorary pallbearers in uniform do the same when not in motion. Men in civilian clothes stand at attention, uncovered, and hold the headdress over the left breast or just hold the empty hand there if no cover is worn. Women in civilian clothes will hold their right hands over their hearts. Female military personnel remain covered during military funerals. All personnel bow their heads at the words, "Let us pray." Active pallbearers remain covered and do not salute while carrying the casket and while holding the flag over the casket during the service at the grave.

BADGE OF MILITARY MOURNING. A straight black crepe or plain black cloth band four inches wide is worn around the left sleeve of the outer garment above the elbow to signify mourning. No badge of military mourning is worn with the uniform except when prescribed by the commanding officer or when specially ordered by the Department of the Army. As family mourners, officers are permitted to wear the sleeve band while at the funeral or enroute to or from the funeral.

THE MILITARY FUNERAL CEREMONY. The military funeral is laced with ceremony that signifies the services and sacrifices the soldier has made with the recognition of the debt the nation owes the deceased. The casket is covered with the American flag. Traditionally, it is transported on a casket carriage known as a caisson; often a light civilian hearse, truck, or ambulance is adapted for this purpose. Six military body bearers carry the casket to the grave, while honorary pallbearers march alongside the caisson. At the cemetery, the casket is placed over the grave and the body bearers hold the flag-pall waist high over the casket. A committal service is read by the chaplain, and then a firing party fires three volleys with rifles. This tradition has been in use since the seventeenth century, and is perhaps linked to the Roman custom of casting earth on the grave and saying the name of the deceased and "Farewell" three times. Following the volley, a bugler stationed at the head of the grave plays "Taps" over the casket to complete the funeral. The body bearers then fold the flag and present it to the next of kin.

Military Weddings

At military weddings, officers wear their appropriate dress uniform complete with medals, ribbons, and badges. The national and unit colors are crossed above and behind the chaplain.

Rank Has Its Privileges

PERKS OF RANK. While in some instances rank has no bearing in the military, differential rank is applied in many ways, none the least of which includes who gets preferential treatment. Thus, generals get better treatment than lieutenants who get better treatment than privates. Such privileges are considered perks for services rendered and for the increased responsibility the higher-ranking person is given. Basics like the type of quarters on base or the quality of transportation are meted out according to rank. The higher the rank, the better and bigger the quarters or the vehicle, and so on.

"I WISH" AND "I DESIRE." When commanding officers state, "I wish" or "I desire," it means, "I order you to do" whatever is the wish or desire.

PLACE OF HONOR. The place of honor is on the right. A junior riding, walking, or seated with a senior is always positioned on the left. The senior enters a door first; if walking together, the junior is expected to walk in step with the senior then step back and allow the senior to "arrive" first.

"SIR/MA'AM." All soldiers addressing an officer or the junior officer addressing a senior officer must use "Sir" or "Ma'am" to precede a report, a query, or to follow the answer to a question—every time, without fail.

COMMANDING OFFICER DEPARTS FIRST. All other officers remain at receptions or social gatherings until the commanding officer has left.

Military Taboos

UNIFORM MUST BE RESPECTED. The uniform represents the soldier, the branch of the military to which he is attached, and the country. While in uniform, soldiers are expected to behave appropriately, especially officers. The cleanliness, crispness, and smartness of the uniform reflects on the soldier's attitude towards himself, the military, and his country.

FRATERNIZATION. Fraternization, the term for relationships other than strictly business, is prohibited between enlisted soldiers and officers. Socialization, gambling, drinking, dating, cohabitation, sexual relationships, etc., are all included in the term "fraternization." It is an offense subject to court martial. The reason for this "tradition" is the compromise (or possibility of) of the chain of command, the appearance of partiality, undermining of order, discipline, authority, or morale. Thus, it is not for minor or merely old-fashioned reasons that fraternization is considered a crime.

Fictionalizing the Military

The following paragraph shows the serious mistakes that were made in the paragraph presented at the beginning of the chapter (on page 3). Particular errors are indicated and explained below.

What's wrong with the following paragraph?

When their car arrived at the port **1**, the nuclear submarine was already docked, the stench of its diesel engines **2** choking the air. The four conspirators flashed their faked credentials **3** to the officer of the day with more bravado than any of them felt, but he merely nodded and led them to the front **4** of the ship **5**. Craning his neck **6** to catch a glimpse of the fly-by of Navy F-15s **7** that screamed overhead, the solitary **8** Marine guard grinned at the officer **9** and motioned **10** with his M-1 rifle **11** to let them pass. At the top of the gangplank, they were greeted by the officer of the deck, whom they'd been drilled to ask for permission to come aboard the ship. Their credentials were briefly inspected **12**, accepted, and before their hearts began beating again, they found themselves ushered through the door **13** to the captain's cabin and offered a stiff drink **14**.

1. A nuclear submarine would be located at a base, not merely at a port.

2. Nuclear submarines do not require diesel fuel; they're nuclear powered.

3. Visitors to a nuclear sub do not flash their credentials; they are inspected carefully, both at the base entrance and at the sub.

4. The "front" of a vessel is called the "bow."

5. Submarines are not called "ships"; they are "boats."

6. A Marine guard does not crane his neck while on duty. Guard duty is a formal affair and Marines take it very seriously.

7. The Navy does not fly F-15s. That's the Air Force.

8. There would be more than one guard at a nuclear sub, which is a high-security situation.

9. Marine guards do not grin while on duty, and never at an officer. Again, that is too informal, and not like a Marine guard.

10. Marine guards do not motion with their weapons.

11 M-1 rifles were standard issue of the 1940-1950s; nuclear submarines were introduced in a later era.

12 Security on a nuclear submarine involves more than brief inspections of credentials.

13 "Doors" are called "hatches" upon any maritime vessel.

14 Visitors will not receive a stiff drink on a nuclear submarine, not even in the captain's cabin.

CHAPTER 2

Understanding the U.S. Army

★ OVERVIEW AND MISSION ★

The United States Army is the largest branch of the military and serves as the land-based fighting machine of the country. Its mission is to fight and win the nation's wars by providing prompt land dominance when and where needed. Officially, this mission is carried out primarily via deterrence, but in reality, the Army is the team in for the long haul. Army operations range from counter-drug operations to local or global warfare.

★ BRIEF HISTORY ★

The first regular U.S. fighting force, the Continental Army, was founded by the Continental Congress on June 14, 1775, to supplement local militias in the American Revolution. It was placed under the control of a five-member civilian board, and U.S. military forces have notably remained in civilian control ever since. In 1789, the civilian Department of War was established, and the U.S. Constitution named the president as commander-in-chief. The Continental Army was officially disbanded in 1783, but a small regular army was established.

Thereafter, the army's size increased during times of crisis, expanded with conscription, and decreased during peacetime. In 2004, there were approximately 500,000 soldiers on active duty.

The U.S. Army has seen action in every major conflict since the Revolution, including the War of 1812, the Mexican War, the Civil War, the Indian Wars, the Spanish-American War, World War I, World War II, Korea, Vietnam, the Gulf Wars, and the Iraq War. Conscription first occurred during the Civil War, Volunteer units were used during the Spanish-American War. Afterwards, a regular army, state militias, and a national army were formed. During World War I, the "National Army" was formed. After the conflict, it was demobilized and replaced with the Regular Army, Organized Reserve Corps, and state militias. In 1941, the Army of the United States was officially established and operated with the Regular Army, the National Guard, the Officer/Enlisted Reserve Corps, and the state militias. The Army of the United States was used again during the Korean War and then demobilized after the draft ended.

Currently, the Army consists of the Regular Army, the Army Reserve, and the U.S. National Guard. The use of the Army Reserve and National Guard has increased since the Vietnam War. The National Guard has been active in such conflicts as the Gulf War, the Kosovo peacekeeping mission, and the Iraq War.

Call Up to War

The sequence of call up to war for components of today's Army is as follows 1) Regular Army volunteer force, 2) Army Reserve total mobilization, 3) full-scale activation of all National Guard forces, 4) re-establishment of the draft, 5) recall of previously discharged officers and enlisted who left under honorable conditions, 6) activation of the state defense forces/state militias, and 7) full-scale mobilization of the unorganized U.S. militia. The final stage requires all "able-bodied males" to be in the service of the Army. The last time this occurred was in 1865 during the end of the Civil War when the Confederate States of America drafted all males into the Confederate Army.

★ MOTTO ★

Members of the U.S. Army are officially termed "soldiers" and their motto is "This We Will Defend."

★ ORGANIZATION ★

With the Army's massive size comes a large, sometimes overwhelming, bureaucracy. It is organized along various lines according to functions, many of which overlap in joint commands. The Army's organization is convoluted and complex, and not easily charted. In this chapter, it is divided into the administrative arena, the business end, and the fighting army's specific commands, units, and numbered armies. Components of each are described in the following sections.

Administration

The man at the top is the secretary of the army, the senior official of the Department of the Army. Since November 2004, this post has been held by Dr. Francis J. Harvey, the 119th secretary. The secretary of the army reports to the Secretary of Defense and is responsible for organizing, training, and equipping the land combat Army force. The secretary of defense reports to the commander-in-chief (the president of the United States). Directly reporting to the secretary of the army is the under secretary of the army, who oversees the Army's business functions. The chief of staff of the Army serves as the chief military advisor for the secretary. Beneath these are layers upon layers of organization.

Business Affairs

Necessary for a large organization to operate smoothly are a number of general business functions. In the Army, these are organized in the following different sections or elements.

CIVIL WORKS (CW). Includes national water resource management, flood control, navigation, the environment, direction of the Arlington National Cemetery and the Soldiers' and Airmen's Home Cemetery, program direction of foreign activities, and the Corps of Engineers.

FINANCIAL MANAGEMENT (FM). This section runs the financial end of Army activities, including budgeting and planning.

INSTALLATIONS, LOGISTICS, AND ENVIRONMENT (ILE). Deals with long-range and strategic planning for Army installations and is also responsible for logistics, environment, safety, occupational health, and chemical munitions demilitarization. Includes downsizing operations and disposing of chemical stockpiles.

MANPOWER AND RESERVE AFFAIRS (MRA). Oversees all the manpower and reserve components of the Army. Recent challenges have included the downsizing of the Army and the need for reserve components to serve in conflicts in Asia and the Middle East, especially Afghanistan and Iraq.

RESEARCH AND DEVELOPMENT AND ACQUISITION (RDA). Manages the Research and Development program of the Army, as well as procurement, contracting, and acquisitions. It must translate technology developments into affordable weapons.

OPERATIONS AND PLANS (DCSOPS). This section establishes requirements for the assignment of forces to different locations (called "force structure stationing actions"). It recommends priorities for and control of the employment of Army forces. It uses threat capability analysis to determine force requirements and is responsible for coordinating all joint and external matters, including operations, readiness, and mobilization.

PERSONNEL (DSCPER). Responsible for Army personnel issues.

LOGISTICS (DCSLOG). This section deals with the logistics of Army issues, including strategic mobility programs.

INTELLIGENCE (DCSINT). Deals with all intelligence-related activities of the Army, including foreign liaison, policy, counterintelligence, foreign intelligence, and reserve affairs. Additional challenges include streamlining of Army intelligence and multiregional threats and global or information warfare.

INSTALLATION MANAGEMENT (ACSIM). An assistant chief oversees this section, which is responsible for running all Army installations. Base construction, as well as base closures, are operated under this element.

Major Army Commands

There are seven specific major Army commands (MACOMs) that provide command, control, communications, and intelligence functions. Four additional commands have unique roles in the Army. A brief summary of each follows.

CORPS OF ENGINEERS (USACE). Provides military constructions for the Army and Air Force, as well as supports other defense and federal agencies. Responsible for numerous civil works concerning water resources such as dams and levees.

CRIMINAL INVESTIGATION COMMAND (UASCIDC). Investigates Army-related crimes, and provides support of crime laboratories as needed.

MEDICAL COMMAND (USAMEDCOM). Provides health care to soldiers, retirees, and family members during peacetime and war (See page 40 for further details).

INTELLIGENCE AND SECURITY COMMAND (USAINSCOM). Covers all intelligence issues and functions as the bridge between battlefield operation systems and national intelligence agencies.

INFORMATION SYSTEMS COMMAND (USAISC). Deals with communications systems, both in war efforts and during domestic emergencies. Includes telecommunications, publications, visual information, and records management.

MILITARY DISTRICT OF WASHINGTON (USAMDW). Responsible for responding to crisis, disaster, or security issues in the National Capital Region.

SPACE AND STRATEGIC DEFENSE COMMAND. This command oversees all Army space-related programs, including the "Star Wars" missile defense plan.

Other Specialized Commands

ARMY RECRUITING COMMAND (USAREC). This is a field-operating agency reporting to the deputy chief of staff for personnel (DCSPER). It is organized into brigades and battalions throughout the country. Recruiting sergeants recruit and process young men and women for the all-volunteer Army.

TOTAL ARMY PERSONNEL COMMAND (PERSCOM). This field-operating agency also reports to the DCSPER. It's responsible for the day-to-day management of Army civilian employees and all active duty personnel.

U.S. MILITARY ACADEMY. This field-operating agency trains the Corps of Cadets at West Point Military Academy. Graduates earn a bachelor's degree and are commissioned as second lieutenants for a lifetime career in the Army. Details of the U.S. Military Academy are included at the end of this chapter.

U.S. ARMY CADET COMMAND. This is another field-operating agency that provides headquarters for the Army Reserve Officer Training Corps (ROTC).

★ THE WAR MACHINE ★

The U.S. Army is composed of several different "armies"; in fact, all units larger than a corps are generically given the name "army." An army in this sense has three levels, dependent upon the size and scope of the conflict: a theater army, a field army, and an army group. Each of these is commanded by a lieutenant general (pay grade O-9) or "full" general (O-10), assisted by a command sergeant major (E-9) and a large staff. A theater army is part of a unified command that includes other branches of the military. Its operational and support responsibilities are assigned by the theater commander. A field army may direct operations of assigned corps and divisions. An army group, composed of two or more field armies under a designated commander, is the largest tactical formation used in combat operations. Formations of this scope have not been used since World War II. *Note:* General Schwarzkopf commanded a field army during Operation Desert Storm; during Operation Iraqi Freedom, a corps was the largest Army organization employed.

The Fighting Units

The fighting components of the U.S. Army are divided into fire teams, squads, sections, platoons, companies, battalions, brigades, divisions, and corps.

FIRE TEAM. A component of a squad composed of four soldiers. Commanded by a corporal (E-4). Composed of a fire team leader, a grenadier, and two riflemen.

SECTION/SQUAD. 8 to 16 soldiers. Function varies, but is usually the smallest element in the Army structure. Commanded by a staff sergeant (E-6) or sergeant (E-5). Composition is dependent upon function. Two squads may compose a section led by a staff sergeant. In a light infantry (nonmechanized) squad, there are usually nine soldiers and a squad leader. In a mechanized infantry squad, there are up to sixteen soldiers, organized into two teams. Each team is assigned to a tactical vehicle (e.g., Bradley Fighting Vehicle). In an armor (tank/cavalry) unit the term *section* is used instead of *squad*. A section consists of two vehicles (e.g., M1A2 Abrams). Each tank has a crew of four.

PLATOON. 16 to 44 soldiers. Functions as the basic combat unit. Commanded by a first or second lieutenant (O-1 or O-2), and assisted by a sergeant first class (E-7). Composed of two to four squads depending on the type of unit; e.g., an infantry platoon consists of three squads; a mechanized infantry platoon consists of four M2A2 Bradley Fighting Vehicles, divided into two sections. A tank platoon consists of two sections of two tanks each. Each vehicle holds up to nine soldiers.

COMPANY/TROOP/BATTERY. 60 to 200 soldiers. A cohesive tactical unit that can perform battlefield functions on its own. Composed of three to five platoons, and fifteen to twenty-five vehicles. For example, an armor tank company is composed of five officers, fifty-seven enlisted soldiers, fourteen M1A2/A3 main battle tanks, and several wheeled vehicles. Commanded by a captain (O-3), and assisted by a first sergeant (E-8). Ground or air cavalry units (armor and aviation units specially trained for reconnaissance missions) refer to these elements as troops. Field artillery and air defense artillery units refer to these elements as batteries.

BATTALION (OR SQUADRON). 300 to 1,000 soldiers. A unit that is both tactically and administratively self-sufficient, thus capable of independent operations of limited duration and scope. Composed of two to six companies. Commanded by a lieutenant colonel (O-5), and assisted by a command sergeant major (E-9). A battalion task force has additional companies attached in direct support to enhance mission capability. An armored or air cavalry unit of equivalent size is referred to as a squadron.

BRIGADES. 1,000 to 10,000 soldiers. Serves as a large unit that can be deployed independently or semi-independently. Also called groups (Rangers or Special Forces) or regiments (armored cavalry regiments). Composed of three or more battalions. Commanded by a colonel (O-6).

DIVISION. 10,000 to 16,000 soldiers. Performs major tactical operations and conducts sustained battles and engagements. Composed of three to five brigades. Numbered (e.g., 1st Armored Division, 82nd Airborne Division) and categorized by type (e.g., light infantry, mechanized infantry, armor, airborne, or air assault). Commanded by a major general (O-8), and assisted by two brigadier generals (O-7), one each for maneuver and support functions. Composed of three tactical maneuver (infantry and/or armor) brigades and a division base of combat support/service elements. There are ten divisions in the active Army and eight in the Reserves/National Guard. In October 1999, the Army established two integrated divisions (the 7th Infantry Division and the 24th Infantry Division) consisting of an active component headquarters commanded by an active component major general (O-8), and three Army National Guard enhanced separate brigades.

CORPS: 20,000 to 40,000 soldiers. Serves as the deployable level of command required to synchronize and sustain combat operations. Also provides the framework for multinational operations. Composed of two to five divisions. Commanded by a lieutenant general (O-9), assisted by a command sergeant major (E-9). There are four corps in the active Army; three with headquarters in the continental United States (I, III, and XVIII Corps) and one in Germany (V Corps).

★ ARMY VALUES ★

The seven core values of the U.S. Army are:

Loyalty: Bear true faith and allegiance to the U.S. Constitution, the Army, your unit, and other soldiers.

Duty: Fulfill your obligations.

Respect: Treat other people as they should be treated.

Selfless Service: Put the welfare of the nation, the Army, and your subordinates before your own.

Honor: Live up to Army values.

Integrity: Do what's right, legally and morally.

Personal Courage: Face fear, danger, or adversity (physical or moral).

The Warfighting Elements

On a larger scale, the Army is organized according to specified armies and commands, either numbered or named according to the region of responsibility; these are responsible for the actual fighting operations.

U.S. ARMY EUROPE AND SEVENTH U. S. ARMY. These function under the umbrella of the U.S. European Command and are responsible for U.S. defense efforts in Europe and for NATO commitments. They command Army units in Germany, Italy, England, and the Netherlands including V Corps, 1st Armored Division, 3rd Mechanized Infantry Division, Southern European Task Force, 21st Theater Support Command, and area support groups with headquarters in Heidelberg, Germany.

U.S. ARMY SOUTH. This functions under the umbrella of the U.S. Southern Command and includes command and control of southern Army forces and the Army element of Joint Task Force Panama. It's organized around eight major commands with light and airborne infantry, aviation, military police, signal, and engineer units. Its headquarters are at Ft. Clayton, Republic of Panama.

U.S. ARMY PACIFIC. This is the Army component of the U.S. Pacific Command, excluding the Korean region. It commands and supports units in Alaska, Hawaii, and Japan, and includes: the 25th Infantry Division (light) and U.S. Army Hawaii; 1st Brigade, 6th Infantry Division (light), and the U.S. Army Garrison, Alaska; the U.S. Army Japan and IX Corps; the 4th Special Operations Support Command; the U.S. Army Chemical Activity, Pacific; the U.S. Army Readiness Group, Pacific; and the 9th Army Reserve Command.

EIGHTH U.S. ARMY. Part of the U.S Pacific Command, this is the Army component of the Combined Forces Command created to deter aggression against the Republic of Korea ("South Korea"). It commands the 2nd Infantry Division, the 17th Aviation Brigade, the 18th Medical Brigade, and the 19th Support Command. It is headquartered in Korea.

U.S. ARMY FORCES COMMAND. This functions within the U.S. Atlantic Command and is responsible for combat readiness of active Army and Army Reserve units, and training and supervision of Army National Guard during peacetime. It provides the Army component of the U.S. Atlantic Command

and the Third U.S. Army component of U.S. Central Command. It also commands Active and Reserve Army Headquarter units in the continental United States (CONUS), Puerto Rico, and Virgin Islands. Additionally, it provides land defense of the continental United States, and also provides support to counter the flow of illegal drugs. It controls the three Army Corps Headquarters (I, III, and XVIII Corps). Its headquarters are at Ft. McPherson, Georgia.

THIRD U.S. ARMY. This provides command and control of Army forces in the USCENTCOM area (covers northeast Africa, Southwest and Central Asia, and the Seychelles), but is deployable worldwide in support of Joint Chiefs of Staff activities, as in Operation Desert Storm. Its headquarters are located at Ft. McPherson, Georgia.

U.S. ARMY SPACE COMMAND. This functions as the Army component of the U.S. Space Command for defense satellite communications systems, and to conduct planning operations with Strategic Ballistic Missile Defense. Headquarters are located in Colorado Springs, Colorado, with subordinate elements in Germany, Okinawa, Hawaii, California, Maryland, and Virginia.

U.S. ARMY SPECIAL OPERATIONS COMMAND. This command provides Special Forces, Rangers, special operations aviation, psychological operations, and civil affairs forces to commanders and U.S. ambassadors as needed. It is also responsible for developing special operations doctrine, tactics, and procedures while serving as the Army component of the U.S. Special Operations Command. Headquarters are at Ft. Bragg, North Carolinia. It has four subordinate commands: the John F. Kennedy Special Warfare Center and School, USA Special Forces Command, U.S. Army Civil Affairs and Psychological Operations Command, and U.S. Army Special Operations Integration Command.

U.S. ARMY RESERVE COMMAND. This command controls the U.S. Army Reserve forces. Its headquarters are in Atlanta, Georgia.

ARMY NATIONAL GUARD. The Army National Guard (ARNG) has dual missions of federal and state components. The federal mission is to provide trained and equipped units to respond to war and national emergencies. The president is authorized to activate the ARNG for federal operations, such as in Bosnia or the Middle East. The state mission for ARNG is to provide a disciplined force ready to respond to state and local emergencies. They are activated by the governor who commands them through the state adjutant general. Civilians serving in the Army National Guard serve on a part-time basis, generally one weekend a month and two weeks during summers.

U.S. ARMY MILITARY TRAFFIC MANAGEMENT COMMAND. This command is responsible for global traffic management, the operation of worldwide water ports, and Department of Defense transportation engineering. It serves as the Army component of the U.S. Transportation Command with subordinate commands in Bayonne, New Jersey; Oakland, California; and Newport News, Virginia. It has active and reserve components worldwide. Headquarters are in Falls Church, Virginia.

★ THOSE MISSING ARMIES ★

The numbering and naming of Army components is complicated enough without the gaps between the numbers. If there is a First, Third, Fifth, Seventh, and Eighteenth Army, logic presumes the existence of a Second, Fourth, Sixth, and all the others, right?

Yes and no. Armies and corps are numbered in sequence, but an army or corps may be deactivated or dissolved when needs change and its particular skill set is no longer required. For example, IX Corps had been active during the Civil War and was then deactivated. It was reactivated during World War I, World War II, and Korea. It was deactivated most recently in 1995.

The Army's Corps

Details of the numbered corps of the Army follow. Each has a different capability and function.

I CORPS. I Corps is headquartered in Ft. Lewis, Washington. The I Corps, called "First Corps" and nicknamed "America's Corps," serves under the U.S. Army Pacific Command. (A "I Corps" was in existence during the Civil War, but differs from that since World War I.) I Corps was active in Korea and more recently in the war on terror in Iraq.

III CORPS. Nicknamed the "Phantom Corps," "America's Hammer," the "Counterattack Corps," or "America's Armored Corps," this is headquartered at Fort Hood, Texas. The III Corps (Third Corps) is the official counteroffensive force of the U.S. Army. Its major units include the 1st Cavalry Division, the 4th Infantry Division, and the 3rd Armored Cavalry Regiment. It has been active since World War I and has developed equipment such as the M1 Abrams tank, M2/3 Bradley Fighting Vehicle, and AH64 Apache helicopter. It is active in training and reserve units.

V CORPS. Headquartered in Heidelberg, Germany, V Corps is the Army's only forward-deployed (stationed abroad) corps headquarters, serving in the European Command. With more than 42,000 soldiers and civilians, V Corps is the Army's contingency force for European and Central Command missions. Deployment occurs from bases in Europe to Central and Eastern Europe, the Mediterranean, Africa, the Middle East, and the Persian Gulf. V Corps provides trained, ready forces as a member of the binational corps with the II German Korps.

XVIII AIRBORNE CORPS. The XVIII Airborne Corps (Eighteenth Airborne) is trained in tactical operational and strategic levels of war and is capable of strategic operations anywhere in the world in eighteen hours. It has been widely recognized as a superbly trained force capable of operating in missions ranging from peace operations to general-purpose war, and can conduct large-scale joint operations. Activities have included Somalia, Panama, Middle East, Haiti, Cuba (for detention of Haitian refugees), and Florida (Hurricane Andrew support). XVIII Airborne Corps is headquartered at Fort Bragg, North Carolina.

COMBAT TRAINING CENTERS. Combat training centers are essential to fully train soldiers for potential battlefield condition against a well-trained opposing force. Centers include the National Training Center (NTC) at Ft. Irwin, California; the Combat Maneuver Training center (CMTC) at Hohenfels, Germany; the Joint Readiness Training Center (JRTC) at Fort Polk, Louisiana; and the Battle Command Training Center (BCTC) at Ft. Leavenworth, Kansas. The NTC and the CMTC train to fight against enemy armored units in mid- and high-intensity battles. JRTC training participants include light infantry and special operations forces (SOF). The BCTC is a high-tech computer simulation designed to train corps and division-level commanders; it uses minimal expense and has little environmental impact. The JRTC and the CMTC also train for additional, nonwar scenarios.

MATÉRIEL DEVELOPERS AND SUSTAINERS. Development of equipment, systems, and weapons-related technology is a part of this massive major Army command headquartered in Alexandria, Virginia. While civilian contracting provides a substantial portion of the Army's matériel needs, this command focuses on aviation (Aviation and Troop Support Command, ATCOM, St. Louis, Missouri), chemical/biological defense (Chemical, Biological Defense Command DBDCOM, Aberdeen Proving Ground, Maryland), missile (Missile Command, MICOM, Redstone Arsenal, Alabama), tanks/automotive vehicles (Tank Automotive Command, TACOM, Warren, Mississippi), smart weapons, simulations training, communications (Communications-Electronics Command, CECOM, Ft. Monmouth, New Jersey), and matériel systems.

Other Branches of the Army

The Army is further divided into functional branches that provide support, logistics, and administration functions.

ADJUTANT GENERAL'S CORPS. Responsible for military law in the Army. See chapter eight for more details.

AIR DEFENSE ARTILLERY AND FIELD ARTILLERY. Field Artillery includes units that use artillery weapons systems to deliver surface-to-surface, long-range, indirect fire. Field Artillery currently uses howitzers and the Multiple Launch Rocket Systems.

ARMOR. This branch deals with all aspects of armor, including tanks, mechanized infantry fighting vehicles, armored cavalry vehicles, self-propelled artillery pieces, and air cavalry helicopters.

AVIATION. Following the establishment of the U.S. Air Force as a separate service in 1947, the Army developed its own aviation assets of light planes and rotary wing aircraft in support of its ground operations. The Korean War gave this drive impetus, and the war in Vietnam saw its fruition as Army aviation units performed reconnaissance, transport, and fire support. Since Vietnam, the role of armed helicopters as tank destroyers has received new emphasis. In recognition of the growing importance of aviation in Army doctrine and operations, Aviation became a separate branch on April 12, 1983, and a full member of the Army's combined arms team.

CHEMICAL CORPS. This corps began as the Chemical Warfare Service after World War I to protect the armed forces from toxic gases that had been used in the war. By 1973, plans were made to disband the unit, but by 1976, it was believed that the Soviet Union had superiority in this arena and the branch was continued. The unit was recategorized as a combat support arm. It now covers all aspects of nuclear, biological, and chemical defense and operations.

CORPS OF ENGINEERS. Described previously on page 30.

FINANCE CORPS. This is essentially the payroll department. Someone has to write the paychecks and do the books, and it's this branch that gets the honors.

INFANTRY. This branch does most of the fighting.

U.S. MILITARY ACADEMY, ALSO KNOWN AS WEST POINT. Described in detail in later section.

MILITARY INTELLIGENCE (MI). Officially a branch since July 1, 1962, its job is to collect all intelligence required for the Army's commanders to accomplish their missions. This branch specializes in imagery intelligence, signal intelligence, human intelligence, measurement and signature intelligence, counterintelligence, and security countermeasures worldwide. Army MI works closely with the Intelligence of the Air Force, Navy, and Marines, and with national intelligence agencies. The Army MI employs over 28,000 persons.

MILITARY POLICE CORPS. The Army's Military Police soldiers provide support to the battlefield through basic law and order, security, and police intelligence operations, much as police do in the civilian world.

ORDNANCE CORPS. This logistics corps develops, produces, and sustains weapons systems and munitions. It was created in 1775. In recent years it has developed rockets, guided missiles, and satellites.

QUARTERMASTER CORPS. The oldest logistics branch of the Army, it originally provided lodging for soldiers and was responsible for designing insignias and flags. It currently provides the following support: general supply, mortuary affairs, food service, petroleum and water, field services (from parachute packing to laundry), and matériel and distribution management.

SIGNAL CORPS. Founded in 1861, this branch develops and tests communications equipment for the battlefield. It began with visual signaling, balloons, and telegraphs, and later moved into aircraft, RADAR (a term coined by the Navy in 1941), FM radio, circuit boards, and communications satellites. It is headquartered at Fort Gordon, Georgia.

SPECIAL FORCES. Includes Army Rangers, Special Forces (Green Berets), and several other smaller forces used in unconventional warfare. See chapter seven on special operations forces for further details.

TRANSPORTATION CORPS. A logistics branch since World War II, it took over the movement of personnel and matériel by truck, rail, air, and sea from the Quartermaster Corps.

Army Medical Department

No discussion of Army organization is complete without a review of the Army Medical Department, a significant component since 1775. This branch is immense, with highly trained individuals serving around the world in well-equipped facilities. During times of war, personnel familiar with battlefield wounds and injuries are on hand to provide prompt treatment. It is cost-effective to combine medical with other military services and ensures the availability of medical treatment in areas where the military may be sent for training or missions.

INSIGNIA. The basic insignia for the Corps of the Army Medical Department is the Caduceus, the traditional emblem of physicians. It features two serpents wound around a winged staff, and is adapted from the Staff of Aesculapius, in which one serpent each represents preventative and corrective medicines. The gold Caduceus alone represents the Medical Corps; a letter or letters superimposed on it refers to the other corps as follows: "D" for Dental Corps, "N" for Nurse Corps, "V" for Veterinary Corps, "MS" for Medical Service Corps (their Caduceus is silver), and "S" for Medical Specialists Corps.

THE MEDICAL CORPS. Medical support was first requested by General George Washington as commander-in-chief of the Continental Army in 1775, and a Hospital Department was formed as forerunner to the Army Medical Department. Army doctors have been pioneers in medicine, such as Dr. Walter Reed, who discovered that yellow fever is transmitted by mosquitoes rather than direct contact; and Dr. William Crawford Gorgas, who used Reed's research to stop the spread of the disease in Panama, making the construction of the Panama Canal possible. The first Distinguished Service Medal was issued in 1918 to Dr. Gorgas when he retired as surgeon general of the Army. Another Army doctor, Dr. Joseph Lovell, created one of the finest collections of referenced medical books to make it easier for doctors to locate information on specific illnesses or treatments; it became the foundation for the National Library of Medicine. During the Civil War, Dr. William A. Hammond collected dead tissue specimens for pathologic study; these samples were the beginning of the Army Medical Museum, and later the Armed Forces Institute of Pathology. Army doctors established the first school of medicine, and published textbooks on surgery, psychiatry, bacteriology, and drug encyclopedias. Army doctors introduced smallpox vaccination, published the first summary on vital statistics, and developed numerous vaccines against diseases of man and animals. They even began the first systematic weather reporting.

The all-physician Medical Corps is responsible for setting physical standards for all individuals entering medical service, maintaining their health while in service, and processing them for discharge or retirement. It is geared toward care of troops who are generally young; prevention of disease and injury is as important as rehabilitation. The head of the Medical Corps is entitled chief, Medical Corps and has the rank of brigadier general, sharing responsibility with the commander, U.S. Army Medical Department Personnel Support Agency. The chief, Medical Corps is also responsible for professional standards, preventative medicine, patient administration, and professional policies and practices for health care. In 1971, a program was initiated to train enlisted personnel to be physician assistants. Graduates of this two-year program are appointed as warrant officers and serve in combat units or in troop health clinics under the supervision of a physician.

THE DENTAL CORPS. All aspects of dentistry are represented in the Army Dental Corps, which was established as a formal branch in 1911. Their mission is to provide dental care necessary to preserve the oral health of the Army in support of its fighting strength. The chief of the Dental Corps has the rank of major general and serves as advisor to the surgeon general and chief of staff of the Army. Since 1978, dental personnel have been organized into Dental Activities (DENTACs) and Area Dental Laboratories (ADLS) which are commanded by Dental Corps officers.

THE VETERINARY CORPS. Veterinarians have been associated with the military services since the mid-1800s when veterinarians were assigned to cavalry units. In 1916, the Veterinary Corps was combined into the Medical Department to centralize control of personnel caring for the Army's animals and inspecting food supplies. As cavalry units became mechanized, the Veterinary Corps evolved to include matters of public health. The chief of the Veterinary Corps has the rank of brigadier general. All members of the corps have graduated from an accredited college of veterinary medicine after being awarded either a doctor of veterinary medicine (DVM) or veterinary medical doctor (VMD). In 1980, when the Air Force Veterinary Service was dissolved, the Army Veterinary Corps assumed the role of Department of Defense Veterinary Services. In 1981, a program was established to train enlisted personnel to be veterinary food inspection technicians. Graduates are appointed as warrant officers who assist Army Veterinary Corps.

MEDICAL SERVICE CORPS. This corps has two functions: to produce scientists and specialists in medicine, and to generate technically qualified officers to keep the Medical Department self-sustaining in administration, supply, environmental sciences, mobilization preparedness, readiness training, and engineering. The Medical Service Corps relies heavily on the ROTC as a source of officers. The chief of the corps, with the rank of colonel, serves as advisor and consultant to the surgeon general; he or she helps assign and plan for Medical Service Corps officers and Medical Department warrant officers.

The current Medical Service Corps was established in 1947 and has four sections: Pharmacy, Supply and Administration, (personnel management, pharmacy, supply operations, and patient administration); Medical Allied Sciences (includes audiology, medical laboratory sciences, microbiology, biochemistry, immunology, and parasitology); Sanitary Engineering (environmental engineering, environmental science, medical entomology, and nuclear medical science); and Optometry.

THE ARMY NURSE CORPS. This branch, established in 1901, is the oldest military nurse corps in the United States and the first women's component of the U.S. Armed Forces. The chief of the corps is a brigadier general who serves as consultant to the surgeon general on staff policies, procedures, and activities. Army nurses serve in seven clinical specialties: community health, psychiatric-mental health, pediatrics, obstetrics, operating room, anesthesia, and medical-surgical nursing, as well as three functional areas: administration, education, and research. In 1976, ROTC graduates first entered the Army Nurse Corps, and in 1981, a joint effort was initiated to increase the number of nursing students in ROTC.

THE ARMY MEDICAL SPECIALIST CORPS. This corps, formulated in 1947, comprises three medical specialties: dietitians, occupational therapists, and physical therapists. ROTC graduates are eligible for commission within the Army Medical Specialist Corps. The chief, Army Medical Specialist Corps holds the rank of colonel and serves as advisor to the surgeon general on relevant matters.

★ RANK AND UNIFORMS ★

Army Rank

Army personnel may be commissioned officers, warrant officers, or enlisted personnel. See appendix B for a comparison of ranks between services.

- Commissioned officers from top to bottom rank as follows: general of the Army (five-star, wartime use only), general (four-star), lieutenant general (three-star), major general (two-star), brigadier general (one-star), colonel, lieutenant colonel, major, captain, first lieutenant, and second lieutenant.

- Warrant officers rank, from top to bottom: chief warrant officer 5, chief warrant officer 4, chief warrant officer 3, chief warrant officer 2, and warrant officer.

- The enlisted personnel rank, from top to bottom: sergeant major of the Army, command sergeant major, sergeant major, first sergeant, master sergeant, sergeant first class, staff sergeant, sergeant, corporal, specialist, private first class, and private.

Army Uniforms

The Army has three types of uniforms: combat dress, service or garrison dress, and full dress.

- The *combat uniform*, also called fatigues, battle dress uniform (BDU), or army combat uniform (ACU), has changed several times since World War II. Since 2005, ACUs are printed with a digital camouflage pattern based on the Marine's uniform. The pattern lacks the color black and is suitable for all nonpolar terrain, especially desert, urban, and woodland areas. The uniform includes suede brown leather boots (the shiny black leather boots required more care and polishing) and a beret for base duties, or a visor cap for noncombat patrols. Kevlar body armor and helmets are used for combat duties. Officers and enlisted wear the same uniform. Sewn-on rank is authorized only for the ACU patrol cap, ACU boonie hat, and the Kevlar camouflage cover. Only chaplains wear their branch insignia on the ACU.

- The *service/garrison uniform* is worn in noncombat conditions, on base, and at informal occasions. It includes a dark green coat and plain, dark green trousers or skirt, with a light green shirt. Enlisted soldiers wear a coin-shaped "U.S." insignia on the right collar tip of their jacket, and an insignia indicating career specialty on the left collar tip, with nothing worn on the lapel; a rank patch is worn on the upper sleeve.

  Commissioned officers additionally wear a black stripe on the outside of each trouser leg, and wear a black band above each cuff on the green jacket. Officers wear a brass "U.S." insignia on each side of the collar, with branch insignia on their lapels. Rank is worn on shoulder epaullettes on the jacket; their berets have their rank insignia, in cut-out brass letters. Since 2001, the black beret previously only given to Army Rangers is included in the general service uniform.

  Regular units wear black shoes; boots, scarves, and pistol belts are reserved for parade dress. Airborne, Ranger, and Special Forces units wear jump boots instead of black shoes. Airborne units wear maroon berets, Rangers wear tan berets, and Special Forces wear green berets.

- The *full dress uniform* is worn for ceremonial duties in most stateside posts. The Army blue uniform has a dark blue, open-fronted coat with white shirt, black necktie, light blue trousers or skirt trimmed in gold, and a dark blue saucer cap. Officers' rank insignia are worn on rectangular epaulettes in the color of their branch of service. Commissioned officers don dark blue trousers or skirts. For "black-tie" events, men wear bowties.

★ JOINING THE ARMY ★

Individuals may join the Army through one of several tracks. They may enlist directly, join as an officer through the Reserve Officers Training Corps (ROTC) or the U.S. Military Academy, or via direct appointment for trained specialists. Soldiers may join as active duty or reserve forces.

ACTIVE DUTY. Active duty is full-time employment, and service commitments range from two to six years. Specific duties, termed "Military Occupation Specialty" (MOS), are vast in the Army's large organization, and range from active fighting positions (e.g., infantryman, parachuting, tank) to active support positions (e.g., logistics, mechanics, weapons development, explosives) to a huge cadre of behind-the-scenes jobs (e.g., administration, accounting, uniform supplies, funeral arrangements).

ARMY RESERVES. Reserve personnel are part-time employees; the soldier keeps a civilian career while training near home, generally one weekend a month with two weeks of annual training. Commitments for Army Reserves range from one to six years; Reservists may be mobilized at any time for active duty. A reserve soldier is "activated" when called to serve in the Army full time. "Mobilization" entails reporting to duty when the soldier receives orders. Once activated, Army Reserve soldiers serve a maximum of two years active duty, unless extended during wartime. "Deployment" means active duty soldiers are moved to a specific area of operations, usually on foreign soil. Activated or deployed Army Reserve soldiers receive the same pay as active duty soldiers of the same rank. Reservists who are mobilized cannot lose their civilian job, according to federal law. As of this writing, the Army Reserve is deployed in Operations Iraqi Freedom, Enduring Freedom, and Noble Eagle.

The Army Reserve is composed of three groups of soldiers: the Selected Reserve, the Individual Ready Reserve, and the Retired Reserve. The *Selected Reserve* is the most readily available group, composed of Troop Program Units, Active Guard and Reserve Soldiers, and Individual Mobilization Augmenters. Troop

Program Units generally train on weekends and once annually; they comprise over 185,000 soldiers in some 2,000 Troop Units. If necessary, all members of the Selected Reserve and up to 30,000 Individual Ready Reserves can be mobilized. Active Guard and Reserve Soldiers are those who serve full time on Active Duty. Individual Mobilization Augmenters are assigned to high-level headquarter jobs where they would serve if mobilized, and usually train annually for two weeks.

Members of the *Individual Ready Reserve* (IRR) are trained soldiers who may be called upon to replace soldiers in Active and Army Reserve units; many have recently left Active Duty and still have an Army Reserve commitment. In all, there are about 163,000 members of the IRR.

The *Retired Reserve* includes some 715,000 retirees from the Army, including Active Army, Army Reserve, and Army National Guard. They remain part of the Army Reserve family.

ENLISTMENT. Soldiers must be between the ages of eighteen and thirty-four (seventeen with parental consent), a high school graduate or equivalent, and must take the Armed Services Vocation Aptitude Battery (ASVAB), the general aptitude test of all the military services. Other tests are given to ensure the candidate is mentally, physically, and morally capable of service.

Documentation the enlistee needs to bring to the Military Entrance Processing Station include Social Security card, driver's license, original or certified copies of marriage, divorce and/or separation orders if applicable; birth certificates for those eighteen or younger; proof of citizenship; high school diploma or GED; and ROTC or college transcript documentation if applicable. The enlistee is given the rank of private and joins either as active duty or reserve personnel. He or she receives a complete physical, is assigned a specialty (called an "MOS"), and is sworn in as a soldier in the U.S. Army.

RESERVE OFFICER TRAINING CORPS (ROTC). High school students can apply for college through the ROTC program, available at numerous institutions throughout the country, after which the soldier has both an officer's commission and a commitment to service in the Army for several years. ROTC scholarships may be awarded for a four-year college program.

Requirements for these scholarships include being a U.S. citizen between seventeen and twenty-six years old; grade point average of 2.5 or greater; high school diploma or GED; SAT score of 920 or greater (1100 recommended), or

ACT score of 19 or greater; and excellent physical condition. College students with at least two years of study remaining can switch to a ROTC program by taking the Army ROTC basic course.

Enlisted soldiers can also become officers by joining the ROTC in the Army's "Green to Gold" program. Army Reservists or Army National Guards can join the ROTC concurrent with their service commitments. ROTC cadets serve as officer trainees in the Reserve or National Guard while completing college, receiving pay and benefits in addition to ROTC allowances. Upon graduation, Reservists are commissioned as second lieutenants in the Army.

DIRECT APPOINTMENT. Individuals with special training, such as in the medical or dental fields, may join the Army via direct appointment.

★ TRAINING IN THE U.S. ARMY ★

Basic Combat Training

Basic Combat Training (Boot Camp or BT) is a nine-week intensive training program in addition to the initial "Reception Week." The goal is to make recruits become soldiers capable of fighting, following orders, and working as a team. Recruits begin as privates (PVT) and graduate to private first class (PFC).

★ YOU'RE IN THE ARMY NOW—NOW WHAT? ★

Luggage: What May Recruits Bring to Training?

This is the list of what recruits can and must bring, without exceptions. It is essentially the same for all branches of the military.

- Clothing: one-day supply of casual, comfortable clothing in good condition (no ragged shorts or halter tops); three sets of white underwear; one pair of plain white, calf-length athletic socks (more will be purchased at the Post Exchange, or PX); one pair of comfortable shoes; standard eye glasses (no fancy designer glasses); all in a small suitcase or gym bag.
- A combination lock or padlock with two keys.

> • Toiletries: disposable razor, shaving cream, toothbrush with case, hair-brush or 6-inch black comb, one washcloth and towel, antiperspirant, shower shoes, toothpaste, dental floss, shampoo, soap, and case.
>
> • Money: Ten to fifty dollars in cash, traveler's checks, or money orders.
>
> • Copies of all orders and documents issued by the recruiter, and identi-fication documents as required.
>
> • Women may additionally bring cotton panties, bras, one full slip, flesh-toned pantyhose, and earring studs (2-inch or less, of pearl, silver, gold, or diamond).
>
> **What Not to Bring**
>
> The Army leaves nothing to chance. Not only do they tell you what to bring, they specify what you must *not* bring. Obvious or not, these items include: family; pets; personal vehicles; expensive items such as cameras, radios, or jewelry; nonprescription drugs; steel hair picks; razor blades; weapons; obscene or pornographic material; alcoholic beverages; playing cards, dice, dominoes; and cigarette or tobacco products.

The first few days in the Army are for processing, basic orientation, and medical exams; the first true week is termed Week 00. During the actual second week (which is officially called Week 1), serious training begins and continues through Week 9 of Boot Camp. The current basic schedule of boot camp is as follows:

Week 00: Reception Week

Day 01: Recruits arrive at Fort Jackson, South Carolina for general orientation.

Day 02: Haircuts. Uniforms and ID cards are issued.

Day 03: Inoculations and dental exams are given.

Day 04: Recruits take first Physical Assessment (PA) tests. Men must run a mile in 8.5 minutes; women must run it in 10.5 minutes.

Day 05: Recruits are schooled in barracks upkeep and drill (marching fundamentals).

Day 06: Recruits prepare for the arrival of the drill
sergeant and the start of Basic Training (BT).

Day 07: Chapel service and a little personal time are scheduled.

Week 01: Fall In

Day 01: Pickup from Reception. In-process paperwork begins. Drill
and Ceremony practice

Day 02: Army Physical Fitness Test (APFT) Diagnostic #1.

Day 03: Drill and Ceremony.

Day 04: Battalion commander and commander sergeant major
conduct Values class.

Day 05: Classroom instruction.

Day 06: Classroom instruction.

Day 07: Personal time, foot march, and chapel services.

Week 02: Direction

Day 01: Unarmed combat exercise.

Day 02: Victory Tower.

Day 03: Teamwork development course.

Day 04: First Aid training.

Day 05: Map reading and land navigation.

Day 06: Compass course.

Day 07: Personal time, foot march, and chapel services.

Week 03: Endurance

Day 01: 5-km foot march.

Day 02: Bayonet instruction.

Day 03: Bayonet assault course and pugil stick training.

Day 04: Nuclear biological chemical (gas chamber) training and obstacle course.

Day 05: Phase One tests.

Day 06: Basic Rifle Marksmanship (BRM) fundamentals training.

Day 07: Personal time, foot march, and chapel services.

Week 04: Marksmanship.

The M16A2 rifle is currently the standard issue weapon of the Army. Recruits must know and respect this weapon. Before live rounds are used, meticulous details and nuances like breathing, stance, and mechanics are discussed and rehearsed (see sidebar below for details).

Day 01: 8-km foot march, Basic Rifle Marksmanship (BRM), procedures and fundamentals.

Day 02: Army Physical Fitness Test (APFT) Diagnostic #2.

Day 03: Basic Rifle Marksmanship grouping.

Day 04: Basic Rifle Marksmanship zero.

Day 05: 10-km foot march, BRM down range feedback.

Day 06: BRM single and multiple target detection.

Day 07: Personal time, foot march, and chapel services.

★ READY, AIM, FIRE: ★ LEARNING TO USE THE M16A2 RIFLE

In the Basic Rifle Marksmanship program, recruits are trained to understand common firing principles and to be proficient, confident marksmen both on a range and in actual combat. Recruits demonstrate the *fundamentals* before approaching any firing line: 1) establish a steady position to observe the target; 2) aim the rifle by aligning the sight system; and 3) fire without disturbing this alignment through improper breathing or during trigger squeeze. Before using live rounds, all personnel are briefed on procedures and safety guidelines.

Shot grouping is practice firing of live rounds. Grouping exercises are conducted on a live-fire range that provides the precise locations of hits and misses on paper targets stapled to cardboard silhouettes. Recruits must place three rounds within a 4-cm circle at 25 meters.

The purpose of *battle sight zeroing* is to align the fire control system (the sights) with the rifle barrel to calibrate the rifle. When done correctly for an M16A2 rifle, the point of aim is the point of bullet impact at 300 meters. "Battle sight zero" is the sight setting that provides the highest hit probability for most combat targets with minimum adjustment to the aiming point.

Down range feedback provides the precise location of bullet strikes at ranges beyond 25 meters.

Single target detection and engagement, a field firing exercise, uses single targets at distances of 75, 175, and 300 meters with fleeting, combat-type, pop-up silhouettes. Time standards add stress and simulate the short exposure times of real combat targets. Likewise, *multiple target detection and engagement* is an exercise that uses multiple targets at the same distances: two or more fleeting, combat-type, pop-up silhouettes appear at the same time, forcing the recruit to decide upon the order of engagement.

In *prequalification*, the recruit completes a difficult course of fire, with single and multiple target engagements at six distances ranging from 50 to 300 meters. These tests integrate all the tasks learned from previous training.

In *qualification,* recruits qualify by shooting at forty targets at distances between 50 and 300 meters in various timed sequences and combinations. A score of twenty-three hits qualifies a recruit as a "Marksman," thirty as a "Sharpshooter," and thirty-six as an "Expert."

Week 05: Trials.

Day 01: Drill sergeant sessions.

Day 02: Basic Rifle Marksmanship prequalification.

Day 03: BRM prequalification.

Day 04: BRM qualification.

Day 05: Phase Two tests begin.

Day 06: Phase Two tests continue. Fit to Win Obstacle Course (see sidebar on page 52 for details).

Day 07: Personal time, foot march, and chapel services.

★ FIT TO WIN OBSTACLE COURSE ★

The Fit to Win Obstacle Course is a valuable, physical fitness training tool used to present recruits with intense physical challenges to develop and test their basic skills. Over the 900-meter course, recruits are required to negotiate and clear up to twenty obstacles while running, jumping, dodging, climbing, traversing, vaulting, balancing, or crawling. As the recruits master various obstacles, they also embody several of the Army core values. By overcoming their own physical limitations and supporting other recruits, they develop a deeper sense of personal courage, respect, and selfless service.

The course includes the following named obstacles: 3-foot Wall, Lane Guide, Ladder on Ground, Cement Culvert, Cargo Net, Low Crawl Wire, 3-foot Across Jump Box, 30-inch Balance Log, Culver, 40-inch Deep Trench, Horizontal Ladder, Over and Under, Hurdles, Night Trench High Crawl, Window Wall, 40-inch Wall, High Stepper, 5-foot Jump.

Week 06: Camaraderie

Day 01: Army Physical Fitness Test (APFT) Diagnostic #3.

Day 02: Post detail sentry duties.

Day 03: Deferred issue.

Day 04: U.S. weapons familiarization.

Day 05: Buddy movement techniques instruction.

Day 06: Squad defensive live-fire exercise.

Day 07: Personal time, foot march, and chapel services.

Week 07: Confidence

Day 01: Drill sergeant sessions. Uniforms.

Day 02: End-of-cycle Army Physical Fitness Test and Phase Tests.

Day 03: Hand grenade training.

Day 04: Live-fire exercise.

Day 05: Threat briefing (explanations of threat levels). Foot march.

Day 06: Confidence Course (see sidebar for details).

Day 07: Personal time, foot march, and chapel services.

★ CONFIDENCE COURSE ★

The Confidence Course is twenty-four exercises divided into four groupings that recruits negotiate with their company. It gives recruits confidence in their mental and physical abilities, while cultivating their spirit of daring. Obstacles vary from easy to difficult, testing physical strength, balance, and mental endurance. Additionally, it offers recruits perspective on how basic training has prepared them for combat. The course is not run against time, but rather is designed to make recruits see how far they've come and how far they're willing to go.

For pictures and schematics of each exercise, go to: http://goarmy.com. It may look a bit like playground equipment, but nothing is child-sized. Remember, recruits are in full uniform, including heavy boots—and the weather *always* permits. It's grueling work year-round to get through the course. The four groupings are indicated by colors.

Week 08: Victory Forge

Day 01: Drill and ceremony competition.

Day 02: Victory Forge: 10-km foot march.

Day 03: Victory Forge: night infiltration course.

Day 04: Victory Forge: 15-km foot march.

Day 05: Personal time and recovery.

Day 06: Personal time and recovery.

Day 07: Personal time, foot march, and chapel services.

Week 09: Graduation

Day 01: Inspection period.

Day 02: Out-processing.

Day 03: Personal time.

Day 04: Personal time and haircuts.

Day 05: Family day.

Day 06: Graduation.

Recruits graduate to private first class (PFC).

Advanced Individual Training

Also known as AIT, Advanced Individual Training begins immediately after BT. Seventeen different schools are available. Recruits get some choice, but individual aptitude, ability, and Army need have the final say as to where recruits go for advance training.

The schools are currently as follows:

ADJUTANT GENERAL CORPS SCHOOL. Includes personnel management, postal operations, reporting, and human resources.

AIR DEFENSE ARTILLERY SCHOOL. Refers to air defense systems, from maintenance to transportation, and includes the PATRIOT Missile System, the Bradley Linebacker system, the Man Portable Air Defense System, and the AVENGER system.

U.S. ARMY ARMOR CENTER. Refers to tanks. Individuals study either Cavalry Scout Operations to identify enemy activity and weapons, or Armor Operations, which currently focuses on the M1A2 tank.

AVIATION LOGISTICS SCHOOL. Helicopter maintenance. Currently, these include the following: AH-64 Apache, UH-60 Black Hawk, CH-47 Chinook, or OH-58 Kiowa.

CHEMICAL SCHOOL. "NBC" refers to Nuclear, Biological, or Chemical weapons. This school trains personnel to identify and detect these weapons, and to operate equipment used in these operations.

DEPARTMENT OF DEFENSE FIRE ACADEMY. This is firefighting and everything related to it.

ENGINEER SCHOOL. This course covers bridge building, structural maintenance, and mapping. Specific areas include Combat Engineer Operations (e.g., bridge building/destruction, minefield placement) and Topographic Engineer Operations (map making).

FIELD ARTILLERY CENTER. Covers cannons, missiles, and rockets.

FINANCE CORPS SCHOOL. Accounting and payroll.

INFANTRY SCHOOL. Combat. This includes small arms, anti-armor, or indirect fire weapons, together with navigation, reconnaissance, minefields, and bunker building.

MILITARY INTELLIGENCE SCHOOL. Intelligence gathering, interpreting, and reporting are covered in this training.

MILITARY POLICE SCHOOL. Military law enforcement. Military Police personnel are usually called MPs.

ORDNANCE MECHANICAL MAINTENANCE SCHOOL. This covers the maintenance of tanks, small arms, Humvees, trucks, generators, air conditioners, as well as the more mundane laundry, bath units, and water purifiers. It may also include machinist or welding training and certification.

ORDNANCE MUNITIONS AND ELECTRONICS MAINTENANCE SCHOOL. Munitions management, explosives disposal, electronics and missile maintenance are all part of this course.

QUARTERMASTER SCHOOL. This is the logistics system that provides soldiers with food, water, petroleum, repair parts, and the like.

SIGNAL CORPS SCHOOL. Covers all types of communications; for example, the automation, transmission, and reception of voice and data transmissions.

TRANSPORTATION SCHOOL. Operation and maintenance of trucks, equipment, and watercraft.

Specialized Schools

More advanced training for highly skilled soldiers includes:

- Airborne School (parachuting)
- Army Medical Department School
- Aviation School (helicopter piloting)
- Chaplain School

- Defense Information School (publications, PR)
- Defense Language Institute (foreign language training)
- Drill Sergeant School
- Equal Opportunity Advisors (EOA) Course (to promote equality and identify discrimination)
- Judge Advocate General's (JAG) Corps (military law/legal issues)
- Jumpmaster School (teach parachuting at Airborne School)
- Pathfinder School (navigation specialists, especially in foreign lands)
- Ranger School (to become an elite member of the Army Rangers). See chapter seven on special operations forces for further details.
- Recruiting and Retention School
- School of Music (the Army Band)
- Special Forces Training (experts in unconventional warfare). See chapter seven for further details.

★ U.S. MILITARY ACADEMY ★

The Military Academy at West Point ("The Academy,") is the Army's prestigious officer development school. It is both a fully accredited four-year college and a military program; cadets are active-duty members of the U.S Army. The demanding "West Point Experience" transforms cadets into leaders and includes academic, military, and physical development. A strong emphasis on moral-ethical development is woven into each area.

THE ACADEMY'S MISSION. "To educate, train, and inspire the corps of cadets so that each graduate is a commissioned leader of character committed to the values of duty, honor, and country and prepared for a career of professional excellence and service to the nation as an officer in the United States Army."

The Military Academy has been developing cadets for two hundred years in four areas deemed critical to military leadership: intellectual, physical, military, and moral-ethical.

ACADEMIC PROGRAMS. The Academy's challenging academic program has over thirty core courses in the arts and sciences, and numerous electives for depth of study in various fields. Because of the technical nature of the program, all graduating cadets receive a bachelor of science degree.

PHYSICAL DEVELOPMENT. The physical program encompasses exercise as well as competitive athletics. Every cadet is required to participate in a sport each semester, whether at the intercollegiate, club, or intramural level. This rigorous program contributes to the mental and physical fitness required for service as an officer in the Army. Sports teams include baseball, basketball (men's and women's), cross country, football, golf, gymnastics, hockey, lacrosse, rifle, sprint football, swimming/diving, soccer (men's and women's), softball, tennis (men's and women's), track, volleyball, and wrestling. Competition against the other military academies offers the greatest rivalries, especially against Navy. Since 1990, the Black Knights have been a part of the Patriot League, together with Navy and other exclusive northeast colleges. Army-Navy football games are hugely popular, and are watched on satellite television wherever military are stationed around the globe. These NCAA games serve the needs of recruitment and fan the flames of school spirit while fostering teamwork, honing leadership skills, and fueling personal excellence.

MILITARY DEVELOPMENT. Cadets learn basic military skills, especially leadership, starting on their first day at West Point. Most of the military training takes place during the summers, with new cadets undergoing Cadet Basic Training—otherwise known as "Beast Barracks"—in the weeks prior to their first semester. In the second summer, they undergo Cadet Field Training. The third and fourth summers are spent in active Army units around the world; in attending advanced training courses such as airborne, air assault, or northern warfare; and in training first and second year cadets as part of the leadership cadre. Military science instruction also provides a solid foundation for officership.

MORAL AND ETHICAL DEVELOPMENT. Moral and ethical development is fundamental to the education program. Formal instruction in the important values of the military profession, voluntary religious programs, interaction with staff and faculty role models, and a strong guest speaker program are provided. The ethical code at West Point is evident in the Academy's motto: "Duty, Honor, Country." Cadets also must adhere to the Cadet Honor Code: "A cadet will not lie, cheat, steal, or tolerate those who do." Strict moral discipline at the Academy results in cadets with a strong sense of purpose, pride, and satisfaction from meaningful service to others.

APPLICATION. Admission is open to all young men and women, but is extremely competitive. Candidates must be nominated by a member of Congress or by the Department of the Army. They are evaluated on their academic, physical, and leadership potential; fully qualified candidates receive appointments to the Academy. Candidates should prepare early, with a well-rounded academic program, excellent physical fitness, and substantial leadership experience.

CURRICULUM. Cadets major in engineering, math and science, or humanities and social sciences with different electives which may include: military science, English, history, leadership, philosophy/ethics, foreign languages, law, chemistry, physical geography, information technology, physics, and design.

CADET LIFE. There is little time for fun, though organized sports may provide an athletic outlet. Over one hundred extra-curricular opportunities are available, from radio production and disc jockeying to a Fine Arts Club. Cadets do not pay for their education, and receive a six-hundred-dollar monthly stipend to cover basics such as laundry, haircuts, and so on. Upon graduation, cadets are obliged to serve at least five years of active duty and three years in a reserve component, for a total of eight years.

STATISTICS. The Academy currently graduates more than 900 new officers annually, providing about one-fourth of the new lieutenants needed each year. The student body, or corps of cadets, numbers 4,000 with approximately 15 percent now women. Over 50,000 cadets have graduated from the Academy during its two centuries of operations.

A favorite expression at West Point is, "Much of the history we teach was made by people we taught." Well-known Academy graduates include Grant, Lee, Pershing, MacArthur, Eisenhower, Patton, Westmoreland, and Schwarzkopf.

★ GOLDEN KNIGHTS ★

In 1959, thirteen men formed the Strategic Army Corps Sport Parachute Team to compete in the Communist-dominated sport of skydiving. The team was officially designated the U.S. Army Parachute Team and adopted the nickname "Golden Knights" because of their record for winning gold medals and of conquering the skies. The team is a recruitment device and serves as the Army's goodwill ambassadors to the world in addition to testing new parachuting equipment and techniques. The team is currently organized into six sections: two demonstration teams (Black and Gold teams); two competition teams (Style and Accuracy; and Formation Skydiving); "Team-Six," the Aviation Team, responsible for transport issues; and Headquarters, which provides team support for scheduling and public relations.

The dramatic air-to-ground show begins with the first jumper leaving the aircraft at 12,500 feet, landing, and then narrating the rest of the show from the ground. The Black and Gold teams demonstrate skills such as: the baton pass; the individual "cutaway" maneuver; the "diamond track," which demonstrates the amount of lateral movement possible while falling; the "diamond formation," in which four jumpers fly with their bodies adjacent to each other without making contact and form a diamond pattern; and the "mass exit," in which many jumpers exit the aircraft at once.

An individual wanting to join the Golden Knights must be an Army soldier, have a minimum of 150 freefall parachute jumps, a class "C" international skydiving license, and an excellent military and civilian record.

★ THE U.S. ARMY BAND—"PERSHING'S OWN" ★

The United States Army Band, also known as "Pershing's Own," provides world-class music in support of all branches of government, the Department of Defense, the Department of the Army, and the U.S. Army Military District of Washington. "Pershing's Own" also provides musical support for a wide spectrum of national and international events including troop support, community and civil relations, recruiting initiatives, and outreach to music education centers.

The band was founded in 1922 by Army Chief of Staff General John J. "Black Jack" Pershing to emulate European military bands prominent during World War I. The band became widely known and critically acclaimed for radio broadcasts, and completed four national tours and an international tour in Spain between 1928 and 1931. In June 1943, the band was sent overseas to perform in North Africa and received a battle streamer for their efforts during the Rhineland Campaign. It is the only Washington-based military band to have participated in a theater of foreign combat. After World War II, the band expanded in scope and diversity, and the Army Ceremonial Band, the Army Chorus, the Army Herald Trumpets, and the Army Strings were established as regular performing units. Well-known entertainers and recording artists played with the Band members in the 1950s, including Eddie

Fisher and Steve Lawrence. Army Band Bugler Keith Clark performing "Taps" at the graveside service of President John F. Kennedy in Arlington National Cemetery. During the 1970s, the Army Blues Jazz Ensemble, the Army Chorale, and the Army Brass Band were officially established as regular performing ensembles.

An official coat of arms and distinctive uniforms were approved to reflect the band's increasing visibility at events of national significance, including the visit of Emperor Hirohito to Alaska with President Nixon, the national Bicentennial Celebration, the Lake Placid Winter Olympics, the return of the former U.S. hostages from Iran, the World's Fair in Knoxville, Tennessee, and the 1984 Olympic Games in Los Angeles.

★ NONMILITARY OPERATIONS ★

The Army will assist in Homeland Security operations as necessary, although this is not common. In August 2005, in the aftermath of Hurricane Katrina and the devastating damage and flooding to New Orleans and Mississippi, the Army deployed all available medical staff in the southeast United States to the region as well as supplied National Guard troops, equipment, and supplies for the relief efforts. Additionally, field hospitals already mobilized to support the Iraqi war were deployed longer than originally scheduled to allow rotating units to help Katrina victims.

INSIDE THE ARMY

"Did You Like Being in the Army?"

**By Virginia "Ginny" Slayton (formerly Mullin),
U. S. Army Major (RET), RN, MS, CCRN**

When people ask me if I liked being in the Army, I say "Yes, I did." After spending over twenty-three years in the military, how could I not enjoy it? I then wonder if the question should have been, "Why did you join the Army?"

I enlisted in the Army in 1977, and later received my commission in the Army Nurse Corps, a "mustang" who went from enlisted to commissioned officer. I learned much in the military and really did grow up in the military. Traveling to many places in the United States, and in Germany, Belgium, and even Korea, I had experiences I could never have imagined. I also had the opportunity to get an education that I still use every day. Personally and professionally, the Army is a large part of my foundation.

The military camaraderie has been the biggest treasure of all. I have become friends with many people that I still keep in contact with, and have seen many laid to rest. Enveloped within this are the traditions, rites of passage, and protocols of both the Army Nurse Corps and the entire military.

I am the patriotic American that gets that red, white, and blue lump in the throat when I hear the "Star Spangled Banner," and the American that gets teary eyed when I see the effects of war on soldiers of all ages. These are all the reasons that I joined the Army and why I love being a part of the Army.

★ CELEBRITY ARMY MEMBERS ★

Some of the more well-known members of the Army include: Burt Bacharach (composer), Irving Berlin (composer), Tony Bennett (singer), Samuel Clemens aka Mark Twain (author), Bob Dole (senator), Clint Eastwood (actor), Dwight D. Eisenhower (president), Andrew Jackson (president), Don Knotts (actor and comedian), Charles Lindbergh (aviator), Colin Powell (secretary of state), Elvis Presley (singer), Ronald Reagan (actor, president), Andy Rooney (writer), George Straight (country singer), Dave Thomas (founder of Wendy's restaurants), Gore Vidal (author), Bobby Vinton (singer), Kurt Vonnegut, Jr. (author), George Washington (first president), and Orville Wright (aviation pioneer).

ARMY STATISTICS

As of September 2005, Army personnel statistics are as follows:

Total Strength:	1,041,340
Active Duty:	488,000
Commissioned Officer:	103,580
Warrant Officer:	15,011
Enlisted:	558,993
Reserve:	189,000

CHAPTER 3

Understanding the U.S. Navy

★ OVERVIEW ★

The United States Navy is the equivalent of the Army but on water. This branch of the military runs America's defense of the seas. While not quite as large, complicated, and convoluted as the Army, the Navy is a huge organization, and with its size comes its own brand of confusing and nearly inexplicable terminology.

★ MISSION ★

The official mission of the Navy is to maintain, train, and equip combat-ready naval forces capable of winning wars, deterring aggression, and maintaining freedom of the seas.

★ BACKGROUND ★

The Continental Navy was established on October 13, 1775, when the Continental Congress in Philadelphia authorized two armed vessels to search for ships supplying the British Army. About fifty ships were operated during the

Revolutionary War; soon after, Congress authorized the construction of six frigates. Several of these were instrumental in the War of 1812, including the USS *Constitution*, the USS *United States*, and the USS *Constellation*.

The overall history of the United States Navy is divided into two major periods: the "Old Navy," a small but well-respected force of innovative sailing ships such as the ironclads during the Civil War; and the "New Navy," the modernized fleet that began in the 1880s and became the most powerful navy in the world. Noting that other countries were building up their navies provided the impetus for constructing a bevy of large, modern warships. The philosophical doctrine of Manifest Destiny also justified the expansion of American interests beyond the continent. The Spanish-American War gave naval warships an opportunity to show their might, and Teddy Roosevelt's Great White Fleet cruise in the early 1900s made it clear that America's naval forces were not to be trifled with. Despite this, the Navy's role in World War I was mainly as convoy escorts, troop transport, and minefield clearing.

The attack at Pearl Harbor by Japanese bombers heavily damaged the American fleet but brought America fully into World War II. By this time, the use of battleships was nearly over. Aircraft carriers, essentially sea-going airbases, were used in the Battle of the Coral Sea and the Battle of Midway, as well as in a range of other smaller fights with Japan in the Pacific. The Navy was used in support of landings in Europe and captured a German submarine in 1944; it assisted in the Philippines and the Japanese surrender on the battleship *Missouri*.

In the 1950s, nuclear-powered ships, along with missiles and jets, were developed specifically for naval use, giving the Navy its reputation for high technology and superior capabilities. Naval aircraft carriers and gunboats were active in Vietnam; during the Cold War, construction of ships expanded to keep up with the Soviet fleet. Today, the world's waters are dominated by the U.S. Navy with its powerful aircraft carriers and supporting watercraft and aircraft. In the 1990s, American naval strategy was to have the ability to engage in two simultaneous, limited wars along separate fronts. Following the September 11, 2001, attacks, the Navy designed several new classes of ships to enable it to meet more diverse missions with a reduced force.

★ ORGANIZATION ★

The Department of the Navy has three primary components: the Navy Department; the Operating Forces, which include the Navy, the Marine Corps, Reserve components, and in time of war, the U.S. Coast Guard; and the Shore

Establishment. The Marine Corps and the Coast Guard are described in chapters four and six, respectively.

The Navy Department

The head of the Navy is the secretary of the navy (SECNAV) who is responsible for an annual budget in excess of $110 billion and over 800,000 personnel. His job is to implement policies established by the president and the secretary of defense. The Honorable Gordon R. England was sworn in as the seventy-third secretary of the Navy on October 1, 2003. He is the second person in history to serve twice. He also served as secretary of the Navy from May 24, 2001, until January 2003 when he joined the Department of Homeland Security.

Answering to the secretary of the Navy are two commanders: 1) the chief of naval operations (CNO), a four-star admiral who is responsible for the Navy Operating forces and the Shore Establishment; 2) and the commandant of the Marine Corps, who commands the Marine Corps. The CNO is also a member of the Joint Chiefs of Staff and serves as the principal naval advisor to the president. Admiral Michael G. Mullen became the twenty-eighth chief of naval operations on July 22, 2005. Assistants to this office include vice chief of naval operations (VCNO), the deputy chiefs of naval operations (DCNOs), and other ranking officers; collectively, these offices are known as the office of the chief of naval operations (OpNav).

The Operating Forces of the Navy

Like the Army, divisions within the Navy overlap with commands and functions sometimes held jointly. The Atlantic Fleet (Second Fleet) and the Pacific Fleet (Third Fleet) are the main fleets. The Fifth, Sixth, and Seventh Fleets are located in the Middle East, in the Mediterranean Sea, and in the Western Pacific and Indian Ocean, respectively. There have been seven numbered fleets, with the first and fourth fleets no longer active.

ATLANTIC FLEET. The Atlantic Fleet (Second Fleet) operates to keep sea lanes open, deter aggression, and defend territory in the Atlantic and Indian Oceans, the Caribbean and Mediterranean Seas, and the Persian Gulf. This fleet includes Naval Surface Forces, Naval Air Forces, Naval Submarine Forces, and other separate commands.

The *Naval Surface Forces* consolidated the former Cruiser-Destroyer, Amphibious, Service and Mine Forces, Atlantic Fleet. It consists of about 110 ships and additional special units, and it employs 35,000 personnel stationed stateside, from Bath, Maine, to Corpus Christi, Texas, and at sea, from the Norwegian Sea in the Atlantic Ocean to the Persian Gulf of the Arabian Sea in the Indian Ocean. Additional surface forces are used in drug interdiction operations in the Caribbean Sea and the Eastern Pacific.

The *Naval Air Forces* is composed of more than 40,000 men and women, six aircraft carriers, seventy aircraft squadrons, and approximately 1,400 aircraft. It provides combat-ready air forces to fleet commanders operating in areas ranging from the North Pole to the Antarctic and from the East Coast of the United States to the Indian Ocean.

The *Atlantic Fleet Submarine Force* numbers forty submarines and over 15,000 officer, enlisted, and civilian personnel providing submarine support to the Atlantic, Arctic, Eastern Pacific, and Indian Oceans, and the Mediterranean Sea. It operates and maintains combat-ready, nuclear-powered strategic deterrent and attack submarines. Fleet ballistic missile submarines carry the highly accurate Trident II D-5 Missile and operate in international waters, ensuring our nation's strategic security. Attack submarines are responsible for antisubmarine warfare, intelligence gathering, insertion of Special Forces, Tomahawk strike missions, mining, and search and rescue. Atlantic Fleet submarine squadrons are located in Groton, Connecticut; Norfolk, Virginia; Kings Bay, Georgia; and La Maddalena, Sardinia, Italy.

PACIFIC FLEET. The Pacific Fleet (Third Fleet) has the mission to keep the sea lanes open, deter aggression, provide regional stability, and support humanitarian relief activities in the Pacific region. Its territory covers over half of the earth's surface, encompassing more than 100 million square miles in the Pacific, Indian, and Arctic Oceans, in waters from the west coast of the United States to the Arabian Gulf. The Pacific Fleet currently includes 200 ships, 2,000 aircraft, and about 240,000 personnel. Navy personnel are stationed in Guam, Hawaii, Japan, Korea, and Singapore, as well as along the northwest and southwest American shores.

U.S. NAVAL FORCES EUROPE (NAVEUR). This provides overall command, operational control, and coordination of U.S. Naval forces in the European theater. Headquartered in London, England, NAVEUR directs naval operations through the Sixth Fleet based in Gaeta, Italy, and support activities ashore through the Navy Region Europe, headquartered in Naples, Italy. NAVEUR's area of responsibility covers about half of the Atlantic Ocean, from the North Pole to Antarctica, as well as the Mediterranean, Black, Barents, Caspian, and Baltic Seas, encompassing ninety-one countries and 21 million square miles of land and sea. The Navy has approximately 24,000 sailors at any one time in Europe. Typically, half serve aboard units of forward-deployed carrier strike groups and expeditionary strike groups, while the rest are assigned to the Navy's shore support facilities.

The operational arm of Naval Forces Europe is the Sixth Fleet; it directs all operations for carrier strike groups and expeditionary strike groups during their rotational deployments from homeports on the East Coast. During the war in Iraq, the Sixth Fleet operated two carrier strike groups led by the aircraft carriers USS *Theodore Roosevelt* and USS *Harry S. Truman*; one expeditionary strike group led by the amphibious assault ship USS *Iwo Jima*; and more than 150 aircraft.

Navy Region Europe is the logistics and support arm of Naval Forces Europe, and is responsible for the maintenance and supply of shore facilities throughout Europe. Major naval facilities that make up Navy Region Europe, include: Naval Activities United Kingdom; Naval Station Rota, Spain; Naval Support Activities in Italy at La Magdalena, Naples, and Gaeta, and in Greece at Souda Bay; and Naval Air Stations in Keflavik, Iceland, and Sigonella, Italy.

U.S. NAVAL FORCES CENTRAL COMMAND. U.S. Naval Forces Central Command's area of responsibility encompasses about 7.5 million square miles and includes the Arabian Gulf, Red Sea, Gulf of Oman, and parts of the Indian Ocean. It includes twenty-seven countries and three critical "chokepoints" at the Strait of Hormuz, the Suez Canal, and the Strait of Bab el Mandeb at the southern tip of Yemen. It is headquartered in Bahrain and commands the Fifth Fleet.

U.S. SEVENTH FLEET. The Seventh Fleet is the largest of the Navy's forward-deployed fleets. Originally established in 1943, it now has forty to fifty ships, over 200 aircraft, and 20,000 Navy and Marine Corps personnel. Forces operate from bases in Japan and Guam, or are rotated from bases in Hawaii or the continental

United States. The Seventh Fleet operates in the Western Pacific, Indian Ocean, and Arabian Gulf to promote peace and stability in this region.

MILITARY SEALIFT COMMAND (MSC). Military Sealift Command is responsible for the coordination of the Department of Defense's common-user air, land, and sea transportation services. Common-user ships carry cargo for more than one military branch; in fact, MSC reports to three separate divisional heads. For Navy transportation matters, MSC reports to the chief of naval operations. For research, development, and acquisition, and for procurement policy and oversight matters, MSC reports to the assistant secretary of the Navy, and to the commander, U.S. Transportation Command.

The Military Sealift Command operates more than 110 ships around the world. These ships use civilian crews, carry the designation "USNS" (United States Naval Ships) and the prefix "T" before the normal hull numbers, and are not commissioned ships. Some MSC ships have small military departments assigned to carry out specialized functions such as communications and supply operations.

NAVAL INSTALLATIONS COMMAND. This division covers naval bases and shore installation management. It's located in Washington, D.C.

OPERATIONAL TEST AND EVALUATION FORCES. Since 1945, this division has provided an independent and objective evaluation of the operational effectiveness and suitability of naval aviation, surface, subsurface, C4I, cryptologic, and space systems in support of acquisition and fleet introduction decisions.

NAVAL SPECIAL WARFARE COMMAND (SEALS). These are the sea, air and land assault forces (see chapter seven on special operations forces for more details). These are *the* Navy SEALs, the tough special operations forces unit of the Navy.

NAVAL NETWORK WARFARE COMMAND. NETWARCOM is the Navy's central operational authority for space systems, information technology, and network operations in support of naval forces afloat and ashore. Other missions include operating and securing an interoperable naval network; coordination and assessment of the Navy's requirements for networking, command-and-control, and information operations; and serving as the operational forces' advocate in the development and implementation of space systems.

NAVAL RESERVE FORCES. This is the division that recruits, trains, and eventually puts to work reserve forces in times of national emergencies.

The Shore Establishment of the Navy

This portion of the Navy covers all operations, installations, and activities that deal with onshore or Navy-wide duties and responsibilities.

BUREAU OF NAVAL PERSONNEL (BUPERS). Covers all aspects of personnel management. It entails such components as budgets, finances, manpower, compensation, and foreign languages.

BUREAU OF MEDICINE AND SURGERY (BUMED). Headquarters command for Navy medicine, whose goal is to provide high quality, economical health care in wartime and in peacetime. Highly trained Navy medicine personnel deploy with sailors and marines worldwide, providing critical mission support aboard ships, in the air, and on the battlefield. Navy corpsmen are especially appreciated for these services to the Marine Corps. Additionally, this division provides health care services to military family members and retirees worldwide.

NAVAL SEA SYSTEMS COMMAND (NAVSEA). The largest of the Navy's systems commands, it engineers, builds, and supports the nation's fleet of ships and combat systems. This command accounts for almost a fifth of the Navy's total operating budget and operates over a hundred different acquisition programs. Staffing includes 37,000 persons working in shipyards and at the undersea and surface warfare centers.

NAVAL AIR SYSTEMS COMMAND (NAVAIR). This command is the equivalent of NAVSEA but for the air division within the Navy. It provides the air power and systems the Navy relies upon.

NAVAL FACILITIES ENGINEERING COMMAND (NAVFAC). Produces and trains engineering professionals who are committed to Navy and Marine Corps combat readiness. With a staff of over 13,000 military, civilians, and contractors who serve as engineers, architects, contract specialists, and professionals, NAVFAC has a "business volume" of over $7.6 billion.

NAVAL SUPPLY SYSTEMS COMMAND (NAVSUP). This command provides the Navy with all its supplies and services. Its workforce numbers more than 24,000 (military and civilians). NAVSUP oversees logistics of supply operations, conventional ordnance, contracting, resale, fuel, transportation, and security assistance, in addition to "quality of life" services such as food and postal services, Navy exchanges, and movement of household goods.

SPACE AND NAVAL WARFARE SYSTEMS COMMAND (SPAWAR). This command is responsible for the acquisitions and management of communications and warfare systems. It has a budget of over $5.4 billion.

STRATEGIC SYSTEMS PROGRAMS. This is the defense program based initially on the Polaris missiles and currently on Trident I and II fleet ballistic missiles.

U.S. NAVAL ACADEMY. Located in Annapolis, Maryland, this is the officer training academy for both the Navy and Marine Corps. (See page 77 for more details.)

NAVAL EDUCATION AND TRAINING COMMAND (NETC). Its mission is to educate and train naval personnel.

NAVAL METEOROLOGY AND OCEANOGRAPHY COMMAND. This command applies oceanographic sciences for military benefits.

OFFICE OF NAVAL INTELLIGENCE. This covers the collection and use of all forms of intelligence for military benefits.

NAVAL STRIKE AND AIR WARFARE CENTER. Located in Fallon, Nevada, this center provides air warfare training under realistic conditions.

NAVAL SECURITY GROUP COMMAND. Responsible for electronic warfare analysis, predeployment readiness training, and support for regionally based naval air and surface forces, including the cryptology division within the Navy.

NAVAL LEGAL SERVICE COMMAND. This division covers all aspects of legal services as required by the Navy.

U.S. NAVAL OBSERVATORY (USNO). The U.S. Naval Observatory is one of the oldest scientific agencies in the country. Established in 1830 as the Depot of Charts and Instruments, its primary mission was to care for the Navy's chronometers, charts, and other navigational equipment. Today it serves as the preeminent authority in the areas of precise time and astrometry, and distributes earth orientation parameters and other astronomical data required for accurate navigation and fundamental astronomy.

NAVAL SAFETY CENTER. This command covers all aspects of safety as it relates to personnel, equipment, occupational safety, and health.

NAVAL RESERVE OFFICER TRAINING CORPS (NROTC). This is the officer training program for college-bound recruits. Officer candidates, or "midshipmen," may enter via the College Program or the Scholarship Program. In the *College Program*, college prefreshmen can apply for the four-year track; freshmen and sophomores can apply for the two-year plan. Once accepted, candidates receive uniforms, naval science textbooks, a hundred-and-fifty-dollar monthly stipend during junior and senior years. The *Scholarship Program* pays tuition and fees, free textbooks, and a monthly stipend of two hundred dollars. Acceptance to this program is based on class rank, exam scores, and extracurricular activities. In addition to other studies, NROTC midshipmen are required to participate in weekly two-hour lessons in military science, in drill, and in hour-long weekly workouts. Following graduation, the midshipmen serve in the Reserves, with an eight-year obligation. College Program midshipmen spend an average of four to five years in active duty, and begin as ensigns, the lowest ranking officers. Recent statistics count one hundred and forty institutions in thirty-five states participating in the NROTC program.

★ CREEDS ★

THE SAILOR'S CREED

I am a United States Sailor.

I will support and defend the Constitution of the United States of America and I will obey the orders of those appointed over me.

I represent the fighting spirit of the Navy and those who have gone before me to defend freedom and democracy around the world.

I proudly serve my country's Navy combat team with Honor, Courage and Commitment.

I am committed to excellence and the fair treatment of all.

THE NAVY RESERVIST'S CREED

I serve voluntarily in the service of my choice … The United States Navy.

I serve willingly, because it is my privilege, as well as my duty, to serve my country.

I serve with pride, because of the heritage passed down to me by our long line of proud Navy volunteers.

I serve with dignity, because I know that to associates among the civilian population, I am the Navy.

I serve with honor, because the Navy's honor is mine to cherish and guard.

I serve with confidence, because I am certain of the ability of my Navy leaders and the future of the Navy.

I serve with fellowship, because I am secure in the unique and splendid comradeship of the Navy.

I ask only that I be given, by my country and my fellow citizens, the opportunity to better prepare myself and to serve in the defense of our beloved nation.

Amen.

★ RATE AND UNIFORMS ★

Rate in the Navy

Unlike the other branches of the American military, Navy personnel are not given the term *rank*; the correct term is *rate*. Navy personnel may be commissioned officers, warrant officers, or enlisted personnel. See appendix B for a comparison of rank between services.

- *Commissioned officers* rank as follows: fleet Admiral (five-star, wartime use only); admiral (four-star); vice admiral (three-star); rear admiral, upper half (two-star); rear admiral, lower half (one-star); captain; commander; lieutenant commander; lieutenant; lieutenant junior grade; and ensign.

  Commissioned officers may be unrestricted line (surface warfare, aviation, submarine warfare, special warfare, or nuclear); restricted line (engineering, aerospace engineering or maintenance, cryptologic, naval intelligence, public affairs, meteorology and oceanography, information, human resources); or staff corps (supply, medical, dental, nurse, chaplain, civil engineer, judge advocate general, navy band).

- *Warrant officers* include, from top to bottom, chief warrant officers 5 to 2; the use of warrant officer 1 has been discontinued.

- *Enlisted personnel* include, from top to bottom: master chief petty officer of the Navy; master chief petty officer; fleet/command master chief petty officer; senior chief petty officer; chief petty officer; petty officer first class; petty officer second class; petty officer third class; seaman; seaman apprentice; seaman recruit.

★ PROMOTION/ADVANCEMENT TIMELINE ★

The following list reflects the time-in-rate required between pay grades for enlisted Navy personnel:

E-1 to E-2: nine months

E-2 to E-3: nine months

E-3 to E-4: six months

E-4 to E-5: twelve months

E-5 to E-6: thirty-six months

E-6 to E-7: thirty-six months

E-7 to E-8: thirty-six months

E-8 to E-9: thirty-six months

Navy Uniforms

- *Utility uniforms* include blue coveralls, used in dirty, laborious environments ashore, or as the primary uniform when underway "at sea." The officers' utility uniforms include a gold or white insignia and gold or silver belt buckle worn with black boots. The petty officers' utility uniforms include a light blue blouse, dark blue trousers, navy belt, and black boots or black leather shoes (sneakers when underway). This uniform is not worn away from a naval installation; it is worn only in transit to and from base or on base or ship.

- The *working uniform*, "working whites" or "working blues," is used by officers, chief petty officers, and petty officers when interacting with the public or in office environments. The working white uniform includes the "Dixie cup" white hat. The "working khaki" uniform, worn by chief petty officers and officers, has a khaki blouse, khaki trousers, khaki belt, and boots or shoes as above. A new working uniform, similar to Army and Marine Corps' uniforms is being tested in colors of gray, black, or blue, as found in the Navy. It may eliminate the service white uniform.

- There are several *dress uniforms*. The *service white uniform* has white trousers or skirt, white shoes, and a high collar white tunic with shoulder boards. The *service dress blue uniform* has black shoes, Navy blue (very dark blue) trousers or skirt, Navy blue coat, and a white shirt with bowtie.

The *rating badge* is a combination of rate and rating. Rate refers to pay grade, and is indicated by the chevrons, or upside-down "V" used in insignia; rating is the occupational specialty, and indicated by a symbol just above the chevrons. A ratings badge is worn on the left, upper sleeve of all uniforms for petty officers. chief petty officers wear collar devices on their white and khaki uniforms, and rating badges on their service dress blues.

Commissioned officers wear their rank devices in different places depending on the type of uniform. For the khakis, or working uniform, pins on the collar are worn. For whites, stripes are worn on the shoulder boards. For dress blues, stripes are sewn on the lower sleeve.

Officers are either considered "line" officers or "staff corps." Staff corps are specialists in career fields—e.g., physicians, lawyers, civil engineers—and wear their specialty insignia on the sleeve of the dress blue uniforms and on their shoulder boards in place of the star worn by line officers. On winter blue and khaki uniforms, the specialty insignia is a collar device worn on the left collar while the rank device is worn on the right. Commissioned warrant officers (line officers or staff corps officers that have advanced through the enlisted rates and have technical expertise in particular fields) wear insignia on the sleeve of the dress blue uniforms and on their shoulder boards. Limited duty officers wear their specialty insignia on the sleeve of the dress blue uniforms and on their shoulder boards in place of the star worn by line officers. On winter blue and khaki uniforms, the specialty insignia is a collar device worn on the left collar while the rank device is worn on the right.

★ CORE VALUES OF THE NAVY ★

Honor: "I will bear true faith and allegiance ..." Accordingly, we will: Conduct ourselves in the highest ethical manner in all relationships with peers, superiors and subordinates; Be honest and truthful in our dealings with each other, and with those outside the Navy; Be willing to make honest recommendations and accept those of junior personnel; Encourage new ideas and deliver the bad news, even when it is unpopular; Abide by an uncompromising code of integrity, taking responsibility for our actions and keeping our word; Fulfill or exceed our legal and ethical responsibilities in our public and personal lives twenty-four hours a day. Illegal or improper behavior or even the appearance of such behavior will not be tolerated. We are accountable for our professional and personal behavior. We will be mindful of the privilege to serve our fellow Americans.

Courage: "I will support and defend ..." Accordingly, we will have: Courage to meet the demands of our profession and the mission when it is hazardous, demanding, or otherwise difficult; Make decisions in the best interest of the Navy and the nation, without regard to personal consequences; Meet these challenges while adhering to a higher standard of personal conduct and decency; Be loyal to our nation, ensuring the resources entrusted to us are used in an honest, careful, and efficient way. Courage is the value that gives us the moral and mental strength to do what is right, even in the face of personal or professional adversity.

Commitment: "I will obey the orders ..." Accordingly, we will: Demand respect up and down the chain of command; Care for the safety, professional, personal, and spiritual well-being of our people; Show respect toward all people without regard to race, religion, or gender; Treat each individual with human dignity; Be committed to positive change and constant improvement; Exhibit the highest degree of moral character, technical excellence, quality and competence in what we have been trained to do. The day-to-day duty of every Navy man and woman is to work together as a team to improve the quality of our work, our people, and ourselves.

★ JOINING THE NAVY ★

Individuals may join the Navy along several tracks: 1) by direct enlistment, 2) joining through the Naval Reserves (NROTC) program, or 3) joining the elite Naval Academy. Additionally, persons trained in particular areas such as medicine or law may obtain a direct appointment to the Navy as an officer. Some of the specifics for each track are listed below:

ENLISTMENT. Enlistees must be between the ages eighteen and thirty-four (seventeen with parental consent), a high school graduate or equivalent, and take the "Naval test drive," which is an informal interview with a recruiter to discuss basics, answer questions, and schedule the Armed Services Vocation Aptitude Battery (ASVAB), the general aptitude test of all the military services. Other tests are given to ensure the candidate is mentally, physically, and morally capable of service. The enlistee begins as an E-1, a seaman recruit.

NROTC. Midshipmen candidates must either apply to a college that participates in the NROTC or already be enrolled at one, take the same battery of tests that enlisted personnel do, and be accepted into the program. Midshipmen then have an eight-year obligation in the Reserve Forces, and begin as ensigns.

NAVAL ACADEMY. Individuals may enter the Navy as officers via the Naval Academy (see below for details).

DIRECT APPOINTMENT. Experienced professionals trained in a range of specialties are always in demand as directly appointed officers. Specialties include medicine, dentistry, engineering, law, and religion. Requirements include a college degree (good grades are required), good health, and age of nineteen to thirty-four.

Competition is tough. College graduates accepted into this track attend thirteen weeks of Officer Candidate School (OCS) at Pensacola, Florida, and begin their careers as ensign. Appointments include a minimum four-year obligation. Professionals with more specialized training attend the six-week Officer Indoctrination School (OIS) in Newport, Rhode Island, and also begin as ensign. Within four to five years, the direct-appointed officer may be promoted to lieutenant.

★ TRAINING IN THE U.S. NAVY ★

PRIMARY TRAINING. The Navy recruit's primary training (Boot Camp) begins at Recruit Training Command in Great Lakes, Illinois, or as a "plebe" (freshman) at the U.S. Naval Academy in Annapolis, Maryland. Recruits must complete nine and a half weeks of basic training, a challenging and demanding experience. Their mentor is the recruit division commander (RDC), an experienced career sailor, specially selected for his or her professionalism, experience, and commitment to excellence. Recruits must satisfactorily complete all phases of training, including academic, physical, and medical standards. If unsatisfactory, he or she may be given a second opportunity to meet the standards in a junior division that allows the recruit to concentrate on particular weaknesses. Failure to make sufficient progress results in discharge.

DAILY ROUTINE. Each day of Boot Camp has a routine much the same as that which occurs in the Army. The schedule is based on ten forty-minute training periods daily. Classes involve academic instruction, training, and administrative activities.

DUTIES AND COMPETITION. Every recruit shares in the general duties, called Service Week. Service Week includes food service duties in the enlisted dining facility, various administrative tasks, deck swabbing, facility maintenance (e.g., lawn care, snow removal), and other necessary jobs to ensure basic living conditions for all.

During Recruit Training, divisions also compete for weekly awards in such categories as athletic skills, scholastics, military drill, personnel inspections, and overall excellence, with flags awarded to the winning divisions. These flags are carried in ceremonial dress parades and reviews. Honor recruits receive special recognition in the dress parades.

GOING ABOARD. Navy recruits reporting for duty on ships or submarines are under strict space requirements and are limited to one seabag to include a specified list of clothing items and very little else.

★ U.S. NAVAL ACADEMY OF ★ THE NAVY AND MARINE CORPS

The premier officer-generating program for both the Navy and Marine Corps is the U.S. Naval Academy, in Annapolis, Maryland. The Naval Academy gives young men and women the academic and professional training needed to be effective Navy and Marine officers in their assignments after graduation. Officer development integrates moral, ethical, and character development of midshipmen in every aspect of the Academy experience. The Naval Academy believes that this approach distinguishes the Academy from all other educational institutions and officer commissioning sources.

MISSION. The mission of the Naval Academy is "to develop midshipmen morally, mentally, and physically."

★ HONOR IN THE ACADEMY ★

The Officer Development Program is designed to develop and strengthen the attributes of integrity, honor, and mutual respect in Academy students. The *Honor Concept* is as follows:

"Midshipmen are persons of integrity: They stand for that which is right. They tell the truth and ensure that the full truth is known. They do not lie. They embrace fairness in all actions. They ensure that work submitted as their own is their own, and that assistance received from any source is authorized and properly documented. They do not cheat. They respect the property of others and ensure that others are able to benefit from the use of their own property. They do not steal."

Violating these principles may be grounds for permanent dismissal from the Academy. The *Honor Treatise* was developed in 1994 to enable plebes and midshipmen to better understand the ramifications of the Honor Concept. It is as follows:

"As a Brigade we cherish the diverse backgrounds and talents of every midshipman yet recognize the common thread that unites us: the trust and confidence of the American people. They have appointed us to defend our country by developing our minds, our bodies, and most especially, our moral character. It is our responsibility to develop a selfless sense of duty that demands excellence both of ourselves and of those with whom we serve. We must honor our loyalties without compromising our ultimate obligation to the truth. Our leadership must set a standard that reflects loyalty to our goals and the courage to stand accountable for all our actions, both those that lead to success and to those that end in failure. We will never settle for achieving merely what is expected of us but will strive for a standard of excellence that reflects the dedication and courage of those who have gone before us. When we attain our goal, we will raise our expectations; when we fall short, we will rise up and try again. In essence, we espouse leadership by example, a leadership that will inspire others to follow wherever we may lead.

Countless challenges and trials lie before us. We believe that those with the strongest moral foundation will be the leaders who best reflect the legacy of the Naval Academy. This is our call as midshipmen: It is a mission we proudly accept."

BACKGROUND. The Naval School was first established (without congressional funding) at Fort Severn in Annapolis, Maryland, on October 10, 1845, with a class of fifty midshipmen and seven professors. The original curriculum included mathematics and navigation, gunnery and steam, chemistry, English, natural philosophy, and French. Five years later it was renamed the United States Naval Academy, with a new curriculum requiring midshipmen to study for four years and to train aboard ships each summer. The campus covers 338 acres, with 4,000 midshipmen enrolled annually. Bachelor of science degrees were first awarded in 1933 as authorized by Congress. The present core curriculum has eighteen major fields of study, including an array of elective courses, advanced study, and research opportunities. The Academy accepted the first women midshipmen in 1976; women now comprise nearly 15 percent of entering plebes. Academic and physical training for women is the same as for men, although the physical standards are slightly reduced.

APPLICATION. Top high school students who are athletic and active in community affairs are considered, but the competition for acceptance into the Naval Academy is tough. A candidate's SAT or ACT scores and class rank are reviewed, and if adequate, he or she is invited to complete the full application process. The official instructions state that the application process "normally includes nomination letters from the candidate's U.S. representative, two U.S. senators, *and* the vice president." Other approved sources of nomination letters include: the president of the United States, active members of the Navy and Marine Corps, members of Reserve Officer Training Corps units, children of deceased or disabled veterans, children of prisoners of war or servicemen missing in action, or children of Medal of Honor awardees.

Background checks, medical exams, and a few other specifics (candidates cannot be married, pregnant, or have children) are required besides the age restrictions of seventeen to twenty-three years old. In return for a five-year post-graduation obligation of active duty, midshipmen receive free education, meals, and a monthly stipend of six hundred dollars to start.

Midshipmen begin their tenure at the Academy with the so-called "Plebe Summer," the seven weeks before freshman year actually begins. Freshmen, or "plebes," begin their days at dawn with an hour of rigorous exercise, followed by training and indoctrination into the Academy. Mental and physical exercises continue past sunset with no leisure time whatsoever. It's an intense welcome into the program. Once the fall semester begins, the midshipmen's schedules are focused on academics, but physical rigor is still a major factor. The routine is much the same for their four years at the Academy. A typical weekday schedule looks like this:

5:30 A.M. Personal fitness workout (optional)

6:30 A.M. Reveille (all hands out of bed)

6:30–7:00 A.M. Special instruction period for plebes

7:00 A.M. Morning meal formation

7:10 A.M. Breakfast

7:55–11:45 A.M. Four class periods, one hour each

12:05 P.M. Noon meal formation

12:15 P.M. Noon meal for all midshipmen

12:40–1:20 P.M. Company training time

1:30–3:30 P.M. Fifth and sixth class periods

3:30–6:00 P.M. Varsity and intramural athletics, extracurricular and personal activities; drill and parades twice weekly in the fall and spring

5:00–7:00 P.M. Supper

7:30–11 P.M. Study period for all midshipmen

11:00 P.M. Lights out for plebes

Midnight Taps for upperclassmen

Add to this strict schedule additional military duties, inspection preparation, and extra academic instruction if necessary. There isn't much time left for sleep, much less for thinking or game playing.

ACADEMICS. Midshipmen at the Academy major in a range of technical or scientific fields. These include traditional areas of study as well as those specific to Naval issues: aerospace engineering, chemistry, computer science, economics, electrical engineering, English, general engineering, general science, history, information technology, mathematics, mechanical engineering, naval architecture, ocean engineering, oceanography, physics, political science, quantitative economics, and systems engineering.

A typical plebe fall semester course load would include: Chemistry I, Calculus I, Writing, Government and Constitutional Development, and Leadership. A typical plebe spring semester would include: Chemistry II, Calculus II, Rhetoric and Literature, American Naval History, and American Naval Science.

Upon graduation, a bachelor of science degree is awarded. Those in the top 10 percent of their class graduate with distinction. Those who have completed special honors programs in one of six selected majors graduate with honors.

Special programs include Trident Scholars, Honors Programs, and the Voluntary Graduate Education Program (VGRP). The *Trident Scholar Program* is an independent study and research available to exceptionally capable midshipmen during their senior year. First class scholars conduct independent research in an area of interest, working with a faculty advisor who is an expert in the field. Trident Scholars carry a reduced formal course load to allow time for in-depth research and for preparation of a thesis.

Other midshipmen with excellent academic and leadership performance can apply for *Honors Programs* offered in history, English, political science, mathematics, oceanography, and economics. Honors students complete a thesis or research project and orally defend it before a panel of faculty members.

In the *Voluntary Graduate Education Program*, midshipmen who have completed course requirements early through any combination of validation and overloading can compete for selection and begin work toward their master's degrees at nearby civilian universities, such as Johns Hopkins and the University of Maryland. Up to twenty midshipmen can participate annually, starting graduate work during first-class (senior) year and completing their master's degree programs within seven months after graduation from the Naval Academy. Fields of study are selected from Navy-approved graduate education programs leading to Navy subspecialty qualification.

PROFESSIONAL DEVELOPMENT. The Academy prides itself on its professional and leadership training. Instructors indoctrinate students with the traditions and customs of naval service, from teaching them to take orders to learning to give them. Classroom studies are backed by many hours of practical experience in leadership and naval operations, including assignments with Navy and Marine Corps units.

PHYSICAL FITNESS. The Naval Academy athletic program receives a priority much different from that at civilian schools. Athletic teams are an integral part of the overall education of midshipmen, providing leadership opportunities, team exercises, cooperative effort, commitment, and individual sacrifice. The primary goal of the physical education curriculum is fitness, which is understood as "vital for midshipman health, personal appearance and well-being" and therefore performance. Additionally, midshipmen take the Physical Readiness Test twice a year. This includes the following minimums for men and women:

	MEN	WOMEN
1.5-mile run (maximum time)	10:30	12:40
Push-ups (minimum in 2 minutes)	40	18
Sit-ups (minimum in 2 minutes)	65	65

ACADEMY SPORTS. Men's varsity sports include baseball, basketball, crew, cross country, football, golf, gymnastics, lacrosse, soccer, sprint football, squash, swimming, tennis, track and field, water polo, and wrestling. Women's varsity sports include basketball, crew, cross country, soccer, swimming, track and field, and volleyball. Co-ed varsity sports include sailing and rifle. Additional club sports are possible for men (boxing, hockey, lacrosse, rugby, and volleyball), for women (gymnastics, lacrosse, tennis, rugby, and softball), or co-ed (combat pistol, cycle, judo, karate, pistol, powerlifting, and triathlon). Sports facilities are excellent and not reserved for only a few midshipmen; all have access to them, whether for team use or individual workouts. The Navy Midshipmen compete in the NCAA Patriot League against Army and other exclusive northeastern universities.

★ NAVY EQUIPMENT ★

The Navy is defined in part by the equipment it uses. Its effectiveness depends less on individual troops than on watercraft and aircraft. An understanding of the Navy depends on comprehending the craft it relies upon.

Commissioned ships are named beginning with "USS" which means "United States Ship." Noncommissioned, civilian-manned vessels of the U.S. Navy are named beginning with "USNS," for "United States Naval Ship." Vessel types are designated using a letter-based hull classification symbol. Ship names are selected by the secretary of the Navy and generally include American states, cities, towns, important people, famous battles, fish, and ideals.

There are several classes of ships in the U.S. Navy fleet. These include:

AIRCRAFT CARRIERS. Aircraft carriers are the strategic arm of the Navy, putting American air power within reach of most land-based military power. American aircraft carriers are the largest, most powerful in the world. Modern aircraft carriers are typically named for politicians; previous aircraft carriers were named for battles or famous fighting ships of the Navy. All have hull classification designations of CV, CVA, CVB, CVL, and CVN. These designations mean the following: "CV" refers to basic aircraft carrier; "CVA" designates attack aircraft carrier (now just "CV"); "CVB" refers to large aircraft carrier (now just CVA); "CVL" is light aircraft carrier; and "CVN" means nuclear-powered aircraft carrier. There are currently sixty-nine aircraft carriers in the Navy fleet with two additional carriers planned or under construction. Twenty-two of these include supercarriers (with much greater capacity than traditional carriers). The supercarrier USS *Nimitz* can carry fifty or more aircraft on its deck.

AMPHIBIOUS ASSAULT SHIPS. Amphibious assault ships ("amphibs," "phibs" or "gator freighters") include a range of classes of warship used to land and support ground forces on enemy territory by amphibious assault. They resemble small aircraft carriers, but their aviation facilities host helicopters to support forces ashore rather than to support strike aircraft. Amphibious assault ships are usually named after World War II aircraft carriers, as earlier ships of this class were actually converted World War II carriers.

Designations include LHA (amphibious assault Tarawa-class), LHD (amphibious assault Wasp-class), LPH (landing platform, helicopter, amphibious assault ships of the Iwo Jima-class), LPD (amphibious assault landing platform dock), LSD (amphibious assault dock landing ship), LSL (amphibious assault, landing ship, logistics), LSM (amphibious assault landing ship, medium), LST (amphibious assault landing ship, tank), LCC (amphibious assault, landing craft, control), LCT (amphibious assault, landing craft, tank), LCU (amphibious assault, landing craft utility), AGF (amphibious assault, auxiliary command ship).

AMPHIBIOUS TRANSPORT DOCKS. These include warships that embark, transport, and land elements of a landing force for a variety of expeditionary warfare missions. Their helicopters, vertical takeoff and landing aircraft, and air-cushion or conventional landing craft support the Marine Corps. The ships transport troops into a war zone by sea, primarily using landing craft, although they also have limited airborne capability. Amphibious transport docks incorporate both a flight deck and a well deck, which can be ballasted and deballasted to support landing craft or amphibious vehicles. They are named mainly for cities. Exceptions include USS *New York* (LPD-21) (named for the state), and USS *Somerset* (LPD-25) (named for Somerset County, Pennsylvania).

DOCK LANDING SHIPS. These are medium amphibious transports that carry more landing craft than the amphibious transport dock above, but have less vehicle space and no helicopter hangar. They transport and launch amphibious craft and vehicles, carry landing craft air cushions (LCACs), and transport Marine troops. They are named after locations in the United States.

SUBMARINES. Submarines are either *ballistic* (carry nuclear submarine-launched ballistic missiles or SLBMs) or *attack* submarines, which carry out missions that include sinking ships and subs, launching cruise missiles, and gathering intelligence. Sea attack subs are typically named for cities; land attack submarines

(Virginia- and Ohio-class) are generally named for states. There are currently about twenty ballistic submarines and sixty attack submarines in the Navy.

CRUISERS. Guided missile cruisers are capable of conducting war via air, surface, or undersea. All modern cruisers are named for battles. Previous cruisers were either named for cities, naval heroes, or states. There are twenty-three cruisers of the Ticonderoga-class.

DESTROYERS. All destroyers since USS *Bainbridge* have been named for naval heroes. Hull designations include DD (guided missile destroyer), DL (destroyer leader), DDG (guided missile frigate), DLG (guided missile destroyer leader), and DLGN (guided missile destroyer leader, nuclear powered).

FRIGATES. Modern frigates are used for antisubmarine warfare or escorting other ships. The Navy is gradually retiring its frigate fleet. They are named for naval heroes.

BATTLESHIPS. All U.S. battleships have been retired. Most battleships were named for states.

AIRCRAFT. Aircraft are also critical to the Navy's success. The following are some of the aircraft used by the Navy: A-4 Skyhawk, AV-8B Harrier II, C-2 Greyhound, E-2C Hawkeye, E-6B Mercury, EA-6B Prowler, FH-1 Phantom, F-14 Tomcat, F/A-18 Hornet, F/A-18E/F Super Hornet, EA-18G Growler, CH-46 Sea Knight, CH-53 Sea Stallion, SH-2 Seasprite, SH-60 Sea Hawk, P-3C Orion, S-3B Viking, V-22 Osprey, T-6A Texan II, and T-45 Goshawk.

MISSILES. The Navy currently uses the Trident, Poseidon, Tomahawk, and Polaris missiles.

★ TOPGUN ★

TOPGUN is the code name and common name of the U.S. Navy Strike Fighter Tactics Instructor (SFTI) course. It was established in 1969 at Naval Air Station Miramar, California in response to disappointing Naval aviator performances in Vietnam. The school originally operated the A-4 Skyhawk and F-5 Freedom Fighter to instruct pilots, including the first American aces of the Vietnam War, Randy "Duke" Cunningham and Willie Driscoll.

During the 1970s, TOPGUN instructors used the F-16 Fighting Falcon to simulate the threat by the Soviet Union's new fourth generation MiG-29 "Fulcrum" and Su-27 "Flanker" fighters. In the 1990s, TOPGUN training expanded to emphasize the air-to-ground strike mission and retired their A-4s, F-5s, and F-16s in favor of F-14s and F/A-18s. In 1996, NAS Miramar was transferred to the Marine Corps, and TOPGUN was moved to the Naval Strike and Air Warfare Center (NSAWC) at NAS Fallon, Nevada. TOPGUN instructors currently fly the F/A-18 Hornet and the F-16 Falcon.

TOPGUN now conducts five six-week trainings annually. TOPGUN trains experienced Navy and Marine Corps aircrews in all aspects of fighter aircraft employment, including tactics, hardware, technique, and the current world threat. The course includes eighty hours of lectures and a rigorous flight schedule pitting student pilots against adversary aircraft flown by TOPGUN instructors. Ultimately, each graduate of the Navy Fighter Weapons School returns to his operational squadron as a Training Officer to carry the latest tactical doctrine back to his unit.

★ BLUE ANGELS ★

The Blue Angels, officially known as the Naval Flight Demonstration Squadron, have been in existence for more than fifty years. The squadron was formed after World War II by the chief of naval operations to keep the public interested in Naval Aviation. The Blue Angels regularly fly in spectator events and perform "fly-overs" for special military occasions, including funerals of important military and government personnel. Their official mission is to enhance Navy recruiting and to represent the Navy and Marine Corps to the rest of the American military and to the world as ambassadors of goodwill. They assumed the nickname "Blue Angels" after a famous New York City nightclub. They often perform with the Army Parachute team, the Golden Knights. Shows are about forty-five minutes long without repeated stunts.

Always on the cutting edge of technology, the Blue Angels change aircraft as new features and equipment become available. Originally, the Blue Angels performed at the Naval Air Station in Jacksonville, Florida, flying the F-6F Hellcat; within a few months, they switched to the F-8F Bearcat, when they introduced their famous "diamond" formation. They began using more powerful and maneuverable planes with jet engines in 1949. From 1953 to 1956, Blue Angels flew F-9/F-8 Cougars; from 1957 to 1968 they used F-11/F-1 Tigers. When McDonnell

Douglas Phantoms became available in 1973, they became the aircraft of choice, quickly followed by the Skyhawks in 1974. For the past ten years, they have flown the F/A-18 Hornet, the first dual-role fighter/attack aircraft now serving on the nation's front lines of defense.

Pilots selected for the Blue Angels team must be active duty Navy or Marine Corps tactical jet pilots with a minimum of 1,350 flight hours. Experience with the F/A-18 Hornet is a plus. Only about 225 pilots have been Blue Angels during their history.

★ SEABEES ★

The Navy Seabee's motto aptly describes their role in the Navy: "We build, we fight." The Seabees are the construction division, building entire bases, roads, airstrips, and many other construction projects to support Naval activities around the world. Early Seabees were recruited from civilian construction trades, and numbered 325,000 during World War II alone. After World War II, their numbers were reduced to about 3,000 men, then increased to about 10,000 for the Korean Conflict. Landing with the assault troops, the Seabees fought enemy fire and deadly tides to quickly provide causeways to benefit the rest of the troops. Because of their invaluable role in this conflict, they were not demobilized after the war ended.

After Korea, the Seabees provided construction assistance and training to underdeveloped countries, becoming the "Navy's Goodwill Ambassadors." This role continued through the Vietnam War, during which the Seabees built roads and public utilities even while fending off enemy fire. The Seabees have constructed Naval bases in Guam, Greece, Japan, Puerto Rico, Sicily, and Spain. Their largest peacetime effort occurred in 1971 on Diego Garcia, a small atoll in the Indian Ocean where the Navy's largest ships and the biggest military cargo jets are accommodated. Some 5,000 Gulf War Seabees served in the Middle East, constructing camps, aircraft landing, and support sites. Their unofficial motto is "Can Do!"

★ SEA CADETS ★

The Naval Sea Cadet Corps (NSCC) is designed to "introduce youth to naval life, to develop a sense of pride, patriotism, courage, and self-reliance, and to maintain an environment free of drugs and gangs." American citizens aged thirteen to seventeen who desire to learn about the Navy, Marine Corps, Coast Guard, and

Merchant Marine can apply, if they are in good health, pass a physical exam, are full-time students in good standing ("C" GPA required), and lack felony convictions. Sea Cadets drill with their units weekly or monthly in divisions, squadrons, or battalions. Organization is based on the surface Navy organization, squadrons are similar to naval aviation, and battalions are based upon Seabees, the construction battalions. The program goal is to foster an understanding of the military command structure as well as teamwork and camaraderie. Classroom instruction in military drill, leadership, and basic seamanship are included, as are regular skill competitions with other units. Cadets are given the rate of seaman recruit; the rate structure parallels the Navy's enlisted structure.

Training begins with Boot Camp, a two-week program of military drill and discipline, physical fitness, seamanship, first aid, naval history, shipboard safety, and leadership. Advanced training includes firefighting, airman school, culinary arts, submarine, mine warfare, construction, SEAL training, explosive ordnance, seamanship, SCUBA training, and leadership. This training is usually held for two weeks during the summer on ships and at shore stations around the world. Foreign exchange programs are also possible. Although there is no service commitment, former Sea Cadets may be eligible to enlist in the Navy at an advanced pay grade, or eligible for scholarships to college.

"ASK THE CHIEF"

By Michael D. Setzer, chief petty officer, U.S. Navy (RET)

As a country boy coming from a poor family in the foothills of the Appalachian Mountains in North Carolina, I learned early in life that hard work was the only way to forge ahead. The U.S. Navy provided both a place for me to work hard and rewards for that hard work, albeit in the early years, the rewards were pitifully small.

Since my father was a very strong and demanding man, I would have been lost without strong leadership. I found that in the Navy and thrived on it. I learned early on in the Navy that if you wanted to keep the chief off your back you had to not only follow his orders, you sometimes had to anticipate what those orders might be and act accordingly. In today's world, you would call that being proactive.

On a Navy ship, "Ask the chief" became a household phrase. Chiefs were strictly in charge and they ran everything in the Navy. No one ever spoke to their division officer until they ran it by the chief beforehand. If you tried to bypass the chief, he would find out about it sooner or later and there would be hell to pay. You didn't have to be a rocket scientist to figure out that the division officer always consulted with the chief before granting favors like special liberty or leave.

You didn't have to "suck up" to the chief, but you did have to respect him and you had to follow his orders. Your chief actually wrote your performance reports, and your next stripe was critically dependent upon it.

It was tough to become a chief, and it was a hard job once I got there. However, being a chief in the U.S. Navy was the most gratifying job I have ever had. The chief ran his division or shop. He decided who was qualified to do which jobs, he assigned work, and was responsible for the end product. He could grant or curtail leave and liberty; he could assign overtime work if necessary, including nights, weekends, and holidays. When one of his men had a discipline issue and "went before the Captain's Mast," the skipper always asked the chief's opinion of what kind of man the defendant was and usually asked for the chief's recommendation for punishment as well. It made good sense to stay on the right side of the chief.

The Navy also prepared me well for my second career, as a field service representative with General Electric A/C Engines, at which I spent twenty years.

To say that the Navy was a way of life for me is a gross understatement. I loved being in the Navy; I even loved Boot Camp. If I had any regrets it would be that I was gone from my family so much of the time, but even that wasn't all bad. I believe that my sons became better men because they learned how to take care of their own problems early in life, when Dad simply wasn't available.

★ CELEBRITY NAVAL MEMBERS ★

Some of the celebrity members of the U.S. Navy include: Neil Armstrong (astronaut, first man to walk on the moon); Humphrey Bogart (actor); George H. W. Bush (former president; former director of the CIA); Bill Cosby (actor, comedian); David Farragut (Civil War admiral); John Paul Jones (Revolution-ary War commander); John F. Kennedy (former president); John McCain (U.S. senator, Arizona); Richard M. Nixon (former president); Jesse Ventura (former Navy Seal, actor, wrestler, former governor of Minnesota).

NAVY STATISTICS

U.S. Navy personnel statistics, as of July 2006, are as follows:

Navy Personnel

Active duty:	353,627
Officers:	53,172
Enlisted:	295,941
Midshipmen:	4,514
Ready Reserve:	131,705
Selected Reserves:	70,347
Individual Ready Reserve:	61,358
Reserves currently mobilized:	4,897
Personnel on deployment:	31,308
Civilian employees:	176,732

Ships and Submarines

Deployable Battle Force Ships:	281
Ships Underway (away from home port):	143
On deployment:	99
Attack submarines:	54
Submarines underway (away from home port):	23
On deployment:	11

CHAPTER 4

Understanding the U.S. Marine Corps

★ OVERVIEW ★

The United States Marine Corps (USMC) has a widely held reputation as a fierce and effective fighting force, and they take pride in their gung-ho attitude. They are indoctrinated with a strong belief in their chain of command and the importance of *esprit de corps*, a spirit of enthusiasm and pride in themselves and the Corps. Simultaneously famous and infamous for this enthusiasm, the Corps uses their reputation to their advantage whenever possible to instill fear in their adversaries.

The Marines serve as America's "first to fight" where rapid deployment, action, and success are critical. Usually, other forces follow once Marines have opened up a site for heavy artillery and troops. Tactics emphasize aggressiveness and offensive warfare, with the Marines supplying ground, marine, and air combat elements, and the Navy providing sea combat elements, transport, and supplies. The highly complex amphibious assault developed and perfected by the Marines relies on absolute obeyance of orders as well as on the initiative of individuals to morph a sometimes disorganized landing force into a cohesive, highly organized assault team.

Regardless of rank, every Marine is first and foremost a rifleman, and all are capable of serving as infantrymen. Because essential decision making occurs in small maneuvers, each Marine is trained as a leader, a philosophy unique among America's military branches. Marines are not used as long-term, heavy artillery fighting troops; that is the Army's job. In fact, many services provided by the Marines could be fulfilled by other branches, but the Marines act as a rapid force where aggression and action are required. The character of the Marines was noted by German soldiers in World War I, who called them "Teufelhunden," or "Devil Dogs," a nickname the Marines proudly retain today.

★ STICKER SLOGAN ★

A bumper sticker summarizes the essence of the USMC: "When it absolutely, positively *must* be destroyed overnight."

The emblem of the Marine Corps is the Eagle, Globe, and Anchor. The eagle is clutching a banner bearing the Marines' motto, "*Semper Fidelis*," Latin for "Always Faithful." It is perched atop a globe depicting the Western Hemisphere. Behind the globe is an anchor, which emphasizes the maritime element.

★ MISSION ★

The National Security Act of 1947 states the current structure, mission, and function of the Marine Corps. Officially, the mission of the Corps is to provide marine forces with combined arms and supporting air components for service with the U.S. Fleet in the seizure or defense of advance naval bases, and for land operations as may be essential to a naval campaign; provide service on armed vessels of the Navy and security detachments for the protection of naval property at naval stations and bases; develop doctrines, tactics, techniques, and equipment employed by landing forces in amphibious operations; provide marine forces for airborne operations; and serve as sentinels over American embassies and consulates around the world.

★ BACKGROUND ★

The Corps was created on November 10, 1775, when a resolution of the Continental Congress in Philadelphia raised two battalions of Marines. The "Continental

Marines" were first recruited at Tun Tavern in Philadelphia by Samuel Nicholas. They served as landing troops for the recently created Continental Navy. Marines worldwide still celebrate November 10 as the Marine Corps birthday. In 1834, the Marines officially became part of the Department of the Navy.

The Marines have been active in every military campaign. The "Marine's Hymn" celebrates the efforts of the Marines "from the Halls of Montezuma to the shores of Tripoli," calling to mind campaigns in the early nineteenth century. In regard to "Tripoli," a group of eight Marines led three hundred Arab and European mercenaries in capturing Tripoli. With respect to "Montezuma," Marines participated in the Mexican-American War and assaulted the Chapultepec Palace, and later served as guards at the Mexican Presidential Palace, "The Halls of Montezuma."

The Marine Corps saw little action during the American Civil War, but were highly active in deployments around the world, such as in Korea, Cuba, the Philippines, and during the Boxer Rebellion in China. Before and after World War I, the Marines were active in the Banana Wars in the Caribbean and Central America. Experience in these campaigns gave them their celebrated skill in counterinsurgency and guerrilla operations.

In World War I, the Marines earned the "first to fight" reputation at the Battle of Belleau Wood. Battle cries such as "Retreat? Hell, we just got here!" by Captain Lloyd Williams, and "Come on, you sons of bitches, do you want to live forever?" by then Gunnery Sergeant (later Sergeant Major) Dan Daly, a two-time Medal of Honor recipient, aided the Marines in driving out German forces and cemented the image of the Marines forever.

In World War II, the Marines played a central role in the Pacific. The Corps expanded from two brigades, to two corps with six divisions and five air wings with 132 squadrons, with about 485,000 Marines. Marines saw heavy battle action during the battles of Guadalcanal, Tarawa, Saipan, Iwo Jima, and Okinawa. The use of the celebrated Navajo code talkers for secret transmissions was a significant asset. Nearly 87,000 Marines were killed or wounded during World War II and eighty-two received the Medal of Honor.

The most recognized and celebrated image from World War II is a photograph of Marines holding the American flag aloft at Iwo Jima. Taken by Joe Rosenthal of the Associated Press, it depicts five Marines and one Navy corpsman raising the American flag on Mt. Suribachi. Secretary of the Navy James Forrestal commented that "... [this event] means a Marine Corps for the next five hundred years."

The Marines were the first American combat troops deployed to Vietnam and the last to leave during the evacuation of the American embassy in Saigon. Marines operated in the I Corps regions of South Vietnam, fighting both a harsh guerilla war against the Viet Cong and a conventional war against North Vietnamese Army regulars.

The Marines have seen substantial activity since Vietnam in Grenada, Lebanon, Kuwait during the Persian Gulf War, Somalia, Bosnia, Afghanistan, and Iraq.

★ ORGANIZATION ★

The Marine Corps is led by the commandant of the Marine Corps, currently General Michael W. Hagee. He serves as a member of Joint Chiefs of Staff and advisor to the Secretary of Defense.

★ LOYALTY ★

A Marine's loyalty is to unit, corps, God, and country—in that order.

Smaller in size than the other branches of the military, the Corps is nevertheless highly effective, in part because of its task-oriented organization. Other branches of the military segregate air, ground, and marine combat units, but the Marine Corps combines them so that any combination of missions can be carried out with maximum efficiency and minimal bureaucratic red tape.

The organization of the Marine Corps is based on flexibility with task forces composed of Marine air-ground task force (MAGTF). MAGTFs may be of varying sizes but all have four elements: the command element (CE)—directs other elements; the ground combat element (GCE)—includes infantry, with tanks and artillery, and sometimes scouts, Force Recons, snipers, and others; the air combat element (ACE)—supplies the air power and may include fixed wing and helicopter aircraft and all personnel associated with them; and the combat service support element (CSSE)—contains communications, combat engineers, motor transport, medical, supply, and other specialized groups.

The smallest type of MAGTF is the Marine expeditionary unit (MEU), (special operations capable (SOC). The command element is the headquarters for the MEU, headed usually by a colonel; the ground command element is a battalion landing team that includes an infantry battalion reinforced with tanks, amphibious and other light armored vehicles, artillery, and engineers; the air command element includes both fixed and rotary-wing aircraft; and the combat service support element generally includes additional artillery, armor, or air squadrons.

Three MEUs are usually assigned to each of the Navy Atlantic and Pacific Fleets, with an additional MEU based on Okinawa. One of the three is usually on deployment, one is training to deploy, and the third is "standing down" (resting and refitting). A Marine Expeditionary Brigade (MEB) is larger than a MEU, and is based on a Marine regiment. It has larger air and support capabilities.

A Marine expeditionary force (MEF) contains a MEF headquarters Group, Marine division, Marine Air Wing, and Marine Logistic Group. There are three MEFs: 1st Marine Expeditionary Force, based out of Camp Pendleton, California; 2nd Marine Expeditionary Force, based at Camp Lejeune, North Carolina; and 3rd Marine Expeditionary Force, based at Camp Kinser, Okinawa, Japan.

The functional organization of an infantry unit begins with a *fire team*, consisting of three Marine riflemen and a team leader. Three fire teams and a squad leader (corporal or sergeant) comprise a *squad*. *Platoons* may be either a *rifle platoon*, containing three squads, a Navy corpsman, a staff sergeant, and a lieutenant as commander; or a *weapons platoon*, containing a 60mm mortar section, an assault section, a medium machine gun section, a Navy corpsman, a gunnery sergeant, and a lieutenant as commander.

A *company* (sometimes called a *battery*) may be a *rifle company*, consisting of three rifle platoons, a weapons platoon, a Navy corpsman, an administrative clerk, a police sergeant (corporal or sergeant), a noncommissioned officer, a company gunnery sergeant, a first sergeant, a first lieutenant as executive officer, and captain as commander; or a *weapons company*, containing an 81mm mortar platoon, an anti-armor platoon, and a heavy machine gun platoon.

Moving up the command structure, a *battalion* consists of three or four companies, commanded by a lieutenant colonel. A colonel commands a *regiment* which is composed of three to four battalions. Next is a *brigade*, commanded by a brigadier general, which is composed of one or more regiments. Above this is a *division* which is composed of three or four regiments, commanded by a major general. Units at the battalion level and above have a sergeant major and executive officer as second in command, with additional officers and personnel for administration, intelligence, operations, logistics, communications, and civil affairs (wartime only). Battalion levels and above may be reinforced with tank or artillery units.

Numbered Divisions

There are four numbered Marine divisions. These include: 1st Marine Division, Camp Pendleton, California; 2nd Marine Division, Camp Lejeune, North Carolina; 3rd Marine Division, Camp Smedley Butler, Okinawa, Japan; and 4th Marine Division, a reserve unit headquartered at New Orleans, Louisiana. During World War II, two additional Marine Divisions were employed: the 5th and 6th, which were active in the Pacific region. These were dissolved after the war ended.

Air Combat Elements

Four air combat elements are available to conduct air operations as needed for air assault, anti-air warfare, offensive air support, electronic warfare, aircraft and missiles, and aerial reconnaissance. Units include squadrons, groups, and wings.

Marine Aircraft Wings

There are four Marine aircraft wings (regiment-sized aircraft-based units) which include: 1st Marine Aircraft Wing, Marine Corps Air Station (MCAS) Futenma, Okinawa, Japan; 2nd Marine Aircraft Wing at MCAS Cherry Point, North Carolina; 3rd Marine Aircraft Wing at MCAS, Miramar, California; and 4th Marine Aircraft Wing, New Orleans, Louisiana (reserve unit).

Marine Logistics Groups

Marine Logistics Groups include: 1st Marine Logistics Group, Camp Pendleton, California; 2nd Marine Logistics Group, Camp Lejeune, North Carolina; 3rd Marine Logistics Group, Camp Smedley Butler, Okinawa, Japan; and 4th Marine Logistics Group, New Orleans, Louisiana (reserve unit).

★ RANK AND UNIFORMS ★

Rank

Rank in the Marine Corps differs slightly from the other services. Marines may be commissioned officers, warrant officers, or enlisted personnel. See appendix B for a comparison of ranks between services.

- Commissioned officers rank as follows: general (four-star), lieutenant general (three-star), major general (two-star), brigadier general (one-star), colonel, lieutenant colonel, major, captain, first lieutenant, and second lieutenant.

- Warrant officers rank, from top to bottom: chief warrant officer 5, chief warrant officer 4, chief warrant officer 3, chief warrant officer 2, and warrant officer.

- Enlisted personnel rank from top to bottom: sergeant major of the Marine Corps, sergeant major, master gunnery sergeant, first sergeant, master sergeant, gunnery sergeant, staff sergeant, sergeant, corporal, lance corporal, private first class, and private. Before Boot Camp is completed, members are referred to only as "recruits," and may not refer to themselves as anything but "This recruit." They *earn* the title of Marine only upon graduation from Boot Camp.

Uniforms

Marines' uniforms are distinctive from those used by the other services.

- For *utility uniforms*, the Marine cover ("hat") has eight sides and corners, and is worn "blocked"—heavily starched, creased, and peaked. The Marine Corps emblem (Eagle, Globe, and Anchor) is printed directly on the front.

    Marines wear the advanced camouflage "MARPAT" uniform ("MARine Disruptive PATtern"), with a digitized pattern of brown, tan, or green colors for woodland or desert environments. They wear cotton, olive green "skivvies" (undershirts) even in the desert. Marines tightly fold their long sleeves so that the lighter-colored underside faces out, known as "white-side out"; and "blouse" their boots, with the trouser cuffs rolled back inside and tightened over the boots with a boot band. Marines do not normally wear any insignia or device on their utility uniforms denoting unit or specialization. Marine officers typically wear rank insignia made of shiny metal on both collars; however, in combat they do not wear rank insignia to avoid being identified by snipers. All Marines wear a color-coded "rigger's" belt, according to their qualification under the Marine Corps Martial Arts Program. Black combat boots are obsolete; Marines now wear light brown suede combat boots.

- The Marine *service uniform*, "business dress," has a button-up khaki shirt and olive-green trousers or skirt. The long sleeved version is worn with a double Windsor-knotted field scarf (necktie). Enlisted Marines wear their rank insignia on the sleeve of the service shirt. Marine officers wear rank insignia on the collar. The Marine class "A" service coat is olive green and has a waist belt. The uniform is worn with either a barracks (service) cover with a bill and a round top, or a garrison cover, which comes to a peak.

- *Mess dress*, or *evening dress*, is the formal attire worn to banquets, balls, and state affairs. It is mainly worn by staff noncommissioned officers (NCOs) and officers. It is required for general and field-grade officers and optional for company-grade and warrant officers. Officer's evening/mess dress has of a hip-length "shell" jacket with a choker collar at the top. The front of the jacket is left open and is worn with high-waisted trousers with a gold and red stripe down each leg. All officers wear a white vest for evening dress. For mess dress, general officers wear a scarlet vest and other officers wear a cummerbund. The senior NCO mess dress includes a regular hip-length mess jacket with oversized rank insignia worn on both sleeves, and high-waisted trousers and a white vest or scarlet cummerbund according to the occasion.

- The Marine blue *dress uniform* is the most elaborate of the American armed forces. It is referred to as "dress blues" and has many forms.

  Dress blue "A" has a midnight blue (nearly black) outer blouse with long sleeves and a choker collar; it's worn with a white barracks cover and with all medals and ribbons. A Mameluke Sword or NCO sword may be worn by officers and noncommissioned officers as authorized. *Dress blue "B"* utilizes ribbons instead of medals and badges. *Dress blue "C"* is the same as for "B" but includes a khaki long sleeve shirt and tie instead of the outer blue coat. Ribbons and badges are normally worn on the shirt. *Dress blue "D"* is the same as "C", but with short sleeve khaki shirt and no tie. All the blues have the same trousers, cover (headgear), and shoes. General officers wear a two-inch wide scarlet "blood stripe" down the outer seam of each leg of the trousers; field and company grade officers wear a 1 ½-inch wide scarlet stripe; NCOs wear a 1 ⅛-inch wide scarlet stripe. General officers wear dark blue trousers in the same color as the coat, while lower ranking officers and NCOs wear sky blue trousers. Women wear the evening dress, a long or short skirt in black for formal affairs. The dress uniform has the colors of the American flag: blue for bravery, red for sacrifice, and white for honor.

★ JOINING THE MARINE CORPS ★

As with the other services, recruits may join the Marines by direct enlistment, through officer training programs, or via direct commission. Besides the U.S. Naval Academy, of which about 15 percent of its graduates become Marines, the Marine Corps obtains its officers through the Officer Candidates School (OCS), or as "mustangs," the term for enlisted Marines who cross over to be come officers.

Recruitment messages differ from those used for the other services. There is no sugar coating of the experience a recruit will undergo as a Marine. Their current slogan, "The Few. The Proud. The Marines," combined with their unique dress blues uniform and images of knights of eras past provide strong clues to the kind of service expected.

★ A SELECTION OF SOME OF ★ THE SLOGANS AND SAYINGS MARINES FAVOR

"We promise you sleep deprivation, mental torment, and muscles so sore you'll puke. But we don't want to sugar coat it." "Pain is temporary. Pride is forever." "Nobody ever drowned in sweat." "The deadliest weapon in the world: a Marine and his rifle." "The most dangerous place is between a Marine and his country." "Marine. Your best friend. Your worst enemy." "It's not an attitude problem. We are that good!" "Marines fear only God. No others." "If you can read, thank a teacher. If you can read in English, thank a Marine!" "Heaven won't take us and Hell's afraid we'll take over!" "To err is human, to forgive is divine. However, neither is Marine Corps policy." "Some people spend an entire lifetime wondering if they made a difference. The Marines don't have that problem." "Gun control: hitting your target." "U.S. Marine. Your freedom. His life without complaint." "When we do our job, people shoot at us."

★ TRAINING IN THE MARINE CORPS ★

Boot Camp—Marine Style

Boot Camp takes place either at Marine Corps Recruit Depot San Diego, or Marine Corps Recruit Depot Parris Island outside Beaufort, South Carolina. Recruits are intentionally brought in at night to add to their nervousness, fear, and intimidation. They immediately encounter their drill instructors (DI), who the Marine Corps describe as "the scariest S.O.B. a recruit ever meets, and the last person he or she ever forgets." The DI, wearing the "Smokey Bear" campaign hat tipped at an impossible angle, appears certifiably insane. He shouts a welcoming speech and demands instant compliance with orders, and recruits quickly learn Boot Camp is nothing like the movies. It's immediately harsh, intense, and extreme, and they'd better be up for the challenge.

Processing begins immediately and includes removal of all contraband (e.g., tobacco, food, vitamins, cards, cologne). Recruits undergo physical exams, receive the infamous thirty-second "cranial amputation" haircuts, and comply with other steps designed to remove individuality. Marine Corps indoctrination combined with complete isolation from outside influence gradually converts individuals into team members. Verbal abuse is constant at every misstep.

Processing continues for three days. Medical and dental exams include urinalysis and HIV testing. Any illegal drug use found in the urinalysis results in immediate expulsion. Processing also includes instruction on receiving orders, Marine and Navy rank structure, chain of command, Naval terminology, the Uniform Code of Military Justice, weapons safety, saluting, standing interior guard, and how to break in boots. Recruits receive an unloaded M16A2 rifle and are taught its handling. During processing and until they are given firing training, recruits carry their rifle with them wherever they go to emphasize its importance to each Marine.

Indoctrination Versus Individuality

A significant part of training in the Marine Corps entails removing the uniqueness each recruit brings to the Corps, and then building up in them the foundation of a Marine. The Marine Corps believes strongly in individuality—once the recruit understands what it means to be a Marine. All Marines are trained first and foremost as warriors, and all are equally suited for the work. During Boot Camp, recruits are addressed as "Private" or called by their last name only. They are not permitted to speak unless spoken to, and "Sir" or "Ma'am" is an obligatory part of every answer they give—loudly and enthusiastically. Furthermore, recruits are forbidden to use the word "I" to refer to themselves. They refer to themselves in the third person, saying, "This recruit requests ..." and so on. Talking among recruits is not permitted during Boot Camp formations. Swatting at pesky sand fleas is likewise not permitted. DIs often hold "funerals" for the slain insect to drive home the message of concentration and self-discipline; Marines should not be bothered by something as trivial as an insect.

Initial Testing, Incentive Training, and Drilling

An initial strength test (IST) is given to be sure the recruit is strong strength to face the grueling training to come. For males, the IST standard entails 2 pull-ups from a dead hang, 44 sit-ups in 2 minutes, and 1.5-mile run in under 13 minutes. For females, the IST requires a 12-second flexed air hang, 44 crunches in 2 minutes, and a 1.5-mile run in less than 15 minutes. Otherwise, women are not given an easier training program; all Marines are expected to have the same basic capability and training.

Where recruits require additional discipline and motivation, drill instructors use incentive training, or "IT," sometimes called "incentive torture." Strict regulations for the use and duration of IT exercises are found in the drill instructor's Recruit Training Pocket Guide, which DIs are required to carry at all times.

Recruits spend a great deal of time marching and drilling, much of it designed to train them to act as a team. Drills teach discipline, develop team spirit, provide combat formations, and are used to move units around in an orderly manner. Conditioning marches also prepare recruits for the Crucible, a 40-mile, march carrying over sixty pounds of combat gear.

Phase One

Boot Camp is divided into three four-week phases. In Phase One training focuses on physical conditioning, self-defense, and close-order drilling. Recruits learn general military skills, begin the Marine Corps martial arts program, take their first 1.5-mile run, learn bayonet techniques, customs and courtesies, take classes on USMC core values and history, and receive an introduction to the M16A2 rifle. And that's just the first week. During the rest of Phase One, recruits also undergo training in the following areas: general military skills, first aid, pugil sticks, physical training, weapons handling, throws and falls, USMC history and terrorism awareness, circuit course, inoculations, confidence course, 3-mile conditioning march, counters to general military skills, USMC Leadership Course, Uniform Code of Military Justice, senior drill instructor inspection, series commander inspection, and initial drill evaluation.

Phase Two

During Phase Two (weeks five through eight), recruits endure four named "Weeks" of training in combat water survival and weapons marksmanship. The first is "Swim Week," which includes combat survival swimming, Marine Corps Martial Arts Program testing, and a 5-mile conditioning march. Next is "Grass Week" which includes an introduction to marksmanship, 35-yard rifle groupings, the endurance course, and a field meet. Then comes "Firing Week" with known distance firing, M16A2 rifle qualifications, the confidence course, a 6-mile conditioning march, and small unit leadership training. Finally, recruits have "Team Week," featuring an obstacle course and 10-mile conditioning march that emphasizes team skills.

Phase Three

During Phase Three (weeks nine through twelve), training steps up with emphasis on basic warrior skills. Specific areas taught during week nine include weapons training, and night firing. During week ten, recruits undergo additional intensive training, which includes: combat endurance course, basic field skills, gas chamber, final drill competition, final physical training test, rappelling tower, company commander's inspection, defensive driving course, land navigation, and the military operations in urban terrain (MOUT) movement course. Week eleven is the infamous Crucible (see page 103), a 54-hour, no-rest intensive test of the recruit's new skills, followed by the warrior's breakfast and core values training. During the final week, recruits have their battalion commander's inspection, a financial responsibility course, a final motivational run, and they participate in the Marine Corps Emblem ceremony and graduation.

Marine Corps Martial Arts Program

The Marine Corps Martial Arts Program (MCMAP) was introduced in 2001. Since 2003, every member of the Marine Corps, regardless of rank, must be at least a tan belt in the program. It is a blend of several martial arts systems—kung fu, karate, jujitsu, judo—with additional bayonet and knife fighting techniques that enable Marines to succeed in hand-to-hand combat using kicks, punches, throws, falls, choke holds, grappling, defense maneuvers, and so on. A Marine learns to fight with his fists, then with a rifle (pugil sticks are used in training), and later learns knife techniques. The philosophy of MCMAP instructors is printed on their sweatshirts: "One Mind. Any Weapon." The program develops leadership skills and teaches the rules of engagement, conduct, and safety, and instructs Marines in a continuum of force. Recruits cannot fail this portion of their training and become a Marine. Anyone who fails may be "recycled" through training up to three more times to try again, but will be sent home if success in this program is not achieved.

Additional MCMAP training is given to Marines during their career, with the following belt colors: gray (46 hours of training), green (55 hours), brown (65 hours), and six degrees of black (71.5 hours for the first degree).

Other Training Programs

Water survival training is essential to a Marine, due to the amphibious nature of service. Whether the water is fresh or salt, whether it occurs in a lake, a swamp, a river, or an ocean, Marines must be ready for the task. This program teaches them to stay afloat, wearing full gear, including their filled combat backpack. They learn to use their equipment to stay afloat, minimize energy use, and maximize mobility. It is critical they learn to survive under all possible conditions where future amphibious operations might be concerned.

Weapons' training is also essential for every Marine. During Boot Camp, every recruit spends a good portion of each day cleaning and disassembling his rifle to learn the intricate details of how it works. Basic techniques of marksmanship are learned during Phase One. These include sighting and aiming, firing positions (prone, sitting, kneeling, and standing), trigger control, rapid fire, sight adjustments, and effects of weather on firing and bullet trajectory. During Phase Two, recruits apply their techniques to firing at targets of known distances. Recruits also learn that Marines do not leave a single bullet casing behind. Each bit of ammunition must be accounted for, via the use of metal detectors if necessary. This practice enforces self-discipline and accountability.

During Phase Three, recruits undergo field-range firing, which gives them training in shooting realistic targets under combatlike conditions. Moving targets at unknown distances give recruits this final bit of expertise with their rifles. Marines are expected to shoot accurately right- or left-handed regardless of their preference, to shoot while wearing a gas mask, to shoot from a slope, a fighting hole ("foxhole") or on a rooftop, and to provide assault fire when approaching an enemy position, including under night conditions. All of these possibilities are stressed and practiced.

★ THE CRUCIBLE ★

The final training a recruit faces is called the Crucible; it serves as the metamorphosis of a recruit into a Marine. It's the grueling, 54-hour event that defines a recruit. It mimics the stress and rigor of combat by challenging recruits to their limits and beyond, using strenuous physical activity combined with food and sleep deprivation and mentally challenging exercises. Recruits are organized into eighteen-member teams, travel 42-miles carrying their full combat gear, sleep no more than eight hours, and eat less than three MREs (Meals, Ready-to-Eat, the prepackaged military-issue meals) during this time. They must solve about thirty problematic exercises and combat-related events, including unknown distance firing, combat assault resupply, casualty evacuation, bayonet assault, night infiltration, and hand-to-hand combat.

The Crucible begins in the middle of the night with a 6-mile forced march in which recruits drag ammunition, water, and food supplies through a combat assault course with simulated (but highly convincing) live weapons firing overhead and grenades exploding nearby, as screams of soldiers echo through loudspeakers. As the resupply exercise is completed, a recruit reads aloud how the actions of a hero (named for each resupply station) exemplified the Corps and its values. Physical feats include crossing over a contaminated area by swinging on ropes from safe zones, falling backwards into the arms of team members, and climbing a wall via a knotted rope. Additional confidence courses follow with problem-solving exercises and unknown-distance firing. After an MRE for dinner, recruits conduct a night infiltration, followed by a 5-mile forced march. Four hours of sleep are permitted.

As the Crucible continues, teamwork becomes essential, with recruits helping others when mates falter. They learn that they become stronger when all contribute to their success. The Crucible terminates with a 9-mile forced march where—despite body odor, filth, blisters, aches, and often hallucinations from lack of sleep and food—they reach the finish line. Waiting for them is the Warrior's Breakfast, an all-you-can-eat feast of steak, eggs. and potatoes, and the knowledge that they'll soon receive their Eagle, Globe and Anchor emblem, and the title of U.S. Marine.

During "Transition Week" which follows the Crucible, recruits recover and begin transitioning to Marine Corps membership. DIs reduce their discipline, expecting it to now come from within the recruits. Recruits undergo a final inspection by the battalion commander, a daunting experience as he scrutinizes their uniforms and drills them with intimidating academic questions. The emblem ceremony is the moment when recruits actually receive the title of "Marine" and see their family for the first time in three months. It is held the day before graduation. Recruits pin the emblems on their covers (hats) and receive the insignia of rank (private E-1 or private first class E-2) according to their enlistment contract. An occasional few receive meritorious promotion to lance corporal (E-3) for demonstrating outstanding leadership.

Following Boot Camp, Marines undergo additional training in the School of Infantry at Camp Lejeune, North Carolina, or Camp Pendleton, Clifornia. Training programs include the Infantry Training Battalion and the Marine Combat Training Battalion.

Infantry Training Battalion

This is a fifty-two-day program for Marines who will serve as "grunts," the infantrymen, machine gunners, mortar men, assault men, and antitank guided missile men. Women do not enter this combat program. During the first two weeks of training, called the Common Skills Package, Marines learn to use equipment including grenades, M249 light machine gun, mines, AT-4 shoulder-fired antiarmor rockets; as well as learn skills such as target engagement, offensive tactics, fire and movement methods, land navigation, NBC (nuclear, biological, and chemical) protection and decontamination, patrolling techniques, and urban warfare.

Additional specialty training is according to "Military Occupation Specialty" or MOS. *Infantrymen* (MOS 0311) are trained in patrolling, defensive and offensive operations, and urban terrain operations. *Machine gunners* (MOS 0331) receive training on the use of heavy automatic weapons including the M240G 7.62 medium machine gun, M2 .50 caliber heavy machine gun, and the Mk 19 40mm automatic grenade launcher. *Mortar men* (MOS 0341) become skilled in the M224 60mm lightweight mortar and the M252 81mm medium extended-range mortar. *Assault men* (MOS 0351) become specialists in rockets and demolitions and use the Mk 153 shoulder-launched, multi-purpose assault weapon (SMAW) and the Javelin fire-and-forget antitank missile. *Antitank guided missile men* (MOS 0352) learn to attack enemy tanks and armored vehicles using a variety of weapons including the tube-launched, optically tracked, wire-guided (TOW) missile.

Marine Combat Training Battalion

Marines may also serve in noninfantry areas, including communications, intelligence, electronic warfare, vehicle repair, nuclear and biochemical defense, and logistics. These persons, and all women enlisted Marines, undergo two weeks of training at the Marine Combat Training Battalion to learn basic infantry skills.

Other Marine Training

All Marines regardless of their MOS are expected to know how to conduct security patrols, to camouflage gear, and to set up defenses.

Additional training is given to Marines in aviation, artillery, engineering, intelligence, and communications. Marines may be selected for further training to become a scout-sniper, force recon, drill instructor, or Marine security guard.

★ COLORS AND INSIGNIA ★

The colors of the Marine Corps are scarlet and gold. They appear on their flag along with the Marine Corps emblem: the Eagle, Globe, and Anchor. The eagle represents service to the country; the globe represents worldwide service; and the anchor represents naval traditions. The emblem, adopted in 1868, is derived from ornaments worn by the Continental Marines and the British Royal Marines, and is usually topped with a ribbon reading "*Semper Fidelis*" ("Always Faithful.") The eagle is not a bald eagle, but a crested eagle, selected because while bald eagles are found only in North America, crested eagles are found, like Marines, through out the world.

★ SWORDS ★

Two styles of swords are worn by Marines. The Marine Corps officer sword is a Mameluke sword, similar to the sword presented to Lt. Presley O'Bannon after the capture of Derne during the First Barbary War. Noncommissioned officers carry one similar to a Civil War U.S. Army infantry officer's sword. Marine NCOs are the only enlisted service members in the American Armed Forces authorized to carry a sword.

★ FORMER MARINES AND EX-MARINES ★

Unofficially, the term "former Marine" refers to an individual who has completed his or her service and has received an honorable or general discharge—a Marine no longer in active duty. However, the Marine ethos is, "Once a Marine, always a Marine." Marines who have retired are commonly called "retired Marines." Only those who have brought dishonor upon themselves are referred to as "ex-Marines," since they are no longer deserving of the title Marine. (For example, Lee Harvey Oswald is considered an ex-Marine.)

Guard Duty

American embassies and consulates around the world are guarded by Marine security guards (MSGs). Guards consider their work extremely important and are not to be trifled with. MSGs usually serve three tours of duty of twelve months each. They are enlisted Marines from the rank of private first class (E-2) to master sergeant (E-8). Marine detachment commanders serve two tours of duty of eighteen months each. They are enlisted in the ranks of staff sergeant (E-6) to master sergeant.

★ DEMONSTRATION TEAMS ★

Drum and Bugle Corps—"The Commandant's Own"

The Marine Corps Drum and Bugle Corps performs martial and popular music for hundreds of thousands of spectators annually. It consists of over eighty musicians dressed in ceremonial red and white uniforms and is considered one of the finest musical marching organizations. It was formed in 1934 to augment the Marine Band.

Music has always been integral to the Marine Corps. Military musicians passed commands to Marines in battle formations during the 1700s and 1800s, using drum beats and bugle calls to signal for attack or to retire for the evening. Through the 1930s, Marine Corps posts still authorized a number of buglers and drummers to play the traditional calls and to ring a ship's bell to signal the time "The Commandant's Own" provides musical support to ceremonies around the nation's capital. During World War II, the corps was awarded the scarlet and gold breastcord by President Franklin D. Roosevelt, which is still proudly displayed on their uniforms.

In the tradition of their "field music" predecessors, the musicians in "The Commandant's Own" are full-fledged Marines with all the required training and infantry skills. These Marines are preselected during enlistment and must pass a demanding audition for service in the Drum and Bugle Corps. Following Boot Camp and Marine Combat Training, they proceed directly to "The Commandant's Own."

During the summer months, they perform in traditional Friday evening parades held at the Marine Barracks, Washington, D.C. and in sunset parades every Tuesday evening at the U.S. Marine Corps War Memorial (Iwo Jima Monument) near Arlington, Virginia. These dramatic military ceremonies symbolize the professionalism, discipline, and *esprit de corps* of the United States Marines.

United States Marine Band—"The President's Own"

The United States Marine Band, known as "The President's Own," is charged with providing music for the president of the United States and often plays during state functions. Founded in 1798 by an Act of Congress, the U.S. Marine Band is America's oldest professional musical organization. "The President's Own" encompasses the United States Marine Band, Marine Chamber Orchestra, and Marine Chamber Ensembles. It performs regularly at the White House and in more than five hundred public performances across the nation each year. *The Marine Band* performs a wide range of music including new works for wind ensemble, traditional concert band literature, and the patriotic marches that made it famous. Many of these marches were written by John Philip Sousa, the "March King" and former director of the Marine Band. Solo performances often highlight its members' virtuosity and artistry.

The Marine Chamber Orchestra performs both popular and classical selections, including compositions for string orchestra and those utilizing various wind instruments. Renown for its dramatic and strong performances, the Marine Chamber Orchestra performs Broadway to classical, from Baroque to modern music.

The Marine Chamber Ensembles feature the virtuoso musicians of "The President's Own" performing in intimate, small ensemble settings. Performers coordinate the programs, with players and repertoire varying from concert to concert. A range of instrumentation may be used, including string or saxophone quartets, clarinet choirs, brass quintets, brass and percussion ensembles, flute and harp or string duos, among others. They perform regular concerts at the George Washington Masonic National Memorial Auditorium in Alexandria, Virginia., and present preconcert recitals before Marine Band and Marine Chamber Orchestra performances throughout the concert season.

Silent Drill Platoon

The Silent Drill Platoon is a twenty-four-man rifle platoon that performs a precision drill exhibition. The Marines execute a series of calculated drill movements using hand-polished M-1 rifles with fixed bayonets. The routine concludes with a unique weapons-inspection sequence demonstrating elaborate rifle spins and tosses. This team of handpicked Marines performs all summer long, executing a completely silent ten-minute drill that exemplifies the discipline and professionalism that identifies all Marines. They begin their training at the historic Marine Barracks in Washington, D.C. (called "8th and I" for its crossroads location) and later move to Marine Corps Air Station, Yuma, Arizona. They perform their routine across the United States and abroad.

★ TOYS FOR TOTS ★

Toys for Tots is an organization run by the Marine Corps Reserve which donates toys to underprivileged children during the winter holiday season. The organization was founded in 1947 by Major Bill Hendricks. The mission is to collect new, unwrapped toys during October, November, and December each year and distribute those toys as Christmas gifts to needy children in the community in which the campaign is conducted. Their goal is to deliver a message of hope to needy youngsters that will motivate them to grow into responsible, productive, patriotic citizens and community leaders. Local Toys for Tots campaign coordinators conduct an array of activities throughout the year, including golf tournaments, foot races, bicycle races, and other voluntary events designed to increase interest and to generate toy and monetary donations.

INSIDE THE MARINE CORPS

"Being a Marine"
By Dick Schading, former sergeant, U.S. Marine Corps

It is hard to explain what it is to be a Marine to someone who is not one. The title "Marine" is not just a word. It is like a living, breathing Corps: a warrior spirit, which connects you with all the rest of the thing, from its historic past to the present, that cannot change for those that will follow in the future. The Corps is a place where honor, tradition, pride, and an inability to fail are not just words or obscure concepts but rather a reality that lasts a lifetime.

The Corps is a place where lifelong friends are made, and sometimes lost, at very young ages. November 10, 1775, will always be a Marine's other birthday for one who has earned the right to call anything associated with the Navy (except the corpsman) rude and demeaning names.

Among the wonderful life lessons learned from the Corps are the facts that taking pride in what you do and how you appear are not character flaws. Working until a job or objective has been completed is expected and is the right way it should be done. Never giving up on friends, jobs, or anything else is in keeping with the training and tradition of the Corps and becomes a part of your character forever.

One of the less-than-wonderful lessons learned from the Corps is that you cannot give up on friends, family, or relationships, even when it's the logical thing to do. Failure, by one's self or by friends and loved ones, is not just an obscure concept, but a crushing experience that is extraordinarily hard to deal with. In combat, errors or mission "failure" sometimes equates to death. Simple mistakes cost lives in the blink of an eye or the flash of an M16. The losses of my young friends so long ago are still very hard to come to grips with, and not preventing these losses are still considered personal failures.

It is said that Marines are made at Parris Island. It is true that the training and fine edge are put on there, and the formal induction into the Corps is begun at graduation with the awarding of the title United States Marine, but I think that the warrior heart and soul of a true Marine are there from birth.

★ CELEBRITY MARINES ★

A short list of famous Marines includes the following: Don Adams (actor), James Baker (secretary of the treasury, secretary of state), F. Lee Bailey (attorney), John Chaffee (U.S. senator, secretary of the Navy), John Glenn (astronaut, U.S. senator), Gene Hackman (actor), Charlton Heston (actor), Lee Marvin (actor), Steve McQueen (actor), George Peppard (actor), Dan Rather (network news anchor), Burt Reynolds (actor), Fred Smith (chairman and CEO, FedEx), John Philip Sousa (musician), Leon Spinks Jr. (boxer), Leon Uris (author), and Montel Williams (talk show host).

MARINE STATISTICS

Statistics regarding Marine Corps personnel are less available than for other branches. As of December 2005, numbers are approximately as follows:

Active duty:	178,000
Officers:	18,000
Enlisted:	160,000
Reserves:	39,000
Reservists on Active Duty:	8,600
Marines Deployed:	25,000

CHAPTER 5

Understanding the U.S. Air Force

★ OVERVIEW ★

The Air Force is responsible for conducting military operations in air and space. It acts in the defense of the nation by deploying aircraft to fight enemy aircraft, bomb enemy targets, provide reconnaissance, and transport other armed services. The Air Force is responsible for strategic nuclear deterrence, and maintains bomb and missile wings capable of delivering nuclear weapons anywhere in the world. It has fighter interceptors assigned to home defense commands in active duty and Air National Guard forces. The vision of the Air Force is "Global Vigilance, Reach, and Power."

★ HISTORY AND BACKGROUND ★

Early U.S. military activities in the air began with Army use of balloons for reconnaissance during the Civil War and the Spanish-American War. In 1907 the Aeronautical Division of the Signal Corps was created. In 1920, the Army Reorganization Act created the Air Service (after 1926, the Air Corps.) In 1941, it became the Army Air Forces. An independent Air Force was established in

1947. It was active in the Korean War, and especially during the Vietnam War through bombing raids, helicopter attacks, and support missions. The Cold War and the arms race with the Soviet Union fueled America's desire for surveillance aircraft, and the space program was expanded to send men to the moon.

The Air Force conducted air strikes in Bosnia in their first North Atlantic Treaty Organization (NATO) mission, and later led NATO airstrikes against Serbia in the Kosovo War. Air power was also supplied during the first Gulf War, in Afghanistan, and in Iraq.

The Department of the Air Force is headquartered at the Pentagon. Separate operating agencies of the Air Force include the Air Force Reserve, the Air Force Intelligence Service, and the U.S. Air Force Academy. In 2005, there were about 350,000 Air Force members.

★ ORGANIZATION ★

The three components of the U.S. Air Force are the Air Force, the Air Force Reserve, and the Air National Guards. The secretary of the Air Force (SECAF) is a civilian who leads the Department of the Air Force. In early 2005, that position was filled by Michael Wynne. His office includes a general counsel, auditor general, inspector general, administrative assistant, public affairs director, legislative liaison director, small and disadvantaged business utilization director, and several committees. The chief of staff, U.S. Air Force, is a presidential appointee and a four-star general; it is currently General T. Michael Moseley. He serves as a member of the Joint Chiefs of Staff and the Armed Forces Policy Council and also serves as principal advisor to the secretary of the Air Force. The senior enlisted is the chief master sergeant of the Air Force, currently Chief Master Sergeant Gerald R. Murray.

Air Force Units

An "air force" is composed of two or more "wings." "Wings" are the basic organizational unit of the U.S. Air Force. Four or more squadrons make a wing with 1,000–5,000 persons. A "squadron" consists of a single type of aircraft. There are generally ten to twenty aircraft in a bomber squadron, eighteen to twenty-four in a fighter squadron, and eight to sixteen in a transport squadron. Formerly, two or more wings made a division, but divisions have become obsolete.

Currently, two or more wings constitute a numbered air force, or NAF. Wings are designated as operational, air base, or specialized mission. There are over one hundred and forty active wings, with about fifty additional either inactive, unnumbered, Air National Guard, or Air Expeditionary Wings.

There are currently sixteen numbered air forces (NAF), including First, Second, Fourth, Fifth, Seventh, Twelfth, Fourteenth, Sixteenth, Eighteenth, Nineteenth, Twentieth, and Twenty-Second, which are described below. NAFs are commanded by a major general. The Third, Thirteenth, and Seventeenth Air Forces were recently deactivated during reorganization in 2004–2005. There may also be groups that report to a wing, serve as an expeditionary unit, or are completely independent.

Major Commands

The Air Force is comprised of nine major commands, thirty-five field operating agencies, four direct-reporting units, plus two reserve components: the Air Force Reserve and the Air National Guard. Major commands are organized by function within the U.S. and overseas and are structured to accomplish specific Air Force goals and objectives. In descending order of command, elements include numbered air forces, wings, groups, squadrons, and flights.

Air Combat Command (ACC)

Located at Langley Air Force Base, Virginia, ACC was combined from Strategic Air Command and Tactical Air Command in 1992. The ACC is the primary provider of air combat forces to America's warfighting commands. ACC operates bomber, fighter, reconnaissance, battle management, and electronic-combat aircraft. It organizes, trains, and equips combat-ready forces for rapid deployment. ACC has four numbered air forces, one Air Force Reserve numbered air force, and several main subordinate units. It also operates fifteen bases, with standing units on thirteen additional bases within the U.S. It is responsible for inland search and rescue within the forty-eight contiguous states. The ACC commander is the component commander of U.S. Air Forces-Joint Forces Command and U.S. Strategic Command.

NUMBERED AIR FORCES WITHIN AIR COMBAT COMMAND

FIRST AIR FORCE: Headquartered at Tyndall AFB, Florida, it provides surveillance, command, and control for air defense forces for the continental United

States in support of NORAD, the North American Aerospace Defense Command. Ten Air National Guard fighter wings are assigned to First Air Force.

EIGHTH AIR FORCE: Headquartered at Barksdale AFB, Louisiana, the Eighth Air Force provides command and control, intelligence, surveillance and reconnaissance, long-range attack, and information operations forces. Eighth Air Force trains, tests, and exercises combat-ready forces for rapid deployment worldwide. It also provides conventional forces to U.S. Joint Forces Command and surveillance capabilities to U.S Strategic Command. It serves as the command element for Air Force-wide computer network communications.

NINTH AIR FORCE: Headquartered at Shaw AFB, South Carolina, the Ninth Air Force controls forces based along the eastern seaboard. It also serves as air-component for a twenty-five nation area within the U.S. Central Command.

TENTH AIR FORCE: Located at Naval Air Station Joint Reserve Base, Ft. Worth, Texas, the Tenth Air Force commands the Air Force Reserve forces throughout the country.

TWELFTH AIR FORCE: Headquartered at Davis-Montham AFB, Arizona, it controls conventional fighter and bomber forces based in the western United States. It also has warfighting responsibility for U.S. Southern Command, and the U.S. Southern Air Forces.

Air Education and Training Command (AETC)

Located at Randolph AFB, Texas, it is responsible for recruiting, training, and educating Air Force personnel. This command affects every member of the Air Force. It includes the Air Force Recruiting Service, two numbered air forces, and the Air University.

SECOND AIR FORCE: Keesler AFB, Mississippi, is responsible for the basic military and technical training for all nonflying enlisted members and support officers. (This training begins at Lackland AFB.) Second Air Force also trains military dogs and their handlers for the Department of Defense, and for the Transportation Security Administration. The Inter-American Academy at Lackland AFB, Texas, also offers courses in aviation studies in Spanish to students from nineteen Western Hemisphere nations.

NINETEENTH AIR FORCE: Located at Randolph AFB, Texas, it conducts flight training and trains air crews and air battle managers. It also conducts survival, escape and evasion training at the 336th Training Group at Fairchild AFB, Washington; a portion of the courses are taught at NAS Pensacola, Florida, and Eielson AFB, Arkansas. Additional training programs include air battle manager training, which includes doctrine, radar, surveillance, wartime operations, and basic fighter control, using simulated aircraft and F-15, F/A-22, AWACS, or JSTARS equipment.

AIR UNIVERSITY: Headquartered at Maxwell AFB, Alabama, it is responsible for professional military education (PME) and continuing education for officers and enlisted members.

Air Force Matériel Command (AFMC)

Located at Wright-Patterson AFB, Ohio, AFMC conducts research, development, testing, evaluation, and management of all Air Force weapon systems. It has three product centers for development, two test centers to evaluate products, and three air logistics centers to service weapon systems from "cradle-to-grave."

Air Force Space Command (AFSPC)

Headquartered at Peterson AFB, Colorado, AFSPC has the responsibility to defend North America via space and intercontinental ballistic missile operations to project American global reach and power. It has four primary missions and one mission support area: 1) space force enhancement (maximize effectiveness of military air, land, sea, and space operations); 2) counterspace (provides space superiority by aiding friendly forces and negating unfriendly forces in the space realm); 3) space force application (weapons systems operating through or from space: nuclear deterrence, missile defense, conventional strike and counterair); 4) space support (launch and satellite operations); and 5) mission support (functions across all mission areas with infrastructure such as communications, training, logistics, and so on).

Air Force Special Operations Command (AFSOC)

Located at Hurlburt Field, Florida, it serves as America's specialized air power, providing special operations forces.

Air Mobility Command (AMC)

Located at Scott AFB, Illinois, AMC is responsible for rapid global mobility and sustainment for the armed forces, providing strategic airlift and aerial refueling for all forces. Mobility aircraft under this command include the C-5 Galaxy, KC-10 Extender, C-17 Globemaster III, C-130 Hercules, KC-135 Stratotanker, and the C-141 Starlifter, with operational support aircraft including the VC-25 (Air Force One), C-9, C-20, C-21, C-32, C-37, C-40, and UH-1.

Pacific Air Forces (PACAF)

Located at Hickam AFB, Hawaii, it provides air and space power for the Asia-Pacific region. Its territory covers the west coast of the U.S. to the eastern seaboard of Africa, from the North Polar region to the South Polar region.

United States Air Forces in Europe (USAFE)

Headquartered at Ramstein AB, Germany, USAFE directs air operations across Europe, Africa, and parts of Asia. In addition to warfighting, it provides humanitarian and peacekeeping missions, and trains and equips Air Force units working under NATO. Combat-ready troops are based from Great Britain to Turkey. Equipment used includes over two hundred fighter, attack, tanker, and transport aircraft.

Air Force Reserve Command (AFRC)

Headquartered at Robins AFB, Georgia, it became the ninth major command in 1997, expanding from a field operating agency. It is integral to the daily Air Force mission of defending the United States through control and exploitation of air and space, and is not merely a force in reserve for possible war needs. It has thirty-five flying wings with their own aircraft, and nine associate units that share aircraft with active duty units. Four additional space operations squadrons share satellite control missions with active units, and over six hundred mission support units are part of the command as well. It has over four hundred aircraft, including the newest models of the F-16, O/A-10, C-5, C-141, C-130, MC-130, HC-130, WC-130, KC-135, B-52, and HH-60, with almost all available for deployment within seventy-two hours. Crews are available for immediate deployment without further training. Components of the reserve program include Ready Reserve, Standby Reserve, and Retired Reserve.

Air National Guard (ANG)

Headquartered at the Pentagon, Washington, D.C., it serves as a joint bureau of the Departments of the Army and Air Force. It serves both a federal and state mission. Federal missions include mobilization during wartime with well-trained and equipped units, as well as mobilization during national emergencies. Peacetime activities include assignments to most Air Force commands for a range of missions including training, mobilization readiness, and humanitarian operations. Units provide nearly half of the Air Force's tactical airlift support, combat communications function, aeromedical evacuations, and aerial refueling. The Air National Guard holds the responsibility for air defense of the entire United States. The state mission of the Air National Guard, when not deployed or otherwise under federal control, includes protection of life and property and the preservation of peace and public safety. While under state control, they report to the governor of the respective state, territory (Puerto Rico, Guam, Virgin Islands), or the District of Columbia. Emergency relief support operations include those required during natural disasters, such as hurricanes, earthquakes, and fires; and search and rescue operations, as well as counterdrug support operations.

★ RANK AND UNIFORMS ★

Rank

Rank in the Air Force is similar to the other services with a few changes. Air Force personnel may be commissioned officers or enlisted personnel. The Air Force does not use warrant officers. See appendix B for a comparison of ranks between services.

- Commissioned officers rank as follows: general of the Air Force (five-star, wartime use only), general (four-star), lieutenant general (three-star), major general (two-star), brigadier general (one-star), colonel, lieutenant colonel, major, captain, first lieutenant, and second lieutenant.

- For enlisted, the ranking is, from top to bottom, as follows: chief master sergeant of the Air Force, chief master sergeant, first sergeant, command chief master sergeant, senior master sergeant, first sergeant senior master sergeant, master sergeant, first sergeant, technical sergeant, staff sergeant, senior airman, airman first class, airman, and airman basic.

Uniforms

Uniforms consist of service dress uniforms, utility uniforms, desert uniforms, and physical training (PT) uniforms.

- The *service dress uniform* has a three-button coat similar to a sport jacket but with silver "U.S." pins on the lapels, matching trousers or skirt, and a service or garrison cap in Air Force blue, worn together with a light blue shirt and Air Force blue necktie. Officers wear metal rank insignia on the coat and slide on loops on the shirt, and enlisted personnel wear sleeve insignia on the jacket and shirt. Before 1993, Air Force blue uniforms strongly resembled the dress uniforms of the Army.

- The *utility uniform* used in combat and work duties is the battle dress uniform (BDU).

- *Desert uniforms* have desert camouflage print.

- The *physical training* (PT) uniform (beginning in late 2006) includes shorts, T-shirt, jacket, and pants in Air Force blue with silver reflective stripes along the leg. The T-shirt has reflective Air Force logos on the chest and back, and the jacket is blue with silver reflective stripes and a reflective chevron on the back. Pants are blue with silver piping and reflective stripes.

★ BASIC MILITARY TRAINING ★

Basic Military Training (BMT) in the Air Force is less intensive than the training in other branches of the U.S. military. It consists of six-and-one-half weeks training at Lackland AFB, Texas. Technical training in career specialties follows and occurs at one of five locations: Goodfellow, Lackland, and Sheppard AFBs, Texas; Keesler AFB, Mississippi; and Vandenberg AFB, California. Commissioned officers attend technical training courses for similar career fields at the same locations.

Basic Military Training begins with paperwork, assignment to a flight, uniform assignments, and haircuts—for men only; women can wear hair to their collars, with bangs to their eyebrows. Within a day or two, recruits are out of civilian clothes and into uniforms. Recruits are assigned to dorms. During the first week, recruits learn reporting and saluting, have medical and dental checks, are issued their ID cards, and begin individual drills. Nonfiring M16s (replicas) are assigned to recruits. Physical conditioning (PC) begins with minimal requirements: Men must complete a 2-mile run within 18 minutes, 45 sit-ups within 2 minutes, and 30 push-ups within 2 minutes; women must complete the run within 21 minutes, and do 38 sit-ups and 14 push-ups in 2 minutes each. During the second week, recruits are trained further in physical fitness, dorm inspections, personal appearance, military insignias, military citizenship, and more. The third week focuses on heritage, military structure, and physical endurance. Marching skills as well as further classroom training in financial management, citizenship, and force structure are provided. In the fourth week, "Warrior Week," the confidence course is given. Military survival skills are instilled in the airmen-in-training, through a grueling seven-day-long course which ends with the ceremonial "Airman's Run," a 2.5-mile run designed to build morale while testing endurance. At the end of Basic Training, recruits graduate to become airmen.

★ AIR FORCE OATH ★

"I,_____,do solemnly swear (or affirm) that I will support and defend the Constitution of the United States against all enemies, foreign and domestic, that I will bear true faith and allegiance to the same, and that I will obey the orders of the President of the United States and the orders of the officers appointed over me according to regulations and the Uniform Code of Military Justice, so help me God. In the Air Force, we live by three core values: Integrity first, Service before self, Excellence in all we do."

Following Basic Training, airmen are provided with technical training in their career field specialties.

Basic Officer Training is a rigorous twelve-week program designed to develop men and women qualified to lead. A typical schedule includes an hour of physical conditioning (PC) before 6:30 A.M., followed by breakfast, then technical skills practice (drill practice, firing range, parades, and leadership reaction course). After lunch, classes in subjects including writing, principals of war, Air Force history, World War II history, leadership, and management are given. After dinner, officer candidates attend flight meetings and deal with issues such as uniform cleaning, preparation, and studying.

PILOT TRAINING. Nineteenth Air Force, with headquarters at Randolph AFB, Texas, conducts Air Education Training Command's flight training. Air Force pilot candidates begin with Introductory Flight Training (IFT). Civilian instructors provide fifty hours of instruction to complete requirements for a private pilot license. Pilot candidates then attend either Euro-NATO Joint Jet Pilot Training (ENJJPT), or Joint Specialized Undergraduate Pilot Training (JSUPT).

Euro-NATO Joint Jet Pilot Training is located at Sheppard AFB, Texas. The course lasts over a year. Air Force officers and other NATO-member officers teach contact, instrument, low-level, and formation flying on the T-37 Tweet, before students move on to the fighter-trainer T-38 Talon, where they enhance their piloting skills.

Joint Specialized Undergraduate Pilot Training students receive primary training at Columbus AFB, Mississippi; Laughlin AFB, Texas; Vance AFB, Oklahoma; or at Naval Air Station Whiting Field, Florida. Students who report to Laughlin and Moody train in the T-6A Texan II; those reporting to Columbus use the T-37; and those who report to Vance will fly either the T-6A or T-37. Whiting Field students fly the T-34 C Turbomentor. Joint training is conducted at Vance and Whiting Field for students from the Air Force and the Navy.

There are four advanced training tracks based on class standing. These tracks include airlift/tanker (training in the T-1 Jayhawk), bomber/fighter track (training in the T-38 Talon), multi-engine turboprop (T-44 turboprop trainer), or helicopter (UH-1 Huey).

★ AIR FORCE FIGHTER WEAPONS SCHOOL ★

Similar to the Navy's TOPGUN School, the Air Force Fighter Weapons School at Nellis Air Force Base, Nevada, provides advanced training in weapons and tactics employment, and conducts extensive technical off-station training and liaison with Combat Air Force units. The school also publishes the quarterly *USAF Weapons Review* with worldwide readership. Aircraft include: A-10, AC-130, B-1, B-2, B-52, F-15C, F-15E, F-16C, F-117, HH-60, MC-130, and MH-53.

Selection to the weapons school is extremely competitive. Of those who qualify and apply, fewer than 5 percent are selected. The program begins with intense classroom study and hands-on training with actual equipment. Technical and tactical expertise, instructor preparation, and teaching ability are emphasized throughout the program. Aircrews deploy nearly every type of conventional ordnance certified for their aircraft, and are exposed to the equipment and procedures they will use in the field.

The program is nearly six months long and ends with the mission employment phase, a simulated wartime scenario. Students are exposed to the entire range of combat air and space capabilities and are required to plan the exercise and to integrate different weapons systems and disciplines to effectively accomplish the objectives of each.

Graduates return to their units as weapons officers, serving as their wing's technical expert in weapons, weapon systems, force integration and employment tactics, and training procedures. As the commander's technical advisor, the weapons officer is the focal point for appropriate training programs that will improve the unit's wartime capability.

★ U.S. AIR FORCE ACADEMY ★

The youngest of our nation's military academies, the U.S. Air Force Academy was instituted in 1954 to "mold future leaders from outstanding young men and women into Air Force officers with knowledge, character, and discipline; motivated to lead the worlds' greatest aerospace force in service to the nation." Of the more than 35,000 cadets that have graduated in forty-four classes, more than half are still on active duty with 4,000 cadets at the Academy at any one time. The Academy is located in Colorado Springs, Colorado.

CHARACTER DEVELOPMENT. As with the other military academies, personal integrity is not only important, it is tantamount. The core values of "Integrity first, Service before self, and Excellence in all we do" are the cornerstone of a cadet's ethical training, in the belief that "these special standards of good conduct are tied to the military profession's unique demand for self-discipline, stamina, courage, and selfless service to the nation." The Honor Oath, taken at the end of Basic Cadet Training, is broader in scope: "We will not lie, steal, or cheat, nor tolerate among us anyone who does. Furthermore, I resolve to do my duty and to live honorably, so help me God." Cadets are expected to report themselves for any code violation, and encourage any other cadet to turn themselves in if they believe they have violated the code as well.

MILITARY DEVELOPMENT. Cadets are taught military art and science, leadership, aviation sciences and airmanship, and professional development. All cadets participate in "airmanship" activities during each year. During the first summer, cadets are introduced to flying through orientation rides in the Cessna 172, and must take an aviation fundamentals course. In the second year, cadets receive experience via sailplane flights. Cadets in their third year take courses in soaring, parachuting, and navigation. Flying activities are complemented by academic studies in astronomy, aeronautics, astronautics, and physics. Most cadets complete the sailplane program; more than half earn parachuting badges. Cadets intending to become pilots complete introductory flight training during their Academy years.

ACADEMIC PROGRAM. Four main academic divisions provide a rigorous classical education which includes basic sciences (biology, chemistry, computer science, mathematics, and physics), humanities (English, foreign language, history, philosophy), engineering (aeronautics, astronautics, civil engineering, electrical engineering, engineering mechanics), and social sciences (behavioral science and leadership, economics and geography, law, management, and political science). Additional interdisciplinary programs include systems engineering and meteorology.

The goal of the academic program is to: "Produce officers who possess breadth of integrated, fundamental knowledge in the basic sciences, engineering, the humanities, and social sciences, and depth of knowledge in an area of concentration of their choice; officers who are intellectually curious; officers who can communicate effectively; officers who can frame and resolve ill-defined problems; officers who can work effectively with others; officers who are independent learners; and officers who can apply their knowledge and skills to the unique tasks of the military profession."

ATHLETIC PROGRAM. The Academy's athletic program is designed to provide its cadets with a realistic leadership experience, as well as mental and physical challenges; to prepare and motivate cadets for a lifetime of service through physical education, fitness training, and testing; and to provide intramural and intercollegiate athletic competition. Cadets take courses in aquatics, combatives, lifetime sports, and conditioning activities, and each must participate in an intercollegiate or intramural sport. There are twenty-seven men's and women's intercollegiate sports to choose from. Many of the men's teams, including basketball and football, compete in the highly competitive Mountain West Conference of the NCAA Division I. All sports compete against nonconference opponents, including many nationally ranked teams. Varsity teams are pitted against some of the top teams in the nation. Men's competitive sports include: basketball, baseball, cross country, fencing, football, golf, gymnastics, ice hockey, indoor and outdoor track, lacrosse, rifle, soccer, swimming, tennis, water polo, and wrestling. Women's competitive sports include basketball, cross country, fencing, gymnastics, indoor and outdoor track, rifle, swimming, tennis, and volleyball. Intramural sports include basketball, boxing, cross country, flag football, flickerball, racquetball, rugby, soccer, softball, tennis, team handball, ultimate Frisbee, volleyball, wallyball, and water polo.

Cadets are additionally required to take three different physical education classes each year. During the freshman year, this includes unarmed combat or boxing, swimming, and weight training. Sophomore cadets take water survival, physical fitness methods, and unarmed combat II. Juniors have courses in two of three "individual" sports (racquetball, tennis, or golf) plus an elective team sport. Senior cadets take another elective team sport and two electives.

ADMISSIONS. The Academy's admission process is competitive and highly selective. Candidates must be between seventeen and twenty-three to apply, American citizens, unmarried with no dependents, of good moral character, and must meet high leadership, academic, physical and medical standards to be considered. Academic performance in high school (rank in class and GPA) and SAT/ACT scores are used to evaluate academic potential. Participation in athletic and nonathletic extracurricular activities is also important. The Academy's physically challenging and team-oriented program requires athletically superior cadets who are active leaders in their community. Medical exams are required. As with the other military academies, nomination from the vice president, a senator, or representative is essential. Nominations from children of deceased or disabled veterans, children of Medal of Honor recipients and Air Force Regular and Reserve components are also possible, but limited on an annual basis. Honor Military Schools and Air Force ROTC may also nominate candidates, with twenty total appointments possible. Women were first admitted to the academy in 1976 as the graduating class of 1980. *Note:* Prospective students with tattoos and piercings should be aware that percings will be removed at the Academy, and if tattoos are "excessive," or contain inflammatory, obscene, racist, sexist, or similar content, the candidate will be rejected outright.

CADET LIFE. The Academy uses the class system. Thus, fourth-class is the same as freshman; third-class is sophomore; second-class is junior; first-class is senior.

As with all military academies, there isn't much time for leisure. There are other restrictions on life as well. Cadets are assigned to one of thirty-six squadrons with an assigned roommate, but may change roommates twice a year. Personal possessions are not permitted at the Academy with very few exceptions. All basic necessities, such as uniforms, bedding, and linens, are furnished when the student enters. As cadets advance through the years, additional items may be authorized. Each cadet is issued a personal computer while at the Academy and is permitted to have stereo equipment beginning the spring semester of the fourth-class (freshman) year. Televisions are permitted for first-class (seniors) only. Third-class cadets may have a coffee pot, and second-class cadets are permitted to have most other electrical appliances. Additionally, fourth-class cadets must follow different restrictions; they are a "lower class" than upperclassmen. Cadets wear uniforms and strict personal grooming is expected. They receive a stipend of seven hundred dollars per month plus a daily allowance of $5.75 per day, which is applied to food service.

Summer training for cadets is mandatory and is organized into three three-week training periods; each cadet is granted one three-week period of leave. During the second summer, combat survival training is taught. Cadets may work with airmen at an operational unit at an Air Force installation, undergo airborne or freefall parachute training or soaring training. During the third and fourth summers, cadets receive leadership training or supervise summer training of junior cadets.

Additional programs include the Cadet Summer Research Program in which selected cadets spend five weeks at various Air Force, Department of Defense, and other research facilities around the world using their classroom knowledge in a research project.

Cadets graduate with a bachelor of science degree and a second lieutenant's commission in the Air Force.

★ AIR FORCE DEMONSTRATION TEAMS ★

Thunderbirds

The Thunderbirds have represented the ultimate in American air power, skill, and precision flying since 1953. They fly high-performance aircraft in demonstrations all over world and are the premier aircraft demonstration team.

The Thunderbirds squadron is an Air Combat Command unit with eight pilots, four support officers, and about 125 active duty, Air National Guard, and Reserve enlisted or civilian members. Officers serve a two-year assignment with the squadron; enlisted personnel serve three to four years. About one-third of the team is renewed annually.

The Thunderbirds demonstration is a mix of six aircraft, performing formation flying and solo routines. Their impressive four-aircraft diamond formation demonstrates the skill of the pilots, and the solo maneuvers demonstrate the ability of the F-16 Flying Falcon, their current aircraft. Aircraft used over the history of the Thunderbirds have included the F-84G Thunderjet, the F-100 Super Sabre, the F-4 Phantom II, the T-38A Talon, and the F-16A Fighting Falcon. As technology and equipment have evolved, the Thunderbirds have changed aircraft, but the demonstration squadron has always opted for the most advanced, most versatile and most awe-inspiring aircraft possible to showcase America's frontline fighters and demonstrate the skill of every U.S. Air Force fighter pilot.

Air Education Training Command (AETC) Demo Team

The AETC Demo Team exhibitions feature a single pilot performing basic maneuvers that student pilots must learn during flight training; they demonstrate the most advanced Air Force trainer, the T-6A Texan II. This impressive aircraft is fully aerobatic, featuring a pressurized cockpit with an anti-G system and an advanced avionics package with sunlight-readable liquid crystal displays.

There are two AETC Demo Teams performing around the country. One performs from the East Coast and is based at Moody AFB, Georgia, and the other is on the West Coast and is based at Randolph AFB, California.

Air Combat Command (ACC) Demo Teams

There are six ACC Demonstration Teams based around the nation, each comprised of one demo pilot, nine maintenance personnel, and four narrators.

The Air Combat Command (ACC) Single-Ship Demonstration Teams perform precision aerial maneuvers in operational fighters. The exhibitions not only demonstrate the unique capabilities of the Air Force high-performance aircraft, but also the professional qualities the Air Force develops in the people who fly, maintain, and support these aircraft.

ACC Heritage Flight

The Heritage Flight program was established in 1997 in honor of the Air Force's fiftieth anniversary. The exhibition features modern, state-of-the-art fighters flying in close formation with World War II and Korean War vintage fighters, such as the P-51 Mustang and the F-86 Sabre. The Heritage Flight mission is to safely and proudly display the evolution of Air Force air power and to support recruiting and retention efforts. Aircraft utilized in Heritage Flight shows include: P-51, F-86, P-47, P-38, P-40, and FU-461.

Air Force Reserve's Aerobatic Show

The Air Force Reserve performs their "Living the Dream" air show to honor three eras of aerobatics in three acts, covering the Barnstormers, Competitors, and the Skydancers. Narration and inspirational music provide a tour of one hundred years of flight. The journey starts with a tribute to the first flight at Kitty Hawk and finishes with present-day, high-energy aerobatics. The performance includes such maneuvers as low knife-edge passes, snap rolls, tumbles, the centrifuge, the double hammerhead, torque rolls, and pilot Ed Hamill's signature maneuver, the Lucky Dog.

★ AIR FORCE DRUM AND BUGLE CORPS ★ AND AIR FORCE BANDS

The Air Force Drum and Bugle Corps has been in existence since 1948 but was transferred to the Air Force Academy in 1963. The Corps's mission is to support Cadet Wing activities, including military formations and Academy football and basketball games. The mission is extended to community concerts, field exhibitions, band festivals, and various military ceremonies, performing an average of thirty-five times a month. The Corps is composed of 120 cadets and has represented the Air Force Academy at such occasions as presidential inaugural parades, Macy's Thanksgiving Day parades, Tournament of Roses parades, and Special Olympics Opening Ceremonies.

Two premier bands include The United States Air Force Band in Washington, D.C., and the United States Air Force Academy Band (formerly the USAF Band of the Rockies) in Colorado Springs, Colorado. Ten additional regional bands are located in eight continental United States locations and at four locations overseas

(Germany, Japan, Alaska, and Hawaii). An additional eleven Air National Guard bands are found at various locations throughout the United States.

INSIDE THE AIR FORCE

"Training, Team, and Family"

By Colonel Bob Boswell, U.S. Air Force (RET)

As the son of a highly decorated combat veteran and career Air Force pilot, I grew up in the military, advancing and learning through the progression of Cub and Boy Scouts, Air Explorers, Civil Air Patrol, and ROTC. It was inevitable that I would enter the military upon graduation and become an Air Force pilot. Flying was fun, and the Air Force provided vast opportunities and adventures that were unmatched by other career paths. Southeast Asia was calling and I answered with two combat tours in Vietnam and three to Guam and Thailand, followed by combat in Desert Storm, with several minor conflicts in South America along the way. I advanced from combat operations to combat crew training, and air refueling to airlift, enjoying a long career in military aviation.

If I had to name two critical elements to this successful and enjoyable career, they would be "training" and "team." The bedrock of Air Force success is its second-to-none education and training. The never-ending cycle from student to leader and back again provides both the technical skills and higher education necessary not only to achieve specific military goals and objectives, but paves the way for success later in life. The Air Force is also a potent "team." The "can-do" attitude of its members is the foundation for the team spirit which transcends all ranks and positions. This is the fabric for the close-knit family of the Air Force and what sets it apart from other organizations. From this association, many life-long friendships are formed.

Reflecting on my thirty-plus years of active duty Air Force service and the twenty-two years of early military association, I have but one conclusion: Those fifty-two years were with the best "family" the world could have provided. As a military retiree, I have maintained this relationship and will forever appreciate my years in the United States Air Force.

★ CELEBRITY AIR FORCE MEMBERS ★

Some of the celebrity members of the Air Force include Buzz Aldrin (astronaut), George W. Bush (president), Jimmy Dolittle (first launch of land-based aircraft from an aircraft carrier), Gus Grissom (astronaut), Glenn Miller (musician), James Stewart (actor), Colonel Paul W. Tibbets (Enola Gay pilot, dropped the first atomic bomb on Japan), Ed White (astronaut), and Chuck Yeager (first to fly faster than the speed of sound).

AIR FORCE STATISTICS

Air Force Personnel as of December 2005:

Active duty:	365,377
Officers:	73,451
Enlisted:	291,926
Civilians:	141,326
Reservists:	331,076
Deployed:	21.1%
Officers:	10,965
Enlisted:	66,225
Deployed Civilians:	6,555

CHAPTER 6

Understanding the U.S. Coast Guard

★ OVERVIEW ★

The Coast Guard is proud to be the nation's oldest continuous seagoing service. It has responsibility for maritime activities within the United States. It plays a major role in homeland security, law enforcement, search and rescue, marine environmental pollution response, and maintenance of river, intracoastal, and offshore aids to navigation. The Coast Guard has been reorganized and relocated several times since its inception in 1790 during the Revolutionary War era.

★ MISSION ★

The Coast Guard has five main missions: maritime safety, maritime mobility, maritime security, national defense, and protection of natural resources. Units may be responsible for multiple missions at any time.

MARITIME SAFETY. Search and rescue operations may include the servicing of small boats out of fuel, finding missing boats or boaters, and aiding larger vessels in trouble or sinking within U.S. and international waters. Smaller boats from 25 to 42 feet are used in inland waters. HH-60 helicopters are used both at sea and inland. The Coast Guard also investigates marine accidents, whether American ships in national or international waters or foreign ships in American waters. Additionally, the Coast Guard operates a Marine Safety Office (MSO) in each major American port. The MSO conducts inspections, responds to pollution incidents, manages waterways, and investigates marine casualties. Its commanding officer is the captain of the port (COTP) for merchant mariners.

Recreational boating safety is also the responsibility of the Coast Guard, which conducts inspections for registration, personal flotation devices, and fire extinguishers, together with the U.S. power squadrons. However, only the Coast Guard can issue citations and forcibly return a boat to port. The International Ice Patrol, organized following the sinking of the Titanic in 1912, locates and reports icebergs in the North Atlantic.

MARITIME MOBILITY. The Coast Guard maintains navigation systems including radio systems, buoys, daymarks, and other visual aids to navigation, in addition to icebreaker ships to clear passages through ice-clogged waterways. A number of drawbridges are operated by the Coast Guard as well.

HOMELAND AND MARITIME SECURITY. Missions are coordinated through the Coast Guard Office of Law Enforcement. The Coast Guard provides port and waterway security for over 350 ports and almost 100,000 miles of waterways. They are the lead agency in maritime drug interdiction, sharing efforts with the Bureau of Immigration and Customs Enforcement. Caribbean Sea efforts are coordinated with the Navy, the Royal Navy (United Kingdom), and the Royal Netherlands Navy. They also enforce U.S. Immigration law at sea, with particular emphasis off the Florida coast, between the Dominican Republic and Puerto Rico, and around Guam. Necessarily, many of these efforts become search and rescue operations. Fisheries law enforcement is another part of the Coast Guard's security efforts.

NATIONAL DEFENSE. During times of war, the Coast Guard is operated by the U.S. Navy. The Coast Guard is also often sent for port security overseas, such as during American operations in the Persian Gulf and elsewhere.

PROTECTION OF NATURAL RESOURCES. It includes pollution education and prevention, as well as response and enforcement. When a ship sinks in Coast

Guard jurisdiction, the rescue of crew members is the first concern, followed closely by containment of any hazardous materials. Inspections of foreign vessels in American waters are included in this responsibility as are efforts to protect living marine resources.

The Coast Guard Auxiliary and the Coast Guard Reserve

The *Coast Guard Auxiliary* is a voluntary civilian service that has assisted the Coast Guard since 1939 in noncombatant and non-law-enforcement activities. Weapons are not permitted on auxiliary vessels. There are nearly 40,000 members of the auxiliary, who use their own vessels (both boats and aircraft), or offer radio operating skills to aid the Coast Guard.

The *Coast Guard Reserve* functions much as the Army, Navy, or Air Force reserve forces with monthly drills and two weeks of service annually unless called up for active duty. All of the Coast Guard's Port Security Units and many of its Naval Coastal Warfare Units are Reserve units.

★ MOTTOS ★

The Coast Guard's motto is "Semper paratus," which means "Always Ready" in Latin.

The unofficial motto of the Coast Guard is, "You have to go out, but you don't have to come back."

★ HISTORY ★

The Revenue Cutter Service was founded in 1790 with the construction of ten ships (called cutters) and recruitment of one hundred revenue officers. Between 1790 and 1798 (when the Navy was created), the Revenue Cutter Service served as the only armed American presence at sea. It was involved in fighting with France from 1798–1799, the War of 1812, and the Mexican War.

Other actions by the Revenue Cutter Service during the early years of America's history included slave trade prevention from 1794 through 1865, with the capture of some five hundred slave ships. The Revenue Cutter Service enforced Jefferson's embargo of American ports to European trade and was also active during the Civil War. Efforts in Alaska during the 1880s included rescue of whalers and miners.

The Coast Guard was officially formed in 1915 by consolidation of the Revenue Cutter Service, the Lifesaving Service, and the Steamship Inspection Bureau, with the Lighthouse Service joining in 1939. Its training center was founded at Sewell Point, Cape May, New Jersey, in the early 1900s, and could accommodate dirigibles as well as airplanes. During Prohibition, cutters assigned at the center, as well as destroyers employed elsewhere, were active in enforcement.

World War II saw a huge expanse of Coast Guard activities, ranging from patrols in Greenland to protect mining interests to protection and rescue operations after German attacks off the American coast. Coast Guard ships sank a dozen German ships, two Japanese submarines, and captured two German surface vessels. The Coast Guard assisted during the evacuation of Korea in the early stages of the Korean War, and aided in halting the enemy's resupply ships during the Vietnam War. During the 1980s and 1990s, the Coast Guard was active in the Caribbean Sea, particularly around Cuba, with immigration issues.

After the September 11 terrorist attacks at home, the Coast Guard was sent to the Persian Gulf to enforce the Iraqi embargo. In 2003, the Coast Guard was transferred to the Department of Homeland Security and assigned homeland defense duties exclusively. It was active in the federal emergency activities following Hurricane Katrina, rescuing over 35,000 persons. About one-third of the entire Coast Guard was deployed to support the hurricane rescue response.

★ IMPORTANT DISTINCTION ★

The Coast Guard is the only branch of the military with civilian arrest and detention powers, which is why it is not under the umbrella of the Department of Defense. Our forefathers did not want the military to have civilian arrest and detention powers, but recognized the need for this within the Revenue Cutter Service. Thus the Coast Guard is distinct from the other branches in this important aspect.

★ ORGANIZATION ★

The Coast Guard is organized into districts, which have undergone changes and reorganization over the years. The current district organization is as follows:

FIRST DISTRICT: Atlantic Region (includes New England states, New York, and northern New Jersey), with its district office in Boston, Massachusetts. Coast Guard Air Station (CGAS) Cape Cod, Massachusetts is under this jurisdiction.

FIFTH DISTRICT: Atlantic Region (includes Pennsylvania, southern New Jersey, Delaware, Maryland, Virginia, and North Carolina) with its district office in Portsmouth, Virginia. This district includes two Coast Guard Air Stations: CGAS Atlantic City, New Jersey, and CGAS Elizabeth City, North Carolina (both an operational and training air station).

SEVENTH DISTRICT: Atlantic Region, (includes South Carolina, Georgia, and eastern Florida) with its district office in Miami, Florida. Four Coast Guard Air Stations are part of this district: CGAS Clearwater, Florida; CGAS Miami, Florida; CGAS Savannah, Georgia; and CGAS Borinquen, Puerto Rico.

EIGHTH DISTRICT: Atlantic Region (includes the inland waters of the U.S. and Gulf of Mexico) with its district office in New Orleans, Louisiana. Coast Guard Air Stations in this district include CGAS Houston, Texas; CGAS Corpus Christi, Texas; Coast Guard Aviation Training Center, Mobile, Alabama.

NINTH DISTRICT: Atlantic Region (includes the Great Lakes) with district office in Cleveland, Ohio. Coast Guard Air Stations include CGAS Detroit, Michigan; and CGAS Traverse City, Minnesota.

ELEVENTH DISTRICT: Pacific Region (includes California, Arizona, Nevada, and Utah) with district office in Alameda, California. Coast Guard Air Stations include CGAS Humboldt Bay, California; CGAS Sacramento, California; CGAS San Francisco, California; CGAS Los Angeles, California; CGAS San Diego, California.

THIRTEENTH DISTRICT: Pacific Region (includes Oregon, Washington, Idaho and Montana) with district office in Seattle, Washington. Coast Guard Air Stations include CGAS Astoria, Oregon; CGAS North Bend, Oregon; and CGAS Port Angeles, Washington.

FOURTEENTH DISTRICT: Pacific Region (includes Hawaii and Pacific territories) with district office in Honolulu, Hawaii. CGAS Barbers Point, Hawaii is part of this District.

SEVENTEENTH DISTRICT: Pacific Region (includes Alaska) with district office in Juneau, Alaska. CGAS Kodiak, Alaska and CGAS Sitka, Alaska are within this district.

In the current organization, "Groups" (large operational centers) within each district merge with Marine Safety Offices to become "Sectors." "Stations" are the designation for smaller boat stations; "Coast Guard Air Stations" use aircraft. Stations report to Sectors, and Sectors and Coast Guard Air Stations report to District offices.

Since 2003, the Coast Guard has been a part of the Department of Homeland Security. It is headed by the Commandant of the Coast Guard, Admiral Thomas H. Collins, who holds the position on a four-year term. He is assisted by the Vice Commandant of the Coast Guard, Vice Admiral Terry Cross; Master Chief Petty Officer of the Coast Guard, Frank A. Welch, the senior enlisted person; and Chief of Staff Vice Admiral Thad W. Allen, who also serves as commanding officer of Coast Guard Headquarters. Vice Admiral Allen was sent to coordinate rescue and relief operations after Hurricane Katrina devastated New Orleans and surrounding areas, and replaced Federal Emergency Management Agency (FEMA)'s Michael Brown shortly after the hurricane. The commander of the Atlantic area and maritime defense zone is Vice Admiral Vivien S. Crea; the commander of the Pacific area and coast guard defense forces west is Vice Admiral Harvey E. Johnson, Jr.

Additional senior leaders of the Coast Guard include Rear Admiral (Upper Half) James C. Van Sice, as the superintendent of the U.S. Coast Guard Academy and chief director of the auxiliary Captain B. Hill.

★ TERMINOLOGY ★

Understanding marine vessels used by the Coast Guard is essential to understanding the service. The terminology for the vessels under its command has fluctuated greatly over the years, which leads to much confusion.

Currently, any Coast Guard vessel over 65 feet long is termed a *cutter*. Over the years, different terms have been used to designate different types or sizes of ships. Through 1915, the Coast Guard referred to the largest vessels as "first class," with smaller craft designated as "second class," "third class," and "launches." With the formation of the Coast Guard in 1915, all larger cutters were referred to as "cruising cutters," smaller vessels were called "harbor vutters," and the smallest craft called "launches." In 1920, the Coast Guard divided the cruising cutter category into "cruising cutters" for the largest sea-going cutters, and "inshore patrol cutters" for coastal vessels. Change again occurred in 1925 when the largest cutters were designated "cruising cutters, first class," and the coastal cutters became "cruising cutters, second class." As Prohibition enforcement became more important, the term "patrol boat" was used to describe any smaller craft. Naval destroyers were acquired and termed, "Coast Guard destroyers."

In 1942, the Coast Guard again changed its designations by adopting the Navy's ship classification scheme whereby a vessel was given a two-letter designation based on the type of ship and its hull number, with the additional letter "W" as prefix. For example, cruising cutters, first class became patrol gunboats, or "WPG." The reason for the use of the "W" is unclear; it may have referred to "weather" patrol, or have been an unused letter of the designation alphabet. Hull numbers were given to each vessel at the same time. After World War II, the large sea-going vessels were classified as WPG (patrol gunboats), WDE (destroyer escorts), and WAVP (seaplane tenders).

In 1965, the names were changed again, and these same vessels were combined into one grouping, WHEC (Coast Guard high endurance cutters). The former cruising cutters, second class became "WPC" (Coast Guard patrol craft). Patrol boats maintained their last designation (WPB) in recognition of the Coast Guard's intention to designate the vessels according to their patrol duration capability.

Current Coast Guard Vessel Designations

WAGB: icebreaker

WHEC: high endurance cutter

WIX: auxiliary; training ship

WLB: seagoing buoy tender

WLBB: inland icebreaker, newly launched in April, 2005

WLI: inland buoy tender

WLIC: inland construction tender

WLM: coastal buoy tender

WLR: river buoy tender

WMEC: medium endurance cutter

WPB: patrol boat

WTGB: large icebreaking tug

WYTL: small harbor tug

Additional boats smaller than cutters used by the Coast Guard include:

ASB: arctic survey boat

DPB: deployable pursuit boat

MLB: motor life boat

RHI: rigid hull inflatable boat with deep-V glass reinforced plastic hulls, both portable and rugged

TANB/BUSL/ANB/ANB: aids to navigation boats

TPSB: transportable port security boat

UTB: utility boat

★ RATE AND UNIFORMS ★

Rate

Rates used in the Coast Guard are essentially those used in the Navy; see appendix B for a comparative listing.

- The term "commodore" is no longer used in the regular Coast Guard, and is replaced by "rear admiral, lower half." (Chief elected officers of the Coast Guard Auxiliary are called commodores, but this is not a military rank.)

- Coast Guard captains, like their Navy counterparts, rate immediately below rear admiral (lower half) and command most large operational units such as sectors, large cutters, large air stations, integrated support commands, training centers, and large headquarters units.

- Note that in maritime tradition, the commanding officer of a ship is also called "captain" regardless of actual rank held. The person in charge of a Coast Guard or Coast Guard Auxiliary boat is the "coxswain."

Uniforms

- The *dress uniform* is similar to the Navy officer uniform, consisting of a blue single-breasted jacket and trousers or skirt in a darker shade than the Air Force uniform. Officer rank insignia parallels that of the Navy, replacing the Navy star with the Coast Guard gold shield on a blue background. Enlisted rate insignia has the Coast Guard shield instead of the Navy eagle on collar and cap devices. Group rate marks (stripes) for junior enlisted members (E-3 and below) follow Navy convention with white for seaman, red for fireman, and green for airman. Distinct from the Navy convention, petty officers (E-6 to E-4) wear red chevrons, and all chief petty officers (E-7 and above) wear gold.

- The *utility uniform* is called the ODU, similar to the battle dress uniform (BDU) worn by the other services. It is blue without camouflage patterns and is worn with steel-toed boots. No "Dixie cup" hats are worn by Coast Guard enlisted personnel as with the Navy; but instead they wear "baseball" caps embroidered with "U.S. Coast Guard" or the name of their ship in gold.

- The Coast Guard Auxiliary wears identical uniforms but with silver stripes to denote office.

★ JOINING AND TRAINING WITHIN ★
THE COAST GUARD

Commissioned officers join the Coast Guard via the U.S. Coast Guard Academy, or Officer Candidate School.

The Coast Guard Academy is located in New London, Connecticut, along the Thames River. It is the only military academy to which no presidential or congressional appointments are made (besides the specialized Uniformed Services University of the Health Sciences). Approximately 170 cadets are commissioned as ensigns annually (see details on page 138).

Officer Candidate School (OCS) is another means whereby officers may join the Coast Guard. OCS is a seventeen-week training program held at New London, Connecticut. Graduates are indebted for three years' active duty. About seventy candidates are commissioned ensigns annually and a few are commissioned as lieutenant junior grade within each class.

Individuals may enlist in the Coast Guard from high school or equivalent training, and receive eight weeks Basic Training at the Coast Guard Training Center Cape May in Cape May, New Jersey. Enlisted personnel receive training in physical fitness, water survival and swimming, wellness and nutrition, self-discipline, military skills, and military bearing. They receive advanced training at class "A" schools for their chosen "rating," the Coast Guard equivalent term for Military Occupational Specialty (MOS). *Note:* Advanced training is available for enlisted chief petty officers (E-7) at the U.S. Coast Guard Chief Petty Officer Academy at New London, Connecticut. Training covers professionalism, leadership, communications and systems, and lifelong learning.

★ U.S. COAST GUARD ACADEMY ★

The U.S. Coast Guard Academy is unique among the service academies in that it educates the future leaders of a humanitarian, not military, force. The United States Coast Guard is the oldest life-saving service in the world. Commissioned officers in the Coast Guard lead and are responsible for a force of men and women who are continually called upon to serve their country and community.

MISSION. The Coast Guard Academy's mission statement is long-winded but covers the ground—er, water: "To graduate young men and women with sound bodies, stout hearts, and alert minds, with a liking for the sea and its lore, with that high sense of honor, loyalty, and obedience which goes with trained initiative and leadership; well-grounded in seamanship, the sciences, and amenities, and strong in the resolve to be worthy of the traditions of commissioned officers in the United States Coast Guard in the service of their country and humanity."

Headquartered in New London, Connecticut, the Academy provides a four-year bachelor of science program with a full scholarship for each individual, similar to the other military academies. It graduates nearly two hundred cadets every year who are commissioned as ensigns in the Coast Guard with a five-year service obligation. The Academy has been in operation for about 125 years.

CORE VALUES AND PHILOSOPHY. The core values of the Academy are based on traditional values and are three-tiered: "Honor—Integrity is our standard. We demonstrate uncompromising ethical conduct and moral behavior in all our personal actions. We are loyal and accountable to the public trust.

Respect—We value our diverse work force. We treat each other with fairness, dignity, and compassion. We encourage individual opportunity and growth. We encourage creativity through empowerment. We work as a team. Devotion to Duty—We are professionals, military and civilian, who seek responsibility, accept accountability, and are committed to the successful achievement of our organizational goals. We exist to serve. We serve with pride."

The basic philosophy of the Academy is: "Belief in your country. Belief in your fellow cadets and Coast Guard personnel. And belief in yourself."

ACADEMIC PROGRAM. The U.S. Coast Guard Academy program is designed to provide a top quality academic foundation in a military environment, resulting in future leaders of America. Major programs of study include one of eight choices: civil engineering, mechanical engineering, electrical engineering, naval architecture and marine engineering, marine and environmental science, operations research and computer analysis, and government and management. Class size is small with an instructor-to-student ratio of 1 to 8. The core curriculum includes the following: Chemistry, Physics, Calculus, Statics and Engineering Design, Nautical Science, Economics, American Government, English Composition and Speech, Criminal Justice, Maritime Law Enforcement, U.S. History, Morals and Ethics, Organizational Behavior and Leadership, Oceanography, and Probability and Statistics. An Honors Program is offered, which may include seminars, in-depth research projects, and internships in Washington, D.C.

ADMISSION TO THE ACADEMY. One of the most selective undergraduate colleges in the country, just three hundred students are selected from about six thousand applicants. Requirements include a strong academic record, especially in math and science, athletic skills, and a community service record. Unlike the other military academies, the Coast Guard Academy does not require congressional nominations.

PHYSICAL PROGRAM. The athletic program is quite extensive for a school of this size—its total cadet force is only 850. The Academy believes that an athlete's strength, stamina, and determination to excel leads to strong leadership capabilities, and thus require cadets to maintain their best possible physical condition through sports and other physical activities.

ACADEMY SPORTS. The Coast Guard Academy is an NCAA Division III school and has men's and women's varsity programs in sports such as: baseball, basketball, crew, cross country, football, pistol, rifle, sailing, soccer, softball, swimming, tennis, track, volleyball, and wrestling. Club sports include rugby, lacrosse, and volleyball. Women's lacrosse, bowling, boxing, and ultimate Frisbee are additional sports activities not quite on the club level. Three additional sports are co-ed: rifle (NCAA), sailing, and pistol.

CADET LIFE. All cadets receive annual stipends of $8,760 per year, to pay for uniforms, equipment, and textbooks; a portion of this is available to the cadet for personal expenses. Cadet lives are run much as at other military academies. The Corps of Cadets is organized into eight companies *(Alfa* through *Hotel)* forming one regiment. Cadets run the Corps through a regimental chain of command, a technique designed to provide sound leadership training as well as respect for higher-ranking individuals. First class (senior) cadets act as regimental staff officers, company commanders, department heads, and division officers. Second class (junior) cadets serve as assistant division officers, providing direct leadership to and supervising third and fourth class cadets. Second class cadets are also responsible for the fourth class training program. Third class (sophomore) cadets serve as mentors, each providing personal oversight of one or two fourth class cadets. Fourth class (freshman) cadets are assimilating into the rigors of military life while developing teamwork skills essential to success in the Coast Guard.

Each company's chain of command is organized to parallel that of the Coast Guard itself. The First class cadet assigned as company commander is responsible to the company officer (a commissioned Coast Guard officer assigned to each company) for the performance of the company. Other first class cadets fulfill junior officer roles and are assigned duties as department heads and division officers to assist the company commander. The second class cadets' roles parallel those of Coast Guard senior enlisted, third class cadets parallel mid-grade petty officers, and fourth class cadets fulfill the role of junior enlisted. The professional and personal development of each class is progressive in nature, ensuring that cadets are capable of meeting the demands and responsibilities at the next level in their development.

SOCIAL AND UNIQUE ASPECTS OF COAST GUARD ACADEMY LIFE. There are a number of interesting aspects of cadet life at the Academy, some of which are described here.

ONE HUNDRETH DAY: Each year near the end of February, typically one hundred days to graduation, the tables turn, and the fourth class become "kings for a day." The second class are given the low-ranking jobs.

CHAIN LINKS: This tradition dates back to the Revolutionary War when a massive chain was drawn across the Hudson River to keep ships from attacking the rebel fort at West Point, New York. General Benedict Arnold, the infamous American traitor, was in command of that fort and one of his betrayals concerned these chains. The chain links currently found in the Academy Museum were donated by members of the family that originally forged them. Today, before home football games, fourth class cadets are challenged to hide the chain somewhere on Academy grounds, and second class cadets have to find it by half-time or else reward the fourth class with some privilege.

HALLOWED WORDS: "Who Lives Here Reveres Honor, Honors Duty." These words, a symbol of the Honor of Academy, are inlaid on the Quarterdeck (at the flagpole in front of Hamilton Hall, which resembles the quarterdeck, or place of honor, on a ship) and should never be tread upon.

LIBERTY BELL: Tradition says that the cadet who rings the black navigational buoy by the museum will be granted good luck.

OBJEE STATUE DRESSUP: A statue of the Academy's mascot, Objee, is traditionally dressed up before a big athletic event.

RING DANCES: The first annual ring dance is used to permit third class cadets to officially don their miniatures, or pins. At the second ring dance, second class cadets are first officially permitted to wear their large class rings. During this occasion, the escort receives the ring which women wear around their necks and men on their lapels. At the dance, each couple proceeds to the ring monument where the escort removes the ring, and dips it into a bowl of water as a christening, symbolizing all the waters patrolled by the Coast Guard.

SQUARE ROOT CLUB: In this rather recent tradition, students suffering academic difficulties dub themselves the Square Root Club, due to the fact that their grade point average is so low that its square root is larger. They make a midnight pilgrimage to the grave of Hopley Yeaton, lighting a candle and smoking a pipe while they sharpen their dividers (nautical chart measuring device) above his crypt. Hopley Yeaton, incidentally, was commissioned by George Washington with command of a Coast Guard vessel, and is considered the "Father of the Coast Guard." He was buried in the 1800s in Lubuc, Maine, but his remains were exhumed in 1975 and placed in a crypt on the plaza in front of the Academy Chapel.

SWABHOOD: Tradition honors the transformation from fourth class cadets ("Swabs") to third class. Cadets advance only when the new year of swabs arrive on campus. As the saying goes, "You are still a swab, until you see a swab."

INSIDE THE U.S. COAST GUARD

"Proud to Serve in the Coast Guard Family"
By MKC Bromley Ball and MK1 Mark Carstens, U.S. Coast Guard

Serving in the U.S. Coast Guard is both an honor and a privilege. The Coast Guard is the smallest branch of the armed forces. It is the only armed service that functions within the Department of Homeland Security. In addition, the Coast Guard also has the smallest budget when compared to the other armed services. Moreover, the multi-missions the Coast Guard performs that include port security, search and rescue, migrant and drug interdiction, recreational and commercial boating safety, maintaining aids to navigation, and licensing U.S. crews working in the maritime industry are its other distinguishing characteristics. It is also important to remember that we perform these missions both at home and abroad. Despite the differences between the Coast Guard and the other armed services, it may appear that the Coast Guard is at a disadvantage. We Coast Guard members do not perceive these differences as negatives. Instead, these differences provide all Coast Guard members a unique opportunity to learn the importance of versatility, hard work, patriotism, and to be a part of a close-knit family that includes both active duty members as well as reservists.

When the Coast Guard shifted to the newly created Department of Homeland Security, the demands placed on the Coast Guard increased significantly. All of our missions are demanding and subsequently entrust a lot of responsibility on all its members regardless of rank. To cope with this high-stress environment, Coast Guard members form close relationships that extend beyond the workplace. These relationships and bonds are constantly reinforced due to the nature of our job and lifestyle. For Coast Guard Reservists, these experiences are no different.

Once a month and for two weeks in the summer, Coast Guard Reservists drill with their shipmates. This volunteer service inherently facilitates close relationships. Because of these close relationships, the Coast Guard Reserve has a high retention rate. In fact, if you ask many reservists why they remain in the reserves, most of these people will say they enjoy the mission and the camaraderie that is associated with our commitment.

With just over forty thousand men and women serving in the U.S. Coast Guard, career members invariably encounter old friends. It is this frequent contact that leads to the reminiscing of old "sea stories," and experiences. Here is where friendships are reinforced and bonds are renewed. This is both a gratifying and satisfying fact of life for Coast Guard members.

For us, we could not think of a better place to serve our country. Unlike the other services, we do not train for what we might do someday; we train for what we do every day. We take great satisfaction in having the opportunity to save lives, protect lives, and make the world a better place. We are able to do our job and, at the same time, to create and maintain life-long friendships. There is a silent but understood notion that members of the Coast Guard look out for each other and take care of their own.

★ CELEBRITY COAST GUARD MEMBERS ★

A short list of celebrity Coast Guard members includes the following: Humphrey Bogart (actor), Beau Bridges (actor), Lloyd Bridges (actor), Sid Caesar (comedian), Walter Cronkite (television anchorman), Jack Dempsey (boxer), Marlene Dietrich (actress), Buddy Ebsen (actor, comedian, dancer), Arthur Fiedler (conductor), Charles Gibson (newscaster), Alex Haley (author), Tab Hunter (actor), Sam Nunn (U.S. senator), Arnold Palmer (golfer), and Ted Turner (businessman).

COAST GUARD STATISTICS

Coast Guard Personnel approximate numbers as of 2006:

Active duty:	39,000
Reserve:	8,000
Auxiliary:	nearly 33,000
Civilian:	8,000

★
CHAPTER 7

Understanding the U.S. Special Operations Forces

★ OVERVIEW ★

The term *special operations forces* refer to all components of the military that have unique capabilities and do not fight by conventional means, hence the designation "special." However, the term *Special Forces* refers exclusively to the United States Army Special Forces, commonly known as the Green Berets. The United States special operations forces (SOF) include: the Army Rangers, the Green Berets (*the* Special Forces), and 160th SOAR (Aviation) "Night Stalkers" of the Army; Delta Force, Navy SEALs, and Special Warfare Development Group (DEVGRU) of the Navy; the Marines' Force Reconnaissance; Air Force Special Forces; and Psychological Operations ("PSYOPS") of the U.S. Army Special Operations Command (USASOC).

Each force has a distinct function and mission for different situations, and due to the nature of these operations, publicly available information is limited. The special operations forces generally serve as small, discrete units that work quite independently of the rest of the military. For this reason, they are highly trained in a range of tactical combat and survival skills.

Women are not permitted to serve in the special operations forces—despite the movie *GI Jane* in which a female SEAL member was depicted.

★ 75ᵀᴴ RANGER REGIMENT—"ARMY RANGERS" ★

The 75th Ranger Regiment, also known as the U.S. Army Rangers, is a special operations force of the United States Army Special Operations Command (USASOC), with headquarters in Fort Benning, Georgia. The regiment is a flexible, highly trained, and rapidly deployable light-infantry force with specialized skills that can be employed against a variety of conventional and special operations targets.

★ MOTTO ★

The motto of the Army Rangers is "Rangers lead the way."

The force specializes in airborne, light-infantry, and direct action operations; conducting raids; infiltration and exfiltration by air, land, or sea; airfield seizure; recovery of personnel and special equipment; and support of general purpose forces. Each Ranger Battalion can deploy anywhere in the world with eighteen hours' notice.

Prospective Rangers begin with the Basic Combat Training and Advanced Individual Training of all Army soldiers. Next, the soldier must complete airborne training. Upon graduation, he will be assigned to the 75th Ranger Regiment to attend the Ranger Indoctrination Program (RIP) or "Ranger School." If the soldier passes each of the required programs, he will receive an assignment to either the 75th Ranger Regiment Headquarters or to one of the three Ranger Battalions.

All members of the Ranger Regiment must pass Ranger School and earn their Ranger Tab before assuming any leadership position within the regiment. The unofficial motto of Ranger students is "With the tab, or on a slab"—meaning, they will return to the regiment with their Ranger Tab or die trying.

Ranger School

Army Rangers are world renown for their toughness. The training course is an intense two months that weeds out all but the best for this kind of soldiering. The training covers three phases designated "Crawl," "Walk," and "Run."

CRAWL PHASE. The "Crawl" phase begins at Ft. Benning, Georgia. It is designed to assess and develop the military skills, physical and mental endurance, stamina, and confidence a soldier requires to accomplish the type of combat missions Rangers face. It teaches self-sustenance, subordinate sustenance and control, and equipment maintenance, skills necessary for the difficult field conditions of training and essential for Ranger missions. If a student is not in top physical condition when he begins the Ranger course, he will be quickly eliminated from the program.

Specific activities include a timed series of push-ups, sit-ups, and a 2-mile run; as well as completing chin-ups, combat water survival test, a 5-mile run, a 3-mile run with an obstacle course, a 16-mile foot march, night and day land-navigation tests; and training in rifle bayonet, pugil stick and combatives (hand-to-hand combat). There is additional training in medical treatment, explosives, terrain reconnaissance, and an airborne refresher jump. The second portion of the crawl phase covers squad combat patrol operations, including ambush and reconnaissance patrols, methods of entering or clearing a room, and air assault operations. Another obstacle course must be completed as well as intensive communications training.

WALK PHASE. Located at Camp Frank D. Merrill in Dahlonega, Georgia, the "Walk" phase is also known as the mountain phase. Each student is given aggressive training in mountaineering techniques and learns to conduct combat patrol operations under mountainous conditions. Students further develop their skills in commanding and controlling a platoon-sized patrol by planning and conducting a range of combat patrol missions. Mountain survival skills are emphasized as the student learns how to sustain himself and subordinates. Difficult physical conditions as well as weather, hunger, mental and physical fatigue, and emotional stress test students further. Mountaineering skills evaluations include a 200-foot night rappel and other grueling tests.

Combat patrol missions are designed against a conventionally equipped threat force in a low-intensity conflict. These patrol missions are conducted day and night over a four-day squad field training exercise (FTX) and a platoon five-day FTX that includes moving cross-country over mountains, conducting vehicle ambushes, raiding mortar and communications sites, crossing a river and scaling a steep mountain. The student's stamina and endurance is pushed to the limit and beyond. At the end of the mountain phase, the students parachute, assault-style, into the third and final phase of their training.

RUN PHASE. Also called the Florida training, the "Run" phase is conducted at Camp Rudder, near Eglin Air Force Base, Florida. This training emphasizes the student's combat arms skills in another extreme physical environment, the jungle or swamp. The student endures continuous exercises in platoon-level patrol operations and are taught to plan and lead small units in a range of combat operations, from water to air to ground, in a low-intensity combat environment against a well-trained, sophisticated enemy. Survival skills in the swamp environment are developed, with a final ten-day FTX that challenges students to apply all skills learned in the form of raids and other combat patrol missions. Students end with an airborne insertion (i.e., parachute drop) back into Fort Benning.

★ THE RANGER CREED ★

Recognizing that I volunteered as a Ranger, fully knowing the hazards of my chosen profession, I will always endeavor to uphold the prestige, honor, and high *esprit de corps* of the Rangers.

Acknowledging the fact that a Ranger is a more elite soldier who arrives at the cutting edge of battle by land, sea, or air, I accept the fact that as a Ranger, my country expects me to move further, faster, and fight harder than any other soldier.

Never shall I fail my comrades. I will always keep myself mentally alert, physically strong, and morally straight, and I will shoulder more than my share of the task, whatever it may be, 100 percent and then some.

Gallantly will I show the world that I am a specially selected and well-trained soldier. My courtesy to superior officers, neatness of dress, and care of equipment shall set the example for others to follow.

Energetically will I meet the enemies of my country. I shall defeat them on the field of battle, for I am better trained and will fight with all my might. Surrender is not a Ranger word. I will never leave a fallen comrade to fall into the hands of the enemy and under no circumstances will I ever embarrass my country.

Readily will I display the intestinal fortitude required to fight on to the Ranger objective and complete the mission, though I be the lone survivor.

Ranger Background

The U.S. Rangers were first employed on the American frontier in 1670 under the direction of Captain Benjamin Church, whose Rangers brought the Indian Conflict known as "King Phillip's War" to a successful conclusion in 1675.

Rangers were officially organized in 1756 by Major Robert Rogers, who recruited nine companies of American colonists to fight for the British during the French and Indian War. The Rangers at that time used the methods of the American frontiersmen, but Major Rogers was recognized as the first to incorporate them into the fighting doctrine of a permanently organized force.

On June 14, 1775, the Continental Congress decreed, "Six companies of expert riflemen be immediately raised in Pennsylvania, two in Maryland, and two in Virginia." The frontiersmen that formed under Dan Morgan were named "The Corps of Rangers" by George Washington and had a reputation for being crack shots. Thomas Knowlton's Connecticut Rangers, a small group of fewer than 150 men, conducted reconnaissance during the Revolutionary War. Knowlton himself was killed leading his men in action during the conflict.

A number of Rangers were operating during the Civil War, with the best known commanded by the Confederate Army. Mosby's Rangers aggressively pressured Union forces with surprise assaults, attacking weak points with skill and frequent victories, as did Ashby's Rangers. For the Union, Mean's Rangers captured the ammunition train of Confederate General Longstreet and a portion of Colonel Mosby's force.

Rangers were activated again during World War II in Tunisia, Italy, Normandy, the Battle of the Bulge, and in the Pacific. Additionally, "Merrill's Marauders" gained fame and glory recapturing the only all-weather airfield in Burma.

In 1980, Rangers and the Delta Force attempted to rescue the hostages from the American embassy in Iran, and although unsuccessful, it resulted in enhanced training. The Rangers have been deployment for such diverse conflicts as Grenada, Panama, Somalia, Saudi Arabia, and other regions of the Persian Gulf.

★ SPECIAL FORCES—"GREEN BERETS" ★

The U.S. Army Special Forces, also known as the Green Berets or simply Special Forces (always capitalized), is a special operations force of the U.S. Army trained for unconventional warfare and special operations. These are *the* Special Forces. Special Forces soldiers are either on a mission or training for one at all times. Their missions are conducted worldwide and are frequently classified. Their activities include stopping acts of terrorism in progress, supporting the global war on terrorism and related humanitarian efforts.

Counterterrorism efforts involve the deployment of Special Forces to preclude, preempt, and resolve terrorist incidents abroad, as well as train other nations' military to fight terrorism. *Direct action missions* are short duration strikes used to seize, capture, recover, or destroy enemy weapons and information, or to recover designated personnel or material. *Foreign internal defense missions* are used to organize, assist, and train the military and national defense forces of foreign governments to protect their citizens from aggressors. *Special reconnaissance missions* involve intelligence gathering to learn about the enemy, in terms of movement and operations. *Unconventional warfare*, or guerilla warfare, includes the training, equipping, advising, and assisting of forces in enemy-held or controlled territory.

★ MOTTO ★

The Green Berets' motto is *"De opresso liber,"* meaning "To liberate the oppressed."

Their official headgear is the green beret, which was originally approved for all the Army. President Kennedy suggested the exclusive use of the green beret as a recognizable symbol to set them apart.

Special Forces Training

Special Forces training almost makes Ranger School look tame. Soldiers wishing to join the Special Forces must have already completed Basic Training, Advanced Intermediate Training, and Airborne School. Then, additional intensive training includes the following:

SPECIAL OPERATIONS PREPARATORY COURSE (SOPC). A thirty-day course taught at Fort Bragg, North Carolina that helps soldiers recruited "off the street" (i.e., not from within the Army structure) to complete the Special Forces Assessment and Selection Course. It focuses on physical training and land navigation skills.

SPECIAL FORCES ASSESSMENT AND SELECTION (SFAS). This is a rigorous twenty-four days of survival training.

SPECIAL FORCES QUALIFICATION COURSE (SFQC). This consists of five phases somewhat illogically numbered Two through Six. Soldiers successfully completing this training are termed "Special Forces."

PHASE TWO: INDIVIDUAL SKILL. Covers land navigation, small unit tactics, and live-fire training.

PHASE THREE: MOS TRAINING. Instruction on specialty skills is given, according to soldier's background, abilities, and interests.

PHASE FOUR: COLLECTIVE TRAINING. This includes Special Forces doctrine and organization, unconventional warfare operations, direct action operations, methods of instruction, and both airborne and airmobile operations. Soldiers are deployed to the Uwarrie National Forest, North Carolina, for an unconventional warfare exercise where they perform as members of the Operational Detachment Alpha team. Skills and performance are evaluated.

PHASE FIVE: LANGUAGE TRAINING. Language training ranges from the Romance languages (e.g., Spanish, French, Portuguese, Italian) to more difficult languages (e.g., Korean, Arabic). Because the mission of the Special Forces includes working directly with foreign forces, language and cultural training is a significant component of their training and distinguishes them from the other special operations forces.

PHASE SIX: SURVIVAL, EVASION, RESISTANCE AND ESCAPE (SERE) COURSE. This is the final portion of the Special Forces training.

Upon graduation from the Special Forces Qualification Course, every Special Forces soldier is issued a knife known as the "Yarborough," named in honor of General William P. Yarborough, the "father of the Green Berets." Each Yarborough is engraved with the name "Yarborough" and a serial number. It is made from CPM S30V steel, an alloy with great strength and superior edge-holding ability. The handles are canvas Micarta, chosen for its toughness, chemical resistance, and wet-grip capabilities. Only current or former Special Forces members are permitted to purchase one. An almost identical knife, the "Green Beret," is available to all other branches of the military and to the civilian market. It differs in that the name "Yarborough" and serial number do not appear on the blade.

Special Forces Organization

There are five active duty Special Forces groups (SFG) and two National Guard groups. Each SFG has a specific regional focus, and its soldiers receive intensive foreign language and cultural training.

FIRST SPECIAL FORCES GROUP. This group has responsibility for the Pacific. The 1st Battalion is stationed in Okinawa, whereas the 2nd and 3rd Battalions are stationed at Fort Lewis, Washington.

THIRD SPECIAL FORCES GROUP. This group is responsible for Africa with the exception of the eastern Horn area and is headquartered at Fort Bragg, North Carolina.

FIFTH SPECIAL FORCES GROUP. This group is responsible for the Middle East, Persian Gulf, Central Asia, and the Horn of Africa. It is headquartered at Fort Campbell, Kentucky.

SEVENTH SPECIAL FORCES GROUP. Responsible for Latin and Central America, and the Caribbean, it is also headquartered at Fort Bragg, North Carolina.

TENTH SPECIAL FORCES GROUP. This group is responsible for mainly Central and Eastern Europe, the Balkans, Turkey, Israel, and Lebanon. The 1st Battalion is stationed near Stuttgart, Germany, and the 2nd and 3rd Battalions are headquartered at Fort Carson, Colorado.

NINETEENTH AND TWENTIETH SPECIAL FORCES GROUPS. These are the National Guard groups of the Special Forces.

Special Forces Teams

Special Forces teams are composed of twelve specifically trained members. The Special Forces Operational Detachment-A, or A-Team, is the core unit; six A-detachments form a Special Forces company. A captain leads the team with a warrant officer as second in command. Five pairs of NCOs trained in each of the functional skills areas of weapons, engineering and demolitions, medicine, communications, operations, and intelligence comprise the remainder of the team. All team members are cross-trained in different skills and are multilingual.

Some of the capabilities of A-teams include: planning and conducting operations separately or as part of a larger force; infiltrating and exfiltrating by air, land, or sea; conducting operations in remote areas and hostile environments for extended periods of time with a minimum of external direction and support; developing, organizing, equipping, training, advising, or directing indigenous forces in special operations; and training and assisting other U.S. and allied forces and agencies. In each Special Forces Company, one of the six A-teams is trained in combat diving and one is trained in military free-fall parachuting. Both methods are used for infiltration.

A-teams are equipped with high-powered communications systems such as tactical satellite communications, burst transmission devices, high-frequency radios, and global positioning systems. Medical kits include field surgical kits, laboratory and dental instruments, sterilizers, resuscitator-aspirators, water-testing kits, and veterinary equipment. Additional key equipment includes individual and perimeter defense weapons, night-vision devices, and electric and nonelectric demolitions. For underwater or waterborne infiltration, SCUBA (Self-Contained Underwater Breathing Apparatus) teams are equipped with open-circuit twin-80s SCUBA tanks, closed-circuit Dragger (re-breather) Lar-V, Zodiac boats, and Klepper kayaks. Military free-fall parachuting teams use ram-air parachutes and oxygen systems.

★ THE SPECIAL FORCES PRAYER ★

"Almighty God Who art the Author of Liberty and the Champion of the oppressed hear our prayer. We, the men of Special Forces, acknowledge our dependence upon Thee in the preservation of human freedom. Go with us as we seek to defend the defenseless and to free the enslaved. May we ever remember that our nation, whose oath 'In God We Trust' expects that we shall requite ourselves with honor, that we may never bring shame upon our faith, our families, or our fellow men. Grant us wisdom from Thy mind, courage from Thine heart, and protection by Thine hand. It is for Thee that we do battle, and to thee belongs the victor's crown. For Thine is the kingdom, and the power, and glory forever. Amen!"

★ 160TH SOAR (A)—"NIGHT STALKERS" ★

The 160th Special Operations Aviation Regiment (SOAR [A]) provides Special Forces teams with aviation support, using highly modified and advanced aircraft to transport them in and out of enemy territory. The 160th SOAR (A) (for "Aviation") is also known as the "Night Stalkers" in recognition of their primarily night-based activities. Their missions include attack, assault, and reconnaissance and are most frequently conducted in secret and at low altitudes. The Night Stalkers were established in 1981 following the disastrous attempt to rescue American hostages in Iran.

Their mission is defined as: "Organize, equip, train, resource, and employ Army Special Operations Aviation (SOA) forces worldwide in support of contingency missions and the warfighting commanders."

They are headquartered at Fort Campbell, Kentucky. The regiment includes the Special Operations Aviation Training Company, 1st and 2nd Battalions (also at Fort Campbell, Kentucky), and the 3rd Battalion at Hunter Army Airfield, Georgia. It has one forward-deployed company in the Pacific Command area.

★ MOTTOS ★

The Night Stalkers' mottos: "Night Stalkers Don't Quit" (NSDQ) and "Death Waits in the Dark."

Soldiers wishing to join the 160th SOAR (A) must have already completed Army Basic Training, Advanced Intermediate Training, and Airborne School. Night Stalker training is an intensive five-week program for enlisted, and up to twenty-eight weeks for officers. Mission qualification can take one to two years. Flight-lead qualification generally requires three to five years of training. The training, called "Green Platoon," teaches advanced first aid techniques, combatives, land navigation, and weapons training combined with intense physical conditioning sessions.

Night Stalkers fly a range of helicopters. These include the AH-6 Little Bird light assault, MH-6 light transport, the MH-60 Black Hawk assault, and the MH-47 Chinook heavy assault helicopters. Night Stalkers have participated in Ranger missions in Grenada, the Persian Gulf, Africa, Panama, Somalia, and elsewhere.

★ PSYCHOLOGICAL OPERATIONS—"PSYOP" ★

The Psychological Operations (PSYOP) group plans and conducts activities worldwide in support of operations during open hostilities short of declared war, as well as PSYOP activities during peacetime. Following the declaration of war, PSYOP assists in the planning and execution of strategic and operational joint force commander's PSYOP activities. There are both active and reserve components. The definition of Psychological Operations is the "dissemination of truthful information to foreign audiences in support of U.S. policy and national objectives." Their motto is: "Persuade, Change, Influence."

Tactics include logic, reasoning, fear, desire, or other emotional "hot buttons" to convince enemy, neutral, and friendly nations and forces to take action favorable to the United States. PSYOP strategic operations include long-range, often global objectives directed towards large audiences. Tactical operations are used for immediate or short-term objectives, such as lowering the morale of enemy forces.

Typical activities of PSYOP include audiovisual and printed material production and dissemination, such as flyers dropped via air. Specialized PSYOP equipment includes powerful television and radio broadcast transmitters, print systems, loudspeakers, and mobile audiovisual vans. PSYOP soldiers are also well trained in regional language and skills.

The effectiveness of PSYOPs missions has varied over time. Generally, the better the intelligence and basic and detailed information about the enemy, the more likely it is to succeed. In Operation Desert Storm, PSYOPs teams disseminated "surrender" leaflets and used loudspeakers to instruct Iraqis how to give themselves up. Nearly 90,000 soldiers did so without any bloodshed, and most were still carrying the PSYOPs leaflets.

The 4th Psychological Operations Group (Airborne), headquartered at Fort Bragg, North Carolina is the only active unit. Two other groups, the 2nd and the 7th Psychological Operations Groups, are in the Army Reserve and contain about three-quarters of the Army PSYOP units.

★ 1ST SPECIAL FORCES OPERATIONAL ★ DETACHMENT-DELTA (AIRBORNE)—"DELTA FORCE"

The U.S. Army 1st Special Forces Operational Detachment-Delta (1stSFOD-D) otherwise known as "Delta Force," is one of two federal units tasked as a versatile counterterrorism force. Their main function is hostage rescue. Also referred to by the Pentagon as the "Combat Applications Group," Delta Force is a highly secretive group recruited mainly from among Army Green Berets or Rangers. Chuck Norris movies aside, it's the most carefully guarded special operations force within the U.S. military.

Information about the Delta Force is tightly controlled and very limited. What is publicly known is as follows: There are three operational squadrons (A, B, and C), a support squadron, a signal squadron that deals with covert eavesdropping equipment as used in hostage rescue situations, an aviation platoon, and the "Funny Platoon." This funny platoon is reported to be the only joint special operations command unit including female operators. Each squadron is divided into smaller units called troops; each troop specializes in HALO, HAHO (High Altitude, Low Opening parachuting skills), SCUBA, or other operational skill. Selection is rigorous with emphasis on mental abilities and toughness. Delta Force numbers are very small—about 800 total. Approximately 225 of these are "shooters" and about 75 are designated snipers.

Headquarters are at Fort Bragg, North Carolina in a remote location of the base where a wide range of training facilities are provided. Training involves close-quarters battle "houses" designed to teach how to assault buildings that have been captured by terrorists. Selective firing (whether or not to shoot a target) as well as the double tap (shooting a target twice to make sure it does not get up) are instilled in the counter-terrorism specialists. The indoor training range, nicknamed "The House of Horrors," is equipped with mock-ups of trains and buses for practice assaults, and even an aircraft mock-up to simulate hijacking situations. It's considered the best special operation training facility in the world.

Delta Force operators *intend* to blend into the civilian population and are distinct from Rangers and other special operations forces. For example, haircuts are not "military"; and standard uniforms are not generally used, even at Fort Bragg. Soldiers are highly flexible and greatly autonomous. Delta Force members commonly carry the weapons of the foreign nation in which they are operating as part of their tools of invisibility. Much of their gear is customized. For example, Delta Force specially rigged a HAHO parachute to permit the jumper to keep his hands at his sides rather than above his head, allowing his arms to function better for prolonged descents.

Delta Force works closely with the 160th SOAR (A) for air support, but they also have their own fleet of helicopters. Using civilian colors and fake registration numbers, their mounted gun pods provide air support as well as transportation. Delta Force also works with the CIA's Special Activities staff.

Delta Forces are believed to have operated in Iraq just prior to the invasion of 2003, as well as in Afghanistan and elsewhere. They are sometimes referred to as "D-boys" or "Operators." Other missions include the invasion of Grenada;

the response to a Kuwaiti Airlines airliner hijacking; and the rescue of a hostage in Panama. In 1997, they were sent to Lima, Peru, with several members of the Special Air Service (SAS), the principal Special Forces organization of the British Army, following the takeover of the Japanese Ambassador's residence. Delta Force operatives were sent to Waco to plan the assault on the Branch Davidian compound, and were employed in Seattle during the World Trade Organization riot during the Clinton administration.

Two Delta Force operators killed in Mogadishu, Somalia, were awarded the Medal of Honor for their actions as depicted in the movie *Black Hawk Down*. They were Master Sergeant Gary Gordon and Sergeant First Class Randall Shughart. Two Navy warships have been since named in their honor.

★ U.S. NAVY SEALS AND U.S. NAVY SPECIAL ★ WARFARE DEVELOPMENT GROUP—"DEVGRU"

The Navy SEALs

The United States Navy Sea, Air, and Land (SEAL) forces are the elite special operations forces of the Navy. "SEALs" stands for "Sea, Air, and Land," which is why the last "s" is not capitalized with the other letters. They are active in unconventional warfare, foreign internal defense, direct action, counterterrorism, and special reconnaissance missions. Specializations include airborne operations, direct action operations, raids, counterterrorism, infiltrating and exfiltrating by sea, air, or land, intelligence gathering, recovering of personnel and special equipment, and underwater demolitions. Readiness is defined by deployment by sea, air, or land anywhere in the world within eighteen hours notice.

★ NICKNAMES ★

SEALs are nicknamed "Frogmen." The Leap Frogs are the Navy SEALs parachuting demonstration squad.

ORGANIZATION. A SEAL platoon includes sixteen men, two of which are officers. Teams may contain eight to ten boat teams. There are currently nine SEAL teams. Of these, eight are officially recognized: One, Two, Three, Four, Five, Seven, Eight, and Ten. See comments on "Team Six" on page 159. Previously, teams were specialized to deploy around the world; they are now deployed as Naval warfare squadrons anywhere. Former deployments have included: Team One and Three in Southeast Asia (Vietnam); Team Two in Europe, and the only team with arctic warfare capability; Team Four in Central and South America, and the only team with an additional language capability (Spanish); Team Five in the northern Pacific; and Team Eight in the Caribbean, Africa, and the Mediterranean. Teams Seven and Ten are new.

TRAINING. Navy SEALs specialize in basic underwater demolition (BUD), and sea, air, or land (SEAL) operations. Recruits endure what may be the toughest military training in the world. Basic underwater demolition/SEAL (BUD/S) training is conducted at the Naval Amphibious Base Coronado in San Diego, and lasts twenty-six weeks. On average, a BUD/S class drops more than 70 percent of its initial enrollment over the duration of the training. BUD/S and the SEALs are voluntary services, and most BUD/S students find they cannot endure the extreme physical and mental demands that SEALs training requires. These students "Drop on Request" (DOR) from the course. BUD/S includes a five-week indoctrination course ("Indoc"), followed by three phases that cover physical conditioning, diving, and land warfare. Officers and enlisted endure the same training.

BUD/S FIRST PHASE. This phase is eight weeks and involves physical conditioning using running, swimming, and calisthenics exercises that becoming increasingly more intensive. Students undergo 4-mile timed runs in boots, timed obstacle courses, and swim distances up to 2 ocean miles wearing fins; they also learn small boat seamanship. During "Hell Week," or the fifth week of training, students participate in five and one half days of continuous training, with a maximum of four hours of sleep. It is the ultimate test of physical and mental motivation, to prove to those succeeding that the human body can do ten times the amount of work the average man thinks possible. The remaining weeks are devoted to teaching various methods of hydrographic surveying and how to prepare a hydrographic chart.

THE SECOND PHASE. This phase is also eight weeks and concentrates on combat SCUBA (Self Contained Underwater Breathing Apparatus) equipment and use. Students are taught two types of SCUBA: open circuit (compressed air), and closed circuit (100 percent oxygen). Emphasis is placed on a progressive dive schedule that will qualify students as combat divers. This skill distinguishes SEALs from all other special operations forces.

THIRD PHASE. In this nine-week phase, students concentrate on land navigation, small-unit tactics, rappelling, land and underwater explosives, and weapons training. The final four weeks of third phase are spent on San Clemente Island, where techniques are applied in a practical environment.

Students successfully completing BUD/S must next attend the Navy's Strategic Air Operations (SAO) School in the desert outside San Diego, in which they become free-fall and HALO-qualified. HALO is parachuting using a High Altitude Low Opening parachute, and is a military term for skydiving. This course lasts three weeks. Successful trainees receive their Naval Special Warfare Classification (NEC) code.

Finally, SEALs students undergo the fifteen-week SEAL Qualification Training at the Naval Amphibious Base Coronado. Upon completion, they become junior SEALs. After an eighteen-month "trial" period with a SEAL unit, individuals are authorized to wear and display the Special Warfare Badge. Commonly called the Trident, or the "Budweiser" since it resembles the Budweiser Eagle, it serves as the SEALs' insignia, and is the largest and most recognizable warfare pin in the United States Navy.

"DEVGRU"—The Invisible Team Six

Team Six was originally created in 1980 as one of two SEAL teams at the time, in response to the American hostage rescue failure in Iran. Rumor has it that it was given the name "Six" to confuse Soviet Intelligence as to the number of teams in existence. It was officially renamed as the U.S. Navy Special Warfare Development Group (NAVSPECWARDEVGRU) or just "DEVGRU." It is the Navy's counterpart to the Army's Delta Force; occasionally both forces train together. DEVGRU's compound is located at Dam Neck, Virginia. Its focus is on maritime operations, with firing ranges, shooting houses, aircraft sections, and other hostage rescue scenarios onsite at their base. The skill of DEVGRU individuals in firearms is legendary.

DEVGRU's organization and numbers are covert knowledge, but it is estimated that there are two hundred DEVGRU operators. It is suggested that they are broken down into four combat assault teams along the lines of the Special Air Service (SAS), the principal special forces organization of the British Army:

mountain, mobility, boat, and HALO. Reports indicate that the four teams are coded Red, Blue, Gold, and Gray. The Gold team is reputed to be the premier team; the Gray team is the transportation unit. There is an additional Green team in training. There is believed to be three hundred-plus personnel involved in administration and equipment testing.

DEVGRU operatives have been active in the Persian Gulf, Bosnia, and Iraq, among other areas.

★ U.S. MARINE CORPS FORCE ★ RECONNAISSANCE—"RECONS"

U.S. Marine Corps Force Reconnaissance ("Force Recons," "Force Marines," or simply "Recons") are the USMC equivalent of the Navy SEALs or Army Special Forces, but their missions differ. Recons perform highly specialized, small-scale, high-risk operations, including amphibious and deep ground surveillance, and specialized technical missions. Essentially, Recons perform intelligence-gathering missions far behind enemy lines by conducting small-unit raids on enemy centers. They also assist in ordnance delivery, such as designating targets for laser-guided bomb units, ground artillery, and naval artillery. They conduct "limited-scale raids," including gas and oil platform (GOPLATs) raids and Military Interdiction operations (MIOs) and may be involved in hostage rescue. Their readiness is defined as "Any shore in the world within six hours' notice."

★ MOTTO ★

Their motto, like that of all Marines, is "Semper fidelis" ("Always Faithful").

TRAINING. Marines may enter Force Recon training after Boot Camp and Infantry Training School. The Basic Recon Course is then followed by advanced training in some of the following schools: airborne (basic and military freefall), jumpmaster, pathfinder, ranger, scout-sniper, combat diver (SCUBA), mountain warfare, jungle operations, demolitions, close-quarters battle, and others. Marines must have superior physical abilities and a near flawless record for Force Recon consideration.

ORGANIZATION. Special Operations forces of the Marines are part of a unit known as Marine Expeditionary Unit, Special Operations Capable [MEU (SOC)], made up of no more than 2,500 men. MEU (SOC)s are composed of: battalion landing teams (BLT), an infantry element which includes the non-Force Division Reconnaissance; Marine medium helicopter squadrons, an air element with a control detachment; and MEU service support groups (MSSG), a support element. Tying these elements together is the command element (CE).

Force Recon platoons are attached to and are a part of the command element (CE). Their position in the MEU (SOC) is not tied to the battalion landing team.

There are currently seven MEU (SOC)s in the Corps. MEU (SOC)s are deployed onboard amphibious ready groups, a group of several ships usually centered upon an amphibious assault helicopter carrier. Up to three groups can be deployed around the world at any given time. Because of this constant mobility, a MEU (SOC) can reach any shore in the world within six hours of an order.

A Recon company operates like a battalion. There is generally a commanding officer (the "CO," a lieutenant colonel), an executive officer (the "XO," a major), and a sergeant major, as well as administrative, intelligence, operations, logistics, and communications components. A company contains six operational platoons, each with a platoon commander (captain) and a platoon NCO (sergeant, staff sergeant, or higher). One of these platoons is a scout/sniper unit retained from the MEU battalion landing team. Navy medical corpsmen are also active in Recon units, and undergo the same training as Force Recon. Medical Corpsmen are highly respected and appreciated by Recons, as they are by all Marines.

GENERAL EQUIPMENT. Some unique weapons and equipment include:

- *Amphibious Assault Vest, Quick-Release* (FSBE AAV QR). This is a lightweight assault vest system that incorporates protection in the form of soft armor coupled with hard ballistic inserts, with cargo retention capabilities. The FSBE kit includes a vest body, throat protector, groin protector, and an assortment of heavy-duty pouches. A fully loaded vest with armor plates is very heavy, and thus only used in high-risk, direct-action missions. The quick release mechanism that makes this vest unique enables a Marine to remove it rapidly in case of emergency.

- *Modular Integrated Communications Helmet* (MICH). This is a lightweight helmet that incorporates excellent ballistic protection with tactical communications ability, i.e., headsets and microphones.

- *MEU (SOC) Pistol*, a M1911A1 .45 pistol. These are made from original service M1911 frames dating back to the 1940s. MEU (SOC) pistols use parts from different high-end manufacturers; they are each hand-built and never exactly the same. They are among the most reliable pistols in the world. Most U.S. special forces operators also prefer the M1911 as their sidearm.

- *Interim Fast Attack Vehicle* (IFAV). This is a militarized Mercedes-Benz G-Class 290 GDT diesel 4x4, like the traditional "Jeep" type truck. The IFAV is considered "an alternative to walking," though it has numerous defensive weapons, including an Mk 19 automatic 40mm grenade launcher.

GREENSIDE OPERATIONS. Greenside operations are deep reconnaissance patrols. Force Recon Marines operate in six-man teams, and must rely on stealth, evasion, and superior training to survive as they are usually too far ahead of the main force for artillery support or quick helicopter extractions. Generally, a greenside operator's kit includes:

- A "boonie" hat; this looks like a fisherman's hat in camouflage pattern.

- Battle dress uniforms, standard camouflage. Force Recon has also received new digitally camouflaged BDUs in both woodland and desert patterns.

- A load-bearing vest (LBV), a vest with pouches for ammunition and supplies.

- A rucksack, a huge backpack for carrying items that do not need to be often accessed. Recon Marines prefer the seventies-era All Purpose Lightweight Individual Carrying Equipment (ALICE) packs over the newer, but less suitable MOLLE (Modular Lightweight Load-carrying Equipment) packs (too small capacity, the external frame was too fragile and often broke in the field, zippers often burst when the pack was stuffed full, and straps were too short for an individual wearing body armor).

- Rations, toiletries, fuel, water, ammunition, etc.

- The primary weapon depends on the Marine's role in the squad. It can range from carbines (M4) to rifles (M16, M14) to squad automatics (M249 SAW).

- A sidearm may be carried, but usually not in a tactical thigh-mounted configuration.

- Boots.

- Armor, or bulletproof vests such as FSBE vests and ballistic helmets, is usually not worn on greenside operations because they are too bulky, trap heat, and generate noise upon movement. Force Recons shown in photos wearing armor and helmets when apparently on greenside operations are actually in training, where the equipment is a safety requirement.

BLACKSIDE OPERATIONS. Blackside, or direct action, operations include tactical recovery of aircraft personnel; gas/oil platform raids; vessel, board, search, and seizure maneuvers; and other missions involving close-quarter battle. Recently, in-extremis hostage rescue activities were also assigned to Force Recon units.

During blackside operations, a platoon includes special operators according to mission specifications (e.g., explosive ordnance disposal personnel, electronic warfare specialists). Force Recon Marines can be inserted into a combat zone on land, using the Interim Fast Attack Vehicle (IFAV); by sea; and by air via HAHO, HALO, helicopter fast rope, etc.

A common blackside operational kit includes:

- *MICH Helmet* and a hands-free communications headset (usually a TELEX Stinger 700) and tactical goggles.

- NOMEX *balaclava*, a hood with a large opening for the eyes. NOMEX is a fire-retardant fabric developed post-Korean War for use by aircraft pilots.

- NOMEX *flight suit* and NOMEX aviator's gloves. These are usually sage-green in color, but there is a khaki version for desert operations.

- *FSBE vest* with attached pouches for magazines, grenades, flashbangs, breaching charges, gas masks, medical supplies, and communications equipment. Ballistic insert plates are used in these operations.

- High-tensile nylon *pistol belt* or rigger's belt with suspenders, used to attach additional pouches or drop-leg devices. This may be worn like a traditional belt to keep up trousers, or as a second belt, specifically for equipment.

- A thigh-mounted *tactical holster* with the MEU (SOC) .45 sidearm, with an underframe flashlight installed. This sidearm is usually attached to the operator's belt via a retention lanyard.

- Another drop-belt thigh pocket on the leg opposite the operator's handedness, either with a "dump" pouch, for easily stowing spent magazines, or additional ammunition and munitions pouches.

- Tactical kneepads and elbow pads, for protection and operator comfort as he moves into various firing positions.

- Boots, or specialized hiking shoes.

- A relatively compact primary weapon.

★ AIR FORCE SPECIAL ★
OPERATIONS FORCES—"AFSOC"

Air Force Special Operations Command (AFSOC), established in 1990, operates Air Force Special Operations Forces and is headquartered at Hurlburt Field, Florida. Air Force Special Operations Forces have four basic tasks: "Forward presence and engagement, information operations, precision employment and strike, and special operations forces mobility." They provide specially trained airmen who are rapidly deployable and equipped with highly specialized aircraft to conduct missions including precision firepower, infiltration, exfiltration, resupply, and refueling. They are also equipped for airborne broadcast of radio and television for Psychological Operations use. Special tactics squadrons combine combat control, combat weather reporting and pararescuemen for unconventional warfare needs. They are also responsible for inland search and rescue in worldwide humanitarian efforts.

AFSOC utilizes nearly 20,000 active duty, reserve, Air National Guard, and civilian personnel. There are five active duty, five reserve components, and over 250 aircraft. Operationally, there are two wings (one special operations and one rescue), three special operations groups, and one test squadron.

MISSION. The mission of AFSOC is "America's specialized air power ... a step ahead in a changing world, providing combat search and rescue and delivering special operations power any time, any place." The three main teams in AFSOC are Combat Control, Pararescue, and Weather teams.

COMBAT CONTROL. Combat Control members are certified FAA air traffic controllers and are trained in special operations tactics. These soldiers deploy to hostile or combat territory to establish airfields and to provide air traffic control, counterterrorism, fire support, special reconnaissance, or humanitarian assistance. Their motto is "First There." Training is a thirty-five week course that includes air combat control, parachuting, survival skills, land navigation, demolitions, field operations, and small unit tactics. Students successfully completing this training wear a scarlet beret. Additional training in advanced skills, advanced parachuting, combat diving, and underwater escape may take another seventeen months or longer.

PARARESCUE. Pararescuemen or "PJ's" are specially trained for personnel recovery and combat search and rescue. They are trained in physical conditioning, parachuting, combat diving, underwater escape, basic survival skills, paramedic skills, and pararescue recovery training. Training takes a minimum of seventy-five weeks. Successful graduates have the right to wear a maroon beret. Their motto is "That Others May Live."

WEATHER TEAMS. The "Weather Warriors" are special operations meteorologists with advanced tactical training that enables them to operate in hostile or combat territory. They gather and interpret weather data, assist in mission planning, and generate route forecasts to support global special operations. They also train foreign national forces and conduct special reconnaissance as needed. They are committed to "deploy into restricted environments by air, land, or sea to observe and analyze all weather data from mud to sun." They frequently operate with SEALs, Rangers, or Special Forces in direct action, reconnaissance, and unconventional warfare and are trained to operate in all climates and weather. Special operations weathermen are recruited only from Airmen already in the weather career field, and all must complete the Army Airborne School of parachuting, as well as basic survival and water survival schools. Finally, they complete a six-month training program in advanced communications, navigation, weapons, and small unit tactics. They wear a gray beret upon completion.

CHAPTER 8

Other Important Aspects of the U.S. Military

This section includes a variety of topics useful to understanding the military that are not covered elsewhere, such as military law, decorations and ribbons, military music, the Tomb of the Unknown Soldier, Missing Man Formation, Department of Veterans Affairs, American Legion, the Veterans of Foreign Wars, and the United Service Organization (USO).

★ MILITARY LAW ★

THE DEPARTMENTS. Judge Advocate General's Corps, also known as JAG, is the judicial arm of the United States Armed Forces, consisting of independent departments in the Air Force, Army, and Navy. Its function is the defense and prosecution of military law as provided in the Uniform Code of Military Justice. Officers of the corps are the chief members of the court-martial and court of inquiry. JAG also provides servicemen and women with a variety of free legal services and supports military combat operations by advising commanders on the law of armed conflict.

MILITARY LAW. The Uniform Code of Military Justice, also known as UCMJ, is the primary legal code through which all internal military justice affairs of the United States are governed. *Note:* The word *uniform* refers to a consistent application of military law. It was authorized by Congress in 1951 to establish identical systems of courts martial in all branches of the military. Naturally, personnel are also subject to the terms of the Constitution and individual state laws where applicable—the UCMJ never replaces state, federal, or other laws.

COURTS-MARTIAL. This is the forum through which judicial cases are tried for the nation's armed forces. The name refers to the panel of military officers selected to serve in a similar capacity as that of a civilian jury. The Uniform Code of Military Justice outlines three distinct types of courts-martial: summary, special, and general.

- *Summary Court-Martial:* This court-martial has jurisdiction over crimes committed by enlisted personnel only, and is the forum for minor offenses such as petty theft. The court-martial is comprised of a single officer, and the maximum sentence is one-month confinement, forfeiture of two-third's pay, and a reduction in rank. This type of court-martial can be refused, in which case the matter is normally referred to a special court-martial.

- *Special Court-Martial.* This intermediate type of court-martial has jurisdiction over crimes committed by any person, including civilians, who are covered by military law at the time the crime was committed. It is a forum for intermediate offenses such as harassment. Members present at the court-martial include the defense counsel, the prosecutor, and the military judge. The court-martial is comprised of three or more panel members, or a judge alone may try it. The maximum sentence is twelve month's confinement, forfeiture of two-third's pay for twelve months, a reduction in rank, and/or a bad conduct discharge (BCD).

- *General Court-Martial.* This court-martial is the forum for the most serious charges, such as homicide or desertion, and it has jurisdiction over crimes committed by commissioned officers, warrant officers, and enlisted personnel. Members present at this court-martial are the defense counsel, the prosecutor, and the military judge. The court-martial is comprised of five or more members, and one-third of these may be enlisted if requested. The maximum sentence that this court may pass is death by execution. This is much like a state superior court or trial division of a supreme court in that it gets any big felony cases.

APPEALS PROCESS. The Uniform Code of Military Justice provides several tiers of appeal. An initial appeal may be reviewed by the convening judge of a court-martial. A second tier of appeal is the Court of Criminal Appeals, a five-member civilian panel appointed by the president of the United States. Sentences involving dismissal, discharge, or confinement of over a year are automatically sent to the Court of Criminal Appeals. Death sentences issued by a court-martial are automatically sent to the president of the United States for appeal.

Here are some common examples of military law vocabulary and their definitions.

Accused: The defendant.

Article 15: Nonjudicial punishment imposed by a commanding officer. Also may be referred to as "NJP," "Mast," and "Office hours," depending upon the service. A person subjected to Article 15 punishment can refuse it in certain cases, which may lead to a court-martial. A court-martial cannot be refused. Refers to Article 15 of the Uniform Code of Military Justice (UCMJ).

Article 32: A formal investigation required before a case may be referred to a general court-martial. It's like a grand jury, but the accused attends and participates. This can be waived.

Bad Conduct Discharge (BCD): The "Big Chicken Dinner." Next-to-worst type of punitive discharge.

Blind: Monetary fine imposed by court-martial.

Convening Authority: Commanding officer of an organization who convenes or authorizes a court-martial. Much like a district attorney but not a lawyer.

Dishonorable Discharge (DD): The worst type of punitive discharge.

Members: Members of the court, i.e., the jury.

Military Judge: A senior military attorney appointed by the Judge Advocate General to serve as judge in a court-martial. Works directly for the Judge Advocate General and is thus independent of the military chain of command.

Staff Judge Advocate (SJA:) Legal advisor to the convening authority, usually working directly for the convening authority. The SJA is similar to a district attorney in function, but final decisions are made by the convening authority. This is usually a senior military lawyer with extensive experience. He may supervise a large staff of attorneys, including trial counsels, but not defense counsel.

The Judge Advocate General (TJAG): Top military lawyer of the service concerned, either a general or admiral.

Trial Counsel: Prosecutor.

★ JAG ★

JAG is also the title of a drama television show which first aired on NBC and was canceled in 1996. It was then picked up by CBS, who aired it for nine more seasons.

★ DECORATIONS AND RIBBONS ★

There are a number of impressive medals and awards given to the military for bravery, service, or skill. The most important medals include the Medal of Honor, the Distinguished Service Cross, the Distinguished Service Medal, and the Silver Star.

DECORATIONS. Not all medals are decorations. *Medal* is a generic term used to describe the three categories of awards: decorations; Good Conduct Medals; and service medals. *Medal* also refers to the distinctive physical device of the metal and ribbon combination that constitutes the tangible evidence of an award. *Decorations* are awarded for valor or meritorious service. They are traditionally in the shape of a star, cross, hexagon, or some heraldic design. A few are round, but round medals are almost always used for service medals. Requirements for these awards includes good conduct or participation in a particular campaign. Decorations may be worn full size, as miniature medals on formal dress, as ribbon bars, or occasionally as an enamel lapel pin worn on civilian suits or on hats by veterans.

RIBBONS. Ribbons are the fabric that suspends a military medal from its fastening device; they may also be awarded without a medal. They are worn individually, or in a bar formed of several. Ribbons are worn in lieu of full-sized medals on the military uniform. Each campaign or war has a unique ribbon to denote duty. Each branch has ribbon-only awards that apply to specific purposes (e.g., Recruiting Duty). Ribbons are worn in order of precedence, i.e. Medal of Honor, Distinguished Service Cross, Silver Star, etc.

DEVICES. Individuals may wear small metal "devices" on the ribbon bar to indicate additional awards, campaigns, or special service. They may be in the form of stars, oak leaf clusters, arrowheads, or numerals. Each branch has their own devices and manner of attachments.

THE AWARDING OF DECORATIONS. Different criteria have been used over the years for certain awards. Awards should be rare and uncommon, and are given to reflect outstanding heroics or uncommonly meritorious service. A serviceperson must be recommended by another person, and his or her application is reviewed through the particular branch of military service, all the way to the top. (Only one medal in the United States military inventory allows a serviceperson to recommend him/herself. That medal is the Outstanding Volunteer Service Medal.) Awards are presented either by the president, or by the top member of the branch of the service the award pertains to.

Lost medals (or any other military item) are the permanent property of the United States government. If you find one, you are obligated to return it to: The Secretary of Defense, Room 3E880, The Pentagon, Washington DC 20301. Requesting a reward for its return is "inappropriate as it should be an honor to return a military medal to its recipient."

The Most Important Decorations

The descriptions of the most important decorations follow, in order of precedence.

MEDAL OF HONOR. Congress established a Medal of Honor for the Navy in 1861, and shortly thereafter, a Medal of Honor for the Army. The purpose was to recognize those who distinguished themselves through gallantry in action or other seaman- or soldier-like qualities. Several thousand were awarded for such actions during the Civil War. At first, criteria for awarding the medal were not specified, and a number of persons received the award for no real acts of heroism; for example, the twenty-nine honor guards who escorted President Lincoln's body back to Illinois in 1865. Criteria were designated in 1876, and further restrictions and procedures were established in 1897, limiting recipients to those who had demonstrated "gallantry and intrepidity" above and beyond that of fellow soldiers. Requests for Medals of Honor had to be made by someone other than the intended recipient, and one or more eyewitnesses were required to testify under oath as to the heroic deed within one year of the act. In 1916, a panel of generals met to review the 2,656 Army Medals of Honor awarded up to that time. They revoked 911 medals, mainly those awarded from Civil War actions. A few of these were later restored, including Mary Walker, the only female Medal of Honor recipient, and Buffalo Bill Cody during the Indian wars.

Only the president of the United States can award this medal. Incidentally, unlike all the other medals, it is worn about the neck on a ribbon.

In 1963, an act of Congress stipulated that the Medal of Honor could only be awarded for service during combat action. The basic criteria was standardized: The act of bravery must have been one of personal bravery or self-sacrifice so conspicuous as to clearly distinguish the individual above his comrades, represent gallantry well beyond the call of duty distinct from lesser forms of bravery, and must include incontestable evidence from at least two eyewitnesses. In the Army and Air Force, recommendations for the medal must be made within two years of the event and the medal awarded within three years. In the Navy, recommendations must be made within three years and the medal awarded within five years. Strict review of the award occurs at all levels of command within each branch of the military, including the secretary of the branch, the chairman of the Joint Chiefs of Staff, the secretary of defense, and the president, who ultimately approves and presents the medal personally.

Fewer than five medals have been awarded for action since the Vietnam War ended. Two were awarded posthumously to two soldiers who died in Somalia, whose story was illustrated in the book and movie *Black Hawk Down*. A third was awarded posthumously to Sergeant First Class Paul R. Smith, U.S. Army for "conspicuous gallantry and intrepidity at the risk of his life above and beyond the call of duty" in Iraq. More than 60 percent of the 850 medals awarded since the end of World War I have been awarded posthumously, underscoring the degree of bravery and personal risk involved.

While it is frequently called the Congressional Medal of Honor, it is officially just the "Medal of Honor." Current statistics of Medal of Honor recipients by service:

Army: 2,400

Navy: 745

Marine Corps: 296

Air Force: 17

Coast Guard: 1

Unknown: 9

Total number of awards: 3,459

Total number of recipients: 3,440

Double awards to one person:

Army: 4

Navy: 8

Marines: 7

DISTINGUISHED SERVICE CROSS (ARMY), THE NAVY CROSS, AND THE AIR FORCE CROSS. These are presented to individuals who display extraordinary heroism while engaged in a conflict with an enemy of the United States; engaged in military operations involving conflict with an opposing military force; or serving with friendly foreign forces engaged in armed conflict with an armed force in which the U.S. is not the belligerent party. The act of heroism must clearly set the individual apart from comrades under similar circumstances. These are presented in the name of the president, although the particular branch of service actually approves and presents them.

DISTINGUISHED SERVICE MEDAL. The Distinguished Service Medal is awarded to any person who, while serving in any capacity with the U.S. military, has distinguished himself or herself by exceptionally meritorious service to the government in a duty of great responsibility. The performance must merit recognition for service that is clearly exceptional. Exceptional performance of normal duty will not alone justify an award of this decoration. For service not related to actual war, the term "duty of great responsibility" applies to a narrower range and requires evidence of conspicuously significant achievement. However, justification of the award may accrue in exceptionally meritorious service in a succession of high positions of great importance. Awards may be made to persons other than members of the Armed Forces for wartime services only, and then only under exceptional circumstances with the approval of the president in each case.

SILVER STAR. It is the third highest award designated for heroism in combat, established as a citation star in 1918. In 1932, it was established as an individual medal. Silver Stars are presented to individuals who are cited for gallantry in action while engaged in a conflict with an enemy of the United States, engaged in military operations involving conflict with an opposing military force, or serving with friendly foreign forces engaged in armed conflict with an armed force in which the U.S. is not the belligerent party. It ranks below that required for a Distinguished Service Cross. The first Silver Star was presented to General Douglas MacArthur in 1932.

THE LEGION OF MERIT. This medal was established by Congress in 1942. It is awarded to any member of the Armed Forces of the U.S. or of a friendly foreign nation who has distinguished himself or herself by exceptionally meritorious conduct in the performance of outstanding services and achievements. The performance must merit recognition for service rendered in a clearly exceptional manner; performance of duties normal to the grade, branch, specialty, or assignment is not an adequate basis for this award. In peacetime, service should be in the nature of a special requirement of an extremely difficult duty performed in an unprecedented and clearly exceptional manner. Justification of the award may accrue by virtue of exceptionally meritorious service in a succession of important positions.

THE DISTINGUISHED FLYING CROSS. Signed into law by President Calvin Coolidge in 1927, this award is presented to individuals serving in any capacity of the military forces who distinguish themselves by heroism or outstanding achievement while participating in an aerial flight. Heroic acts must include voluntary action in the face of danger, well above the actions of others at the same time.

THE BRONZE STAR. Established by executive order by President Roosevelt in 1944, it is awarded to individuals who distinguish themselves by heroism, outstanding achievement, or meritorious service not involving aerial flight, while serving in a combat theater in any capacity of the armed forces.

THE PURPLE HEART. Originally the "Badge of Military Merit" established by George Washington in 1782, it was revived as the Purple Heart by the War Department in 1932. It is awarded to any person serving in any capacity of the armed forces who is wounded or killed in action as a result of an act of an opposing force, in an international terrorist act, or while serving as part of a peacekeeping force. It does not necessarily involve heroism or gallantry in action.

The Purple Heart differs from all other decorations in that an individual is not "recommended" for the decoration; rather he or she is entitled to receive it upon being killed or wounded in a manner meeting specific criteria that include while held as a prisoner of war or while being taken captive.

Several other specifics must be met. A "wound" is defined as an injury to any part of the body from an outside force or agent. A physical lesion is not required; however, the wound for which the award is made must have required treatment by a medical officer, and records of medical treatment must have been made a matter of official record. Individuals wounded or killed as a result of "friendly fire" in the "heat of battle" will be awarded the Purple Heart if the "friendly" projectile or agent was released with the intent of inflicting damage or destroying enemy troops or equipment.

- *Examples of injuries meriting award:* Injury caused by enemy bullet, shrapnel, or other projectile created by enemy action; injury caused by enemy placed mine or trap; injury caused by enemy released chemical, biological, or nuclear agent; injury caused by vehicle or aircraft accident resulting from enemy fire; concussion injuries caused as a result of enemy generated explosions.

- *Examples of combat related injuries which do not qualify for the Purple Heart:* Developing a service-connected disability, such as post-traumatic stress disorder, months or years after having been engaged in enemy combat; suffering environmental injuries in a combat zone, such as frostbite or sunburn; injured while performing a mission related to combat, but not in direct contact with enemy forces, such as falling and breaking a bone while on a patrol or being involved in a vehicle accident while traveling through a combat zone; a physical disability which occurred relating to combat with the enemy, such as hearing loss resulting from enemy artillery shelling; an injury which occurred in combat, but was as the result of taking cover or retreating, such as diving into a fox hole for shelter; a malicious injury caused by another allied solider, such as being shot deliberately as the result of an argument; injury by the enemy through sheer negligence of duty, such as intentionally walking into a marked enemy minefield, or deliberately exposing oneself to enemy fire with a desire to be wounded or killed; any self-inflicted wound, even if it was during combat with an enemy.

THE MERITORIOUS SERVICE MEDAL. This award was established in 1969. It is awarded to any member of the Armed Forces of the United States or to any member of the Armed Forces of a friendly foreign nation who, while serving in a noncombat area after January 16, 1969, has distinguished himself or herself by outstanding meritorious achievement or service.

THE AIR MEDAL. President Franklin D. Roosevelt established this award in 1942 for individuals who distinguish themselves by heroism, outstanding achievement, or meritorious service while engaged in aerial flight, but not of a degree that would justify the Distinguished Flying Cross. In 1964, the bronze "V" device was authorized for use on Air Medals awarded for acts of heroism involving conflict with an armed enemy.

Each branch of the service has a medal that may be awarded to members for heroism not involving actual conflict with the enemy. They rank above the Bronze Star. They include the Soldier's Medal (Army, established in 1926), the Navy and Marine Corps Medal (1942), and the Airman's Medal (established in 1960).

Replacing Decorations

Decorations that have been lost can usually be replaced at no cost. See appendix A for addresses for each specific service.

★ MILITARY MUSIC ★

The military institution has historically used songs of patriotism, heroism, and conquests as a motivational and brotherhood-inspiring technique. Each branch of the military has its own associated song, and each member can (and often does) sing it at any time the occasion demands or the situation inspires.

U.S. Army Song

"The Army Goes Rolling Along" was written in 1908 by then-field artillery First Lieutenant Edmund L. Gruber while stationed in the Philippines, and was called the "Caisson Song." The original lyrics reflect routine activities in a horse-drawn field artillery battery. "Caissons" are battle wagons used to transport artillery and supplies in a conflict and to carry the dead from the field afterwards. The song was transformed into an energetic march by John Philip Sousa in 1917 and renamed "The Field Artillery Song." In 1952, the Army adopted it as the official Army song and changed the title. The lyrics give homage to Army's past, present, and future operations. "The Army Goes Rolling Along" is played at the conclusion of every Army ceremony, and all soldiers are expected to stand and sing. The tune, if not most of the lyrics, are known far and wide. Several of the verses are included here.

The Army Goes Rolling Along

INTRO:

March along, sing our song, with the Army of the free
Count the brave, count the true, who have fought to victory
We're the Army and proud of our name
We're the Army and proudly proclaim

VERSE:

First to fight for the right
And to build the Nation's might
And The Army Goes Rolling Along
Proud of all we have done,
Fighting till the battle's won,
And the Army Goes Rolling Along.

REFRAIN:

Then it's Hi! Hi! Hey!
The Army's on its way
Count of the cadence loud and strong (TWO! THREE!)
For where e'er we go,
You will always know
That the Army Goes Rolling Along.

The Navy Hymn

The Navy's song is "Eternal Father, Strong to Save." The lyrics were originally a poem written in 1860 by William Whiting, an Englishman, for a student who was sailing to America. The melody was composed by another Englishman, Rev. John Bacchus Dykes, in 1861. Because it is always sung at the U.S. Naval Academy in Annapolis, Maryland, it's usually referred to as the "Navy Hymn." It is also sung on ships of the Royal Navy (U.K.). It was played at the funerals of President Franklin D. Roosevelt and President John F. Kennedy, in recognition of their service to the Navy. Roosevelt was secretary of the Navy, and Kennedy was a PT boat commander in World War II.

The Navy Hymn

Eternal Father, strong to save,
Whose arm hath bound the restless wave,

Who bidd'st the mighty ocean deep
Its own appointed limits keep;
Oh, hear us when we cry to Thee,
For those in peril on the sea!

O Christ! Whose voice the waters heard
And hushed their raging at Thy word,
Who walked'st on the foaming deep,
And calm amidst its rage didst sleep;
Oh, hear us when we cry to Thee,
For those in peril on the sea!

Most Holy Spirit! Who didst brood
Upon the chaos dark and rude,
And bid its angry tumult cease,
And give, for wild confusion, peace;
Oh, hear us when we cry to Thee,
For those in peril on the sea!
O Trinity of love and power!

Our brethren shield in danger's hour;
From rock and tempest, fire and foe,
Protect them wheresoe'er they go;
Thus evermore shall rise to Thee
Glad hymns of praise from land and sea.

Submarine Verse of the Navy Hymn

The lyrics to the Submarine Verse of the Navy Hymn were written by the Reverend Gale Williamson. They are as follows:

Bless those who serve beneath the deep,
Through lonely hours their vigil keep.
May peace their mission ever be,
Protect each one we ask of thee.
Bless those at home who wait and pray,
For their return by night or day.

The Marines' Hymn

"The Marines' Hymn" is symbolic of the very best our nation has to offer in defense of the land we love. To Marines, it's a reverent reminder of the sacrifice and courage shown on the battlefield. Marines stand at attention when they hear "The Marines' Hymn," and many become emotional when they hear it played. Marines of all ages stop and reflect on the warrior Marines that have gone before them when they hear this music.

According the U.S. Marine Band, the precise history of "The Marines' Hymn" is unclear. The music may have originated in an "opera bouffe" titled *Geneviéve de Brabant* by the French composer Jacques Offenbach. This opera was first produced in Paris in 1859 and was expanded from its original two acts to three in Paris in 1867. This version included a duet titled "Couplets des hommes d'armes," from which the music for "The Marines' Hymn" is thought to have been taken.

The history of the lyrics is even less definitive. Tradition says an unknown Marine on duty in Mexico wrote the first verse in 1847, predating the music by some twenty years. Possibly the music was taken from a Spanish folk song that predated the opera, and probably the first verse was written sometime after 1867.

The opening lines of the first verse of the hymn refer to the Marines' capture of Derne Tripoli following the war with the Barbary Powers in 1805, and to the Marines' participation in the 1847 capture and occupation of Mexico City and the Castle of Chapultepec, otherwise known as the "Halls of Montezuma." They are sung in reverse order of the actual events for lyrical reasons—it "sings" better.

The earliest known appearance of the first verse in print was in a June 23, 1918, article in the *Kansas City Journal*. The earliest known printing of the words and music together was in an uncopyrighted sheet music edition marked "Printed but not published by USMC Publicity Bureau" and is dated August 1, 1918.

While many campaigns in which Marines have taken part have inspired new, "unofficial" verses, in 1929 the commandant of the Marine Corps authorized the following as the official version:

The Marines' Hymn
From the Halls of Montezuma
To the shores of Tripoli;

We fight our country's battles
On the land as on the sea[1];
First to fight for right and freedom
And to keep our honor clean;
We are proud to claim the title
Of United States Marine.

Our flag's unfurl'd to ev'ry breeze
From dawn to setting sun;
We have fought in ev'ry clime and place
Where we could take a gun;
In the snow of far off northern lands
And in sunny tropic scenes;
You will find us always on the job—
The United States Marines.

Here's health to you and to our Corps
Which we are proud to serve;
In many a strife we've fought for life
And never lost our nerve;
If the Army and the Navy
Ever look on Heaven's scenes;
They will find the streets are guarded
By United States Marines.

---

[1] On November 21, 1942, the Commandant of the Marine Corps approved a change in the words of the fourth line, first verse, as follows:

"In the air, on land, and sea"

This change was proposed by former Gunnery Sergeant H.L. Tallman, who had participated in many combat missions with the Marine Corps Aviation Force over the Western Front in World War I. The proposed change was made at a meeting of the First Marine Aviation Force Veterans Association in Cincinnati, Ohio.

★ SINGULAR MARINE ★

Although the eighth line of "The Marines' Hymn" is frequently sung (by non-Marines, generally), as "of United States Marines," the U.S. Marine Band cites the final word in the singular. The "title" refers to the individual, not to the branch. In the other lines, the word "Marines" refers to the branch and thus is correctly plural. Today, "The Marines' Hymn" is widely recognized and many people lacking a military background can recite its words—with or without a plural in the eighth line.

Air Force Song

In 1938, *Liberty* magazine sponsored a contest for a spirited, enduring musical composition to become the official Army Air Corps song. Of 757 scores submitted, Robert Crawford's was selected by a committee of Air Force wives. The song (informally known as "The Air Force Song" but now formally titled "The U.S. Air Force") was officially introduced at the Cleveland Air Races on September 2, 1939. Robert Crawford sang in its first public performance.

"The Air Force Song" has traveled far and wide. On July 30, 1971, the first page of the score that Crawford had submitted to the selection committee in July, 1939, was carried to the surface of the moon aboard the Apollo 15 *Falcon* lunar module by Colonel David R. Scott and Lieutenant Colonel James B. Irwin. In addition, as the *Falcon* blasted off the moon, a rendition of "The Air Force Song" was broadcast to the world by Major Alfred M. Worden, who had a tape recorder aboard the *Endeavor* command module. Scott, Irwin, and Worden comprised the first and only "All-Air Force" Apollo crew.

The Air Force Song (The U.S. Air Force)

Off we go into the wild blue yonder,
Climbing high into the sun;
Here they come zooming to meet our thunder,
At 'em boys, Give 'er the gun! (Give 'er the gun now!)
Down we dive, spouting our flame from under,
Off with one helluva roar!
We live in fame or go down in flame. Hey!
Nothing'll stop the U.S. Air Force!

Minds of men fashioned a crate of thunder,
Sent it high into the blue;
Hands of men blasted the world asunder;
How they lived God only knew! (God only knew then!)
Souls of men dreaming of skies to conquer
Gave us wings, ever to soar!
With scouts before and bombers galore. Hey!
Nothing'll stop the U.S. Air Force!

BRIDGE:
"A Toast to the Host"
Here's a toast to the host
Of those who love the vastness of the sky,
To a friend we send a message of his brother men who fly.
We drink to those who gave their all of old,
Then down we roar to score the rainbow's pot of gold.
A toast to the host of men we boast, the U.S. Air Force!
Zoom!

Off we go into the wild sky yonder,
Keep the wings level and true;
If you'd live to be a grey-haired wonder
Keep the nose out of the blue! (Out of the blue, boy!)
Flying men, guarding the nation's border,
We'll be there, followed by more!
In echelon we carry on. Hey!
Nothing'll stop the U.S. Air Force!

Of note, Robert Crawford didn't actually write the words "Hey!" but instead wrote "SHOUT!" without specifying the word to be shouted. Wherever they appear, the words "U.S. Air Force" have been changed from the original "Army Air Corps."

Coast Guard Song

The original words and music to "Semper Paratus" were written in 1927 by Captain Francis S. Van Boskerck, USCG. In 1969, the first line of each chorus was modified. The current verse, together with a second chorus, were written by Homer Smith, 3rd Naval District Coast Guard Quartet, and Lieutenant Walton Butterfield, USCGR in 1943. Additional verses are not included here.

Semper Paratus (Always Ready)

From Aztec shore to Arctic zone,
To Europe and Far East.
The Flag is carried by our ships,
In times of war and peace.
And never have we struck it yet,
In spite of foe-men's might,
Who cheered our crews and cheered again,
For showing how to fight.

We're always ready for the call,
We place our trust in Thee.
Through surf and storm and howling gale,
High shall our purpose be.
"Semper Paratus" is our guide,
Our fame, our glory too.
To fight to save or fight to die,
Aye! Coast Guard, we are for you.

Taps

No discussion of military music is complete without mentioning "Taps." It is played at all military burial and memorial services, when the national flag is lowered, and to signal "lights out" at the end of each day. The tune for "Taps" is sad, implying a long and restful sleep, usually in death. It is a simple and melancholy twenty-four note bugle call.

The music and lyrics of "Taps" goes back to the Civil War. A bugler or drummer traditionally signaled the end of the day by playing a tune called "Lights Out." In June of 1862, Union General Daniel Adams Butterfield suffered heavy casualties during the Seven Days battles in Virginia, losing some six hundred men and becoming wounded himself. Butterfield wanted to honor his men with music more compelling and appropriate than "Lights Out" and wrote a tune for his bugler, Private Oliver Wilcox Norton, to play. It became Butterfield's preferred "end of day" music, and was quickly adopted by other camps. The Army made it their official bugle call after the Civil War, and it was named "Taps" in 1874.

"Taps" was played at a military funeral soon after Butterfield composed it. Union Captain John Tidball, head of an artillery battery, ordered it to be played for the burial of a cannoneer killed in action. To avoid revealing his position to the enemy, Tidball substituted "Taps" for the traditional three rifle shots over the grave. "Taps" was quickly adopted by the Confederate Army as well, and was later played at the funeral of Confederate General Stonewall Jackson. In 1891, the Army officially called for "Taps" to be played at military funeral ceremonies.

The first lyrics of "Taps" were "Go To Sleep, Go to Sleep." Over the years, other versions have been created. There are no official words to the music. The first and most well-known verse is presented here:

Taps

Day is done, gone the sun,
From the hills, from the lake,
From the skies.
All is well, safely rest.
God is nigh.

★ TOMB OF THE UNKNOWN SOLDIER ★

The Tomb of the Unknown Soldier, also called the Tomb of the Unknowns, is a monument in Arlington National Cemetery dedicated to soldiers who have died without their remains being identified. It was constructed after World War I and consists of a white marble sarcophagus over the grave of an unidentified soldier who died in the Great War (World War I).

The sarcophagus is highly symbolic. The east side faces Washington, D.C. with three Greek figures that represent peace, victory, and valor carved into it. Six wreaths are carved into the north and south faces to represent six major battles of World War I: Chateau-Thierry, The Ardennes, Oisiu-Eisue, Neuse-Argonne, Belleau Wood, and The Somme. Inscribed on the western face are the words: Here Rests In Honored Glory An American Soldier Known But To God.

Additional crypts in the immediate vicinity include unknowns from World War II and Korea. Another crypt held an unknown soldier from Vietnam whose remains were identified and removed in 1998.

The Unknown of World War I

On Memorial Day, 1921, four unknowns were exhumed from four World War I American cemeteries in France. An American Army sergeant, who was decorated for valor and received the Distinguished Service Medal, selected one of the four for placement into the tomb. The remaining three were interred in the Meuse Argonne Cemetery in France. The selected casket was brought to the United States aboard the USS *Olympia*. President Warren G. Harding officiated at the internment ceremonies. The World War I Unknown Soldier was awarded the Victoria Cross by Admiral of the Fleet Lord Beatty on behalf of King George V of Great Britain.

The Unknowns of World War II and the Korean War

The WWII Unknown was selected from remains exhumed from four cemeteries in Europe, Africa, Hawaii, and the Philippines. Of these, two unknowns were selected representing the European or Pacific Theater and were taken aboard the USS *Canberra*. The Navy's then only active duty recipient of the Medal of Honor elected the unknown of World War II, and the other casket was buried at sea. Four unknowns from the Korean War were disinterred from the National Cemetery of the Pacific in Hawaii and one was selected. When both unknowns from Korea and World War II were brought to the Arlington National Cemetery, President Eisenhower awarded each the Medal of Honor.

The Unknown of Vietnam

The Unknown of Vietnam was selected and interred in 1984 with President Reagan presenting the Medal of Honor at the funeral. DNA technology changed the situation, however, and in 1998, the remains were exhumed and identified as Air Force First Lieutenant Michael Joseph Blassie. His remains were returned to his family and the crypt which once held his remains has been replaced. The original inscription of "Victory" and the dates of conflict have been removed, and the memorial now reads "Honoring and Keeping Faith with America's Missing Servicemen."

The Tomb Guards

It is a supreme honor to serve as a sentinel for the Tombs of the Unknowns, and is carried out with grave solemnity and utmost respect for the dead. This honor is given to the 3rd U.S. Infantry Regiment of the Army, also called the Old Guard. The Tomb has been guarded continuously, twenty-four hours a day, seven days a week, since 1930, and the sentinels follow a prescribed ritual full of symbolism. The sentinels do not wear rank insignia on their uniforms so that they do not outrank the Unknown soldiers, whatever their rank might have been. The guard walks a slow, perfectly paced, twenty-one steps across the Tomb, in reference to the twenty-one-gun salute, the highest honor given any military dignitary. On the twenty-first step, he turns and faces the Tomb for twenty-one seconds, for the same reason. He turns to face across the Tomb and changes his weapon to the outside shoulder. After twenty-one seconds, the first step is repeated. During summer months, the guard is changed every half hour, and during the winter months, every hour. It is a simple ceremony, but extremely moving.

The Tomb Guards undergo a range of personal sacrifices for this honor. They work on team rotations of twenty-four hours on, twenty-four off, then twenty-four on, and ninety-six hours off. Sentinels generally take up to eight hours to prepare their uniform for the next day's work. Uniforms are made of pure wool, regardless of season. There is no lint permitted on the uniforms, or wrinkles or folds. Uniforms are inspected in front of a full-length mirror for perfection. Shoes are specially made with very thick soles for heat and cold protection, with long metal heel plates that sound a loud click as the guard comes to a halt. Guards also undergo physical training, Tomb Guard training, cut their hair before the next work day, and shave twice daily. The physical requirements include height and size: the guards must be between 5'10" and 6'2" with a waist size 30" or less. Additionally, they must commit to one year of service as a guard. There have been three female sentinels and one female platoon leader at the Tombs of the Unknowns.

During the first six months of duty, a guard cannot speak to anyone and is not permitted to watch television. During this period, all off-duty time is spent studying nearly two hundred notable persons interred in Arlington National Cemetery. After nine months of duty and passing a detailed test, guards may be issued the Tomb of the Unknown Soldier Guard Identification Badge. There have been less than 550 issued since 1959, making it the second-least awarded badge in the Army (after the Astronaut Badge). After two years, the guard is given a wreath pin for his lapel signifying his service as guard of the Tomb. Guards cannot disgrace the uniform or the Tomb in any way or they must relinquish their wreath pin. There have been nine cases where the pin was returned.

During 2003, Hurricane Isabelle struck the Washington, D.C. area. Although the Tomb Guards were permitted to suspend their assignment, they respectfully refused and completed their mission through the hurricane.

★ MISSING MAN FORMATION ★

The Missing Man Formation is used as a ceremonial fly-by for the interment of deceased veterans of the Armed Forces, who, in their military career, performed duties as aircrew members onboard military aircraft. At their funeral (or at demonstrations and airshows), they are honored with a fly-by performed by fellow military aviators in a formation of four aircraft. As the four aircraft approach the viewers from the south, one aircraft flies out of formation towards the west, signifying the deceased's final flight towards the setting sun and thus, heaven.

The first public demonstration of the Missing Man Formation was during the Vietnam War in 1969 when the U.S. Air Force Thunderbirds flew the maneuver to honor the men and women who were then POWs. Other aerial demonstration squadrons, both military and civilian, have adopted the formation and perform it during ceremonial events such as National POW-MIA Recognition Day, Memorial Day, during funerals, and at the interrment of repatriated remains of prisoners and missing. Aside from the fixed wing maneuver, a rotary wing version is flown by National Guard and Reservists with exceptional beauty and solemnity.

One of the simplest aerial maneuvers to perform, it nonetheless elicits deep emotion from the viewers.

★ DEPARTMENT OF VETERANS AFFAIRS ★

The Department of Veterans Affairs (the VA) is a federal department dedicated to providing for American veterans and their families or survivors. The VA assists with service-related disabilities, enables veterans to return to civilian life, honors veterans for sacrifices, and contributes to public health. VA hospitals can be found in most large cities.

The VA sponsors the following programs: health programs, veterans benefits administration, advisory committees, Center for Faith-Based and Community Initiatives, Center for Women Veterans, Debt Management Center, homeless assistance programs, Records Center and Vault, Veterans Industries, Virtual Learning Center, and VHA Home Financing.

The VA home loan provides veterans with the opportunity to buy a home with a low down payment. All veterans who have served in active duty since 1940 or have served more than 180 days of continuous active duty will qualify. The VA loan may be used again to purchase successive homes under the same low down payment conditions, but the first loan must be paid off in order to obtain a second loan, and so on.

THE G.I. BILL. A law referred to as "the G.I. Bill" provided benefits for veterans of the Vietnam War and other officers who served in active duty between January 31, 1955, and January 1, 1977. The law provides a permanent system of education, home loans, job placement, job preferences in federal employment, burial flag, and medical care for veterans who served more than 180 days. It provides education and home loan benefits for personnel who remain on active duty. It terminated on December 31, 1976.

★ AMERICAN LEGION ★

The American Legion was chartered by Congress in 1919 as a patriotic, mutual-help, wartime veterans' organization. It now serves as a community-service organization with about three million members in some fifteen thousand American Legion Posts worldwide. Posts are divided into fifty-five departments representing each of the fifty states, the District of Columbia, Puerto Rico, France, Mexico, and the Philippines. Most cities and even small towns have an American Legion Post.

The American Legion's national headquarters is in Indianapolis, Indiana, with additional offices in Washington, D.C. In addition to thousands of volunteers serving in leadership and program implementation capacities in local communities, the national organization has a regular full-time staff of about three hundred employees. The legion is dedicated to Americanism and serving those men and women who served our nation in the military.

As with all things military, the emblem of the American Legion is highly symbolic. Rays of the sun form the background of the emblem, and suggest that the Legion's principles will dispel the darkness of violence and evil. A wreath forms the center, in memory of those brave comrades who gave their lives for liberty. A star symbolizes the victory symbol of World War I and honor, glory, and constancy. Two large rings additionally stand for the rehabilitation of sick and disabled servicemen as well as denoting the welfare of America's children. Two small rings outside the star indicate loyalty and Americanism and service to our communities, our states, and our nation.

The American Legion operates a library in Indianapolis, established in 1923. While the organization and building are not public, the Library staff welcomes Legionnaires—veterans and nonveterans alike—and researchers, students, and genealogists to visit and research their subject. The American Legion also operates a museum that recognizes and celebrates the military contribution. The American Legion's Family Support Network is available for military families, while spouses are deployed, for basic challenges such as grocery shopping, child care, lawn care, and car repair.

The American Legion sponsors community programs, such as a nationwide youth baseball program, Boys State and Girls State to promote civic responsibility and awareness in high school students, scouting, an oratorical contest for constitutional awareness and leadership development, shooting sports, emergency funds for members, temporary financial assistance for veteran's children, and scholarships. Members may participate in prescription drug, medical, and dental coverage programs as well.

American Legion members naturally feel very strongly about the American flag and will gladly take any worn or tattered flag for proper disposal, generally by burning.

★ VETERANS OF FOREIGN WARS (VFW) ★

Like the American Legion, the Veterans of Foreign Wars (VFW) have numerous posts throughout the country and the world. They are especially active on Independence Day and on Veteran's Day, and they sponsor flag education programs nationwide. The Military Assistance Program (MAP) provides moral and financial support to military service members worldwide, such as "adopting" military units or donating TV-VCR units for American soldiers deployed abroad. It also provides emergency financial assistance and transitioning services, such as relocation and employment assistance.

VFW service officers process thousands of veteran's claims, and have recovered hundreds of millions of dollars in disability compensation claims for veterans. Service officers, who must pass rigorous testing and annual certification, also assist veterans in discharge upgrades, record corrections, education benefits, and pension eligibility. In addition, they regularly inspect VA health care facilities and national cemeteries; their employment specialists monitor laws concerning veterans' preference in federal employment. The VFW provides up-to-date information on diabetes, post-traumatic stress disorder, Agent Orange exposure, and Persian Gulf syndrome. It has more than one hundred trained service officers to assist any veteran, or their dependents, to obtain federal or state entitlements. It has active lobbyists on Capitol Hill for veterans' benefits.

The VFW also partners with the National Rifle Association, the U.S. Chamber of Commerce, the International Association of Firefighters, and the Salvation Army, as well as scouting programs. Local chapters have numerous citizenship awareness programs and sponsor two writing contests, the Voice of Democracy Scholarship Competition, and the Patriot's Pen Essay Contest.

★ UNITED SERVICE ORGANIZATIONS (USO) ★

The USO (United Service Organizations) serves as a home-grown, entertainment-based link between the American people and the U.S. military. Active during both peacetime and in war, the USO brings a special kind of entertainment and comfort to service members and their families to boost morale. It's a nonprofit, congressionally chartered, private organization that relies on donations to fund USO activities. The USO is not part of the U.S. government but is supported by the president of the United States and the Department of Defense; each president has been the honorary chairman of the USO since its inception. Its mission is to "provide morale, welfare, and recreation-type services to our men and women in uniform." It was established in 1941 when President Franklin D. Roosevelt challenged six private organizations—the YMCA, YWCA, National Catholic Community Service, the National Jewish Welfare Board, the Traveler's Aid Association, and the Salvation Army—to handle the on-leave morale needs for members of the Armed Forces.

Bob Hope

One can hardly think of the USO without the image of Bob Hope coming to mind. He served as the USO's ambassador of good will for six decades and headlined some sixty tours. His first performance for service members was May 6, 1941, at March Field, California, and his first tour was in 1942, in Alaska and the Aleutian Islands. He appeared in combat zones from 1943 on, and began a Christmas USO tour tradition of visiting military bases and veterans' hospitals every December. This tradition lasted thirty-four years. As the king of the "one-liners," his particular brand of humor gave American servicemen and women a comfortable dose of home with a load of belly laughs. In honor of his remarkable efforts to entertain and honor the American military, President Lyndon Johnson bestowed upon him the Presidential Medal of Freedom in 1969. Bob Hope's final USO tour was in December 1990, bringing Christmas cheer to troops in Operation Desert Shield in Saudi Arabia and Bahrain. In 1997, the USO successfully lobbied Congress to designate Bob Hope as the first honorary veteran of the U.S. Armed Forces. He was also given an honorary knighthood by Britain's Queen Elizabeth in 1998. He died on July 27, 2003.

Other Entertainers

Thousands of other entertainers have voluntarily participated in USO tours. "Entertainers" have included musicians, comedians, actors, and sports figures, among many others. A few recent notables include Wayne Newton, Robin Williams, Drew Carey, Bruce Willis, Brooke Shields, and David Letterman. Longtime USO entertainers, including the Dallas Cowboys' Cheerleaders, continue to donate their time and talents to entertain the troops.

The USO Today

Today, the USO operates at 122 locations around the world. It recently opened centers in Kuwait and Qatar to support service members of Operations Enduring and Iraqi Freedom, and other centers in Vicenza, Italy, and at the Dallas/Forth Worth and Raleigh/Durham International Airports. USO has a regular presence in ten countries and twenty-one states, relying on a cadre of over thirty-three thousand volunteers. In fact, the ratio of volunteer-to-paid staff is more than 20 to 1. Over five million visits by military personnel and family members to USO centers were logged in 2004. In addition to the ever-popular shows, its programs include "newcomer" briefings for troops and family members, family crisis counseling, support groups for families separated by deployments, housing assistance, libraries and reading rooms, cultural awareness seminars, airport service centers, recreational activities, and nursery facilities. While the USO has diversified over time, its goal remains the same: to bring a touch of home to our men and women in uniform, "Until Every One Comes Home."

CHAPTER 9

Changes in the U.S. Military

By Richard Schading, former sergeant, U.S. Marine Corps

★ FRONTIER BEGINNINGS ★

Even before the Declaration of Independence was written, citizen soldiers were serving in the militia on the American frontier. There, as allies of their English masters, the early Americans protected the towns and farms from Indian and French invaders, and helped expand the frontiers of the future nation. Our military began not only as a means to apply force when and where it was needed, but was and still is a reflection of the morals and traditions of the American way of life.

These early frontier soldiers created new units, such as the Rangers, that were the forerunners of today's special operating forces. These special units, as opposed to the standard units, did not fight and march shoulder-to-shoulder in large formations as the great European armies of the time did. Instead, they moved quickly and stealthily through forests and fields, living off the land to fight enemies on their own terms. They set an example of bravery and ingenuity that reflects the freedom-loving and independent spirit that is still a character of the American military today.

★ MILITARY JUSTIFICATIONS ★

The most obvious reason for a strong military is protection from dangers, both foreign and domestic. This military mission has remained basically the same throughout our history, but the tools and personnel that conduct the mission are always evolving to reflect changes in technology and society. During the American Revolution, the Army and the Navy consisted of a small professional corps together with conscripted men in the ranks that were poorly trained, equipped, and paid. Their weapons were mainly smooth-bore, muzzle-loading, black powder weapons, small arms, and artillery alike. Transport was horse-drawn on land and by sail on the seas, and medical treatment for the sick and injured was probably more dangerous to the patient than the cause of the disability in the first place. Only the officer corps had significant education, but for the mission and technology of the time, little formal training was needed for the ranks to stand in line and advance into the guns of the enemy. The military also offered "three hots and a cot" (three meals and a bed), security, training, and a steady if meager income, which remained basically the same until the American Civil War.

★ CHANGES DUE TO CIVIL WAR ★

At the beginning of the American Civil War, both the North and the South used smooth-bore, black powder weapons, mainly sail-driven ships and horse-drawn land transport. The Old World traditions of movement and maneuver were still followed in America as they were in the armies of the world powers. Troops were used in massed formations of infantry (except for in groups like the Rangers) that marched shoulder to shoulder, many ranks deep. Battles were conducted in open fields, with blocks of infantry maneuvered to seek an advantage, supported by horse-drawn, smooth-bore artillery firing solid shot explosive shells, and in defense, grape shot. Rapid maneuver was provided by heavy- and light-cavalry units that could sweep down on isolated infantry units; they were also used for reconnaissance and communications. Battles were usually won by the army with the best training and discipline. The army that could maintain its formation, absorb casualties without breaking, and fire the most lead into the massed lines of the enemy was usually the winner.

The American Civil War changed the way wars would be fought forever. Part way through the war. And new weapons were developed that made massed formations suicidal and the numbers of casualties of exposed troops unacceptable.

The minié ball, a large-caliber bullet capable of being fired from a rifled musket, was accurate hundreds of yards farther than the old smooth-bore muskets had been, and so exposed the massed troops to deadly fire much longer than before, causing greater casualties. Rapid-firing and more accurate artillery contributed to the folly of standing two armies across from each other and trading vollies.

Tactics were changed to take advantage of cover and concealment and reduce exposure to fire.

The Civil War also led to changes as a result of war needs. Steam power, although already in place, became widely used in the rail movement of supplies and troops; the use of steam power quickly changed the Navy from sail to power vessels. The need for weapons and supplies forced improvement in industry and production methods required to maintain the war effort.

The Civil War ushered in the age of modern technology; we were suddenly able to move farther and faster, produce products more rapidly, and communicate through wires—and thus could conduct war on a different level.

★ POST-CIVIL WAR DEVELOPMENTS ★

After the Civil War, the Army and Marine Corps were downsized and used primarily as garrison (i.e., barracks) troops. The Navy, however, steadily increased in size and quality, and gradually became a power on the world stage.

The sinking of the USS *Maine* in Havana Harbor (either by accidental explosion or by sabotage) led to hostilities between Spain and America. The fighting occurred primarily in Cuba, a Spanish territory, and in the Philippines in the Pacific.

On the ground, a small professional army was quickly augmented with enthusiastic volunteer regiments such as future president Lt. Col. Theodore Roosevelt's Rough Riders. The infantry was equipped with the new smokeless powder .30-40 Krag Jorgensen bolt action rifle with a five-round magazine. There was no smoke to reveal the position of the infantrymen nor was there a thick cloud of smoke to block his aim. The new rifles provided accurate and more rapid fire than ever before in the American lines. The Navy, using all metal, coal-fueled, steam-powered ships, soundly defeated the highly regarded Spanish fleet in the battle of Manila Bay under the command of Admiral Dewey, proclaiming to the world that the American Navy had arrived. The Marines demonstrated the need for assault troops when they made an amphibious landing on Guantanamo Bay to secure a coaling station for the fleet.

The Americans also used, for the first time in effective numbers, rapid-fire crew-served weapons such as the Gatling multibarrel gun, and regiments of light-infantry artillery used the breech loading 1.65" Hotchkiss gun. The Hotchkiss gun provided close, accurate, rapid fire, but because it still used black powder, it revealed its position to the enemy. Shortly after the Spanish-American War, a centerfire smokeless cartridge was developed to alleviate that problem.

One of the achievements from the Spanish-American War was that America was no longer acknowledged as a second-rate colony, but as a power to be reckoned with. As always, the war accelerated developments in not only arms and ammunitions but in medicine and other areas associated with the war effort. During this war, disease produced more casualties than enemy action, with malaria and typhoid fever affecting many. However, because the medical community had recognized some of the causes of infection, instruments began to be sterilized, dressings were changed frequently and kept clean, and disinfectants were regularly used. The mortality rate for wounded soldiers was half that of the American Civil War.

The Spanish-American War was also the first time that the Red Cross insignia appeared on the arms of medical personnel. The International Red Cross was formed as a result of meetings held in Switzerland and established the first of the Geneva Conventions.

★ AMERICA IN WORLD WAR I ★

Despite its emerging might, America's isolationist policies kept it from entering the First World War until several years of bloody conflict between the traditional European powers had passed. This isolationism left the American military ill-prepared for war when it was activated in 1917, following Germany's use of unrestricted submarine warfare in which no ships were considered neutral, including American ships.

By the time America entered the war, hostilities had degraded into a brutal stalemate with opposing forces in trenches across from each other with a shell-scarred "no-man's-land" in between. Weapons were developed during the war to either defend or overcome the opponent's trenches. Machine guns were used for the first time in large numbers and inflicted heavy casualties on troops trying to cross the barbed wire strung across the no-man's-land. Hand grenades were effectively used from the trenches due to the consistent, reliable, and precise fuze (the internal triggering "pin" used to initiate the explosion) that had recently been developed by the British. Massed artillery was used in huge rolling bombardments that altered the landscape. Even more frightening, poison gases were used for the first time in attempts to kill and disable the enemy. First employed by the French, then by the

Germans in retaliation, poison gases were most heavily used later by the British. It was an ugly war with no clear advantage to any of the combatants.

Doughboys and Buffalo Soldiers

It was into this stalemate that the mainly conscripted and briefly trained American doughboys arrived in France in mid-1917. They used a mixture of American, French, and English equipment, and although led by General John "Blackjack" Pershing, were not allowed to fight independently. The American units were fed piecemeal into the lines, joining French and British units in trench warfare.

Although there had been the all-black "Buffalo Soldiers" in the Army after the Civil War, the American military did not allow black troops to participate in combat units during the First World War. Black troops were only used in segregated support and supply units, although the 93rd Infantry Division was a "colored" segregated division activated in December 1917 and sent to France. They were incorporated into the French army and fought well.

The American Navy was relegated to convoy duty throughout the war. American airpower was very limited and the units that performed well did so with French and British aircraft. Tanks were introduced late in the war and met with mixed success, but showed promise and led the way for later developments.

Overall, American participation in World War I was limited. Only one great naval battle was fought at Jutland in 1916 between British and German Dreadnaughts and the armored cruisers produced in the naval arms race before the war. America mobilized a total of 4.3 million men during World War I, of which about 350,000 became casualties. Of these, about 126,000 were killed in action. These numbers look small when compared to the losses of the other combatant nations. More than 65 million men were mobilized around the world to participate in the Great War, and of these, 37 million became casualties with over 8.5 million killed in action.

World War I effectively ended the rules of the old monarchies, many in power since the Crusades; led to the Russian Revolution, and ultimately Communism; and left the old powers exhausted and nearly bankrupt.

Because of her late entry into the war, America was not as severely affected. On the contrary, once put on a war footing, industry revealed the true might of America which emerged from the war as an enormous power.

★ THE SECOND WORLD WAR ★

The Great War was followed by a worldwide depression that slowed progress in the military and throughout society. The next war that loomed on the horizon would dwarf the European war in scale and destruction. The depression led to socioeconomic stress that gave dictators such as Hitler in Germany and Mussolini in Italy the opportunity to come to power. They presented a picture of a brighter future to suffering, impoverished people and developed a cultlike following. The Second World War started as did the first, in Europe with Nazi Germany occupying several neighboring countries and forcing England, Russia, and France to honor defense treaties.

The war was not limited to Europe alone. Japan felt the sting of limited access to fuels and metal ores. Under the military dictatorship lead by Hideki Tojo in the name of the emperor, Japan invaded Korea and China in the late 1930s to create what would become the Pacific theater of World War II. On December 7, 1941, the Japanese bombed the Naval, Army, and Army Air Corp facilities at Pearl Harbor, inflicting serious losses of both men and material. In response, President F. D. Roosevelt and the Congress declared war on Germany, Italy, and Japan on December 8, 1941.

Gearing Up

At the beginning of the war, the American military was led by a small corps of professionals and was vastly undermanned, stocked with aircraft, ships, tanks, and other equipment that were outdated. As has also always been the case, America quickly mobilized, adding millions of men to the armed forces and equipping them with what would prove to be some of the finest materials of the war.

After several early setbacks in both the Pacific and Atlantic/European theaters, American industrial might was coupled with a well-led and dedicated military to spearhead the way to victory. Along the path, however, sacrifices were made at home by the civilian population as well as by military personnel. Food, gas, and other commodities were rationed. For the first time, a large portion of the female population left the home to work in positions vacated by males serving in the military, never to return peacefully to the kitchen again.

In the European theater, North Africa and Italy battles were fought using ever-better equipment in ever-increasing numbers. The infantry used semiautomatic M1 Garand rifles and wore metal helmets. They ate "K rations." These were prepared, canned, and packaged meals, ready to eat while in combat areas. Tracked vehicles were commonplace on the battlefield. The Allied Forces' M4 Sherman tanks were never a match for larger German tanks but were produced in such large numbers that they overwhelmed the superior German equipment. The days of horse-drawn supplies and artillery were over shortly after the war began with the introduction of efficient truck and half-track vehicles to move supplies and equipment.

Air Power

At the beginning of the war, air campaigns were conducted using inadequate planes, but by 1943–1944, American know-how had caught up with and surpassed the opposition both in number and in quantity. Heavy bombers like the B-17 and B-24 were used to bomb opposition industry and turn cities into rubble. The bombers were escorted to their targets and back by perhaps the two finest fighters of the war, the P-51 Mustang and the P-47 Thunderbolt, which gave air superiority to the Allies.

Antiaircraft defenses were vastly improved during the war with the development of larger caliber, rapid-fire weapons. The invention of the proximity fuze, a fuze which caused the round to explode when close to a target, eliminated guesswork for altitude and the need to obtain a direct hit on enemy aircraft.

Radar was developed by the British early in the war and was used by American forces on aircraft, ground stations, and ships to provide early warning of approaching enemy craft as well as their ranges and altitudes.

A Changed Navy

Great changes occurred in the Navy. At the onset of the war, the battleship was still king of the fleets with plans and tactics devised around its use. By war's end, the battleships were used for antiaircraft fire or as floating storage in support of invasion. Only once did American battleships slug it out with the Japanese during the Philippine campaign late in the war. They were replaced as the hammer of the fleet by aircraft carriers whose powerful air squadrons could reach enemy targets hundreds of miles away. The carriers used new aircraft types such as the F-6F Hellcat fighter, F-4-U Corsair fighter, SBD Dauntless dive bomber, and TBF Avenger torpedo bomber like the one President George H. W. Bush was shot down in.

Other improvements that were developed for use by the Navy included sonar for underwater detection of submarines that helped defeat the German U-boats. New forward-facing depth charges, and late in the war, sonar-guided torpedoes, were launched from aircraft against submarines. Many prefabricated "Liberty" ships were assembled in a matter of days to bring supplies and troops to the battlefront. New amphibious ships were developed for landing troops under fire on hostile beaches such as Normandy, Iwo Jima, Guadalcanal, and Tarawa. Tracked amphibious vehicles could crawl ashore and deposit troops on dry land, compared to the early Higgins boats that had to drop a forward-facing ramp in the face of enemy fire in several feet of water. Flat-bottomed ships were developed that could deposit tanks, artillery, and other vehicles right on the beach.

Amphibious Landings

The Marines perfected the art of amphibious landings on hostile shores. Small, aggressive forces could rapidly land and attack using tracked, flat bottom boats (precursors of the AMTRAGS) that brought Marines right to shore. Communications and supplies were prepacked in transports to be brought quickly to the beach as needed. The Marine Air Ground Team was created with forward observers to direct air strikes when and where they were needed to support the ground troops.

Technologies Resulting From the War

Additional developments during World War II that had lasting effects included jet aircraft, rockets like the German V-2 that were the precursors of the ICBMs of the Cold War, and vastly improved radio and television. In business applications, the methods of modern management for projects were developed as well as the early software for the first computers. Towards the end of the war, America won the race to unleash the power of the atom. Two atomic bombs were dropped on Japanese cities and led directly to the end of the World War II—and the start of the Cold War.

The success of the all-black air combat Tuskegee Airmen opened the doors for future black Americans in the military. Segregation in the military officially ended in 1948 with President Harry S. Truman's Executive Order 9981. The Tuskegee Airmen were in high demand throughout the newly formed United States Air Force and began to fill the ranks in the other services as well.

The Second World War had a devastating impact throughout the world. More than 62 million persons lost their lives in the war, of which 52 million were part of the combatants' militaries. The United States had nearly 500,000 men killed in the war and nearly all communities and families were affected in some way.

The United Nations

The United Nations was formed after the war to provide a world organization to oversee disputes and give order and structure to mutually support its members. When, just five short years after the Second World War ended, North Korean forces invaded their neighbors to the south and started the Korean conflict, the United Nations called on member nations to aid South Korea.

★ KOREA'S CONTRIBUTION ★

Once again, America was at war. Unfortunately, millions of soldiers, sailors, Marines, airmen, and Coast Guardsmen had mostly returned to their homes and jobs, leaving the military in the hands of a small professional corps. Many of the ships, aircraft, and tanks had been mothballed in storage for future use; time was needed to re-equip and man the fighting units. North Korean forces drove the South Korean army and its allies nearly off the peninsula before the first Marine division could land and shore up the line. General Douglas MacArthur landed American forces at Inchon Harbor in a brilliant move that trapped the North Korean troops in the southern portion of the peninsula. Resupplied and newly equipped American, British, Turkish, and other allied troops routed the retreating North Korean forces, inflicting heavy casualties along the way. The North Koreans were pursued nearly to the Manchurian border, where General MacArthur assured nervous President Truman that the Communist Chinese would never enter the war.

Chinese Communist forces soon poured across the Yalu River into Korea, driving American and allied forces back to the 53rd parallel and nearly trapping the entire 1st Marine Division near the Chosin Reservoir in the process. Only a fighting retreat to the coast and evacuation by the Navy saved the division. For his folly and insubordination to President Truman, MacArthur was quickly replaced.

The war degraded into a stalemate while peace talks were conducted; an armistice was signed in 1953. To this date, the war has not officially been ended and Korea remains divided along the 53rd parallel.

The Korean War was the first conflict to initiate the widespread use of jet aircraft in combat. American F-86 Air Force Saber jets fought Soviet-made MiG-15 fighters along with the Navy's first carrier-borne jet fighters, the Panther. Helicopters were used as medical evacuation ambulances to MASH (Mobile Army Surgical Hospital) hospitals set up near the front lines. These hospitals provided quality care for the wounded and ensured a greater survival rate than ever before. The Korean conflict committed nearly 2 million American troops to fight on the peninsula without the nation ever declaring war. Nearly 34,000 American servicemen lost their lives and billions of dollars and resources were spent fighting a war "that never was."

★ THE COLD WAR ★

The rest of the 1950s and early 1960s was a massive arms race between the opponents of the Cold War. The Communist block, led primarily by the Soviet Union (USSR), China, and their satellite countries, was in conflict with the democratic powers, especially the U.S., the U.K., France, and other NATO allies. America and the USSR built ever-bigger atomic weapons and longer-range delivery systems in what was called the "mutually assured destruction doctrine." The doctrine was based on the belief that a country would probably not attack if its own destruction were guaranteed through greater retaliatory strikes from its enemies. Very large-standing, well-equipped armies, navies, and air forces were maintained by the draft, which assured that nearly all able-bodied American men would serve at least two years in one of the military branches. The units were led by a corps of professionals that maintained the training and quality standards for the services.

The early 1960s experienced a near-nuclear disaster after a showdown with the USSR over missiles in Cuba that could reach American cities. Because of fears that excessive aggression would lead to a conflict that no one really wanted, small politically controlled conflicts were deemed a better way to stop the spread of communism. This led the way to the next undeclared war, in Vietnam.

★ VIETNAM CHANGED SOCIETY ★

The Vietnam conflict began harmlessly enough with a few hundred American military advisors training South Vietnamese units to fight the Viet Cong rebels funded by North Vietnam. American involvement escalated into a fifteen-year investment and became one of the most divisive events in American history. Over the course of the conflict, 2.6 million Americans served in Vietnam. One in ten became a casualty with more than 58,000 killed in action.

The conflict was mishandled from the beginning, with the White House controlling the war down to small unit operations instead of allowing battle-savvy commanders on the ground to do so. Even so, the military performed well and never lost a major battle. The war was "lost" in the arena of public opinion and politics. The Air Force and Navy conducted long-term bombing operations that were less effective than required because many valuable targets were ruled off-limits for political reasons. Losses were heavy in terms of aircraft shot down and pilots and crew lost. The North Vietnamese developed one of the most sophisticated antiaircraft defense systems (antiaircraft artillery, surface-to-air missiles, and fighter interceptor MiGs) in the world with help from the USSR and China.

Vietnam was also the first conflict with uncensored news coverage that presented photos and televised portrayals of combat, and thus a true image of war that the American public had never before seen. The long duration of the conflict coupled with daily news coverage, lists of casualties, and gruesome pictures wore on the American public and led to a broad peace movement that started on college campuses and spread across the country. Eventually public pressure, costs, and lack of any obvious success caused President Richard Nixon to withdraw the majority of U.S. combat troops in 1973, which later resulted in the 1975 downfall of South Vietnam.

Helicopters and Special Operations Forces

Besides causing changes in American society and politics, Vietnam was the first war to have widespread use of helicopters. More than 14,000 helicopters were used in Vietnam, primarily by the Army and Marine Corps. They were effective for rapid troop movements of both large and small units and gave commanders new freedom and speed in battlefield conditions. Units were quickly resupplied by helicopters, and the wounded could be evacuated to modern, efficient hospitals within two hours. Troops were maintained in the field on C-rations, which were improved over K rations and designed to keep fighting men functioning under stressful conditions.

The Navy SEALs, Army Rangers, Recon Marines, and Green Berets served well in Vietnam and established their roles for later conflicts. The Navy developed a force of gunboats and other armored and armed watercraft to fight in the Mekong Delta. "Swift boats" patrolled the coast and intercepted supplies coming from the sea. Giant B-52 bombers dropped tons of munitions on North and South Vietnam from bases as far away as Guam.

Agent Orange

In an attempt to destroy Viet Cong and North Vietnamese Army hiding places, the American government defoliated large areas using the herbicide Agent Orange. Unfortunately, a contaminant in the manufacturing process called dioxin proved deadly to those exposed. The material caused cancers and other problems for veterans long after their return home, including birth defects in their children.

★ GOODBYE DRAFT, HELLO VOLUNTEERS ★

The disillusionment with government and the military towards the end of the Vietnam War led to the end of the draft, leaving the military to rely solely on volunteer forces. This had the eventual effect of greatly improving the force in terms of diversity, quality, and commitment. To encourage more volunteers, the military offered increased pay and educational opportunities. It became a "way out" for poor, nonwhite Americans who took great advantage of the opportunities it afforded, as well as a place for "better off" families to send their sons and daughters for training and personal development. Gradually, the military became the best-trained, best-educated, and best-equipped in the history of the country. The all-volunteer military was much smaller than the military had been previously. To compensate for the lack of numbers in the regular forces, the National Guard and Reserve Forces were upgraded in both quality of training and equipment to represent a real force for use in emergencies. They now represent about half of America's military capabilities.

★ RAPID FIGHTING FORCES ★

Military doctrine evolved from reliance on large, sluggish units to more mobile, hard-hitting forces that could be deployed in a matter of days to respond to emergency situations anywhere in the world. The Army's 82nd and 101st Airborne Divisions and the U.S. Marine Corps are examples of rapid, self-contained troops that can be sent quickly. The special operations forces became more important in planning and carrying out operations due to the increased number of small conflicts and interventions around the world, such as in Libya and Grenada. The invasion of Panama showcased the abilities of Delta Force operatives, while peacekeeping missions in Bosnia and Somalia gave Guard and Reserve forces deployment experience. With American involvement in the Gulf region conflicts, larger-scale forces were again deployed with ever-improving equipment.

★ SMART BOMBS AND GPS ★

Patriot missiles were first used in combat during the Gulf War, with much-touted but less than significant results against Soviet-made SCUD missiles. The so-called "smart bombs," or self-guiding munitions, were also employed with great success, minimizing collateral damage while improving target destruction. Technologies such as portable Global Positioning System units as well as the Airborne Warning and Control System (AWACS) and satellite communication systems were key tools in enabling coalition units to navigate easily across the desert and direct smart bombs.

★ TECHNOLOGY-DRIVEN CHANGES ★

Gone forever are the days of shoulder-to-shoulder formations and trench warfare. In large-scale operations, there is currently less need for hand-to-hand combat and much greater use of high technology to attack enemies and destroy from a distance. For smaller and initial operations, however, the self-contained special operations force and similar units are more critical and play an important role. As always, military needs continue to drive major advancements in technology, medicine, and many other fields. It is no small surprise to recall that the development and production of fledgling antibiotics such as penicillin skyrocketed during World War II as needs for "miracle medicines" grew. While much of the new technology may have eventually reached the same level of advancement without the military demand, the pace of development was certainly accelerated by the military machine.

★ STILL THE SAME ★

While technologies, equipment, and style of fighting wars have evolved over the years, there are several aspects of the American military that have not changed. In times of crisis or national emergency, the ranks have been quickly filled with men and women either by conscription or volunteers, who willingly put themselves in harm's way for the duration. The respect and honor due their fallen comrades is something a military member never takes lightly. Honoring fellow soldiers goes to the core of the military man and woman, and they understand better than anyone else the depth of the sacrifice that military service requires.

There has also always been a highly trained professional corps within each of the military services to lead forces into battle with courage, strength, and determination. This career corps remains a highly dedicated group of men and women who believe fervently in the American way of life. Our military's leaders are passionate adherents to the traditional tenets of discipline, self-sacrifice, and honor. America's military has always been closely connected with the visions of our forefathers for freedom and individual rights. More than any other group of Americans, our military is willing to sacrifice their own lives for these freedoms.

CHAPTER 10

The Geneva Conventions

★ OVERVIEW ★

The Geneva Conventions are a series of documents generated by the world's leading nations and inspired by the founder of the Red Cross that detail the rules of international warfare. All nations who agree to them must abide by these rules. They include customary laws that apply to all conflicts, certain laws that apply to certain conflicts, and laws based on other international treaties. These include particulars like treatment of prisoners of war.

Notation

Writers, note the name "Geneva Conventions" ends in an "s" because it is a plural noun. The Conventions are a series of documents, and when someone has violated the provisions, it's the Geneva Conventions that have been violated. However, if one is referring to a *particular* Convention, it's singular.

What's the Big Deal?

The Geneva Conventions are important in modern warfare because they form the rules to which all fighting must conform. In the past, "all's fair in love and war" might have been a convenient mantra for persons unwilling to face consequences for their behaviors during wartime. In modern times (i.e., the last 150 years), this is no longer an acceptable excuse. *All* is not fair anymore, at least not in war, and there are serious consequences for those not playing by the rules. Military personnel, from the leaders at the top, down to the newest recruits, must understand these rules.

Who Enforces the Geneva Conventions?

For specifics, see the section titled "Grievance Procedures" on page 211. International organizations, watchdog groups, tribunals, as well as national organizations and elected officials, can bring attention to and enforce compliance with the Conventions as well as bring punishment to the offending parties. Unfortunately, it is often too late to help the victims (who are usually already dead), but the procedure does serve as a deterrent to future crimes as well as punishment for past crimes.

★ BACKGROUND LEADING UP TO ★
THE GENEVA CONVENTIONS

Throughout history, the concept of war crimes has appeared only sporadically. In 6 BC, the Chinese warrior Sun Tzu recommended that armies and lands be captured rather than destroyed, and that prisoners of war be treated kindly. The writings of Hugo Grotius and his contemporaries regarding humanitarian treatment of civilians in the early 1600s helped to lessen, somewhat, the horrors of war in Europe during that era. In America, a Confederate major in 1865 was hanged for executing prisoners of war. Only after the Nuremberg trials following World War II did serious efforts begin by the world community to enforce the current standards of "fairness" and "acceptability" of war-related acts. Principles from the Nuremberg trials were adopted to develop the international standards of law incorporated in the rewritten 1949 Geneva Conventions.

The first Geneva Convention was signed in 1864 to protect the sick and wounded in wartime. Henri Dunant, the founder of the Red Cross, inspired the first Convention, and the International Committee of the Red Cross has played an integral part in drafting and enforcing the Conventions since then.

Treaties were signed in 1899 concerning the technologies of asphyxiating gases and expanding bullets, and an additional thirteen treaties were signed in 1907. The Geneva Gas Protocol was signed in 1925 to prohibit the use of poison gas and biological (bacteriological) warfare. Two more treaties were signed in 1929 that considered treatment of wounded and prisoners of war. In 1949, four Geneva Conventions extended protection to those shipwrecked at sea and to civilians. The Hague Convention on the Protection of Cultural Property was ratified in 1954. In 1977, the United Nations Convention on Military or Any

Other Hostile Use of Environmental Techniques was signed, together with two Additional Protocols to the Geneva Conventions of 1949, which extended their protections to civil wars.

Violations of Conventions

Human rights organizations have accused many countries of breaching the Conventions over the years. These include Israel (whose Mossad is notorious for interrogative torture against Palestinians) and the United States in Vietnam (mass destruction of civilian villages, mass defoliation with Agent Orange, use of napalm and poison gas, prisoner execution), and more recently in Guantanamo Bay and in the Abu Ghraib prison in Iraq. Also, China, Russia, Pakistan, Saudi Arabia, Iran, Chile, South Africa, Cuba, Uganda, Colombia, and many others have been accused of crimes including torture, biological and chemical weapons, executions, civilian massacres, assassinations, terrorism, and more. It is unfortunate that public outcry against offenders is often the only significant consequence of such breaches of the Conventions.

★ A VIOLATION OF THE GENEVA ★ CONVENTION BY AMERICA

The International Court ruled in 1966 that the use of the atomic weapons by the United States in Japan during World War II was illegal then. It also ruled that the *threat* of the use of nuclear weapons was also illegal. The use and threat of use of nuclear weapons is still considered illegal under international law.

★ LAWS OF WAR ★

In modern times, there are three types of laws of war: customary wars, which apply to all conflicts; laws set down by one or more of the Geneva Conventions or Additional Protocols; and laws set down by other international treaties, which are beyond the scope of this discussion.

Customary Laws

Regardless of whether nations have signed the Geneva Conventions, the following are considered modern laws of war, and all combatants are expected to uphold them: Warring parties must protect prisoners of war and wounded combatants from murder, discrimination, mutilation, cruel treatment, torture, humiliating and degrading treatment, and sentencing or execution without a fair trial.

Additionally, the following are forbidden toward any persons in an area of armed conflict: torture, mutilation, rape, slavery, arbitrary killing, genocide, crimes against humanity (e.g., forced disappearance, deprivation of humanitarian aid), and war crimes (e.g., apartheid, biological experiments, hostage taking, attacks on cultural objects, depriving people of the right to a fair trial).

International Rules Regarding Combatants

The Geneva Conventions and Protocols distinguish between combatants and civilians. The two groups must be treated differently by the warring sides, and combatants must be clearly distinguishable from civilians. This benefits civilians because warring sides can avoid targeting them. Also, soldiers cannot be prosecuted for murder by shooting a clearly identified enemy soldier. A civilian who shoots a soldier can be prosecuted, as can a soldier shooting a civilian. Thus, uniforms and weapons must be clearly worn and displayed by combatants.

Medical and religious personnel are excepted from this rule: Both are considered noncombatants, even if in uniform. Medical personnel may also carry small arms for self-defense if illegally attacked.

Mercenaries, defined as soldiers not nationals to any party to the conflict, who are paid more than local soldiers, are specifically excepted as well.

Combatants who willfully violate the rules about clear separation between combatants and noncombatants endanger the civilian population, and are no longer protected by the Geneva Conventions.

Protections Offered by the Geneva Conventions

Combatants who act within the guidelines of the Geneva Conventions have the following protections: Prisoners of war must be treated humanely. No torture or medical/scientific experimentation is permitted. They must also be protected from violence, intimidation, insults, or public curiosity. No public display of prisoners of war is permitted.

Prisoners may be questioned in the prisoner's native language, but need only give name, rank, birth date, and serial number. Refusing to answer further may not result in threats or maltreatment.

POWs must be evacuated away from the combat zone, must never be used as human shields, and must not be exposed unnecessarily to danger.

POWs may not be punished for acts they committed during the fighting unless the opposing side would have punished its own soldiers for those acts as well.

International Rules Regarding Civilians

Both the Fourth Geneva Convention and two Additional Protocols extend protection to civilians during wartime. Specifically, they provide:

- Civilians are not to be attacked, either directly or indiscriminately.
- No property is to be destroyed unnecessarily.
- Deportation is not permitted, regardless of motive.
- Civilians must not be used as hostages.
- Personal dignity is not to be attacked.
- Torture, rape, or enslavement is not permitted.
- Collective punishment and reprisals are not permitted.
- No differential treatment is permitted to civilians with respect to race, religion, nationality, or political allegiance.
- Warring parties must not use or develop biological or chemical weapons.
- Children under fifteen years old must not be permitted to participate in hostilities or be recruited into armed forces.

International Rules Regarding Journalists

Until the 1949 Conventions, journalists were considered civilian members of the armed forces, who often wore uniforms and were treated as any other prisoner of war when captured. In the First, Second, and Third Geneva Conventions, war correspondents received the same protections as combatants. They were not to be treated as spies and did not have to respond to interrogation. If sick or wounded, they must be given medical attention and when captured, must be treated humanely.

The 1977 Protocols specifically recognized journalists as civilians, and due all civilian protections. Currently, journalists cannot be deliberately targeted, detained, or mistreated; they must be treated as any other civilian. It follows that journalists must distinguish themselves from combatants by not wearing uniforms or openly carrying firearms.

★ GRIEVANCE PROCEDURES ★

When an individual or a group of people feel their rights have been violated under the Conventions, they may turn to a number of organizations for support. These include:

- The International Committee of the Red Cross
- The United Nations, the U.N. High Commissioner for Refugees, the U.N. High Commissioner for Human Rights, and the U.N. War Crimes Commission
- Amnesty International
- Doctors Without Borders
- Committee on the Rights of the Child
- War Crimes Tribunal on Former Yugoslavia
- International Tribunal for Rwanda
- Inter-American Court on Human Rights
- Inter-American Commission on Human Rights
- Human Rights Watch
- Local human rights groups, military commanders, and elected officials

★ DETAILS OF THE GENEVA CONVENTIONS ★

In essence, the Conventions are as follows:

CONVENTION I: ("For the Amelioration of the Condition of the Wounded and Sick in Armed Forces in the Field," Geneva, 12 August 1949) describes provisions regarding the care of sick and wounded armed forces in the field.

CONVENTION II: ("For the Amelioration of the Condition of Wounded, Sick, and Shipwrecked Members of the Armed Forces at Sea," Geneva, 12 August 1949) describes provisions for care of sick and wounded armed forces at sea.

CONVENTION III: ("Relative to the Treatment of Prisoners of War," Geneva, 12 August 1949) describes treatment of prisoners of war.

CONVENTION IV: ("Relative to the Protection of Civilian Persons in Time of War," Geneva, 12 August 1949) describes provisions regarding civilian treatment during war.

PROTOCOL I: ("Additional to the Geneva Conventions of 12 August 1949, and relating to the Protection of Victims of International Armed Conflicts," 8 June 1977) extends protection for victims of international armed conflicts against racist regimes, wars of self-determination, and wars against alien oppression.

PROTOCOL II: ("Additional to the Geneva Conventions of 12 August 1949, and relating to the Protection of Victims of Non-International Armed Conflicts," 8 June 1977) describes protections of victims of internal armed conflicts.

Each Convention and Protocol has a variety of articles and annexes. For the entire text of the Geneva Conventions, see the International Red Cross Web site (see also appendix A).

At the beginning of each Convention appear the following provisions: "The signatory parties agree to respect the Convention. The provisions of the Convention are implemented in peacetime but apply in all cases of declared war or any other armed conflict which may arise between two or more of signatory parties. Even though only one party in conflict may be a signatory party to the present Convention, the signatory party(-ies) shall remain bound to the Convention." If an armed conflict occurs within a nation who is bound by this Convention, the following provisions apply: 1) noncombatants, including those who have laid down their weapons, are to be treated humanely. The following actions are prohibited towards these persons: any violence, especially murder, mutilations, and torture; hostage taking; outrages against personal dignity, including humiliating and degrading treatment; and sentencing and execution without a regular, fair court trial; 2) the wounded and sick must be collected and cared for. An impartial body such as the International Red Cross may be permitted to carry out this need.

For a table listing current signatories to the Geneva Conventions, see the International Red Cross Web site at www.icrc.org.

★ PROTOCOL I ★

Included within Protocol I are several points particularly worth noting:

- *Perfidy,* or pretending to the enemy that he will be protected under international law and then betraying that confidence, is prohibited; this includes using a white flag to feign surrender, pretending to be a civilian, pretending to be incapacitated or wounded, or by unlawfully using the International Red Cross or United Nations emblems. *Ruses of war,* such as camouflage, decoys, mock operations, and misinformation are not prohibited. It is also illegal to hide behind enemy symbols (e.g., flags, emblems, insignia).

- It is prohibited to order "no survivors" in an operation.

- A person who is *hors de combat,* that is, who has surrendered his arms or is unconscious and incapable of defending himself, must not be attacked.

- Parachutists cannot be attacked during their descent if they eject from an aircraft in distress, and they must be allowed to surrender before being attacked unless it is clear they are "engaging in a hostile act" (attacking). Airborne troops in action have no such protection from this provision.

- Combatants must distinguish themselves from civilians and carry their weapons openly.

- *Spies,* those persons engaged in espionage, are never "prisoners of war" when captured and can be treated as a spy. Military forces gathering information while in uniform are not "spies"; they are considered spies only when the information is collected through false pretenses or deliberate clandestine manners. Moreover, the person may only be treated as a spy, losing prisoner of war status, if he is captured while engaging in espionage; he must be "caught in the act" to be treated as a spy.

- *Mercenaries* are neither combatants nor prisoners of war; they specifically include: any person specially recruited locally or abroad to fight in an armed conflict, who actually takes part in the hostilities and is motivated by private gain (i.e., is a paid warrior), and who is neither a member of either party of the conflict nor a resident of the territory under control of either combating parties, or who has been sent by a state on official duty as a member of the armed forces.

- *Children* under fifteen years old cannot be recruited or allowed to take a direct part in the hostilities; but if they do and become prisoners of war, they are protected.

- If a breach of the Conventions or Protocols was committed by a subordinate, the superior(s) may be liable for disciplinary action if they knew or could have concluded that the subordinate was committing or planning to commit a breach and they did not take all possible measures to prevent or repress the breach. Commanders must ensure that members of their armed forces are aware of their obligations under these Conventions and Protocols.

- The country whose armed forces commits the crime(s) is responsible for all acts committed by its members and is liable to pay compensation.

★ GLOSSARY A

Terms, Abbreviations, and Acronyms Used by the U.S. Military

TERMS

Abort: To terminate a mission or aircraft takeoff/landing for any reason other than enemy action.

Acknowledgment: Response to a message, indicating it has been received and understood.

Acquire: To detect and locate a target in order to eliminate it.

Activation: Order to active duty (other than for training) in the federal service.

Active duty: Full-time duty in the active military service of the United States. This includes members of the Reserve components serving on active duty or full-time training duty, but does not include full-time National Guard duty.

Advance force, advance guard: Small force sent ahead for reconnaissance, minesweeping, preliminary site seizure, air support, etc.

Air assault: Movement of assault forces (combat, combat support, and combat service support) to engage and destroy enemy forces or to seize and hold key terrain.

Air expeditionary wing: A wing or wing section administered by an air and space expeditionary task force by Department of the Air Force orders for a joint operation.

Air defense: All defensive measures designed to destroy attacking enemy aircraft or missiles in the Earth's envelope of atmosphere, or to nullify or reduce the effectiveness of such attack.

Air defense warning conditions: A degree of air raid probability according to the following code. *Yellow:* Attack by hostile aircraft and/or missiles is probable. *Red:* Attack by hostile aircraft and/or missiles is imminent or is in progress. *White:* Attack by hostile aircraft and/or missiles is improbable.

May be called either before or after air defense warning yellow or red. The initial declaration of air defense emergency will automatically establish a condition of air defense warning other than white for purposes of security control of air traffic.

Air interception: Aircraft making visual or electronic contact with another nonfriendly aircraft. Air intercept has five phases: 1) climb phase (airborne to cruising altitude), 2) maneuver phase (receipt of initial vector to target until beginning transition to attack speed and altitude), 3) transition phase (increase or decrease of speed and altitude necessary for attack), 4) attack phase (turn to attack heading, acquire target, complete attack, turn to breakaway heading), 5) recovery phase (breakaway to landing).

Air interdiction: Air operations conducted against the enemy.

Air supply: Delivery of cargo, equipment, and supplies by air.

Airborne: Troops trained for assault via parachuting or touchdown following transport by air or equipment designed for use by airborne troops during or after an assault.

Airfield: Any area used by aircraft for takeoff and landing. "Aerodrome" is the NATO equivalent. *Not* an "airport."

Airhead: Designated area within hostile territory seized in assault phase of airborne operation used as base for supply and evacuation.

Alert: 1. Readiness for action, defense or protection. 2. A warning signal of a real or threatened danger, such as an air attack. 3. The period of time during which troops stand by in response to an alarm. 4. To forewarn; to prepare for action.

All-out war: "General war" is the preferred, politically correct term; it means combatants are using all their resources as their survival is in jeopardy.

Amphibious: Relating to military operations launched from sea and landing on shore. Examples include amphibious forces, amphibious assault, and amphibious raids.

Antiterrorism: Defensive measures used to reduce the vulnerability of individuals and property to terrorist acts, to include limited response and containment by local military forces.

Any Service Member mail: Mail sent by the general public to an unspecified service member deployed on a contingency operation as an expression of patriotic support. This practice was discontinued after the October 2001 anthrax-laced letter threats.

Approach clearance: Authorization for pilot to commence approach to an airport.

Approach sequence: The order in which two or more aircraft are cleared for an approach.

Apron: Designated area on an airfield for loading or unloading cargo or passengers, refueling, parking, or maintenance.

Area of operations: An operational area defined by the joint force commander for land and naval forces. Areas of operation do not typically include the entire operational area of the joint force commander, but are large enough for component commanders to accomplish their missions and protect their forces.

Arm or de-arm: Procedures to place ordnance or explosive device in ready or safe conditions (rocket launchers, guided missiles, guns).

Armed Forces Radio and Television Service: AFRTS, A worldwide radio and television broadcasting organization that provides U.S. military commanders overseas and at sea with sufficient electronic media resources to effectively communicate theater, local,

Department of Defense, and service-unique command information to their personnel and family members.

Armed Forces of the United States: A collective term for all components of the Army, Navy, Air Force, Marine Corps, and Coast Guard.

Armistice: In international law, a suspension of hostilities by agreement between warring parties.

Arms control: Any international agreement governing the numbers, types, and performance characteristics of weapon systems (including the command and control, logistics support arrangements, and any related intelligence-gathering mechanism) and the numerical strength, organization, equipment, deployment, or employment of the Armed Forces retained by the parties. It includes disarmament.

Army base: A base or group of installations for which a local commander is responsible, consisting of facilities necessary for support of Army activities including security, internal lines of communications, utilities, plants and systems, and real property for which the Army has operating responsibility.

Army corps: A tactical unit larger than a division and smaller than a field army. A corps usually consists of two or more divisions together with auxiliary arms and services.

As you were: Command from superior indicating, "You are no longer required to be at attention."

Assault: 1. Climax of an attack, closing with the enemy in hand-to-hand fighting. 2. In amphibious operations, the time between arrival of the major assault forces and the accomplishment of the assault mission. 3. A short, violent, well-ordered attack against a local objective. 4. The beginning of an airborne operation.

Aye-Aye: This means precisely this: "I understand and I will obey." It is two "I's" in that sentence spelled out phonetically. This does not mean, "okay," or "I agree," or "Yes, sir." It means you know what you were just instructed to do and you will carry out the assignment given.

Base pay: The amount a service member earns per month based on rank and years of service.

Battalion: A unit containing multiple companies. It is typically commanded by a lieutenant colonel. Battalions are normally assigned to a regiment.

Battery: Tactical and administrative artillery unit or subunit corresponding to a company or similar unit in other branches of the Army. Also, guns, torpedo tubes, searchlights, or missile launchers of the same size or caliber or used for same purpose, or operating as an entity.

Beach: The portion of shoreline designated as the landing zone for amphibious operations, regardless of whether there's sand at the waterline.

Beachhead: Designated area in hostile territory necessary as base for supply and evacuation.

Beacon: Light or distinctive electronic signal used for determining bearings, courses, or location.

Billet: Shelter for troops; to give quarter to troops.

Biological agent: A microorganism that causes disease in personnel, plants, or animals or causes the deterioration of matériel.

Biological ammunition: A type of ammunition, the filler of which is primarily a biological agent.

Biological threat: A threat that consists of biological material planned to be deployed to produce casualties in personnel or animals or damage plants.

Biological weapon: An item which projects, disperses, or disseminates a biological agent.

Black: In intelligence, a term used to indicate illegal concealment, not cover by trees, etc.

Black list: An official counterintelligence listing of actual or potential enemy collaborators, sympathizers, intelligence suspects, and other persons who endanger security.

Blood chit: A small sheet of material depicting an American flag and a statement in several languages to the effect that anyone assisting the bearer to safety will be rewarded.

Blue Bark: U.S. military personnel, U.S. citizen civilian employees of the Department of Defense, or their dependents who travel in connection with the death of an immediate family member. It also applies to designated escorts for dependents of deceased military members.

Bona fides: Good faith. In evasion and recovery operations, the use of verbal or visual communication by individuals who are unknown to one another to establish their authenticity, sincerity, honesty, and truthfulness.

Bridgehead: Area of ground held or to be gained in enemy territory.

Brig: Prison.

Burn: To deliberately expose the true status of a person under cover.

By your leave: A phrase spoken by a junior when overcoming a senior prior to passing or a request to be allowed to leave, usually followed by "Sir" or "Ma'am."

Cannibalize: To remove useful parts from one item of equipment to repair another.

Captain's mast: Nonjudicial punishment exercised by a ship captain.

Carpet bombing: Heavy, intensive bombing of an area.

Carry on: An informal order to continue what you were doing before being interrupted (usually by the appearance of a commissioned officer).

Casualty: Any person declared lost by death, illness, injury, or just plain missing, in seven official categories: 1) dead, 2) duty status-whereabouts unknown, 3) missing, 4) very seriously ill or injured, 5) seriously ill or injured, 6) incapacitating illness or injury, or 7) not seriously injured.

Chain of command: Succession of commanding officers from a superior to a subordinate through which command is exercised.

Chairman of the Joint Chiefs of Staff: A general or admiral appointed by the president to serve as his senior military advisor. He works with the secretary of defense and has no direct authority over the individual services but directs the Unified Commands.

Challenge: Process conducted to determine whether a character is friendly or hostile.

Check: Term meaning,"Yes," "Affirmative," or "I agree."

Chemical weapon: Together or separately, 1. A toxic chemical and its precursors; 2. A munition or device, specifically designed to cause death or other harm through toxic properties of those chemicals specified in (1), above, which would be released as a result of the employment of such munition or device; 3. Any equipment specifically designed for use directly in connection with the employment of munitions or devices specified in (2), above.

Chemical warfare: Military operations involving the use of lethal and incapacitating munitions/agents and the warning and protective measures associated with them.

Chevron: A basic insignia with a V-shaped pattern; the number of "stripes" in the chevron indicates the level of rank.

Chit: Any piece of paper authorizing something (light-duty chit, leave chit, etc.) within the military.

Civil disturbance: Group acts of violence and disorder prejudicial to public law and order.

Clandestine operation: Any operation conducted to assure secrecy or concealment. It differs from *covert operation* in that emphasis is on concealment of the operation rather than on concealment of the sponsor.

Classified information: Official information that requires protection against unauthorized disclosure in the interests of national security.

Classified matter: Official information or matter in any form or of any nature which requires protection in the interests of national security.

Clear: 1. To approve or authorize, or to obtain approval or authorization for a person or persons with regard to their actions, movements, duties, etc; 2. To give one or more aircraft a clearance; 3. To give a person a security clearance; 4. To fly over an obstacle without touching it; 5. To pass a designated point, line, or object; the end of a column must completely pass the designated feature before the latter is "cleared"; 6. To operate a gun so as to unload it or make certain no ammunition remains or to free a gun of stoppages; 7. To clear the air to gain either temporary or permanent air superiority or control in a given sector.

Coalition: An ad hoc arrangement between two or more nations for common action.

Cold war: A state of international tension wherein political, economic, technological, sociological, psychological, paramilitary, and military measures short of overt armed conflict involving regular military forces are employed to achieve national objectives.

Collateral damage: Unintentional or incidental injury or damage to persons or objects that would not be lawful military targets in the circumstances ruling at the time; it is not unlawful if not excessive in light of the overall military advantage anticipated from the attack.

Color guard: The ceremonial escort for the flag, as of a country or organization.

Color salute: Dipping the colors (flag) in honorary acknowledgment.

Colors: The flag of a specific unit upon which the battle streamers are mounted. Also, the time of day when the national flag is hoisted or lowered from the flagpole. All personnel stop

and render appropriate honors during this period.

Combat fatigue: Total exhaustion from battle often accompanied by shakes, staring, manic-depressive behavior, nightmares, and flashbacks.

Combat zone: That area required by combat forces for the conduct of operations; also, the territory forward of the rear area boundary.

Combating terrorism: Actions, including antiterrorism (defensive measures taken to reduce vulnerability to terrorist acts) and counterterrorism (offensive measures taken to prevent, deter, and respond to terrorism), taken to oppose terrorism throughout the entire threat spectrum. Also called CBT.

Come about: Change course, turn around.

Command: 1. The authority that a commander in the Armed Forces lawfully exercises over subordinates via rank or assignment, including the authority and responsibility for resources and the use of military forces to accomplish assigned missions; 2. An order given by a commander; 3. A unit or area under the command of one individual.

Command and control: The exercise of authority and direction by a properly designated commander over assigned and attached forces in the accomplishment of the mission. Command and control functions are performed through an arrangement of personnel, equipment, communications, facilities, and procedures employed by a commander in planning, directing, coordinating, and controlling forces and operations in the accomplishment of the mission.

Command element: The core element of a Marine air-ground task force (MAGTF) that is the headquarters. It is composed of the commander, general or executive, and special staff sections; headquarters section; and communications support, intelligence, and reconnaissance forces necessary to accomplish the MAGTF mission.

Commission: To put in or make ready for service or use, as to commission an aircraft or a ship; a written order giving a person rank and authority as an officer in the Armed Forces; or the rank and the authority given by such an order.

Company: A military unit smaller than a battalion, but larger than a platoon, commanded by a captain, with generally 100–250 men; artillery equivalent: battery; cavalry equivalent: troop.

Compromise: Exposure of clandestine personnel, installations, or other assets or of classified information or material, to an unauthorized person.

Compromised: A term applied to classified matter, knowledge of which has passed to an unauthorized person or persons.

Concertina wire: Uncoiled barbed wire.

Conflict: An armed struggle between organized groups within a nation or between nations to achieve limited political or military objectives. Conflict is often protracted, confined to a restricted geographic area, and constrained in weaponry and level of violence. Limited objectives may be achieved by short, focused, and direct application of force.

Contingency operation: A military operation designated by the secretary of defense in which members of the Armed Forces are or may become involved in military actions, operations, or hostilities against an enemy of the U.S. or against an opposing force. Under law, a contingency operation exists if a military operation results in the callup to (or retention on) active duty of members of the uniformed services during war or national emergency declared by the president or Congress.

Conventional weapon: A weapon that is neither nuclear, biological, nor chemical.

Counterattack: Attack by a defending force against enemy attacking force.

Convoy: A number of merchant ships and/or naval auxiliaries usually escorted by warships and/or aircraft.

Counterdrug: Active measures taken to detect, monitor, and counter the production, trafficking, and use of illegal drugs.

Counterintelligence operations: Activities used to identify, exploit, neutralize, or deter foreign intelligence collection and terrorist activities directed against the Department of Defense (DOD).

Counterreconnaissance: All measures taken to prevent hostile observation of a force, area, or place.

Countersabotage: That aspect of counterintelligence designed to detect, destroy, neutralize, or prevent sabotage activities through identification, penetration, manipulation, deception, and repression of individuals, groups, or organizations conducting or suspected of conducting sabotage activities.

Countersubversion: Detecting, destroying, neutralizing, or preventing subversive activities through the identification, exploitation, penetration, manipulation, deception, and repression of individuals, groups, or organizations conducting or suspected of conducting subversive activities.

Counterterrorism: Offensive measures taken to prevent, deter, and respond to terrorism.

Coup de main: An offensive operation that uses surprise and simultaneous multiple operations to achieve success in one swift stroke.

Cover: 1. Giving protection to a person, plan, operation, formation, or installation from the enemy intelligence effort and leakage of information; 2. Shelter or protection, either natural or artificial; 3. Headgear (hats).

Covering fire: Fire used to protect troops when they are within range of enemy small arms. In amphibious usage, fire delivered prior to the landing to cover preparatory operations such as underwater demolition or minesweeping.

Covert operation: An operation so planned and executed as to conceal the identity of, or permit plausible denial by the sponsor. A *covert operation* differs from a *clandestine operation* in that emphasis is placed on concealment of identity of sponsor rather than on concealment of the operation.

Crew chief: Petty officer in charge of a detail (group) of personnel.

Crisis: An incident or situation involving a threat to the United States, its territories, citizens, military forces, possessions, or vital interests that develops rapidly and creates a condition of such diplomatic, economic, political, or military importance that commitment of U.S. military forces and resources is contemplated in order to achieve national objectives.

De facto boundary: An international or administrative boundary not legally recognized, but is a practical division between separate national and provincial administering authorities.

De jure boundary: An international or administrative boundary whose existence and legality is recognized.

De-arming: An operation in which a weapon is changed from a state of readiness for initiation to a safe condition. Also called safing.

Death gratuity: Six month's pay given to the beneficiaries of a serviceman who died in active duty.

Debarkation: The unloading of troops, equipment, or supplies from a ship or aircraft.

Debrief: To receive a report (orally) regarding an event. The person doing the talking is being *debriefed*; the person getting the oral report is *debriefing* him.

Deception: Measures used to mislead the enemy by manipulation, distortion, or falsification of evidence to induce the enemy to react in a manner prejudicial to the enemy's interests.

Declassification: The determination that, in the interests of national security, classified information no longer requires any degree of protection against unauthorized disclosure, coupled with removal or cancellation of the classification designation.

Decoy: An imitation in any sense of a person, object, or phenomenon that is intended to deceive enemy surveillance devices or mislead enemy evaluation.

Decrypt: To convert encrypted text into its equivalent plain text by means of a cryptosystem. This does not include solution by cryptanalysis. *Note:* The term "decrypt" covers the meanings of "decipher" and "decode."

Defense Information Systems Network: Integrated network, centrally managed and configured to provide long-haul information transfer services for all Department of Defense activities. It is an information transfer utility designed to provide dedicated point-to-point, switched voice and data, imagery, and video teleconferencing services.

Defense readiness condition: DEFCON, a system of progressive alerts used between the chairman of the Joint Chiefs of Staff, commanders, and services. Readiness conditions specified by DEFCON 5, 4, 3, 2, 1, where 1 is the highest level of alert.

Delayed Entry Program: A program under which an individual may enlist in a Reserve component of a military service and specify a future reporting date for entry on active duty in the Active component that would coincide with availability of training spaces and with personal plans such as high school graduation.

Demilitarized zone: A defined area in which military forces or military installations is prohibited.

Demobilization: The process of transitioning a conflict or wartime military establishment and defense-based civilian economy to a peacetime configuration while maintaining national security and economic vitality.

Demonstration: An attack or show of force on a front where a decision ("victory") is not sought, but is made with the aim of deceiving the enemy.

Denial measure: An action to hinder or deny the enemy the use of space, personnel, or facilities. It may include destruction, removal, contamination, or erection of obstructions.

Denied area: An area under enemy or unfriendly control in which friendly forces cannot expect to operate successfully within existing operational constraints and force capabilities.

Department of the Air Force: The executive part of the Department of the Air Force at the seat of government and all field headquarters, forces, Reserve components, installations, activities, and functions under the control or supervision of the secretary of the Air Force.

Department of the Army: The executive part of the Department of the Army at the seat of government and all field headquarters, forces, Reserve components, installations, activities, and functions under the control or supervision of the secretary of the Army.

Department of the Navy: The executive part of the Department of the Navy at the seat of government; the headquarters, U.S. Marine Corps; the entire operating forces of the U.S.

Navy and of the U.S. Marine Corps, including the Reserve components of such forces; all field activities, headquarters, forces, bases, installations, activities, and functions under the control or supervision of the secretary of the Navy; and the U.S. Coast Guard when operating as a part of the Navy.

Deployed nuclear weapons: When used in connection with the transfer of weapons between the Department of Energy and the Department of Defense, this term describes those weapons transferred to and in the custody of the Department of Defense. Additionally, it refers to those nuclear weapons specifically authorized by the Joint Chiefs of Staff to be transferred to the custody of the storage facilities or carrying or delivery units of the Armed Forces.

Deployment: Leaving the normally assigned duty area, usually as a unit, to serve temporarily in another area.

Deterrence: The prevention from action by fear of the consequences. Deterrence is a state of mind brought about by a credible threat of unacceptable counteraction.

Deterrent options: A course of action, developed on the best economic, diplomatic, political, and military judgment, designed to dissuade an adversary from a current course of action or contemplated operations.

Diplomatic authorization: Authority obtained at government-to-government level through diplomatic channels.

Diplomatic and/or consular facility: Any Foreign Service establishment maintained by the U.S. Department of State abroad. It may be a "mission" or "consular office," or given a special designation for particular purposes, such as "United States Liaison Office." A "mission" is an embassy maintained to conduct normal, continuing diplomatic relations between the U.S. government and other governments. A "consular office" is any consulate that may participate in most foreign affairs activities.

Direct action: Short-duration strikes and other small-scale offensive actions by special operations forces or special operations-capable units to seize, destroy, capture, recover, or inflict damage on designated personnel or matériel.

Directive: A military communication in which policy is established or a specific action is ordered; a plan issued with a view to putting it into effect. Broadly, any communication which initiates or governs action, conduct, or procedure.

Disaffected person: A person who is alienated or estranged from those in authority or lacks loyalty to the government; a state of mind.

Disarmament: The reduction of a military establishment to some level set by international agreement.

Dislocated civilian: A broad term that includes a displaced person, a stateless person, an evacuee, an expellee, or a refugee.

Diversion: The act of drawing the attention and forces of an enemy from the point of the principal operation; an attack, alarm, or feint that diverts attention. Also, a change made in a prescribed route for operational or tactical reasons.

Diversionary attack: An attack wherein a force attacks, or threatens to attack, a target other than the main target for the purpose of drawing enemy defenses away from the main effort.

Division: A tactical unit/formation as follows: A major administrative and tactical unit/formation which has the necessary arms and services required for sustained combat, larger than a regiment/brigade and smaller than a corps; a number of naval vessels of similar type grouped together for operational and administrative command, or a tactical unit of a naval aircraft squadron, consisting of two or more sections; an air division is an air combat organization normally consisting of two or more wings with appropriate service units. The combat wings of an air division will normally contain similar type units; an organizational part of a headquarters that handles military matters of a particular nature, such as personnel, intelligence, plans, and training, or supply and evacuation.

Doctrine: Fundamental principles by which the military forces guide their actions in support of national objectives. It is authoritative but requires judgment in application.

Dog tags: Originally metal disks embossed with personal information that could be left with a body on the field of battle for identification. Eventually, it evolved into a rectangle with round corners and a small notch on one side so it could be set on the teeth of a deceased soldier and kicked into the head so that the enemy could not strip the dead soldier of his identity. Current versions lack the notch.

Double agent: Agent in contact with two opposing intelligence services, only one of which is aware of the double contact or quasi-intelligence services.

Echelon: A subdivision of a headquarters, e.g., forward echelon, rear echelon, or separate level of command (e.g., compared to a regiment, a division is a higher echelon; a battalion is a lower echelon). Additionally, a subunit of a command to which a combat mission is assigned; e.g., attack echelon, support echelon, reserve echelon.

Electromagnetic deception: The deliberate radiation, re-radiation, alteration, suppression, absorption, denial, enhancement, or reflection of electromagnetic energy in a manner intended to convey misleading information to an enemy or to enemy electromagnetic-dependent weapons, thereby degrading or neutralizing the enemy's combat capability. Among the types of electromagnetic deception are: *Manipulative electromagnetic deception:* Actions to eliminate revealing, or convey misleading, electromagnetic telltale indicators that may be used by hostile forces; *Simulative electromagnetic deception:* Actions to simulate friendly, notional, or actual capabilities to mislead hostile forces; and *Imitative electromagnetic deception:* The introduction of electromagnetic energy into enemy systems that imitates enemy emissions.

Electronic warfare: Any military action involving the use of electromagnetic and directed energy to control the elec-tromagnetic spectrum or to attack the enemy. The three major subdivisions within electronic warfare are: electronic attack, electronic protection, and electronic warfare support. *Electronic attack:* That division of electronic warfare involving the use of electromagnetic energy, directed energy, or antiradiation weapons to attack personnel, facilities, or equipment with the intent of degrading, neutralizing, or destroying enemy combat capability and is considered a form of fires. Electronic attack includes: 1) actions taken to prevent or reduce an enemy's effective use of the electromagnetic spectrum, such as jamming and electromagnetic deception, and 2) employment of weapons that use either electromagnetic or directed energy as their primary destructive mechanism (lasers, radio frequency weapons, particle beams). *Electronic protection:* Electronic warfare involving passive and active means taken to protect personnel, facilities, and equipment from any effects of friendly or enemy employment of electronic warfare that degrade, neutralize, or destroy friendly combat capability. *Electronic warfare support:* Electronic warfare actions used to search for, intercept, identify, and locate or localize sources of intentional and unintentional radiated electromagnetic energy. Electronic warfare support data can be used to produce signals intelligence, provide targeting for attack, and produce measurement and signature intelligence.

Encipher: To convert plain text into unintelligible form by means of a cipher system.

Engage: In air defense, a fire control order used to direct or authorize units and/or weapon systems to fire on a designated target.

Engagement: An attack with guns or air-to-air missiles by an interceptor aircraft, the launch of an air defense missile by air defense artillery and the missile's subsequent travel to intercept it, or a tactical conflict.

Escort of the Colors: Honorary ceremony of escorting the national colors by a color guard.

Espionage: The act of obtaining, delivering, transmitting, communicating, or receiving information about the national defense with an intent, or reason to believe, that the information may be used to the injury of the United States or to the advantage of any foreign nation. Espionage is a violation of title 18, United States Code 792-798 and Article 106, Uniform Code of Military Justice.

Espionage against the United States: Overt, covert, or clandestine activity designed to obtain information relating to the national defense with intent or reason to believe that it will be used to the injury of the United States or to the advantage of a foreign nation.

Evacuation: The process of moving any person who is wounded, injured, or ill to or between medical treatment facilities. Also, the clearance of personnel, animals, or matériel from a given locality or the controlled process of collecting, classifying, and shipping unserviceable or abandoned matériel, U.S. or foreign, to appropriate reclamation, maintenance, technical intelligence, or disposal facilities.

Evasion: The process whereby individuals who are isolated in hostile or unfriendly territory avoid capture with the goal of successfully returning to areas under friendly control.

Evasion and escape: The procedures and operations whereby military personnel and other selected individuals escape from a hostile area.

Evasion and escape intelligence: Processed information prepared to assist personnel to escape if captured by the enemy or to evade capture if lost in enemy-dominated territory.

Evasion and escape net: The organization within enemy-held or hostile areas that operates to receive, move, and exfiltrate military personnel or selected individuals to friendly control.

Execution planning: The phase of a planning process that details how a plan will be put into action.

Exercise: Military maneuver or simulated wartime operation involving planning, preparation, and execution. It is carried out for the purpose of training and evaluation.

Exfiltration: Removal of personnel or units from areas under enemy control by stealth, deception, surprise, or clandestine means.

Expedition: A military operation conducted by an armed force to accomplish a specific objective in a foreign country.

Expeditionary force: An armed force organized to accomplish a specific objective in a foreign country.

Explosive ordnance: All munitions containing explosives, nuclear fission or fusion materials, or biological and chemical agents. This includes bombs and warheads; guided and ballistic missiles; artillery, mortar, rocket, and small arms ammunition; all mines, torpedoes, and depth charges; demolition charges; pyrotechnics; clusters and dispensers; cartridge and propellant actuated devices; electro-explosive devices;

clandestine and improvised explosive devices; and all similar or related items or components explosive in nature.

Extract: To recover or pick up; e.g., helicopters "extract" injured or special ops personnel. Opposite of "insert."

Extraction zone: A specified drop zone used for the delivery of supplies and/ or equipment by means of an extraction technique from an aircraft flying very close to the ground.

Faker: A friendly aircraft simulating a hostile in an air defense exercise.

Fall in: To assemble in formation.

Fall out: To leave formation.

Field of fire: The area which a weapon or group of weapons may cover effectively with fire from a given position.

Fighting load: Necessary items such as individual clothing, equipment, weapons, and ammunition that are carried by the combat soldier.

Fire: Command given to discharge a weapon, or the act of detonating a main explosive charge via a firing system.

Fire in the hole: A warning called out when an explosive is about to go off.

Fire mission: An artillery mission.

Fire support team: An Army team provided by the field artillery component to each maneuver company and troop to plan and coordinate all indirect fire means available to the unit, including mortars, field artillery, close air support, and naval gunfire.

Firefight: An exchange of small arms fire between opposing units.

Firing squad: Squad of men assigned to execute someone condemned to death or to honor a dead comrade by firing a certain number of rounds over his grave.

First strike: The first offensive move of a war, now generally associated with nuclear operations.

Five Paragraph Order: An element of the Army and USMC small units tactics, specifying instructions to a unit prior to potential enemy engagement. It includes five paragraphs that are presented orally and that specify: the Situation (i.e., who are the enemy and who are friendly forces), the Mission, the Execution Plan, Administration/Logistics (or Service Support), and Command/Signal.

Fix: To determine position.

Flag officer: An officer with rank of general, lieutenant general, major general, or brigadier general in the U.S. Army, Air Force, or Marine Corps; or admiral, vice admiral, or rear admiral in the U.S. Navy or Coast Guard.

Fleet: An organization of ships, aircraft, Marine forces, and shore-based fleet activities under one command.

Fleet Marine Force: A force of combined arms comprising land, air, and service elements of the Marine Corps, which is an integral part of a U.S. Fleet. Has the status of a type command.

Flight level: Altitude, given in three digits which represents hundreds of feet; e.g., flight level 350 represents an altitude of 35,000 feet.

Force: 1. An aggregation of military personnel, weapon systems, equipment, and necessary support, or a combination; 2. A major subdivision of a fleet.

Force packages: Bombs and/or missiles.

Foreign national: Any person other than a U.S. citizen, U.S. permanent or temporary legal resident alien, or person in U.S. custody.

Formation: 1. An ordered arrangement of troops and/or vehicles for a specific purpose; 2. An ordered arrangement of two or more ships, units, or aircraft proceeding together under a commander.

Forward air controller: Officer who controls aircraft from a forward (advanced) position in support of ground troops.

Forward observer: An observer operating with front line troops and trained to adjust ground or naval gunfire and pass back battlefield information.

Forward operating base: An airfield used to support tactical operations without establishing full support facilities. The base may be used for an extended time period. Support by a main operating base will be required to provide backup support for a forward operating base.

Forward operating location: Similar to a forward operating base but without the in-place infrastructure, primarily used for counterdrug operations.

Free fire zone: Any area in which permission is not required prior to firing on targets.

Friendly: A contact positively identified as friendly.

Friendly fire: Accidentally firing at one's own side.

Frustrated cargo: Shipment of supplies or equipment which is stopped en route and requires further authorization or instruction to move on.

Functional kill: To render a targeted installation, facility, or target system unable to fulfill its primary function.

Garble: An error in transmission, reception, encryption, or decryption that changes the text of a message or any portion thereof in such a manner that it is incorrect or undecryptable.

Garrison force: All units assigned to a base or area for defense, development, operation, and maintenance of facilities.

General military intelligence: Intelligence concerning the military capabilities of foreign countries or organizations, or topics affecting potential U.S. or multinational military operations, relating to: armed forces capabilities, area and terrain intelligence; transportation; military matériel production and support industries; military and civilian command, control, communications, computers, and intelligence systems; military economics; insurgency and terrorism; location, identification, and description of military-related installations; and threats and forecasts. This specifically excludes scientific and technical intelligence.

General orders: Permanent instructions, issued in order form, that apply to all members of a command, as compared with special orders, which affect only individuals or small groups. General orders are usually concerned with matters of policy or administration.

General quarters: The highest condition of alert onboard ship; it pulls the crew from their normal work assignments to a warfighting stance.

General war: Armed conflict between major powers in which the total resources of the belligerents are employed, and the national survival of a major belligerent is in jeopardy.

Germ warfare: Biological warfare.

Go/no go: Condition or state of operability of a component or a system where "go" means functioning properly, and "no go" means not functioning properly.

Grand slam: All enemy aircraft originally sighted are shot down.

Graves registration program: A program that provides for search, recovery, tentative identification, and evacuation or temporary interment. Temporary interment is only authorized by the geographic combatant commander. Disposition of personal effects is included in this program.

Gravity extraction: Extraction of cargoes from aircraft by influence of their own weight, i.e., parachuting.

Ground combat element: The core element of a Marine air-ground task force (MAGTF) that is task-organized to conduct ground operations. It is usually constructed around an infantry organization but varies in size from a small ground unit to one or more Marine divisions under the direction of the MAGTF commander. The ground combat element itself is not a formal command.

Guard: A security operation whose primary task is to protect the main force by fighting to gain time while also observing and reporting information, and to prevent enemy ground observation of and direct fire against the main body by reconnoitering, attacking, defending, and delaying.

Guerrilla: A group of irregular, predominantly indigenous personnel organized along military lines to conduct military and paramilitary operations in enemy held or hostile territory. *Guerrilla force:* A group of irregular, predominantly indigenous personnel organized along military lines to conduct military and paramilitary operations in enemy-held, hostile, or denied territory.

Guerrilla warfare: Military and paramilitary operations conducted in enemy-held or hostile territory by irregular, predominantly indigenous forces.

Hard missile base: A launching base that is protected against a nuclear explosion.

Hard target: Buildings or military installations. "Soft targets" are humans.

Hardened site: A site, normally constructed under rock or concrete cover, designed to provide protection against the effects of conventional weapons.

Heavy drop: A system of delivery of heavy supplies and equipment by parachute.

Hostage: A person held as a pledge that certain terms or agreements will be kept. The taking of hostages is forbidden under the Geneva Conventions.

Hostile: In combat and combat-support operations, a person, equipment, structure, or item belonging to or produced by someone declared to be with the "enemy."

Hostile act: A hostile act is an attack or other use of force by any civilian, paramilitary, or military force or terrorist(s) against the United States,

its personnel, and its property. When a hostile act is in progress, the government has the right to use necessary force, in self-defense by all necessary means available to deter, neutralize, or to destroy the threat.

Hostile intent: The threat of a hostile act against the U.S., U.S. nationals, and their property.

Human intelligence: A category of intelligence derived from information collected and provided by human sources.

Humanitarian and civic assistance: Assistance to the local populace provided by predominantly U.S. forces in conjunction with military operations and exercises. This assistance is specifically authorized by title 10, United States Code, section 401, and funded under separate authorities. Assistance provided under these provisions is limited to: 1) medical, dental, and veterinary care provided in rural areas of a country; 2) construction of rudimentary surface transportation systems; 3) well drilling and construction of basic sanitation facilities; and 4) rudimentary construction and repair of public facilities.

Identification, friend or foe: System using electromagnetic transmissions to distinguish friendly forces from foes;

friendly forces' equipment automatically responds with a pulse.

Improvised nuclear device: A device incorporating radioactive materials designed to result in the dispersal of radioactive material or in the formation of nuclear-yield reaction. Such devices may be fabricated in a completely improvised manner or may be an improvised modification to a U.S. or foreign nuclear weapon.

In country: Serving in any current combat zone or on duty outside the United States and its territories.

In the line of duty: Actions performed in accordance with military regulations and orders.

Incident: In information operations, an assessed event of attempted entry, unauthorized entry, or an information attack on an automated information system. It includes unauthorized probing and browsing; disruption or denial of service; altered or destroyed input, processing, storage, or output of information; or changes to information system hardware, firmware, or software characteristics with or without the users' knowledge, instruction, or intent.

Incoming: An alert that something is coming at you, often enemy fire or artillery.

Indirect fire: Mortar and artillery fire used against targets not directly visible; shells are fired at a high trajectory.

Individual Ready Reserve: A manpower pool consisting of individuals who have had some training, who have served previously in the Active component or in the Selected Reserve, and have some period of their military service obligation remaining. Members may voluntarily participate in training for retirement points and promotion with or without pay.

Infiltration: The movement through or into an area or territory occupied by either friendly or enemy troops or organizations. Methods of infiltration are: *black* (clandestine), *grey* (through legal crossing point but under false documentation), and *white* (legal).

Insurgency: An organized movement aimed at the overthrow of a constituted government through use of subversion and armed conflict.

Insurgent: Member of a political party who rebels against established leadership.

Intelligence: The product resulting from the collection, processing, integration, analysis, evaluation, and interpretation of available information concerning foreign countries or areas; also, information and knowledge about an adversary obtained through observation, investigation, analysis, or understanding.

Joint Chiefs of Staff (JCS): A panel comprising the highest-ranking members of each major branch of the armed services in any particular country. Their primary responsibility is to ensure the readiness of their respective military services. The JCS also act in an advisory military capacity for the president of the United States and the secretary of defense. In addition, the chairman of the JCS acts as the chief military advisor to the president.

Litter: A basket or frame utilized for the transport of injured persons.

Litter patient: A patient requiring litter accommodations while in transit.

Manning the rails: When entering or leaving port or when rendering special honors the ship's compliment will dress in full dress uniforms and stand along the rails or in the rigging at the position of attention.

Manual of Arms: The prescribed movements involving the use of weapons, including swords, in parades and ceremonies.

Marine One: The call sign of the Marine aircraft in which the president of

the United States is either a passenger or pilot.

Marine Expeditionary Unit: The smallest of the expeditionary organizations is built around a Battalion Landing Team and a Composite Air Squadron; MEUs consist of approximately 2,500 Marines.

Matériel: All items (including ships, tanks, self-propelled weapons, aircraft, etc., and related spares, repair parts, and support equipment, but excluding real property, installations, and utilities) necessary to equip, operate, maintain, and support military activities without distinction as to its application for administrative or combat purposes.

Medevac: Medical evacuation. There are three categories: 1) *Emergency:* Near death evacuees; 2) *Priority:* Serious, nonambulatory evacuees; and 3) *Routine:* Ambulatory or dead evacuees.

Military deception: Actions executed to deliberately mislead the enemy. The five categories of military deception are as follows: 1. *Strategic military deception*: Military deception planned and executed by and in support of senior military commanders to result in adversary military policies and actions that support the originator's strategic military objectives, policies, and operations. 2. *Operational military deception*: Military deception planned and executed by and in support of operational-level commanders to result in adversary actions that are favorable to the originator's objectives and operations. Operational military deception is planned and conducted in a theater to support campaigns and major operations. 3. *Tactical military deception:* Military deception planned and executed by and in support of tactical commanders to result in adversary actions that are favorable to the originator's objectives and operations. Tactical military deception is planned and conducted to support battles and engagements. 4. *Service military deception:* Military deception planned and executed by the services that pertain to service support to joint operations. Service military deception is designed to protect and enhance the combat capabilities of service forces and systems. 5. *Military deception in support of operations security (OPSEC):* Military deception planned and executed by and in support of all levels of command to support the prevention of the inadvertent compromise of sensitive or classified activities, capabilities, or intentions. Deceptive OPSEC measures are designed to distract foreign intelligence away from, or provide cover for, military operations and activities.

Missing: A casualty status for which the U.S. Code provides statutory guidance concerning missing members of the military services. Excluded are personnel who are in an absent-without-leave, deserter, or dropped-from-rolls status. A person declared missing is categorized as follows. *Beleaguered:* The casualty is a member of an organized element that has been surrounded by a hostile force to prevent escape of its members. *Besieged:* The casualty is a member of an organized element that has been surrounded by a hostile force, compelling it to surrender. *Captured:* The casualty has been seized as the result of action of an unfriendly military or paramilitary force in a foreign country. *Detained:* The casualty is prevented from proceeding or is restrained in custody for alleged violation of international law or other reason claimed by the government or group under which the person is being held. *Interned:* The casualty is definitely known to have been taken into custody of a nonbelligerent foreign power as the result of and for reasons arising out of any armed conflict in which the Armed Forces of the United States are engaged. *Missing:* The casualty is not present at his or her duty location due to apparent involuntary reasons and whose location is unknown. *Missing in action:* The casualty is a hostile casualty, other than the victim of a terrorist activity, who is not present at his or her duty location due to apparent involuntary reasons and whose location is unknown.

Noted: An answer meaning "understood" when receiving a list of instructions.

Pay grade: A relational term consisting of the letter E, O, or W and the level of pay assigned to that grade.

Platoon: A unit consisting of four squads. It is assigned to a company and is generally commanded by a lieutenant. It is the basic working unit in Boot Camp where its leaders are drill instructors.

Phonetic alphabet: A list of standard words used to identify letters in a message transmitted by radio or telephone. The following are the authorized words, listed in order, for each letter in the alphabet: ALFA, BRAVO, CHARLIE, DELTA, ECHO, FOXTROT, GOLF, HOTEL, INDIA, JULIETT, KILO, LIMA, MIKE, NOVEMBER, OSCAR, PAPA, QUEBEC, ROMEO, SIERRA, TANGO, UNIFORM, VICTOR, WHISKEY, X-RAY, YANKEE, and ZULU. Most terms used during World War I and World War II were different and are as follows: ACK, BEER, CHARLIE, DON, EDWARD, FREDDIE, GEE, HARRY, INK, JOHNNIE, KING, LONDON, EMMA, NUTS, ORANGES, PIP, QUEEN, ROBERT, ESSES, TOC, UNCLE, VIC, WILLIAM, X-RAY, YORKER, ZEBRA.

Post: As a noun, it is a place where a soldier or Marine is assigned, such as a sentry post or an embassy. Also used extensively by the Army to designate bases not named forts. As a verb, it is a command in marching for specific officers to take their assigned positions or the act of placing a sentry on post or assigning a Marine to an embassy.

Post Exchange: Also called PX, the place where military personnel shop on base. On Army and Air Force installations, they are correctly termed Army and Air Force Exchange Service (AAFES); on Navy bases, they are called Navy Exchange, and on Marine Corps bases they are called Marine Corps Exchange.

Presidential Reserve Callup Authority: Provision of a public law (U.S. Code, Title 10 (DOD), section 12304) that provides the president a means to activate, without a declaration of national emergency, up to 200,000 members of the Selected Reserve and the Individual Ready Reserve (of whom up to 30,000 may be members of the Individual Ready

Reserve), for up to 270 days to meet the support requirements of any operational mission. Members called under this provision may not be used for disaster relief or to suppress insurrection. This authority has particular utility when used in circumstances in which the escalatory national or international signals of partial or full mobilization would be undesirable. Forces available under this authority can provide a tailored, limited-scope, deterrent, or operational response, or may be used as a precursor to any subsequent mobilization.

Prisoner of war: A detained person as defined in Articles 4 and 5 of the Geneva Convention Relative to the Treatment of Prisoners of War of August 12, 1949; particularly, one who, while engaged in combat under orders of his or her government, is captured by the armed forces of the enemy. As such, he or she is entitled to the combatant's privilege of immunity from the municipal law of the capturing state for warlike acts which do not amount to breaches of the law of armed conflict.

Prisoner of war personnel record: A form for recording the photograph, fingerprints, and other pertinent personal data concerning the prisoner of war, including that required by the Geneva Conventions.

Propaganda: Any form of communication in support of national objectives designed to influence the opinions, emotions, attitudes, or behavior of any group in order to benefit the sponsor, either directly or indirectly. *Black* propaganda is propaganda that purports to emanate from a source other than the true one. *Grey* propaganda is propaganda that does not specifically identify any source. *White* propaganda is propaganda disseminated and acknowledged by the sponsor.

Psychological operations: Planned operations to convey selected information and indicators to foreign audiences to influence their emotions, motives, objective reasoning, and ultimately the behavior of foreign governments, organizations, groups, and individuals. The purpose of psychological operations is to induce or reinforce foreign attitudes and behavior favorable to the originator's objectives.

Psychological warfare: The planned use of propaganda and other psychological actions having the primary purpose of influencing the opinions, emotions, attitudes, and behavior of hostile foreign groups in such a way as to support the achievement of national objectives.

Radar: A radio detection device that provides information on range, azimuth, and/or elevation of objects.

Rank: The military authority of an individual within the structure of the organization. Rank is represented by insignia showing relative authority.

Rate: Any of the ranks within the Navy or Coast Guard enlisted structure.

Reconnaissance: A mission undertaken to obtain information about the activities and resources of an enemy or potential enemy, or to secure data concerning the meteorological, hydrographic, or geographic characteristics of a particular area.

Request mast: Every sailor and Marine's right to be heard. At every step up the chain of command any sailor may request to see the next person in authority all the way to the top. When a request mast is asked for, the individual does not have to explain why, but he or she must make the request at every step up the ladder.

Resistance movement: An organized effort by some portion of the civil population of a country to resist the legally established government or an occupying power and to disrupt civil order and stability.

Restricted area: An area (land, sea, or air) in which there are special measures employed to prevent or minimize interference between friendly forces; or an area under military jurisdiction in which special security measures are employed to prevent unauthorized entry.

Restricted data: All data (information) concerning design, manufacture, or use of atomic weapons, the production of special nuclear material, or the use of special nuclear material in the production of energy.

Reveille: A signal to awaken, get out of bed, and begin the day, traditionally a bugle call.

Rules of engagement: Directives issued by military authority that define the circumstances and limitations under which U.S. forces will initiate and/or continue combat engagement with other forces encountered.

Ruse: In military deception, a trick of war designed to deceive the adversary, usually involving the deliberate exposure of false information to the adversary's intelligence collection system.

Sabotage: An act with intent to injure, interfere with, or obstruct the national defense of a country by injuring or destroying any national defense or war matériel, premises, or utilities, including human and natural resources.

Sanitize: To revise a report or other document in such a fashion as to prevent identification of sources, or of the actual persons and places with which it is concerned, or of the means by which it was acquired. Usually involves deletion or substitution of names and other key details.

Search and rescue: The use of aircraft, surface craft (land or water), submarines, specialized rescue teams, and equipment to search for and rescue personnel in distress on land or at sea.

Search and rescue incident classification: Three emergency phases into which an incident may be classified or progress, according to the seriousness of the incident and its requirement for rescue service. *Uncertainty phase:* Doubt exists as to the safety of a craft or person because of knowledge of possible difficulties or because of lack of information concerning progress or position. *Alert phase:* Apprehension exists for the safety of a craft or person because of definite information that serious difficulties exist that do not amount to a distress or because of a continued lack of information concerning progress or position. *Distress phase:* Immediate assistance is required by a craft or person because of being threatened by grave or imminent danger.

Security classification: A category to which national security information and material is assigned to denote the degree of damage that unauthorized disclosure would cause to national defense or foreign relations of the United States and to denote the degree of protection required. There are three such categories: *Top secret:* National security information or material that requires the highest degree of protection and the unauthorized disclosure of which could reasonably be expected to cause exceptionally grave damage to the national security. Examples of "exceptionally grave damage" include armed hostilities against the United States or its allies; disruption of foreign relations vitally affecting the national security; the compromise of vital national defense plans or complex cryptologic and communications intelligence systems; the revelation of sensitive intelligence operations; and the disclosure of scientific or technological developments vital to national security. *Secret:* National security information or material that requires a substantial degree of protection and the unauthorized disclosure of which could reasonably be expected to cause serious damage to the national security. Examples of "serious damage" include disruption of foreign relations significantly affecting the national security; significant impairment of a program or policy directly related to the national security; revelation of significant military plans or intelligence operations; and compromise of significant scientific or technological developments relating to national security. *Confidential:* National security information or material that requires protection and the unauthorized disclosure of which could reasonably be expected to cause damage to the national security.

Security clearance: An administrative determination by competent authority that an individual is eligible, from a security standpoint, for access to classified information.

Sedition: Willfully advocating the duty or necessity of overthrowing the U.S. government or any political subdivision by force or violence.

Selected Reserve: Units and individuals within the Ready Reserve designated as essential to wartime missions, with priority over all other Reserves.

Shell shock: Any nervous mental symptom resulting from war.

Short round: An artillery shell that falls short of its intended target, often

because of defective gunpowder or a miscalculation.

Short title: A short, identifying combination of letters and/or numbers (i.e., acronyms) assigned to a document or device for purposes of brevity and/or security.

Sick bay: The location on ship where sick and injured people are treated.

Situation report: A report giving the situation in the area of a reporting unit or formation.

Sortie: Round-trip mission by single aircraft.

Special Days and Times: A few letters are used to designate times or days that specific events are planned. Days designated C-, D-, and M- end at 2400 hours Universal Time (Zulu time) and are assumed to be twenty-four-hours long for planning. These special days or times include: *C-day:* The unnamed day on which a deployment operation begins; may include troops, cargo, weapon systems, or a combination using any or all types of transport. *D-day:* The unnamed day on which operations commence or are scheduled to commence. *F-hour:* The effective time of announcement by the secretary of defense to the military departments of a decision to mobilize Reserve units. *H-hour:*

The specific hour on D-day at which a particular operation commences. *L-hour:* The particular hour on D-day at which a deployment operation will commence. *M-day:* The day on which full mobilization commences or is due to commence. *N-day:* The day an active duty unit is notified for deployment or redeployment. *R-day:* Redeployment day, the day on which redeployment of major combat, combat support, and combat service support forces begins in an operation. *S-day:* The day the president authorizes Selective Reserve call-up (less than 200,000). *T-day:* The effective day the presidential declares a National Emergency and authorizes partial mobilization (under 1,000,000 personnel exclusive of the 200,000 callup). *W-day:* Declared by the National Command Authorities, W-day is associated with an adversary decision to prepare for war (unambiguous strategic warning).

Special operations: Operations conducted by specially organized, trained, and equipped military and paramilitary forces to achieve military, political, economic, or informational objectives by unconventional military means in hostile, denied, or politically sensitive areas. These operations include all military operations, conducted independently or in coordination with operations of conventional, nonspecial operations forces. Political-military considerations frequently shape special operations, requiring clandestine, covert, or low visibility techniques and oversight at the national level. *Special operations* differ from *conventional operations* in degree of physical and political risk, operational techniques, mode of employment, independence from friendly support, and dependence on detailed operational intelligence and indigenous assets.

Squad: A unit consisting of a three fire teams. It is assigned to a platoon and is usually led by a sergeant or staff sergeant.

Strategic psychological activities: Planned psychological activities in peace, crisis, and war which pursue objectives to gain the support and cooperation of friendly and neutral countries and to reduce the will and the capacity of hostile or potentially hostile countries to wage war.

Stealth: Rendering aircraft "invisible" to detection equipment through special technology.

Subversion: Action designed to undermine the military, economic, psychological, or political strength or morale of a regime.

Subversive activity: Anyone lending aid, comfort, and moral support to individuals, groups, or organizations that advocate the overthrow of incumbent governments by force and violence is subversive and is engaged in subversive activity. All willful acts that are intended to be detrimental to the best interests of the government and that do not fall into the categories of treason, sedition, sabotage, or espionage will be placed in the category of subversive activity.

Subversive political action: A planned series of activities designed to accomplish political objectives by influencing, dominating, or displacing individuals or groups who are so placed as to affect the decisions and actions of another government.

Superstructure: That portion of a ship above the main deck. The decks are numbered up from the first deck above the main weather deck, the 01 level. Therefore the 05 level is five decks above the main weather deck. The bridge is located in the superstructure.

Suppression fire: Fire directed at an enemy position to keep them from using their own weapons, often applied to allow portions of a friendly unit to reposition without being hit by enemy fire.

Surface-to-air guided missile: A surface-launched (from the ground) guided missile for use against air targets.

Surface-to-surface guided missile: A surface-launched guided missile for use against surface targets.

Surveillance: The systematic observation of aerospace, surface, or subsurface areas, places, persons, or things, by visual, aural, electronic, photographic, or other means.

Table of allowance: An equipment allowance document that prescribes basic needs and availabilities of organizational equipment, and provides the control to develop, revise, or change equipment authorization inventory data.

Tactical nuclear weapon employment: The use of nuclear weapons by land, sea, or air forces against opposing forces, supporting installations or facilities, in support of operations that help accomplish a military mission of limited scope.

Tactical unit: An organization of troops, aircraft, or ships that is intended to serve as a single unit in combat. It may include service units required for its direct support.

Target: An area, complex, installation, force, equipment, capability, function, or behavior identified for possible action.

Task force: A temporary or semi-permanent grouping of units, under one commander, formed to conduct a specific operation or mission.

Terrorism: The calculated use of unlawful violence or threat of unlawful violence to induce fear and intended to coerce or to intimidate governments or societies for political, religious, or ideological reasons.

Terrorist: An individual who uses violence, terror, and intimidation to achieve a result.

Terrorist groups: Any element, regardless of size or espoused cause, that commits acts of violence or threatens violence for political, religious, or ideological reasons.

Terrorist threat condition: A chairman of the Joint Chiefs of Staff-approved program standardizing the Military Services' identification of and recommended responses to terrorist threats against U.S. personnel and facilities. This program facilitates inter-service coordination and support for antiterrorism activities; also called THREATCON. There are four THREATCONs above normal. THREATCON ALPHA applies when there is a general threat

of possible terrorist activity against personnel and facilities, the nature and extent of which are unpredictable, and circumstances do not justify full implementation of THREATCON BRAVO measures. THREATCON BRAVO applies when an increased and more predictable threat of terrorist activity exists. The measures in this THREATCON must be capable of being maintained for weeks without causing undue hardship, affecting operational capability, and aggravating relations with local authorities. THREATCON CHARLIE applies when an incident occurs or intelligence is received indicating some form of terrorist action against personnel and facilities is imminent. Implementation of measures in this THREATCON for more than a short period probably will create hardship and affect the peacetime activities of the unit and its personnel. THREATCON DELTA applies in the immediate area where a terrorist attack has occurred or when intelligence has been received that terrorist action against a specific location or person is likely; normally declared as a localized condition.

Terrorist threat level: An intelligence threat assessment of the level of terrorist threat faced by U.S. personnel and interests in a foreign country. The assessment is based on a continuous intelligence analysis of a minimum of five elements: terrorist group existence, capability, history, trends, and targeting. There are five threat levels: *negligible, low, medium, high,* and *critical.* Threat levels are not the same as terrorist threat conditions (THREATCON). Threat level assessments are provided to senior leaders to assist them in determining the appropriate local THREATCON.

Theater of operations: A sub-area within a theater of war defined by the geographic combatant commander required to conduct or support specific combat operations. Different theaters of operations within the same theater of war will normally be geographically separate and focused on different enemy forces. Theaters of operations are usually of significant size, allowing for operations over extended periods of time.

Theater of war: Defined by the National Command Authorities or the geographic combatant commander, this is the area of air, land, and water that is, or may become, directly involved in the conduct of the war. A theater of war does not normally encompass the geographic combatant commander's entire area of responsibility and may contain more than one theater of operations.

Threat identification and assessment: The Joint Operation Planning and Execution System function that provides timely warning of potential threats to U.S. interests; intelligence collection requirements; the effects of environmental, physical, and health hazards, and cultural factors on friendly and enemy operations; and that determines the enemy military posture and possible intentions.

Toe chain: The smaller of two chains holding the dog tags. It can be draped around the big toe to identify a casualty while the tag on the larger chain goes to Graves Registration.

Transport aircraft: Aircraft designed primarily for the carriage of personnel and/or cargo. Transport aircraft may be classed according to range: *Short-range*: Not to exceed 1200 nautical miles at normal cruising conditions (2222 km); *Medium-range:* Between 1200 and 3500 nautical miles at normal cruising conditions (2222 and 6482 km); or *Long-range:* Exceeds 3500 nautical miles at normal cruising conditions (6482 km).

Treason: Violation of the allegiance owed to one's sovereign or state; betrayal of one's country.

Troops: A collective term for uniformed military personnel (usually not applicable to naval personnel afloat).

Two-person rule: A system designed to prohibit access by a single individual of nuclear weapons and certain designated components by requiring at least two authorized persons, each capable of detecting incorrect or unauthorized procedures with respect to the task to be performed.

Type unit: A type of organizational or functional entity established within the Armed Forces and uniquely identified by a five-character, alphanumeric code called a unit type code.

Unclassified matter: Official matter which does not require the application of security safeguards, but the disclosure of which may be subject to control for other reasons.

Unconventional warfare: A broad spectrum of military and paramilitary operations, normally of long duration, predominantly conducted by indigenous or surrogate forces that are organized, trained, equipped, supported, and directed in varying degrees by an external source. It includes guerrilla warfare and other direct offensive, low visibility, covert, or clandestine operations, as well as indirect activities (subversion, sabotage, intelligence activities, and evasion and escape).

Uncover: To remove the headgear.

Unified Commands: Units under the control of the Joint Chiefs of Staff containing elements from all of the U.S. Armed Forces. They are normally commanded by a four-star general or admiral and are given the title commander in chief.

Uniform Code of Military Justice: The system of justice for the military services, a federal law enacted by Congress. It replaced the "Rocks and Shoals" system of justice practiced previously in the Naval service.

Uniformed services: The five armed services (Army, Navy, Air Force, Marine Corps, and Coast Guard) plus the commissioned corps of the U.S. Public Health Service and the U.S. Coast and Geodetic Survey.

Unilateral arms control measure: An arms control course of action taken by a nation without any compensating concession required of other nations.

Urgent priority: A category of immediate mission request that is lower than *emergency priority* but takes precedence over *ordinary priority*; e.g., enemy artillery or mortar fire that is falling on friendly troops and causing casualties or enemy troops or mechanized units moving up in such force as to threaten a breakthrough.

Use of force policy: Policy guidance issued by the commandant, U.S. Coast Guard, on the use of force and weapons.

U.S. national: U.S. citizen and U.S. permanent and temporary legal resident aliens.

Vital area: A designated area or installation to be defended by air defense units.

War reserves: Stocks of matériel amassed in peacetime to meet the increase in military requirements consequent upon an outbreak of war. War reserves are intended to provide enough interim support essential to sustain operations until resupply can occur.

Warhead: That part of a missile, projectile, torpedo, rocket, or other munition which contains either the nuclear or thermonuclear system, high explosive system, chemical or biological agents, or inert materials intended to inflict damage.

Wartime load: The maximum quantity of supplies of all kinds which a ship can carry.

Wave: A formation of forces, landing ships, craft, amphibious vehicles or aircraft, required to beach or land about the same time.

Weapons of mass destruction: Weapons capable of a high order of destruction and/or of being used in such a manner as to destroy large numbers of people. Weapons of mass destruction (WMD) can be high explosives or nuclear, biological, chemical, and radiological weapons.

Weapons readiness state: The degree of readiness of air defense weapons that can become airborne or be launched to carry out an assigned task. Weapons readiness states are expressed in numbers of weapons and numbers of minutes. Weapon readiness states are defined as follows: two, five, fifteen, or thirty minutes or one, or three hours, such that weapons can be launched within x (length of time) minutes or hours.

Wing: 1. An Air Force unit composed normally of one primary mission group and the necessary supporting organizations; 2. A fleet air wing is the basic organizational and administrative unit for naval-, land-, and tender-based aviation. Such wings are mobile units to which are assigned aircraft squadrons and tenders for administrative organization control; 3. A balanced Marine Corps task organization of aircraft groups and squadrons, together with appropriate command, air control, administrative, service, and maintenance units. A standard Marine Corps aircraft wing contains the aviation elements normally required for the air support of a Marine division.

Zone of fire: An area into which a designated ground unit or fire support ship delivers, or is prepared to deliver, fire support. Fire may or may not be observed.

COMMON ABBREVIATIONS AND ACRONYMS

A&P: Administrative and personnel

A/C: Aircraft

A/G: Air to ground.

A/O: Area of operations

A2C2: Army airspace command and control

AAFES: Army and Air Force Exchange Service

AAMDC: Area air and missile defense command

AAV: Amphibious assault vehicle

AAW: Antiair warfare

AB: Airbase

ABN: Airborne

ABNCP: Airborne Command Post

AC: Active component

ACCS: Air command and control system

ACE: Airborne command element (USAF)

ACK: Acknowledgment

ACU: Assault craft unit

ACV: Air cushion vehicle; armored combat vehicle

AD: Active duty

ADA: Air defense artillery

ADE: Air defense emergency; assign digit editing

ADIZ: Air defense identification zone

ADMIN: Administration

AE: Assault echelon

AEW: Airborne early warning; air expeditionary wing

AF: Amphibious force

AFB: Air Force base

AFR: Air Force Reserve

AFRTS: American Forces Radio and Television Service

AFSC: Air Force Specialty Code, the Air Force equivalent of an MOS

AFSOF: Air Force special operations forces

AG: Adjutant general (Army)

AMCIT: American citizen

AMMO: Ammunition

ANG: Air National Guard

AOB: Advanced operations base

AOC: Air operations center

AOL: Area of limitation

AOS: Area of separation

AR: Army Reserve

ARA: Aerial rocket artillery

ARFOR: Army forces

ARNG: Army National Guard

ARSOF: Army special operations forces

ASVAB: Armed Services Vocational Aptitude Battery (skills test) required to join the armed forces

AT: Antiterrorism

AWACS: Airborne Warning and Control System

BAQ: Basic Allowance for Quarters

BAS: Basic Allowance for Subsistence

BDA: Battle damage assessment

BDE: Brigade

BDU: Battle dress uniform

BDZ: Base defense zone

BEQ: Bachelor enlisted quarters (barracks)

BI: Battle injury

BMDO: Ballistic Missile Defense Organization

BOQ: Bachelor officer quarters

BP: Battle position

BS: Battle staff; broadcast source

BSU: Blood supply unit

C2: Command and control

C-2W: Command and control warfare

C4 Systems: Command, control, communications, and computer systems

CA: Civil affairs; combat assessment

CANUS: Canada–United States

CAO: Casualty assistance officer

CAR: Chief of the Army Reserve

CAW: Carrier air wing

CAX: Combined arms exercise

CAX: Computer-assisted exercise

CB, C-B: Chemical-biological

CBR: Chemical, biological, and radiological

CBRT: Chemical-biological response team

CBT: Combating terrorism

CBTZ: Combat zone

CBTZ: Combat zone

CBU: Cluster bomb unit

CBW: Chemical and biological warfare

CBW: Chemical and biological warfare

CC&D: Camouflage, concealment, and deception

CC: Command center; correctional custody

CD: Counterdrug

CDR: Commander

CEE: Captured enemy equipment

CFR: Code of Federal Regulations

CG: Commanding general

CGIS: Coast Guard Investigative Service

CHAMPUS: Civilian Health and Medical Program for the Uniformed Services

CI: Counterintelligence

CIC: Combat information center

CINC: Commander in chief

CINCENT: Commander in chief Central Command. (In the Gulf War, it referred to General Schwarzkopf.)

CIV: Civilian

CMC: Commandant of the Marine Corps

CMD: Command; cruise missile defense

CMO: Chief medical officer

CNO: Chief of Naval Operations

CO: Commanding officer

COA: Course of action

COE: Army Corps of Engineers

COGARD: Coast Guard

COIN: Counterinsurgency

COMINT: Communications intelligence

COMSEC: Communications security

COMSEC: Communications security

CONUS: Continental United States

CONUSA: Continental United States Army

CP& I: Coastal patrol and interdiction

CP: Command post

CPO: Chief petty officer

CS: Chief of staff

CSA: Chief of staff, United States Army

DA: Department of the Army

DART: Disaster Assistance Response team

DEROS: Date of expected return from overseas

DFT: Deployment for training

DH: Death due to hostilities

DI: DIA Directorate for Intelligence Production; drill instructor

DIA: Defense Intelligence Agency

DISUM: Daily intelligence summary

DITSUM: Defense intelligence terrorist summary

DNI: Director of Naval Intelligence

DNIF: Duty not involving flying

DO: Duty officer (AF)

DOA: Dead on arrival

DOD Civilian: Civilian Department of Defense employee

DOD: Department of Defense

DON: Department of the Navy

DOR: Date of rank

DOS: Date of separation

DUSTWUN: Duty status— whereabouts unknown

DVA: Department of Veterans Affairs

DZ: Drop zone

E&E: Escape and evasion

EA: Engagement area

EAD: Earliest arrival date

EAP: Emergency action plan

EAS: End of active service

EAT: Earliest arrival time

ECCM: Electronic counter-counter measures

ELINT: Electronic intelligence

ENL: Enlisted

EPA: Evasion plan of action

EPW: Enemy prisoner of war

EUSA: Eighth U.S. Army

EW: Electronic warfare

FA: Field artillery

FAAD: Forward antiair defense

FDO: Flight deck officer

FEZ: Fighter engagement zone

FLOT: Forward line of own troops

FLS: Naval forward logistics site

FMCR: Fleet Marine Corps Reserve

FMF: Fleet Marine Force

FOD: Foreign object damage

FRD: Formerly restricted data

FSU: Former Soviet Union; forward support unit

FWD: Forward

G/A: Ground-to-air

GBR: Ground-based radar

GC: Geneva Convention(s)

GCM: General court-martial

GI: Government issue

GUARD: U.S. National Guard and Air Guard

GW: Guerrilla warfare

GWOT: Global War on Terrorism

HAZ: Hazardous cargo

HAZMAT: Hazardous materials

HE: High explosive

HEAT: High explosive antitank

HQ: Headquarters

HW: Hazardous waste

IC: Inspected and condemned by inspector; initials that were marked on equipment unfit for military service

IC3: Integrated command, control, and communications

IFRC: International Federation of Red Cross and Red Crescent Societies

IG: Inspector general

III: Incapacitating illness or injury

INCOC: Infantry noncommissioned officer's course

INF: Infantry

INTERPOL: International Criminal Police Organization

JAG: Judge Advocate General

LES: Leave and earnings statement

LF: Landing force; low frequency

LNO: Liaison officer

LRRP: Long-range reconnaissance patrol

LZ: Helicopter landing zone

MACG: Marine air control group

MACOM: Major command (Army)

MAF: Mobility air forces

MAG: Marine aircraft group

MAJCOM: Major command (USAF)

MARDIV: Marine division

MASH: Mobile Army surgical hospital

MAW: Marine aircraft win

MCCDC: Marine Corps Combat Development Command

MEB: Marine expeditionary brigade

MEDCOM: U.S. Army Medical Command

MEDEVAC: Medical evacuation

MEF: Marine expeditionary force

MEU: Marine expeditionary unit

MIA: Missing in action

MIB: Military Intelligence Board

MILDEC: Military deception

MILSPEC: Military performance specification

MNF: Multinational Force

MO: Medical officer

MOS: Military Occupational Specialty

MP: Military police

MP: Military police

MRE: Meal, ready-to-eat

MSG: Marine security guard

MTW: Major theater war

MWSG: Marine wing support group

MWSS: Marine wing support squadron

NAS: Naval air station

NASA: National Aeronautics and Space Administration

NATO: North Atlantic Treaty Organization

NAVFOR: Navy forces

NBC: Nuclear, biological, and chemical

NBI: Nonbattle injury

NCA: National command authorities

NCIS: Naval Criminal Investigation Service

NCO: Noncommissioned officer

NCOIC: Noncommissioned officer in charge

NDA: National defense area

NDAA: National Defense Authorization Act

NDRF: National Defense Reserve Fleet

NFA: No-fire area

NFO: Naval flight officer

NG: National Guard

NIE: National intelligence estimate

NJP: Nonjudicial punishment

NMD: National missile defense

NOFORN: Not releasable to foreign nationals

NOK: Next of kin

NOP: Nuclear operations

NORAD: North American Aerospace Defense Command

NSL: No-strike list

NTU: New threat upgrade

NUCINT: Nuclear intelligence

OB: Observation balloon

OCS: Officer Candidate School

OD: Officer of the day

OIC: Officer in charge

OP: Observation post

OP3: Overt peacetime psychological operations program

OPTINT: Optical intelligence

OPZONE: Operation zone

OR: Operational readiness

OSD: Office of the secretary of defense

OSIA: On-site inspection activity

OSS: Office of Strategic Services (precursor to CIA)

OTS: Officer Training School

PIO: Public information officer

PO: Petty officer

POTUS: President of the United States

POV: Privately owned vehicle

POW: Prisoner of war

PRCA: Presidential Reserve callup authority

PRU: Pararescue unit

PSYOP: Psychological operations

PSYWA: Psychological warfare

PT: Physical training

PTSD: Post-traumatic stress disorder

PX: Post exchange

R&R: Rest and recuperation

RECON: Reconnaissance

RET: Retired

RFA: Restricted fire area

ROE: Rules of engagement

S&D: Search and destroy

SA: Staging area

SAI: Sea-to-air interface

SAR: Search and rescue

SDIO: Strategic Defense Initiative Organization

SDO: Staff (or squadron) duty officer

SEABEE: Navy construction branch

SEAL: Sea-air-land special operations force of the Navy

SECAF: Secretary of the Air Force

SECARMY: Secretary of the Army

SECDEF: Secretary of Defense

SECNAV: Secretary of the Navy

SECSTATE: Secretary of state

SF: Special Forces

SIO: Senior intelligence officer

SITREP: Situation report

SJA: Staff judge advocate

SNCO: Staff noncommissioned officer

SNF: Strategic nuclear forces

SOC: Special operations capable

SOF: Special operations forces

SOPA: Senior officer present afloat

SP: Shore patrol

SRB: Service record book

SRU: Search and rescue unit

START: Strategic Arms Reduction Treaty

TA: Theater Army

TAF: Tactical air force

TAW: Tactical airlift wing

TDY: Temporary duty

TNF: Theater nuclear force

UA: Unauthorized absence

UCMJ: Uniform Code of Military Justice

UD: Undesirable Discharge

UDT: Underwater demolition team

UNSC: United Nation Security Council

USA: United States Army

USACE: United States Army Corps of Engineers

USAF: United States Air Force

USAFR: United States Air Force Reserve

USAR: United States Army Reserve

USCG: United States Coast Guard

USG: United States government

USIA: United States Information Agency

USM: United States Marine Corps

USMCR: United States Marine Corps Reserve

USN: United States Navy

USNR: United States Navy Reserve

USNS: United States Naval ship

USW: Undersea warfare

UW: Unconventional warfare

UXO: Unexploded explosive ordnance; unexploded ordnance

VA: Veterans Administration.

WATCHCO: Watch condition

WEZ: Weapon engagement zone

WMD: Weapons of mass destruction

WMP: War and mobilization plan

XO: Executive officer, second in command

★
GLOSSARY B

Slang and Expressions
Used by the U.S. Military

Slang expressions used in the military are generated out of humor, cynicism, sarcasm, and other emotions as a means to deal with ugly, stressful, painful, or difficult conditions that are a part of military life. Without humor, many service personnel would face greater difficulty in handling the strife of active military operations. The humor ranges from mild to sick; again, bear in mind the source and the situation from which these terms were derived. Many people may consider some of these terms offensive. If you are easily offended, you may like to skip this section.

We have attempted to include a selection of common, interesting, or colorful terms that civilians may have heard but not understood, or that civilians may never have come in contact with. Of course, this selection is by no means complete. Additionally, many terms may have changed by the time this reference is in print, and others may have gone out of fashion. New conflicts, equipment, and situations breed more terminology on a continual basis. Some terms are identified if they pertain or arose during a particular conflict.

COMMON MILITARY SLANG AND EXPRESSIONS

4-Striper: A Navy or Coast Guard captain, referring to the four wide stripes worn on the cuffs of the blue uniform by captains.

86: To throw away or get rid of something. From the number of the form originally used to remove an item from a stock record.

90-Day Wonder: Unflattering term for an OCS graduate. Refers to the early practice of training commissioned officers in three months rather than the four years in the Naval Academy or the four-year part-time training in ROTC. Also, "90-day blunder."

1369: The MOS for Vietnam service in USMC, an unlucky number.

1900: Homosexual, from the paragraph in the Separations Manual in the 1970s and 1980s that discusses homosexuals.

A month and a month: Punishment via court-martial, with a month in the brig and a month's salary docked from one's pay.

Abdul: Turks or Arabs (males), depending on era and conflict. From World War I on.

Ack-Ack: Antiaircraft artillery (World War II), referencing the phonetic alphabet "A." Also, "Triple A" in the Gulf Wars.

Across the wire: Term applied when American forces crossed into Laos, Cambodia, or North Vietnam.

Admiral's doorbell: The yellow button in an F/A-18 cockpit that jettisons all the external stores in an emergency. If you hit it, you'll be "ringing the admiral's doorbell" to explain why.

Aiming stakes: Stripes on an officer's helmet which aided snipers in selecting commanding officers more than it actually helped friendly forces.

Air bear: Member of military police.

Air to mud: Air-to-ground fire.

Air start: Blow job.

Airedale: Insulting term for a Navy flier.

Airplane driver: Pilot.

A.J. squared away: A Marine with everything in place and in order; i.e., the perfect Marine and the opposite of "Joe Shit, the Rag Man."

Ali Baba: An enemy combatant, a looter, or any bad guy. (Iraqi Freedom)

Alibi: A round fired to compensate for a previous miss.

Alpha-Bravo: Ambush. From phonetic letters for first letters in syllables.

Alpha Unit: A Marine's spouse.

Aluminum Cloud: The F-14, because it's so large.

Ambush academy: Courses in jungle warfare.

AMF: Phonetic for "Adios, motherfucker." Good-bye.

Anchor clanker or anchorhead: U.S. Coast Guardsperson.

And a wake-up: The day you leave an ongoing duty assignment; usually when leaving a combat zone or leaving the service, used to count down to the transition. For example, if today is Monday and you leave on Friday, you would have "three days and a wake-up" to go.

Angels: Altitude, e.g., "Angels 20" refers to aircraft at 20,000 feet. (Gulf War)

Angles: Gaining angles on a dogfight opponent involves maneuvering for a shot. The ultimate in an angles fight is an angle of zero, straight up the enemy's tailpipe.

Ant Hill: An outpost with major communications assets apparent from the large number of antennae in the vicinity.

Ape: Air Force military police, from AP, air police.

Apple knocker: Farm boy.

Applesauce enema: Tactful rebuke from a superior.

Area bird: West Point cadet assigned to walk the yard in punishment.

Army brat: Child of Army serviceperson, particularly of an officer.

Army dick: Military police.

Arty: Artillery.

ARVN: Army of the Republic of Vietnam or member thereof.

Ash and trash: (also *ash and trash*): A one-helicopter supply mission in Vietnam.

Ashtray: The desert. Think of hotel ashtrays filled with sand.

Ass hanging out: Refers to someone displaying ignorance or stupidity.

Assholes to elbows: Troops or persons crowded close together.

Attaboy: American soldier. (World War I)

Aussie: Australian.

Baby navy: U.S. Coast Guard.

Back to the taxpayers: Where you send a wrecked aircraft.

Bad paper: Other than honorable discharge.

Bag: Flight suit or anti-exposure suit.

Ballgame: Encounter with the enemy; a firefight.

BAM: Pejorative for a female Marine ("broad-assed Marine").

Bandaid: Navy corpsman.

Bandit: Dogfight adversary positively identified as a hostile aircraft.

Bat decoder: A sheet of paper carried on all fight operations that is the key to current airborne communication codes.

Bat turn: A tight, high-G change of heading, in reference to the rapid 180-degree Batmobile maneuver in the old *Batman* television series.

Bathroom stationery: Toilet paper.

Battle rattle: Full combat gear.

BB stacker: Anyone dealing directly with ordnance.

BCD: Bad conduct discharge. Also, "big chicken dinner," but meaning the same thing.

Beach: The desert. (Gulf Wars)

Bedpan commando: Navy corpsman.

Beetlecruncher: Army soldier.

Believer: Dead enemy soldier.

Best girl's on the tow rope: Good weather on the homeward cruise.

Big boy: Any large round.

Big red: The desert sun. (Gulf Wars)

Bigot: Code for very top secret.

Bilge rat: The unfortunate sailors who drain and maintain the bilge on ship or a Marine who was assigned to bilge duty as a form of nonjudicial punishment.

Bingo: Minimum fuel for a comfortable and safe return to base. An aircraft can fly and fight past bingo fuel in combat situations, but at considerable peril.

Bird, ball, and hook: Slur referring to the Marines emblem of Eagle, Globe, and Anchor.

Bird colonel: A full colonel.

Bird farm: Aircraft carrier.

Birdmen: A pejorative term for airmen.

Birdshit: Paratroopers (because they fall from the sky).

Blanket party: Uncommon but effective method of encouraging a screwup to mend his ways: While sleeping, his platoon mates cover him with a blanket and hit the body inside—an unauthorized and punishable activity.

Black hat: Airborne instructor.

Blast: A parachute jump. First parachute jump after Parachutist (Jump) School, i.e., the sixth parachute jump, is a "Cherry Blast." A person qualified to wear the Master Parachutist Badge is a "Master Blaster." "Hollywood Blast" is a parachute jump, usually done simply for pay purposes, without all the encumbering equipment necessary in real or simulated airborne assaults.

Blind pig: Huge shell from a trench mortar.

Blooper: M79, 40mm grenade launcher and the soldier who fires it.

Blue canoe: A portable (chemical) toilet.

Blue ticket: One step above dishonorable discharge, granted for medical issue or mental instability, so-called for the blue paper it was printed on.

Blue water sailor: Sailor on the deep seas (Navy), as opposed to members of the Coast Guard ("shallow water sailors").

Blueblood: Former enlisted Marine who accepted a commission.

Bluesuiter: High-ranking officer in the Air Force whose duty requires the wearing of the Class A (dress) uniform daily.

Boards Out: When speed brakes are extended on an aircraft.

Bobtail: Dishonorable discharge. The term alludes to the trimming off of the portion of one's discharge papers that contain the "dishonorable" wording.

BOHICA: "Bend over, here it comes again." You're about to get screwed.

Bone dome: Kevlar helmet.

Boot: A green recruit.

Boots and utes: Utility uniform (field uniform) and boots, used especially in physical training.

Brains: Intelligence officer.

Brass: Officers (who generally wear brass buttons on their uniforms).

Brass Louie: Lieutenant.

Brig chaser: A Marine, now normally an MP, assigned to guard a prisoner while being transported to a location outside the brig, often for a work detail.

Brig rat: A prisoner or someone who is frequently in trouble.

Brown hat: Drill sergeant.

Brown round: Drill sergeant's hat.

Bubble chaser: Dishwasher or anyone with kitchen duty.

Bubblehead: Submariner.

Buck private: A private, or the lowest-ranking government employee. (World War I, World War II)

Buck sergeant: Sergeant.

Bucket brigade: U.S. Coast Guard.

Bullet bait: Green soldier.

Bullet-stopper: A Marine.

Bumfucknowhere: Or "Bumfuck Egypt," meaning in the middle of nowhere—very remote.

Bunion breeder or bunion buster: Infantryman.

Bushmasters: Jungle-skilled warriors.

Bust caps: A firefight; the actual firing of a weapon.

Butter bars: The insignia for a second lieutenant; from the appearance of the individual yellow bars on each shoulder or lapel.

Buzzer: Signal corpsman.

C and S: Clean and sober, the way a sailor was supposed to be after liberty.

Cabbage: Paper money, for its green color.

Cadillac: Marine Corps-issued boots—transportation for recruits and infantry Marines.

Camel spider: Tarantula. Gulf War.

Cammies: Government-issued camouflage uniforms.

Can: Airplane.

Cannon cocker: A Marine in the artillery or a Navy gunner's mate.

Cannon fodder: Soldiers.

Canoe U: The U.S. Naval Academy.

Cashiered: Dishonorably discharged from the military as a result of court-martial.

Cat 4: Applicants who scored next to the lowest on the entrance exams. Under normal circumstances, they are not allowed to enlist, but during times of war and when recruiting is diffi-cult, a number of them are allowed to join. In the 1960s, the Pentagon utilized Project 100,000 in which a great number of Cat 4 enlistees were taken in. For classification purposes, the category was further broken down to 4a, 4b, or 4c, nicknamed by recruiters as "animal," "vegetable," or "mineral."

Cat 9: A reference to someone as "beyond dumb" since Category 4 is the lowest of the scores on the entrance exams.

Centurion: An aviator who has made one hundred shipboard landings on one carrier; a centurion patch is then issued and proudly worn on the flight jacket.

CFB: Clear as a fucking bell.

Chancre mechanic: Medic or corpsman.

Charlie: A Viet Communist soldier, abbreviated VC or Victor Charlie, thus Charlie.

Charlie tango: Control tower, in alphabet code.

Check six: Look directly behind you. Twelve o'clock means directly in front, six o'clock means directly behind, etc.

Cheese: To brown nose, to suck up to superior personnel.

Cherry Boy: A newcomer to the Orient.

Cherubs: Altitude less than 1,000 feet, measured in hundreds of feet ("cherubs two" means 200 feet).

Chicken of the sea: Submariners, whose job it is to avoid detection.

Chi-Com: Chinese Communists. (Vietnam)

Chief: Unofficial form of address for any Warrant Officer (WO1 to CW5).

Chink: Pejorative for Chinese.

Choggie: A Korean who carried supplies for the American military.

Chuck: A reference to white Marines by black Marines. (Vietnam)

Cinderella liberty: Liberty that ended at midnight.

Civil serpent: Civil servant.

Class 1 download: Bowel movement.

Clerks and jerks: Clerical workers, as opposed to those who do the dirty work in the field.

CNX: "Cank." Cancel.

Coffin nails: Cheap cigarettes.

Combat dump: A bowel movement before flying; also called "sending a Marine to sea."

Coolie: Asian laborer hired for manual work.

Cosmoline gang: U.S. Coast Guard, who carried large drums of cosmoline to keep guns from rusting.

Crash and dash: Aircraft landing followed by immediate takeoff.

Crate: Aircraft.

Crispy critters: Persons burned to a crisp by napalm. (Vietnam)

Crow hooks: Chevrons of an NCO. (Civil War)

Crunchies: Infantrymen, for the sound their feet made on the ground when marching.

Cut one's cable: To die or be killed. (Navy)

Cut the painter: To die; a term derived from a ship's painter or mooring line, which when cut, lets the ship drift out to sea.

CYA: Cover your ass.

D and D: Drunk and dirty, notation when a seaman returned to ship in unclean and unsober condition.

Daisy pusher: Fatal injury.

Darbies: Wrist or leg iron on prisoners.

Dark greens: African American Marines.

Dash ten: An operator's manual for any piece of military equipment, vehicle, or aircraft.

Dash two: The second plane in a two-or-more aircraft formation; the wingman.

Davy Jones's Locker: The bottom of the sea, where a dead soldier's body goes. Davy Jones is traditional naval parlance for the Devil of the Seas.

Dead dog: Empty beer bottle.

Dear John letter: Since World War II, this refers to letters from loved ones at home advising that the relationship is over.

Deck ape: Anyone in the Deck Force onboard ship (those sailors who chip paint, swab decks, etc.).

Delta delta: Dependent daughter, from phonetic alphabet.

Delta hotel: Dependent husband, from phonetic alphabet.

Delta sierra: Dumb shit, from phonetic alphabet.

Delta whiskey: Dependent wife, from phonetic alphabet.

Desk pilot: Qualified pilot assigned to desk duty.

Deuce: Common utility truck (2.5-ton truck—from "deuce-and-a-half).

Devil doc: Nickname for Navy hospital corpsmen assigned to Marine Corps field units.

Devil dogs: Marines, from the German nickname for Marines, *teufelshunden*.

Dick cheese: Term used for someone of little or no value as a person or a member of a unit or team.

Diddy pin: Single gold bar of rank of a second lieutenant, from similarity to diaper "diddy" pins.

Dink: Enemy or, generically, Vietnamese. (Vietnam)

DIP: Die in place. Defend the position until you die.

Dirt sailor: Seabee, naval construction team member.

Dirty: Aircraft configured for landing with gear and flaps down.

Dit-dat artist: Morse code operator.

Dive bomb: To clean an area, diving on trash like a dive bomber aims for its target.

Do a rug dance: A long, amorous good-bye.

Doc: Navy enlisted medical corpsmen assigned to duty with Marine Corps combat units. These sailors are generally given the same respect that one Marine gives to another Marine. In fact, Navy corpsmen who earn service medals during duty with the Marine Corps are authorized to wear a miniature Eagle, Globe, and Anchor on their ribbon—something not even authorized for Marines.

Dodo: AF cadet who has not yet soloed, after the flightless extinct bird.

Dog robber: An aide to a general officer whose duties are so varied as to defy explanation.

Dog tags: ID tags issued to soldiers that resemble dog licenses.

Doggies: A pejorative term for soldiers.

Dolphins: Term for submariners, also "pukin' fish," "tin tunas."

Dot: Refers to how a distant aircraft looks on the horizon. "I'm a dot" means "I'm out of here."

Down range: Physically in a combat zone.

Drill: Drill sergeant.

Drill injector: Drill Instructor.

Drink: Any body of water.

Duck walk: Walking with the knees bent 90 degrees.

Eagle farts: Payday.

El Cid: The CIA.

Eleven Bang-Bang (or Body Bag, Brav, Bullet Catcher, or Bush): An infantryman, from the MOS code for infantry.

Eleven Charlie: A mortarman, from the MOS code.

Eleven on a side: British Army officer's regulation thin moustache, said to have eleven hairs on each side.

Emma gee: Slang for machine gun or gunner.

E-nothing: Serviceman who's essential value is less than E-1 ranking.

Exercise the landing gear: To walk.

Eyewash: Superficial improvements or additions.

Fat friend: Military observation balloon.

Fatal pill: Cannonball.

Feet wet/dry: The former means "over water," the latter "over land."

Fiddler's Green: Heaven for a mariner. Opposite of Davy Jones's Locker.

Field day: Barracks cleanup.

Field grey: German.

FIGMO: "Fuck it, got my orders."

Fish: Torpedo.

Flatfoot: Pejorative for U.S. Coast Guardsperson.

Fluff-n-buff: Cammies that were dried (fluff dry) and not pressed, and boots that were brushed (buffed) but not spit polished, or the person wearing such an outfit.

Flyby: A missile that misses.

Flying elephant: Military observation balloon.

Flying fish: Rifle grenade.

Flying gadget: Cadet.

FNG: Fucking new guy.

FOAD: "Fuck off and die."

Foxtrot: Alphabet code for obscenity "fuck."

Foxtrot bravo: Fucking bastard.

Frag: To kill, especially via grenade.

Freedom bird: Any plane carrying American troops home.

Fresh fish: Green recruit.

Freshwater navy: U.S. Coast Guard.

Fritz: A German.

Frog: A Frenchman.

Front leaning rest position: The position for push-ups.

Fruit salad: Ribbon bars worn on the left breast of the uniform, especially when in large quantity.

FTA: Fuck the Army.

FTN: Fuck the Navy.

FUBAR: Fucked up beyond all recognition.

FUJIBAR: "Fuck you buddy, I'm just a Reservist."

Full bird: Full colonel (O-6).

FUMTU: Fucked up more than usual.

Fur ball: A confused aerial engagement with many combatants.

GAF: Give a fuck.

Garters: Leg irons worn by prisoners.

Geese: Enemy bomber formation.

Get a hat: To leave.

Ghost turds: Blanket lint, that accumulates as if by magic.

Gink: Vietnamese person.

Glad bag: Body bag.

Go juice: Jet fuel.

Go over the hill: To desert or go AWOL.

Go west: To die, "to go into the sunset." Refers to individuals or aircraft.

Goat: Cadet at the very bottom of the class; the lowest-ranking officer.

Goat locker: Navy Chief Petty Officer's quarters.

Gob: Enlisted Navy man.

Gob gully: Naval route.

Goes away: What something does when you hit it with a missile.

Gofasters: Sneakers.

Gomer: Marine; also a North Vietnamese person.

Gone Elvis: Missing in action. Refers to frequent sightings of Elvis despite his death decades ago.

Gone goose: Ship that is deserted, assuming it will soon be destroyed.

Good cookie: Marine Corps Good Conduct Medal.

Good to the last drop: Paratroopers.

Goodie: Booby trap.

Goofy discharge: Discharge for mental instability.

Gook: Pejorative for Asian.

GOYA: Get off your ass.

Grandma: 15-inch howitzer, so named because it is short and stout.

Grassed: A cavalryman thrown from his horse.

Gravel cruncher: Infantryman.

Graveyard watch or graveyard duty: Duty time from midnight to four or six A.M.

Grease: To kill (Vietnam).

Green apple: The control knob for the cockpit's emergency oxygen supply.

Green banana: Same as a Dear John letter. (World War II, Pacific region)

Green Machine: The Army and its bureaucracy.

Greenie beanies: Army Special Forces, due to their green berets.

Ground squirrel: Nonflying member of the aviation Corps.

Groundhog: Nonflying member of the Air Force; also, any infantryman.

Group tighteners: A nonexistent search and fetch item for rookies.

Grunt: Infantryman, especially Marines, but includes anyone undergoing combat under ugly, dirty conditions.

Gun bunny: Pejorative term for someone in the field artillery.

Gung ho: Person eager and ready to accomplish whatever task necessary.

Gungy: Gung ho, but usually to express in an "inexperienced, just-out-of-recruit-training" way.

Gunny: Gunnery sergeant.

Guppy: Someone not SCUBA trained.

Gut truck: Food vendor on wheels, especially in training areas

Gyppo: Pejorative for Egyptian.

Half-loot: Second lieutenant.

Haj, Haji or Haçi: An Iraqi citizen; local good guy. (Gulf Wars)

Hang out the laundry: Drop paratroopers from a plane.

Hard charger: Seasoned combat Marine.

Heine: A German. From common name Heinrich.

High and tight: The traditional Marine haircut.

Hike: A march.

HMFIC: Head Mother Fucker in Charge.

Hollywood Marines: Recruits who went to Boot Camp at Marine Corps Recruit Depot, San Diego.

Holy Joe: Chaplain or religious man.

Hoo-ah: A spirited cry, which can mean nearly anything positive. Short for "Heard, Understood, and Acknowledged."

Hooch: A soldier's dwelling in-country, from hut to barracks (originated in Vietnam).

Hooligan navy: Pejorative for U.S. Coast Guard.

Hoosegow: Jail.

Hop: A mission, or flight.

Horizontal exercise: To sleep.

Hospital corners: A method of making a rack (bed) where the top blanket is squared off at the corners leaving one 45 degree angle on each corner.

House mouse duty: Assignment of assisting the DI with menial tasks, such as making up the DI's bunks, polishing his sword, and so on.

Huffed: Death by parachuting or falling from aircraft in flight.

Hump: To march or move on foot in combat gear.

Hundred and worst: 101st Airborne Division.

Hurry up and wait: Phrase describing military routine.

Iddy-umpty: Signal corpsman.

Idiot seat: Copilot's seat in a two-seater aircraft.

In the tub: Washed out of a training program.

Indian night noises: Ominous creaks, shudders, or other sounds of an aircraft in flight.

Ink stick: Ink pen.

Iodine spiller: Navy corpsman.

Irish pennant: Loose thread.

Ivan: A Russian or the Russian Army.

Jack or Jackie: A sailor (enlisted Navy man); also money.

JANFU: Joint Army-Navy fuck up.

Jarhead: A Marine.

Jazz it: Fly too close to the ground.

Jerry: German.

Jesus nut: The last nut holding a helicopter blade in place. When it fails, the crew will be joining Jesus.

Jody: Traditionally the civilian who moves in on your girl while you are serving your country.

Joe Shit: The generic screwup.

Johnny: A Turk.

Jump ship: To leave a ship without official authorization; to go AWOL.

Kick: Dishonorable discharge.

Kiwi: Nonflying member of Air Corps.

Kiwi injection: A good, sharp, quick kick in the rear.

Klick: Kilometer.

Kraut: Anything German.

LC: Line crosser, a defector. (Gulf Wars)

LEAPEX: A jump-through-your-ass project, exercise, or drill. Something unnecessary that needs to be done immediately.

Leather bumper: Cavalryman.

Leatherneck: Marine.

Leg: Derogatory term used in airborne units meaning a person or a military unit that is not qualified for parachute operations. The "sanctioned" term is NAP (Non-Airborne Personnel).

Lights out: Radar off.

Lost and found badge: Army name tag.

LPC: "Leather Personnel Carriers," i.e., shoes or boots.

Maggie's drawers: The red flag waved at a Marine Corps firing range, which signals a miss.

Maggot: Small, fast airplane that guards reconnaissance planes.

Martin-Baker fan club: If you eject, you're a member (a reference to the Martin-Baker company, manufacturer of ejection seats). An official list of members is maintained.

Meat fleet: Hospital ship(s).

Moonbeam: Flashlight.

Mosquito wings: An E-2 rank insignia (one stripe).

Mother: Howitzer smaller than a grandma; usually a 12-inch howitzer.

Muddy water sailors: U.S. Coast Guard.

Mummy sack: Same as body bag.

Mustang: Former enlisted Army person who becomes an officer.

Muzzle monkeys: Pejorative term for artillerymen; derived from the fact that artillerymen would sometimes have to hang from the Howitzer barrel as a counterweight so the gun could be turned. Usually used by infantrymen.

Navy showers: The process and duration aboard ship for showering: 1) wet down, 2) soap up, 3) rinse off, using no more than one to two minutes of water—salt water may be abundant, but fresh water is precious.

NFG: No fucking good.

Ninety-day wonder: Second lieutenant.

Non-qual: A Marine who did not qualify as an expert, sharpshooter, or marksman on the rifle range. Non-quals do not graduate from Boot Camp.

Number One: The best. Used by Vietnamese to compliment infantrymen

they liked, e.g., calling them "Number One GI."

Number Ten: The worst. Used by Vietnamese to insult infantrymen they disliked, e.g., calling them "Number Ten GI;" the logic was that if Number One was the best, Number Ten must be the worst.

Nylon letdown: Ejection and subsequent parachute ride.

O-club: Officer's club.

O-dark-thirty: Early in the morning.

Old issue: Old soldier.

On the pegs: Under arrest.

One-up: Lance corporal, with one stripe.

One-winger: Air or combat observer, who wears a one-winged insignia.

Ooohraah: A sound made by a Marine to indicate agreement or to provide encouragement.

Orderly room: First sergeant/CO's office.

Oscar: The name of the dummy used for man overboard drills. Also, the flag that is hoisted when there is a man overboard (the flag for the letter *O*).

030SHIT: Pronounced "Oh three, Oh shit," this is the Military Occupational Specialty of a junior infantry officer.

Over the hill: Unauthorized absence.

Page 11: The page in the Marine's service record book containing a chronological listing of favorable and unfavorable actions. The entries can range from listing a DUI to records of courts-martial to warnings about the length of the grass at your assigned quarters. Positive entries include everything from a thank-you letter from a community agency to a Medal of Honor. Page 11 entries stay with a Marine for life.

Passing gas: What an aerial tanker does by refueling other aircraft.

Pearl-diver: Dishwasher.

Philippine haircut: A slit throat.

Piece: Rifle.

PIW: Person in the water. (Coast Guard term)

Plumber: An inept pilot.

Poge: Military personnel who are in a position to grant minor favors. It may be spelled various ways, such as pogey, pogie, pogy, pogee.

Pogey bait: Junk food. Expression refers to "bribing" office poges with junk food for purpose of granting minor favors.

Pom-pom: Large caliber (40mm) machine gun used as antiaircraft.

Poolee: An unofficial rank assigned by recruiters to newly enlisted recruits in the delayed entry program and awaiting departure to recruit training.

Pound one's ear: To sleep.

Powwow: Meeting of senior officers.

Pucker factor: A measure of the stress in any situation. The higher the pucker factor, the more stressful.

Pukes: Pejorative by Marines for members of the U.S. Navy.

Puzzle palace: The Pentagon or any headquarters.

Rack time: Sleep.

Raghead: Pejorative for any Arab person.

Regimental monkey: Drum major.

REMF: Rear Echelon Mother Fucker. A staff person

Remington raider: Office personnel, a reference to the widely used Remington typewriters.

Ring knocker: A graduate of the Naval Academy, Military Academy, or Air Force Academy, who "absentmindedly" taps the ring to be sure it is noticed.

Riveter: Any machine gun.

Rock: Idiot (i.e., as stupid as a rock).

Rotor head: Helicopter pilot.

Rubber duck: A parachute jump with inflatable boat by SEALs; the jumpers are not in the boats. The boat is a Zodiac bound onto a wooden platform with gear in it and a parachute attached.

Sammy: Infantryman. Used as an American cousin to Tommy, the nickname for the British soldier. (World War I)

Sand box: Iraq, particularly the southern part.

Seagoing bellhop: Derogatory term for Marines.

Sealed (or sewed) in a blanket: Dead and buried at sea (wrapped in a blanket).

Seaweed: U.S. Coast Guardsperson.

Sewer pipe sailor: A member of the submarine service.

Sham shield: Specialist rank insignia.

Shoe: Short for "blackshoes," a derogatory term for nonflying personnel; aviators wear brown shoes.

Six, The: A full colonel, from the pay grade (O-6).

Six, six, and a kick: The ultimate general court-martial punishment consisting of six months forfeiture of pay, six months confinement at hard labor, and a dishonorable discharge.

Skippie: A not-too-bright Marine.

Slope: Pejorative for any Asian person.

Small Boat and Barge School: The U.S. Naval Academy.

Smoking hole: An airplane crash site.

Snap in: Practice, especially on a rifle range.

Snuffy: A low ranking enlisted Marine.

Soup sandwich: Not squared away, not sharp or crisp.

Squid: A pejorative term for sailors or Coast Guardpersons.

SSS: Shit, shower, and shave. Four S's refer to the three plus "shove off."

Stew builder: Cook.

S-3: Staff officer.

Stripes: Chevrons that indicate rank on a soldier's sleeves.

Strip the stripes: To be demoted (i.e., to lose the stripes indicating rank).

S-2: Intelligence officer.

Swabbie: Sailor.

SWAG: Scientific, wild-assed guess.

Swamp Lagoon: A pejorative term for Camp Lejeune, North Carolina.

Swimmer: Coast Guardsman who rescues the drowning person.

Tail-end Charlie: The last person or element in a line or column.

Tango uniform: Phonetic for "Tit's up," meaning dead drunk.

Tell it to the Marines: Expression of great skepticism. "Tell it to the Marines," was a Marines recruitment poster slogan. (World War I)

Three-starrer: Vice admiral.

Three-striper: Navy commander, Army sergeant (both wear three stripes or chevrons).

Tickler: Grenade.

Toilet seat: Pejorative term for the "marksman" shooting badge. It is the lowest of three levels of marksmanship qualification and the badge is shaped like a square target.

Tommy or Tommy Atkins: British soldier. (World War I)

Toothpick: Bayonet, from French slang for bayonet (World War I).

Top: First sergeant.

Top kick: First sergeant.

Track lube: A tanker's term for infantrymen.

Trench talk: Military slang, especially obscene.

Trooper(s): Airborne soldiers or cavalrymen.

Tuna boat driver: A pejorative term used by tankers in reference to Amtrac drivers.

Twinkie: Marine aviation personnel. (Korean War)

Uncle Sam's Canoe Club: The U. S. Naval Academy ("Canoe U") or more broadly, the U. S. Navy.

Uncle Sam's Misguided Children: Marines refer to themselves this way, using the acronym for USMC.

Vice: Vice admiral.

WAF: Woman (or women) in the Air Force.

Waltzing Matilda: Pejorative for an Australian person.

Washed out: To be killed.

Waste: To kill.

Whale shit: According to many drill instructors, the only thing lower than a recruit.

White discharge: Any discharge other than dishonorable (medical, honorable).

White hat: An enlisted sailor, from the headgear worn with the enlisted uniform.

Windjammer: Army bugler.

Wing wiper: A pejorative term for a Marine assigned to an aviation unit.

Winger: A Marine assigned to an Air Wing.

Wookie monster: Woman Marine.

Yard bird: Prisoner.

Zero: Any officer (taken from the pay grades O-1 to O-10).

Zip or zipper head: Pejorative for any Vietnamese person. (Vietnam)

Zoomie: A pejorative term for Marines assigned to an aviation unit or all members of the Air Force.

FOOD SLANG

MREs, the abbreviation for *meals, ready-to-eat*, is the official term for the military's field rations. They consist of a concentrated, dehydrated package of a complete meal requiring only heating or rehydrating. A simple chemical heating package that does not require matches is included in MREs. MREs include a main course, like spaghetti or beef stew, together with cheese, jelly, or peanut butter, crackers or similar bread item, a small fruit item like applesauce, a small candy, drink powder (e.g., Kool-Aid, coffee, cocoa), Chicklets gum, a tiny bottle of Tabasco sauce, salt/pepper, matches, and small package of toilet paper. Rumor has it that the Chicklets are really laxatives; it's a good idea if true since MREs are often constipating. A version of these is the LRPR, or Long-Range Patrol Ration, a lightweight compact ration in flexible packaging that can be eaten hot or cold, wet or dry. The ration contains a main entrée, cereal or fruitcake bar, sweet, coffee, cream, sugar, toilet paper, matches, and a spoon.

MREs have been nicknamed "meals refusing to exit," "meals rejected by Ethiopians," or "meals rejected by Ethiopia," among others. Actually, in 1991, the Pentagon offered MREs that were surplus from the Gulf War to needy countries; Ethiopia was one of the few to accept.

C-rats/C-rations were field rations that predated the MREs (developed just prior to World War II). Six cans per person per day held three meal units, three sets of biscuits, coffee powder, and a few pieces of candy. They packed 3,500 calories and were constipating, but kept troops sustained. *K rations* meant dry foods, e.g.,

Airwing Alpo: MRE containing corned beef hash and meatballs with BBQ sauce.

Albatross: Chicken.

Angel cake and wine: Bread and water served to prisoners in solitary confinement.

Armored cow: Canned milk.

Army strawberries: Prunes.

Artillery: Beans. (World War I)

Baby dicks: Hot dogs contained in MREs.

Baby food: Breakfast cereals, especially oatmeal.

Bag nasty: A meal delivered in a paper bag, especially during Marksmanship Training at Boot Camp.

Bags of mystery: Sausages.

Bail-out ration: Compact emergency ration designed to fit into the pocket of a paratrooper. They contained chocolate, dextrose tablets, concentrated bouillon, and chewing gum.

Baltimore lead: Beef liver.

Battery acid: Coffee.

Battle breakfast: Heavy breakfast of steak and eggs served before going to battle stations.

Beans and dicks: Beans and hot dogs in C-rats. Also "Army chicken."

Beef, grease, and shrapnel: C-ration meal of beefsteak, potatoes, and gravy.

Blankets: Pancakes.

Blockade mutton: Dog meat, as used during the British blockade of Germany during World War II.

Blonde and sweet: Coffee with cream and sugar.

Blood: Ketchup.

Boodle: Sweets: cake, candy, etc.

Bottled sunshine: Beer.

Bug: Any solid item in a soup. (World War II)

Bug juice: Colored, sweetened water served on ships or in mess halls; also bad whiskey. (World War II)

Bullets: Beans or dry peas.

Bully beef: Canned meat. (World War II)

Buzzard meat: Chicken or turkey.

Cackle jelly: Chicken eggs.

Camel meat: MRE containing any unappealing entrée.

Can of worms: Canned spaghetti.

Canned horse: Canned corned beef.

Cards: Cornbread cooked in large flat sheets. (Civil War)

Chalk: Powdered milk.

Chicken berry: Egg.

City cow: Canned milk.

Com rats: Commuted rations; money paid for those who don't eat in the mess hall on base.

Corned dog: Canned corned beef.

Crash: Omelet.

Deep sea chicken/turkey: Canned tuna or salmon.

Deep six turkey: Canned salmon.

Depth bomb: Egg.

Desecrated: Dehydrated, as in dried vegetables which were boiled to revive them, a pun on desiccated (1800s).

Dog fat: Butter.

Dog food: Corned beef hash.

Dynamite pills: Potent laxatives.

Embalmed meat: Canned corned beef.

Fisheyes: Tapioca.

400W: Maple syrup (resembling thick engine oil).

Galvanized Guernsey: Canned milk.

Gas bombs: Rotten eggs.

Gedunk: Ice cream. (World War II)

Golf balls and bullets: C-rats with meatballs and beans.

Grapeshot: Pudding. (World War II)

Grass: Salad.

Great unknown: Hash, meat loaf.

Ham and motherfuckers: Ham and lima beans.

Hand grenade: Hamburger.

Hay: Sauerkraut

Horse potato: Sweet potato or yam.

Ink: Black coffee.

Irish grapes: Potatoes.

Iron ration: Canned rations.

Java or Joe: Coffee.

Jawbreaker: Army biscuit.

Knee pad: Pancake.

Leather: Meat.

Liberty cabbage: Sauerkraut. (World War I)

Monkey meat: Canned beef.

Punk: Bread. (World War I)

Redeye: Tomato ketchup.

Repeaters: Any gas-producing food.

Rollers: Hot dogs.

Sea dust: Table salt.

Sewer trout: Any bland fish.

Shivering Liz: Jell-O. (World War II)

Sinker: Heavy biscuits or doughnuts.

Sliders: Hamburgers. "With lids" refers to cheeseburgers.

SOS: Shit on a shingle, a breakfast meal consisting of creamed chipped beef served on toast.

Swamp seed: Rice.

Willie in the can: Canned corned beef. (World War II)

★ GLOSSARY C

Military Equipment

Equipment employed by the U.S. military is in a constant state of flux due to needs and technological improvements. This section attempts to provide a reasonable listing of some of the main equipment currently, commonly, or recently in use with a short description. As is common in the military, many items are given acronyms or letter-and-number descriptors. Items are separated by category.

Where they occur, the letters "A," "N," "M", "F," "C," or "SOF" following the description refer to use by the Army, Navy, Marines, Air Force, Coast Guard, or special operations forces, respectively.

★ AIRCRAFT ★

Aerial Tanker / Transport Tanker / Cargo Aircraft

C-2: Greyhound. The C-2A Greyhound is a twin-engine cargo aircraft used to provide logistics support to aircraft carriers for the Navy. It can deliver a payload of up to 10,000 pounds of cargo, passengers, or both, and litter patients if necessary. It uses a crew of three to four, has a ceiling of 30,000 feet and has a range of 1,300 nautical miles. (N)

C-5: Galaxy. This is a gigantic cargo aircraft, one of the largest in the world. It can carry fully equipped, combat-ready military units to any point in the world on short notice and then provide field support required to help sustain the fighting force. It can carry outsize and oversize cargo intercontinental ranges and can take off or land in relatively short distances. Ground crews can load and off load the C-5 simultaneously at front and rear cargo openings. The Galaxy carries nearly all of the Army's combat equipment, including bulky items, to anywhere needed. It is aerial-refueling capable. (A)

C-9A/C: Nightingale. The C-9 is a twin-engine, T-tailed, medium-range, swept-wing jet aircraft used primarily for Air Mobility Command's aeromedical evacuation mission, and is the only aircraft in the inventory specifically designed for the movement of litter and ambulatory patients. It can carry forty litter patients. (F)

C-17: The C-17 Globemaster III is the most recent and flexible cargo aircraft in the airlift force. It can deliver troops and cargo to bases or in deployment areas as well as perform tactical airlift and airdrop missions. (F)

C-20: The C-20 is a twin-engine, turbofan aircraft acquired to ferry high-ranking government and Department of Defense officials. Secure and clear passenger communication capability exists. (N)

C-21: Learjet. The C-21 is a twin turbofan engine aircraft used for cargo and passenger airlift. The aircraft is the military version of the Lear Jet

35A business jet. It is also capable of evacuating wounded. It is equipped with an automatic navigation system to enhance crew efficiency. (F)

C-27A: Spartan. The C-27A Spartan is a twin turboprop engine aircraft used for rugged, medium-size airland transport of cargo or passengers. The aircraft is particularly suited for short-to-medium range tactical operations into semi-prepared airfields as short as 1,800 feet. The C-27A is an all-weather, day/night transport with capabilities to perform medical evacuation missions. It can carry twenty-four litters and four medical attendants, or thirty-four ground troops. (F)

C-32: The C-32 is primarily used as a transport aircraft for the vice president ("Air Force Two"), the first lady, and members of the Cabinet and Congress. It is a modified version of the Boeing 757-200 commercial intercontinental airliner with the passenger cabin divided into four sections. The forward area has a communications center, galley, lavatory, and ten business-class seats. The second section is a fully enclosed stateroom for the use of the primary passenger. In the third section is the conference and staff facility with eight business class seats. The rear section of the cabin contains general seating with thirty-two business-class seats. It is a "high-standing" aircraft, which means it is high off the ground, making it easier to secure the plane and its passengers. Inside the aircraft, state-of-the art communications systems are available to the vice president and other passengers. (F)

C-37A: The C-37A is a twin-engine, turbofan aircraft used for special air missions for high-ranking government and Defense Department officials. (F)

C-40 B/C: The C-40 B/C is another transport aircraft for American leaders, particularly combatant commanders and members of the Cabinet and Congress. The aircraft also perform other operational support missions. It is designed to be an "office in the sky" for senior military and government leaders. Communications systems are state of the art. (N, F)

C-47: Skytrain or Dakota. Large cargo aircraft derived from the DC-3. It was nicknamed "Gooney bird" in Europe. (N, F)

C-130 or HC-130: Nicknamed "Hercules," this is a medium range, troop and cargo transport designed for air-drop or airland delivery into a combat zone as well as conventional airlift. The E model has additional fuel capacity for extended range. The inflight tanker configurations are designated as C-130 and HC-130, also used for aerial

rescue missions. The gunship version is designed AC-130. (N, M, F, C)

C-135: Stratotanker. Used by the Air Force since 1956, primarily for air refueling. (F)

C-141: Starlifter. The C-141 Starlifter fulfills a range of airlift needs: long distance airlifting of combat, delivering forces and equipment by air, land, or airdrop; resupplying forces; and transporting wounded troops back to medical facilities. The C-141B is a "stretched" C-141A with in-flight refueling capability. It is now primarily used for Reserve and National Guard forces. (F)

Cargo aircraft: These refer to military aircraft used for transport of troops and/or equipment.

Cargo carrier: These are highly mobile, air-transportable, unarmored, full-tracked cargo and logistic carriers capable of fording inland waterways up to 40 inches deep and accompanying and resupplying self-propelled artillery weapons.

KC-10: Extender. The KC-10 Extender is primarily used for aerial refueling, but can simultaneously carry fighter support personnel and equipment on overseas deployments. It carries almost twice as much fuel as the KC-135 Stratotanker. (F)

KC-130: The KC-130 is a multi-role, multimission tactical tanker/transport that provides support for Marine Air Ground Task Forces. It provides in-flight refueling to both tactical aircraft and helicopters as well as rapid ground refueling when required, and aerial delivery of troops and cargo, emergency resupply into unimproved landing zones within the objective or battle area, airborne Direct Air Support Center, emergency MedEvac, tactical insertion of combat troops and equipment, evacuation missions, and support of special operations capable Marine Air Ground Task Forces. (M, F, SOF)

KC-135: The KC-135 Stratotanker is primarily used for air refueling. It can carry over 150,000 pounds of fuel over 1,500 miles at a ceiling altitude of 50,000 feet. About 550 are used by the Air Force. (F)

HC-130P/N: This aircraft is an extended-range, combat search-and-rescue version of the C-130 Hercules transport. It is used for extending the range of combat search-and-rescue helicopters by providing air refueling. Secondary mission capabilities include performing tactical delivery via airdrop or airland of pararescue specialist teams, small bundles, small watercraft, or ATVs; and providing direct assistance to a survivor in advance of the arrival of a recovery vehicle. It is usually flown at night to avoid detection (F, C, SOF)

MC-130E Combat Talon I and MC-130H Combat Talon II: These two aircraft are used for infiltration, exfiltration, and resupply of special operations forces and equipment in hostile territory. They are additionally used for psychological operations and helicopter air refueling. Both have terrain-following and terrain-avoidance radars capable of operating as low as 250 feet in adverse weather conditions. They can locate, and either land or airdrop on small, unmarked zones with pinpoint accuracy, day or night. The MC-130E can carry up to fifty-three troops or twenty-six paratroopers, whereas the MC-130H can transport up to seventy-seven troops or fifty-two paratroopers or up to nearly sixty wounded or injured persons. (SOF)

MC-130P: Combat Shadow. This aircraft is used for clandestine flights refueling special operations helicopters. It generally is flown at night to avoid detection. It also is used for airdrop of special operations teams, leaflets, or equipment. (F, SOF)

Attack Aircraft

Attack aircraft are military aircrafts designed for attacking ground targets. They are deployed in *force application* and *air control* roles. The *force application* role includes three different types of mission goals. *Strategic attack* is to destroy or neutralize the enemy's ability to produce or sustain military forces or his will to use those forces. *Interdiction* is to destroy, delay, or disrupt existing enemy surface forces when they are too far from friendly surface forces. *Close air support* is the support of offensive or defensive surface operations against close enemy forces.

A-3: Skywarrior. The only strategic bomber built expressly for the Navy, it was relied upon greatly during the 1950s. It was one of the heaviest aircraft used on aircraft carriers. It was nicknamed the "Whale" because of its size, and later the "The Electric Whale" when it was converted to electronic warfare use. It required a crew of three and flew at a flight ceiling of 41,000 feet. (N)

A-4: Skyhawk. A light attack aircraft (single-engine, turbojet) designed for use from aircraft carriers to deliver nuclear or non-nuclear weapons, conduct reconnaissance missions, or provide troop support. It can be air refueled and has all-weather attack capability. It was used heavily in the Vietnam War, and John McCain (U.S. senator, Arizona) flew A-4s until he was shot down over Vietnam. About 3,000 were constructed, with some 500 converted for trainer mode. They were all retired by 2003. (N, M)

A-6: Intruder. All-weather, attack aircraft in service from 1962 to 1997. It was a medium carrier-based attack aircraft and served in Vietnam, Libya, Lebanon, and part of the Gulf War. It had a crew of two and flew at a ceiling of over 40,000 feet. Cost was $43 million each. (N, M, F).

A-7: Corsair II. Light attack aircraft based on the F-8 Crusader. It is a single-seat, single-turbofan engine, all weather designed to operate from aircraft carriers and capable of carrying a range of nuclear or conventional ordnance, and air-to-air or air-to-ground missiles. They were used in Vietnam through the Gulf War and had the unflattering nickname "SLUF" (Short Little Ugly Fucker). Cost was just under three million dollars each. (N, F)

A-10: Thunderbolt II. Nicknamed the "Hog" or "Warthog," it is a twin-engine, subsonic, turbofan, tactical fighter/bomber that employs variety of air-to-surface launched weapons in close air support. It can use short fields or unimproved surfaces for usual takeoff/landing. It is long-endurance capable in the target area and air-refueling capable. It has a 30mm (internal) cannon (Gatling gun) capable of destroying a range of armored vehicles with a range of 800 miles. It was developed in response to needs in Vietnam. (F)

A-37: Dragonfly. Modified from a Cessna T-37 with more powerful engines and other modifications. Used in Vietnam for close air support, helicopter escort, and night interdiction. It can carry high-explosive bombs, cluster munitions, unguided rockets, napalm tanks, and more. It can also be fitted with two additional external flue tanks. It was nicknamed "Super Tweet." (A)

AC-47: Spooky. A fixed wing gunship that was a modified C-47 used for heavy firepower, it was fitted with three 7.62mm General Electric miniguns. It provided close air support for ground troops and could fly slowly through a combat zone and put one round into every square foot. It was nicknamed "Puff the Magic Dragon." It was replaced with the AC-119 and AC-130 gunships. (A)

AC-119: Shadow/Stinger, also nicknamed "Creep." A fixed wing gunship used in Vietnam with a crew of 6-8. (F)

AC-130: Hercules. The AC-130 is a gunship used for close air support, air interdiction, and force protection. It is heavily armed with side-firing weapons integrated with sophisticated sensor, navigation, and fire-control systems that provide precise firepower or area saturation and is suitable for night or adverse weather flights.

AV-8B: Harrier II. A single-engine, vectored-thrust, turbojet, vertical and/or short takeoff and landing light attack aircraft, designed to operate from land bases and aircraft carriers in a close air support role. It is capable of carrying a variety of conventional and/or nuclear weapons. It uses a crew of one with a range of about 700 miles. (M)

Bomber Aircraft

Bomber aircraft are military aircraft designed to attack ground targets by dropping bombs. *Strategic bombers* are used for long-range strike missions against strategic targets such as supply bases, bridges, factories, and shipyards (e.g., the B-17 Flying Fortress and the B-52 Stratofortress). *Tactical bombers* are smaller aircraft with shorter range that generally operate in conjunction with ground troops. *Ground attack* or *close air support aircraft* are used over a battlefield or to attack tactical targets such as airfields (e.g., A-10 Warthog). Fighter-bombers can be used for air-to-air combat or air-to-ground combat (e.g., F/A-18 Hornet).

B1-B: Nicknamed "Lancer," the B1-B bomber is the backbone of America's long-range bomber force, and was developed as a replacement for the B-52 bomber. It is described as able to "rapidly deliver massive quantities of precision and nonprecision weapons against any adversary, anywhere in the world, at any time." It can use subsonic and supersonic flight as a versatile, multimission weapon system. It has a strong defense system that includes electronic jamming equipment, radar warning receiver (ALQ-161), and countermeasures (decoy tactics including chaff and flares). (F)

B-2: Nicknamed "Spirit," but more frequently called the Stealth Bomber, this aircraft can deliver both conventional and nuclear weapons. It rapidly provides heavy firepower anywhere on the globe. Its low-observable, or "stealth," characteristics enable it to penetrate highly sophisticated defenses, thus providing an effective deterrent and combat force. Its stealth attributes are derived from a combination of reduced detection, including infrared, acoustic, electromagnetic, visual, and radar features. (F)

B-29: Superfortress. The B-29 Superfortress was designed in 1940 as an eventual replacement for the B-17 and B-24. Technically a generation ahead of all other heavy bomber types in World War II, the Superfortress was pressurized for high altitudes and featured remotely controlled gun turrets. Most important, its four supercharged engines gave it the range to carry large bomb loads across the Pacific Ocean in World War II. It was also used in Korea and later fitted with a flying boom for experiments in air-to-air refueling.

B-36: Peacemaker. An intercontinental bomber designed during World War II but not fully operational until 1951. The last B-36 was built in August 1954. Retired in 1959, there were almost 500 B-36 aircraft in the U.S. bomber fleet. It was replaced by the more modern B-52, but served as a major deterrent to aggression. The fact that the B-36 was never used in combat was indicative of its value in "keeping the peace." (F)

B-45: Tornado. The B-45 Tornado was a jet-powered bomber contracted by the Army after finding secret documents of similar German jet aircraft during World War II. The

B-45 served well as a reconnaissance aircraft during the Korean War. The Tornado performed classified, deep-penetration photographic-intelligence missions over many Cold War communist countries. (F)

B-47: Stratojet. A high-altitude, medium-range, subsonic bomber. Over 2,000 B-47s were built from 1952 through 1956. It was the first pure jet strategic bomber and utilized a crew of three. It used rocket assist on takeoff and a tail chute to slow down the aircraft during landings. Although it was one of the more beautiful airplanes to grace America's skies, it was a medium-range bomber with limitations on space, payload (warhead capacity), and range. (F)

B-52: Nicknamed "Stratofortress" but also called "BUFF" for "big, ugly, fat fucker" in Air Force parlance. It is a long-range, heavy bomber capable of flying at high subsonic speeds at altitudes up to 50,000 feet and can carry nuclear or precision-guided, conventional ordnance with world-wide precision navigation capability. In a conventional conflict, the B-52 can perform strategic attack, air interdiction, offensive counter-air, and maritime operations. During Desert Storm, B-52s delivered 40 percent of all the weapons dropped by coalition forces. Originally deployed in 1955, it is aerial-refueling capable. (F)

B-58: Hustler. This was a high-speed jet bomber capable of supersonic flight that served between 1960 and 1970. It emitted a sonic boom as it flew overhead in supersonic flight. It was fitted with a 20mm cannon and could carry over 1,400 pounds of conventional or nuclear bomb.

SBD: Dauntless. The SBD Dauntless was the U.S. Navy's main scout bomber and dive bomber from mid-1940 until 1943, when it was replaced by the SB2C Helldiver. Together, their extremely effective dive bombing technique, known as "Helldiving" led to their nickname "Helldivers," although there was another aircraft officially designated the Helldiver. (A, N, M)

TBF: Avenger. The TBF Avenger was a torpedo bomber, developed initially for the Navy and Marine Corps and used by a large number of air forces around the world. It entered service in 1942, and saw action during the Battle of Midway. (N, M)

Electronic Warfare / Surveillance / Reconnaissance Aircraft

Electronic warfare aircraft are designed for any or all of three purposes: for offensive jamming of the electromagnetic spectrum used by the enemy to prevent their use of it for communications, for defensive use by protecting their own use of the electromagnetic spectrum, and as support to collect information about the enemy or provide information about friendly forces (reconnaissance aircraft).

E-2, E-2 C: Hawkeye. The E-2 Hawkeye is the Navy's all-weather, aircraft carrier-based tactical airborne early warning (AEW) aircraft. It is also used for surface surveillance coordination, strike and interceptor control, search and rescue guidance, and communications relay. There is currently one squadron of four Hawkeyes in each carrier air wing. It has been in operation since 1964. (N).

E-3: Sentry, or AWACS. The E-3 Sentry is an airborne warning and control system (AWACS) aircraft that provides all-weather surveillance, command, control, and communications as needed by commanders of U.S., NATO, and other Allied air defense forces. The E-3 Sentry is a modified Boeing 707/320 commercial airframe. It is used to gather and present broad and detailed battlefield information, which can be sent on to the president immediately. It is also used in support of air-to-ground operations by providing information

for interdiction, reconnaissance, airlift, and close-air support for friendly ground forces. As an air defense system, the E-3 detects, identifies, and tracks airborne enemy forces from long distances. Its mobility gives it greater survivability as an airborne warning and control system. It can remain airborne for over eight hours, with additional endurance possible through in-flight refueling. The Air Force currently has over thirty E-3 Sentry aircraft. (F)

E-4B: The E-4B serves as the National Airborne Operations Center for the president and secretary of defense. During national emergencies or in the event of the destruction of ground command control centers, the aircraft can provide a "highly survivable" command, control, and communications center from which to direct U.S. forces, execute emergency war orders, and coordinate actions by civil authorities. It is a four-engine, swept-wing, long-range, high-altitude airplane capable of in-flight refueling. The main deck has six functional areas: a command work area, conference room, briefing room, an operations team work area, and communications and rest areas. It may carry a crew of up to 114 people. Its advanced communications system provides worldwide communications. At least one E-4B is always on alert at one of many selected bases throughout the world for the president and secretary of defense. It can remain airborne for over twelve hours before in-flight refueling. Four E-4B aircraft are in operation at this time.

E-6: Mercury. TACAMO, or Take Charge and Move Out, the E-6 is the airborne portion of the TACAMO Communications System. It provides survivable communication links between the National Command Authority (NCA) and Strategic Forces. The E-6 is a derivative of the commercial Boeing 707 aircraft. (N)

E-8C: The E-8C Joint Surveillance Target Attack Radar System, known as Joint STARS, functions as an airborne battle management, command and control, intelligence, and surveillance and reconnaissance system. Its primary mission is to provide theater ground and air commanders with ground surveillance to support attack operations and targeting that contributes to the delay, disruption, and destruction of enemy forces. It can gather and display detailed battlefield information on ground forces, relaying this information immediately to the Army and Marine Corps common ground stations and to other ground command, control, communications, computers, and intelligence (C4I) nodes. It is used in a range of mis-

sions from peacekeeping operations to major theater war. It uses a crew of four, plus up to eighteen specialists according to mission. (F)

EA-6B: Prowler electronic warfare aircraft. The EA-6B Prowler is the primary electronic warfare aircraft used by the Navy and the Marines to support strike aircraft and ground troops by interrupting enemy electronic activity and obtaining tactical electronic intelligence area. It can also attack surface targets using its AGM-88 missiles. It is nicknamed the "Queer" because of the distinct electromagnetic protective coating on the canopy. There are about 125 Prowlers in use today, but they are expected to be replaced by the EA-18G Growler by 2009. (N, M)

EA-18G: Growler, an electronic warfare version of the F/A-18F Super Hornet. (N, M, F).

EC-130E/J: Commando Solo, a specially modified, four-engine Hercules transport that conducts information operations, psychological operations, and civil affairs broadcasts in AM, FM, HF, TV, and military communications band for the Air Force Special Operations Command. A typical mission consists of a single-ship orbit offset from the desired target audience, either military or civilian personnel. It has enhanced navigation systems, self-protection equipment, and air-refueling capability, and it is capable of broadcasting radio and color TV on all worldwide standards. (A, F, SOF)

EC-130H: The Compass Call is an airborne tactical weapon system using a modified version of the C-130 Hercules airframe. The system serves in electronic warfare, suppressing enemy defenses and in offensive counter information. The system also supports tactical air operations, providing conventional and special operations support. It carries a combat crew of thirteen and is in-flight refueling capable. (SOF)

EC-130V: Hercules. The EC-130V Hercules AEW&C aircraft was first developed for the Coast Guard in 1992 for counternarcotics missions requiring great endurance. It has also been used for search and rescue, fisheries patrols, and as a support aircraft for NASA space shuttle launches. Due to budget cuts in the Coast Guard, the EC-130V program was terminated and the EC-130V was transferred to the USAF as the NC-130H for further development, including upgrading. (F, C)

ELINT: Electronic intelligence, which means intelligence gathering via electronic means. This can refer to gathering information regarding enemy's radar, missile systems, or aircraft. It is often gathered in advance of a conflict to locate surface-to-air missiles and antiaircraft artillery systems so that responses can be plotted in advance. It is also used to locate ships and command-and-control centers.

ES-3: Shadow. Jet used to collect and disseminate tactical reconnaissance information. The ES-3 was a carrier-based, subsonic, all-weather, long-range, electronic reconnaissance aircraft. It operated primarily with carrier battle groups providing Indications and Warning (I&W) support to battle group and joint theater commanders. They were removed from active service in 1999. (N)

RC-135U: The RC-135U Combat Sent is a reconnaissance aircraft used to provide reconnaissance information for the president, secretary of defense, and Department of Defense leaders. The Combat Sent deploys worldwide and is used in peacetime and contingency operations. Aerial-refueling capable, it requires a crew of twenty-two or more.

RC-135V/W Rivet Joint: This reconnaissance aircraft is used for real-time, on-scene intelligence collection and analysis. The aircraft is an extensively modified C-135. The Rivet Joint's features include its onboard sensor suite that permits the detection, identification, and geolocation of a range of electromagnetic signals. The information can be forwarded via its communication system. (F)

SR-71: Senior Crown, also "Blackbird." Developed for the Air Force as reconnaissance aircraft more than thirty years ago, SR-71s are still the world's fastest and highest-flying production aircraft. The aircraft can fly more than 2,200 mph (Mach 3-plus) and at altitudes of over 85,000 feet. The airframes are built almost entirely of titanium and titanium alloys to withstand heat generated by sustained Mach 3 flight. Although most news reports characterize the SR-71 aircraft as "radar evading," it actually has one of the largest radar targets ever detected on the FAA's long-range radars. Because of its limitations (it only operates in good weather and cannot transmit the images it collects directly to those who need them), it probably will not be reactivated. (F)

SV-3: Viking. The Lockheed S-3 Viking is a jet aircraft used to hunt and destroy enemy submarines and provide surveillance of surface shipping. The S-3B version includes improvements to sensors, avionics, and weapons systems over the S-3A, such as the capability of launch the AGM-84 Harpoon antiship cruise missile. It can be fitted with aerial refueling stores (ARS), or "buddy stores," external fuel tanks that refuel other aircraft, to act as an airborne tanker. The ES-3A electronic reconnaissance version was fitted for electronic warfare and reconnaissance. Because of the high-pitched sound of the aircraft's engines reminiscent of a vacuum cleaner, it is nicknamed the "Hoover." (N)

U-2: The U-2 is the classic spy plane, providing very high-altitude (over 70,000 feet), all-weather surveillance and reconnaissance, day or night. It has a crew of one, or two if in trainer mode. There are about forty U-2 aircraft in active use. It flew as "2nd Weather Reconnaissance Squadron (Provisional)," out of Adana Air Base in Turkey, primarily to gather intelligence on the Soviet Union. Later, pilot Gary Powers was shot down over the Soviet Union and accused of espionage. The aircraft was used over Cuba to confirm Soviet offensive missile sites.

WC-130 Hercules: This is a high-wing, medium-range aircraft used for weather reconnaissance missions. It can stay aloft up to fifteen hours with a range of about 3,500 miles and a flight ceiling of 33,000 feet. It requires a crew of six with ten currently in use by the reserve forces.

WC-135W: The WC-135W "Constant Phoenix" is an atmospheric collection aircraft in support of the Limited Nuclear Test Ban Treaty of 1963. It is a modified C-135B, which can detect radioactive clouds in real time. It can seat up to thirty-three persons, with varying crew numbers. It has a range of 4,000 miles with a flight ceiling of 40,000 feet. There is currently one in use by the active forces.

Experimental Aircraft

X-planes: These are a series of experimental aircraft used for testing new technologies, generally kept highly secret during development. The Bell-X-1 was the first plane to break the sound barrier in 1947. Most never go into full production. One exception was the X-35 produced by Lockheed Martin, which became the Joint Strike Fighter.

Fighter Aircraft

Fighter aircraft are designed for air-to-air combat.

F-4: Phantom II. The Phantom II is a fighter/attack aircraft. It is a twin-engine, supersonic, multipurpose, all-weather jet fighter/bomber that can operate from both land and aircraft carriers, and employs both air-to-air and air-to-surface weapons and is nuclear-weapons capable. It was used for air interdiction and close air support as well as fleet defense for such missions as laser bombing, electronic bombing, and radar bombing. The Phantom was used by both Thunderbirds (F-4E) and Blue Angels (F-4J) demonstration teams. All have been retired by Air Force, Navy, and Marines. They served as an unmistakable icon of the Cold War. Nicknamed "Double Ugly," "Rhino," "Wild Weasel," or "Fast Mover." (N, M, F)

F-4U: The F4U Corsair was a fighter used as carrier aircraft during World War II and the Korean War. (N)

F-5: The F-5A Freedom Fighter or F-5E Tiger II is a supersonic warplane of world-class quality for the air-to-ground role. The F-5A has two 20mm cannons in the fuselage nose, and two AIM-9 Sidewinders at the wingtips. The F-5E carries two 20mm M39A2 cannons and two AIM-9 Sidewinder missiles at the wingtips. The F-5 lost in competition with F-16 for the Air Force contract. Many have been exported to foreign nations. (N)

F-6F: Hellcat. The Grumman F6F Hellcat began as an improved F-4F Wildcat, but eventually resembled the Wildcat but with no shared parts. Used by the Navy during WWII as the primary aircraft carrier fighter. (N)

F-8: Crusader. The F-8 Crusader was the last U.S. fighter designed with guns as its primary weapon. The F-8A entered service in 1957. The RF-8G Crusader aircraft, the "Eyes of the Fleet" operated by photo reconnaissance squadrons (VFP) and featured camera ports on the side of the fuselage and a forward-firing camera. The RF-8 remained in service longer than the fighters, equipping reserve units through late 1986. (F)

F-14: Tomcat. The F-14 Tomcat is a supersonic, twin-engine, variable sweep-wing, two-seat strike fighter. It is primarily used for air superiority, fleet air defense, and precision strike against ground targets. The first F-14 flight was in 1970. About eighty were also sold to Iran. (N)

F-15A: Eagle. This is a twin-engine supersonic, turbofan, all-weather tactical fighter, capable of using a variety of air-launched weapons in air-to-air combat. It is air-refuelable and long-range capable. It has electronic systems and weaponry to detect, acquire, track, and attack enemies. The F-15's electronic warfare system provides both threat-warning and automatic countermeasures against selected threats. (N, F)

F-15E: Called the "Strike Eagle," and sometimes nicknamed the "Beagle," this aircraft is a dual-role fighter designed to perform air-to-air and air-to-ground missions. An array of avionics and electronics systems gives the F-15E the capability to fight at low altitude, day or night, and in all weather. It can detect, target, and engage air-to-air targets while the weapons systems officer identifies the ground target. It can be armed with AIM-7F/M Sparrows, AIM-9M Sidewinders and AIM-120 advanced medium-range air-to-air missiles (AMRAAM) for the air-to-air role and handles most of the air-to-ground weapons. There are over 200 in the Air Force inventory. (F)

F-16: The Fighting Falcon, also nicknamed "Electric Jet," "Lawn Dart," and "Viper." This single-engine, supersonic, turbofan, all-weather, multipurpose, tactical fighter/bomber is capable of employing nuclear/nonnuclear weapons. Air superiority is its primary mission with air interdiction and close air support secondary. It is air-refueling capable. The F-16 is a compact, multirole fighter aircraft. It is highly maneuverable and is useful in air-to-air combat and air-to-surface attack. The F-16A is a single-seat model and the

F-16B is a two-seat model. It is unusual in that it was constructed under an agreement between the U.S. and Belgium, Denmark, the Netherlands, and Norway. There are about 1,300 F-16s in the military. (N)

F-22A: The F-22A Raptor is a fighter aircraft that combines stealth, maneuverability, and integrated avionics. It is used in air-to-air and air-to-ground missions. It is unmatched by any known or projected fighter aircraft. It features a sophisticated sensor suite allowing the pilot to track, identify, shoot, and kill air-to-air threats before being detected. In the air-to-air configuration, the Raptor carries six AIM-120 AMRAAMs and two AIM-9 Sidewinders. It also is well suited in air-to-ground mode. It can "supercruise" at supersonic airspeeds (above 1.5 Mach) without the need for afterburners. It combines stealth technology with supercruise for the advantage of surprise. It uses a crew of one.

F-35: Joint Strike Fighter. The F-35 Joint Strike Fighter (JSF) is a military fighter aircraft jointly designed by the United States and the United Kingdom. It is intended to replace the current generation of strike fighters, particularly the Harrier jump jets: the AV-8 Harrier II (U.S.), Harrier GR7/9 (U.K.), and the Sea Harrier (U.K.), along with the conventional A-10 Thunderbolt II, F/A-18 Hornet and the F-16 Fighting Falcon. It is intended as a multirole strike fighter used for close air support and tactical bombing and air-to-air combat. It is expected to be available by 2008. The Air Force plans to purchase around 1,800 F-35s; the Navy, 480; and the Marine Corps, 480. (N, M, F)

F-105: Thunderchief. Used extensively in Vietnam as close support aircraft and in bombing of North Vietnam, it has a modified fuselage to accommodate a second man. It was used briefly by the Thunderbirds and is nicknamed "Thunderthuds," "Thuds," or "Wild Weasel."

F-111: A twin-engine, supersonic, turbofan, all-weather tactical fighter, capable of employing nuclear and non-nuclear weapons, it is able to operate from very short, relatively unprepared air strips.

F-117A: Nighthawk. This is the first stealth-equipped jet and is also a precision-strike aircraft that can deploy laser-guided weapons. It is a single-seat fighter jet that is air refuelable. It has sophisticated, integrated navigation and attack systems plus an automated mission planning system. There are over fifty in Air Force inventory. (F)

F/A-18: Hornet. Twin engine, supersonic, fighter/attack aircraft. The C models (single seat) and D models (dual seat) have all-weather intercept, identify, and destroy capability. It is equipped with an electronic self-protection jammer, is both air-to-air and air-to-ground capable, and is designed to operate from both land bases and aircraft carriers. (N, M)

F/A-18E/F/G: The Super Hornet is an all-new fighter and attack aircraft similar in appearance to the F/A-18C/D Hornet. It was designated "F/A-18" for political reasons, because Congress was unwilling to sponsor new military systems at the time. It is nicknamed the "Super Bug" or "Rhino."

Helicopters / Rotary Aircraft

AH: Attack helicopter.

AH-1: Attack helicopter AH-1 Cobra is also called the "Huey Cobra," "Cobra," or "Snake." It has parts in common with the UH-1 helicopter, including the engine, transmission, and rotor system. The Army has replaced this with the AH-64 Apache, but the Marines continue to rely on this helicopter, mainly because it is simpler to maintain and has a smaller shipboard footprint (space required onboard ship for transit). It is primarily used against armored targets, with its narrow front making it more difficult to hit with enemy guns. (M)

AH-1W: Super Cobra. The AH-1W Super Cobra is a day/night marginal-weather attack helicopter. It is a two-place, twin-engine helicopter capable of land- or sea-based operations. The AH-1W provides fire support and fire support coordination to the landing force during amphibious assaults and subsequent operations ashore. It can fire TOW, Hellfire, and Sidewinder missiles. (M)

AH-6J: Little Bird. This variant of the AH-6 carries a pod on either side of the fuselage that can be fitted with a range of guns, missiles, or rockets. In lieu of pods, the MH-6 troop ship variant is rigged with exterior benches on both sides of the cabin for carrying up to six men, three on each side. It is used by the Army's 160th Special Operations Aviation Regiment (SOAR). The NOTAR no-tail-rotor version is frequently used by law enforcement because of its very low noise levels. (A, SOF)

AH-64: Apache. The Apache is the Army's main attack helicopter. It was first used in combat during the invasion of Panama (1989). The Apache AH-64 and AH-64D have been active in the Gulf War and American actions in Afghanistan and Iraq. Useful against tanks, they are vulnerable to ground forces. It carries a cannon, a range of missiles and/or rockets. It is day or night and all-weather capable. (A)

Antiarmor helicopter: A helicopter used in destruction of armored targets

CH: Cargo helicopters.

CH-3E: Sea King. The CH-3E was the USAF version of the Sikorsky S-61 amphibious transport helicopter developed for the U.S. Navy. The USAF initially operated six Navy HSS-2 (SH-3A) versions of the S-61 in 1962, eventually designating them CH-3A/Bs. They were so successful the USAF ordered seventy-five, modified as CH-3Cs, featuring a new rear fuselage design with a ramp for vehicles and other cargo; later, they were updated with more powerful engines and redesignated as CH-3Es and about fifty more were built. Still later modifications included armor, defensive armament, self-sealing fuel tanks, a rescue hoist, and in-flight refueling capability for combat rescue missions gave it the new designation HH-3Es. They were used extensively in Vietnam, nicknamed the "Jolly Green Giant." (N, F)

CH-21B: Shawnee. The CH-21B was an assault helicopter used by the Army in Vietnam, that could transport twenty-two fully-equipped troops or twelve stretchers if medevac. It was armed with 7.62mm or 12.7mm door guns, but was slow and eventually replaced with the UH-1 and CH-47 Chinook. (A)

CH-37: Mojave. The Sikorsky S-56 was called the CH-37 Mojave by the Army or HR2S-1 (and later CH-37 C) by the Marines, was a large, heavy-lift helicopter in the 1950s. It was used for assault transport for the Marines. It was capable of ferrying twenty-six fully-equipped troops. (A, M)

CH-46E: Sea Knight. Medium assault transport helicopter used by the Navy for shipboard delivery of cargo, personnel, and search and rescue. Used by the Marines for all-weather, day-or-night assault transport of combat troops, supplies, and equipment. About 525 were produced for the Marines and Navy combined. (N, M)

CH-47: Chinook Cargo helicopter. The CH-47 Chinook is a versatile, twin-engine, tandem-rotor, heavy-lift helicopter used for troop, artillery, and supplies transport. Nicknamed "Big Charlie" or "Jolly Green Giant," it was used in Vietnam and also by the Royal Air Force. (A, N, M).

CH-53A/D: Sea Stallion. Heavy assault transport helicopter. The CH-53D Sea Stallion is designed for the transportation of equipment, supplies, and personnel during the assault phase of an amphibious operation and subsequent operations ashore. Capable of both internal and external transport of supplies the CH-53D is shipboard, adverse-weather, and day/night capable. It is used now by Marines as a medium-lift helicopter (N, M)

CH-53D E: Super Stallion. Heavy assault transport helicopter, it can carry up to fifty-five passengers. (M)

CH-54: Tarhe. Sky crane helicopter.

H-34: Choctaw. The Sikorsky H-34 Choctaw (also called the Sikorsky S-58) was a helicopter originally designed for the Navy for antisubmarine warfare, modified from the Sikorsky UH-19 Chickasaw. It is a utility transport helicopter, with no armament on board. It carries twelve to sixteen troops, or eight stretcher cases if medevac. Variations included the SH-34 Seabat, the H-34 Choctaw, and the UH-34 Seahorse. Production included 1,800 for Navy and Marines. (N, M)

H-46: Sea Knight. A variant of CH-46.

HEL-H: Heavy helicopter.

HEL-L: Light helicopter.

HEL-M: Medium helicopter.

HELO: Helicopter.

HH-60: Jayhawk. The HH-60 Jayhawk is a twin-engine, medium-range, search-and-rescue helicopter, based on the airframe of the Sikorsky S-70. It is also used for drug interdiction, cargo lift, and special operations. (C, SOF).

HH-60G: Pave Hawk. The Pave Hawk is a medium-lift helicopter used for day or night operations in hostile environments to recover downed aircrew or other isolated personnel during war. It is additionally used for civil search and rescue, emergency aeromedical evacuation, disaster relief, international aid, counterdrug activities, and NASA space shuttle support. It is a highly modified version of the Army Black Hawk helicopter with upgraded communications and navigation. It is inflight refueling-capable. (SOF)

HH-65: Dolphin. A short-range helicopter used for search and rescue, enforcement of laws and treaties (including drug interdiction), polar ice breaking, marine environmental protection (including pollution control), and military readiness. It can be carried onboard medium- and high-endurance Coast

Guard Cutters and can operate up to 150 miles off shore. (C)

MH-53J/M: Pave Low II. The Pave Low is a large, powerful, and advanced helicopter equipped with terrain-following and terrain-avoidance radar, a forward-looking infrared sensor, and an inertial navigation system with global positioning system. It is used for infiltration, exfiltration, and resupply of special operations forces requiring low-level, long-range, undetected penetration, day or night, in adverse weather. It has a range of 600 nautical miles and is in-flight-refueling capable. There are about forty in the Air Force inventory. (A, SOF)

SH-2: Seasprite. The SH-2 Seasprite is a multimission, medium-weight helicopter with undersea warfare capabilities, in operation since 1950. Navy inventory is six new plus rebuilds. (N)

SH-3: Sea King. A twin-engine, all-weather helicopter used by the Navy Reserves to detect, classify, track, and destroy enemy submarines, and is used for logistical support and search and rescue. (N)

TH-6B: A Navy trainer helicopter. (N)

UH: Utility helicopter.

UH-1/N: UH-1 Huey, and UH-1N Iroquois. An assault Utility Helicopter, the "Huey" or "Slick Huey" is a light-lift utility helicopter with a wide range of uses, including emergency airlift and disaster response forces, security surveillance, space shuttle support, and search and rescue. It is generally flown with one or two pilots and is night flying capable. There are over sixty in use by the active forces. (N, M)

UH-3: Sea King. The Sikorsky UH-3 Sea King or S-61 is a twin-engine, multi-purpose helicopter. It has served with the Navy and elsewhere. It was originally intended for shipboard use with foldable rotors, for antisubmarine warfare, but has also been used for search and rescue, transport, communications, and other roles. The Navy no longer uses it for antisubmarine warfare (it was replaced with the SH-60 Seahawk). A Sea King is the official designation of the president's helicopter (operated by the Marines) and is referred to as "Marine One" when the president is aboard. It uses a crew of four, can carry up to fifteen passengers, and can land on water. (N, M)

UH-60: Black Hawk helicopter. The Black Hawk is the Army's front-line utility helicopter used for air assault, air cavalry, and aeromedical evacuation units. It can carry eleven combat-loaded, air assault troops, or move a 105-millimeter howitzer and thirty rounds of ammunition. First deployed in 1978, the Black Hawk's advanced technology makes it easy to maintain in the field. The Black Hawk performs well under many missions, including air assault, air cavalry, and aeromedical evacuations. In addition, modified Black Hawks operate as command and control, electronic warfare, and special operations platforms. It replaced the UH-1 series in the combat assault role. Several variants and modifications are used by the Navy for various missions. The Army has about 1,500 UH-60 variants. (A, N, F, SOF)

Observation Aircraft

OH-58/D: Kiowa Scout, or Kiowa Warrior (D variant). It is used as a reconnaissance, surveillance, and intelligence-gathering helicopter. It has seen action from Vietnam to Iraq.

OV-10: Bronco: Light, twin turboprop, twin-seat, observation and support aircraft. May be equipped with machine guns and light ordnance for close air support missions.

P-3C: Orion. Long-range antisubmarine warfare aircraft. (N)

Trainer Aircraft

These are mainly trainer versions of other aircraft.

T-1A: Jayhawk. This is a medium-range, twin-engine jet trainer used during advanced undergraduate pilot training for students learning airlift or tanker aircraft. It is also used for navigator training for the Air Force, Navy, and Marine Corps. It requires a crew of three. Cost forty-one million dollars each. Nearly 200 are in the Air Force inventory alone. (N, M, F)

T-2: Buckeye. The T-2C Buckeye jet trainer aircraft was used for basic jet flight training with excellent safety and reliability. It has been used to train over eleven thousand students to pilot eighteen different models of Navy jet aircraft, but has been grounded since 1997 and will be replaced by the T-45 Goshawk. (N, M)

T-3: Firefly. A propeller-driven aircraft used by the Air Force AETC to screen pilot candidates by exposing them to military-style traffic patterns, aerobatics, and spins. It replaced the T-41 aircraft which is incapable of performing these maneuvers. It also teaches students takeoffs and landings, stalls, slow flight, ground operations, and mission planning. The Air

Force has 110 aircraft in use since 1994. (F)

T-6A: The T-6A Texan II is a single-engine, two-seat aircraft used to train Navy and Air Force students in Joint Primary Pilot Training (JPPT). The T-6A will be used to train JPPT students, providing the basic skills necessary to progress to one of four training tracks: the Air Force bomber-fighter or the Navy strike track, the Air Force airlift-tanker or Navy maritime track, the Air Force or Navy turboprop track, and the Air Force-Navy helicopter track. About five hundred are expected to be in Air Force inventory by the 2010. (N, F)

T-34: Turbo Mentor. The T-34C aircraft is an unpressurized, tandem-cockpit, low-wing, single-engine monoplane used in primary flight training for student pilots attached to the Chief of Naval Air Training. (N)

T-37B: The T-37B "Tweet" is a twin-engine jet used for training joint specialized undergraduate pilot students in basic aircraft handling, instrumentation, formation, and night flying. There are over four hundred in the Air Force inventory. (F)

T-38A: The T-38A Talon is a twin-engine, high-altitude, supersonic jet trainer used to fill a range of training needs because of its design, cost, low maintenance, excellent performance, and exceptional safety record. (N, F)

T-43A: The T-43A is a medium-range, swept-wing jet aircraft equipped with modern navigation and communications equipment to train navigators for strategic and tactical aircraft. It was modified from the Boeing 737. (F)

T-45: Goshawk. The T-45A is the Navy version of the British Aerospace Hawk aircraft, used for intermediate and advanced portions of the Navy pilot training program for jet carrier aviation and tactical strike missions. The T-45A replaces the T-2 Buckeye trainer and the TA-4 trainer with an integrated training system that includes the T-45 Goshawk aircraft, operations and instrument fighter simulators, academics, and training integration system. It carries one instructor and one student. (N)

TA-4: Skyhawk. Light attack trainer.

Vertical Takeoff

V-22: Osprey. The V-22 Osprey is a joint service, multimission aircraft with vertical takeoff and landing (VTOL) capability. It is designed to perform VTOL missions like a conventional helicopter while also having the long-range cruise abilities of a twin turboprop aircraft. The Marine version, MV-22B will serve as assault transport for troops, equipment, and supplies, and will operate from ships or from expeditionary airfields ashore. Navy plans to use the V-22 for combat search and rescue, delivery and retrieval of special warfare teams, along with fleet logistic support transport. The CV-22 operated by the U.S. Special Operations Command will conduct long-range special operations missions, combat rescue, and other special missions. The V-22 Osprey will replace the Marine Corps's CH-46E and CH-53D and possibly other aircraft. Despite several accidents which killed over two dozen persons, production is scheduled for 360 units designated for the Marine Corps, 48 for the Navy, and 50 for the Air Force. The aircraft requires a crew of three. (N, M, SOF)

V/STOL: Vertical and/or short takeoff and landing aircraft. These are aircraft that take off like a helicopter (vertically) but fly like a plane or jet (horizontally).

VTOL: Vertical takeoff and landing-capable aircraft.

VTOL-UAV: Vertical takeoff and landing unmanned aerial vehicle.

★ ARMS AND ARTILLERY— ★ GENERAL TERMINOLOGY

Guns are classified according to use, size, and tradition, which vary according to the different military branches. Any gun below a 20-millimeter bore size is generally classified as a small arm. Individual weapons include assault rifles in caliber 5.56 or 7.62mm. Light support weapons include machine guns, single-shot grenade launchers, and automatic grenade launchers. Machine guns are available in caliber 5.45, 5.56, 7.62, 12.7, and 14.5mm. Single shot grenade launchers have a caliber of 40mm, and generally fire a HE (high explosive) grenade to a maximum range of about 400 meters. Automatic grenade launchers have a caliber of 30 or 40mm, and fire ammunition of a HE (high explosive) or a HEDP (high explosive dual-purpose) type with a maximum range to 2200 meters.

Some general terms, ordered by size, follow.

Pistol: A pistol is a hand-operated firearm having a chamber integral with or permanently aligned with the bore.

Revolver: A revolver is a hand-operated firearm with a revolving cylinder containing chambers for individual cartridges.

Rifle: A rifle is a shoulder firearm which can discharge a bullet through a rifled barrel 16 inches or longer. The spiral parallel grooves in the bore impart spin in the projectile, providing stability and extended range.

Carbine: A carbine has a barrel under 16 inches in length typically used by cavalry, artillery, engineers, or others who require a weapon for self-defense and emergencies. Accuracy and ballistics tend to be inferior to the full version of the rifles they were adapted from.

Assault rifle: Assault rifles are rifles capable of single-shot or automatic fire using a short cartridge that provides accurate fire and more controllable recoil force than a standard rifle cartridge. By reducing the cartridge case and propellant, the cartridges weigh less and soldiers can carry more. These shorter rifles were developed in response to the recognition that most fire fights take place at ranges under 400 yards. The small size of the assault rifle and its ability to fire at up to 800 rounds per minute has led to it being adopted by various forces as a replacement for the submachine gun.

Machine pistol: A machine pistol is a firearm designed to fire fully automatically by a single pull of the trigger.

Submachine gun: A lightweight one-man weapon capable of automatic fire,

firing a low-powered pistol cartridge with limited range and accuracy.

Machine gun: A general-purpose machine gun functions as either a squad light automatic weapon (light machine gun) when mounted on a bipod and fired from the shoulder or as a sustained fire long-range weapon (heavy machine gun) when mounted on a tripod or light vehicle and provided with an optical sight.

Small Arms

Small arms refer to weapons of small caliber usually requiring only one person to operate, as opposed to crew-served weapons. This is not a precise term as some crew-served weapons, such as smaller machine guns, are often called small arms. Any gun below a 20-millimeter bore size is generally classified as a small arm. Small knives also fall into this category.

Knives and Bayonets

001 Baker Fighting Stiletto: World War II stiletto knife. (A)

Bayonet: A knife-like weapon attached to the muzzle of a rifle used for hand-to-hand combat.

Cornelius pilot survival knife: Carried by pilots of all services, a 6-inch blade was later shortened to 5-inch length. Knife/scabbard with sharpening stone is in attached pouch.

Fairbairn Sykes Commando Dagger: Thin sharp bladed dagger, 11.5-inch long with 6.75-inch long blade that was introduced to American troops with Shanghai Marines pre-World War II in China. Used by OSS/Marine raiders, etc. (M)

Imperial M3: World War II trench knife, with 6-3/4-inch blade.

KBAR: Designated Mk-2, this is the Marine Corps fighting knife, a large, heavy, bladed weapon with a leather grip. (M)

Knuckle knife: Dagger with a studded steel guard over the grip. Used in trench warfare during World War I. (A, M)

M4: Bayonet/fighting knife used with the M-1 carbine, produced in the 1940s–1960s.

M5: Shotgun bayonet of the Vietnam era. (A, M)

M6: Bayonet knife for M16 rifle during Vietnam. (A, M)

M7: Bayonet/Bowie knife combination. 6.5-inch blade with 11.5-inch overall length, stainless-steel blade with metal scabbard, used with the M-14 rifle in Vietnam. (A, M)

M9: Bayonet used with the M16 rifle in Desert Storm. (A, M)

M1905: Sword bayonet with 16-inch blade for World War I Springfield rifle and later used on World War II M-1 rifles. Bayonet later shortened to 10-inch in WWII.

OSS Stiletto M-010: Knife used by OSS field agents.

SOG: Navy SEALs knife. (N)

Stiletto: A long, narrow-bladed dagger.

Pistols

.22: .22-caliber light pistol.

.38: A six-shot revolver, manufactured by Colt, Ruger, and Smith & Wesson. The 2-inch barrel weapons are used by Criminal Investigation Division and counterintelligence personnel. This weapon can be fired by cocking the hammer (single-action) or with a trigger pull that brings the hammer back before releasing it (double-action).

.45: .45-caliber pistol.

M9: Beretta 9mm pistol with fifteen-round magazine that replaced the M1911A1 in the 1990s, it is a lightweight, semiautomatic weapon that serves as the standard Army sidearm. (A, M)

M1911A1: A .45-caliber automatic pistol that is recoil-operated and magazine-fed. Used from World

War I until the 1990s, it has been replaced by the M9. (A, M)

Rifles

BAR: Browning Automatic Rifle, .30-caliber [30-06], an air-cooled weapon capable of firing 200–350 rounds/minute, it was assigned one per squad. Also called the M1918A1 automatic rifle, it was first used in World War II and until Vietnam. It was replaced by the SAW or M249 (see page 304). (A, M)

M1/M2/M3: Garand. An air-cooled, gas-operated, clip-fed, semiautomatic shoulder weapon .30-caliber carbine rifle. It replaced the Springfield M1903 and was itself replaced by the M14. The M1 carbine has a shortened cartridge similar to a .38-caliber pistol round. The M1 carbine was developed to provide better protection to service troops than standard issue pistols when caught under surprise attack during envelopment movements by enemy forces and was the primary infantry weapon of World War II and Korea. The carbine filled a need for a weapon heavier than a pistol, but lighter than a rifle for issue to company-grade officers and NCOs. The variant M1A1 features a folding metal buttstock, an excellent lightweight weapon for use by paratroops. The M2 is selectable for either semi- or fully-automatic fire

and the M3 was modified for sniper use. (A, M)

M4: Carbine rifle caliber 5.56mm. Lightweight for quick action and can be fitted with a grenade launcher. Collapsible for storage, it has a rear sight for better control to the maximum range of ammunition. (A, M)

M14: A 7.62mm rifle, the M14 is an air-cooled, gas-operated, magazine-fed, shoulder weapon. It is designed primarily for semiautomatic fire as an infantry weapon in use between Korea and early Vietnam. It replaced the M1 and was itself replaced by the M16. (A, M)

M16: The M16 rifle is 5.56mm and is a lightweight, air-cooled, gas-operated, magazine-fed, shoulder weapon with both semiautomatic and full automatic fire. It was nicknamed "black magic" because it was made of black plastic and steel. (A, M)

M82: Sniper rifle. The M82 rifle is a high powered heavy sniper rifle used widely around the world. It is also called the "Light Fifty" for its .50-caliber BMG (12.7mm) load. The weapon has two variants, the original M82A1 (and A3) and the bullpup M82A2. The M82A2 is no longer manufactured. (M, SOF)

M1903: Springfield bolt-action .30-caliber rifle that was replaced by the

M1 in the mid-1930s. The Marine Corps used them in early World War II until after Guadalcanal. (M)

M1918: Browning Automatic Rifle, known universally as the BAR. (See *BAR* on page 302.)

Remington 870: Shotgun. (M, SOF)

Heavy Arms—Crew-Served Weapons

Machine Guns

.50: .50-caliber machine gun.

.50-caliber M-2 HMG: Browning Heavy Machine Gun.

.57-caliber antitank gun: "Buffalo gun."

Bandolier: A linked belt of machine gun ammo or other ammunition.

Bazooka: Antitank weapon used in World War II with a rocket method of propulsion. One man loaded and aimed it, and the other carried it on his shoulder and fired it.

Gatling gun: The Gatling gun was the first successful rapid-repeating firearm, and combined reliability, high-firing rate, and ease of loading into a single device. It was introduced during the Civil War. Modern equivalents are guns with a similar rotating barrel design. It is not technically a machine gun as it relies on a hand crank (externally powered), whereas machine guns operate entirely on the power of the fired cartridge (internally powered). (A, M)

Gun: Artillery or other weaponry in which the barrel does not contain rifling (lands and grooves) used to spin a projectile for greater accuracy.

M2: "Ma Deuce," a .50-caliber (12.7mm) machine gun. World War II-era automatic, belt-fed, recoil-operated, air-cooled, crew-operated machine gun, it is crew-transportable with limited amounts of ammunition over short distances, capable of single-shot (ground M2) as well as automatic fire. Unit replacement cost is $14,000. (A, N, M, F)

M2A1: Submachine gun, .45-caliber automatic weapon. "Grease gun."

M3A1: Shoulder-fired, blowback operated .45-caliber submachine gun with thirty-round magazine known as the "grease gun." A favorite of garrison officers. Standard onboard weapon for most tank crews.

M10: Tank destroyer World War II. 76mm, and later, 90mm gun to counter larger-gunned German tanks. Sacrificed overall armor for speed and gun size. No overhead protection. (A)

M37: .30-machine gun, an interim modification to the M1919A4 .30-caliber machine gun for use as a tank machine gun. Ammunition could be fed from either side giving the machine gun more flexibility in tank mountings than either the M1919A4 or M1919A5. The M37 has a rate of fire of 400–550 spm. The model M37C was used as an aircraft gun on the OH-13 Sioux and OH-23 Raven on the skid-mounted M1 armament subsystem.

M60: 7.62mm machine gun. "Hog-60." Air-cooled, belt-fed, gas-operated, fully automatic, shoulder-fired, standard-infantry machine gun with bipod and replacement barrels. (A, M)

M67: 90mm recoil-less rifle. (SOF)

M85: .50-caliber machine gun. The M85 replaced the M2 .50 caliber machine gun, which was too large. The M85 had a quick-change barrel and a dual rate of fire for use against aircraft (1000–1100 spm) or ground targets (400–500 spm). The M85 became the standard tank machine gun for many years. Adapted for tripod mounting, for use at low rate of fire as a flexible machine gun. Operationally unreliable and ineffective against the present generation infantry fighting vehicles (e.g., the Warsaw Pact BMP mechanized infantry combat vehicle). (A, M)

M240: Medium machine gun, 7.62mm, left-hand feed, gas-operated, air-cooled, fixed head space weapon designed for use in aircraft and on ground. The M240G is the standard Marine Corp version. Unit replacement cost is $6,000. (A, M)

M249: SAW or Squad Automatic Weapon, it replaced the BAR after Vietnam. The SAW is a gas-operated, belt/magazine-fed, air-cooled, automatic, shoulder-fired light machine gun of 5.56mm. There are typically nine SAWs in a basic infantry platoon. (A, M)

M1919A4: Browning .30-caliber machine gun, air or water cooled. The Army's standard battalion level machine gun until the mid-1950s, it was replaced by the M60 7.62mm machine gun. (A)

OCSW: Objective Crew-Served Weapon is an ultra-light, two-man portable, crew-served weapon system an integrated machine gun system that couples the firepower of air bursting munitions with optoelectronic fire control to provide all-environment operation and enhanced lethality. It gives high levels of incapacitation and suppression of enemy soldiers up to 2,000 meters away and can damage lightly armored vehicles, watercraft, and slow-moving aircraft beyond

1,000 meters. Likely to replace the MK19 grenade machine gun and the .50-caliber M2 machine gun.

Predator: Short range assault weapon. (A, M)

★ GROUND VEHICLES ★

AMTRAC: Acronym for amphibious armored, tracked, personnel carrier. (M)

Drone: A land, sea, or air vehicle that is remotely or automatically controlled.

Tracked: A vehicle that runs on its own tracks rather than on wheels, such as tanks.

Assault Vehicles / Tanks

ACAV: Armored cavalry assault vehicle.

AFV: Armored fighting vehicle.

Amazing Grace: Army cavalry's 63-ton tank. (A)

APC: Armored personnel carrier. Lightly armored, highly mobile, full-tracked vehicle, amphibious and air-droppable, used for transporting personnel and their individual equipment during tactical operations. Can be fitted or modified to serve as a mortar carrier, command post, flame thrower, antiaircraft artillery chassis, or limited recovery vehicle.

Armored reconnaissance airborne assault vehicle: A lightly armored, mobile, full-tracked vehicle serving as a main reconnaissance vehicle in infantry and airborne operations and as a principal assault weapon of airborne troops.

LAV-25: Light armored vehicle with a 25mm chain gun and 7.62mm machine gun. It is air-portable by fixed wing aircraft or helicopter, and water/amphibious capable. (M)

M1: Abrams tank, also called a Cadillac or fast mover. Main battle tank of the Army, it was first used successfully in the first Gulf War. Too large to be brought more than one at a time by the C5 Galaxy, they were brought in by cargo ship so were delayed, but were still highly successful. (A, M)

M2: Bradley Infantry Fighting Vehicle. An armored, full-tracked vehicle designed to carry mechanized infantry into close contact with the enemy, it can keep up with the Abrams tank, has medium- and long-range firepower capable of defeating any vehicle on the battlefield, and is adequately armored to protect the crew from artillery and small arms threats. It serves as a sophisticated weapons platform capable of providing tremendous firepower in direct support of the infantry it carries. It is armed with the M242 25mm "Bushmaster" Chain Gun and the M240C machine gun, which fires 7.62mm rounds. (A)

M3: Stuart Light tank. A 12-ton tank used by U.S. and British and in the Pacific by Marines in early World War II. Its armor was too thin for success against German armored forces but it was fast and good for scouting and especially useful in tight spaces in the Pacific campaigns. (A, M)

M3A5: Grant tank. Used in early World War II in North Africa, the Grant tank has one 75-mm main gun with limited movement in the hull, and a 37-mm gun in a small turret. (A)

M4: Sherman tank. Medium tank used in World War II in great numbers. Has a 75mm gun with inadequate armor. German tanks were superior but numbers overcame quality. (A, M)

M6: Linebacker infantry fighting vehicle. (A)

M24: Chaffee light tank used in WWII, it had a 75mm M-6 gun.

M26: Pershing main battle tank used in Korea had a 76mm gun. (A, M)

M48: Main battle tank used in Vietnam, originally with a 90mm American gun but later upgraded to a British 105 gun. Still in use around the world. (A, M)

M48A3: A battle tank in Vietnam with a 90mm main gun, coaxial-mounted .30-caliber machine gun and a cupola-mounted .50-caliber machine gun with a crew of four. (A)

M60: Patton battle tank. The main American battle tank post-Vietnam to Gulf War, it was also used by Marines in first Gulf War. (A, M)

M113A1: Gavin. A lightly armored, full-tracked, air-transportable personnel carrier designed to carry personnel and certain types of cargo. Developed in the late 1950s, it is capable of amphibious operations in streams and lakes, extended cross-country travel over rough terrain, and high-speed operation on improved roads and highways. (A)

M551A1: Sheridan. Armored reconnaissance airborne assault vehicle. The M551 Sheridan was developed to give the Army a light-armored reconnaissance vehicle with heavy firepower. Although airdrop-capable, the aluminum armor was thin enough to be pierced by heavy machine-gun rounds, and the vehicle was particularly vulnerable to mines. It had limited use in Vietnam, where many deficiencies were revealed. Sheridan-equipped units participated in Operation Just Cause in Panama (1989), and were deployed to Saudi Arabia during Operation Desert Shield. (A)

Ontos: Ontos, LRM variant, was a light, antitank, tracked armored vehicle used in Korea and Vietnam. It had six 106mm recoilless rifles. (A, M)

Stryker: Series of eight-wheeled, all-wheel-drive, armored combat vehicles used by the Army as the first new military vehicle since the M2 Bradley. Armament includes M2 .50-caliber machine gun, MK19 grenade machine gun, TOW antitank guided missile, M240B machine gun. Questions about the sufficiency of its armor have been raised.

Other Ground Vehicles

ATV: All-terrain vehicle.

Dinkie: Two-seated dune buggy used in the Gulf War.

Humvee: High-mobility multipurpose wheeled vehicle (HMMWV). Successor to jeep and used heavily in the Gulf Wars.

LACV-30: Large air-cushion vehicle, i.e., hovercraft.

LVTP-7: Amphibious tractor (Amtrack) transported Marines from an LST or LPD to and over the beachhead, if necessary. Nicknamed "Large Vulnerable Target," they were renamed AAVP-7 "Tuna Boats." (M)

Polaris ATV: The Polaris all-terrain vehicle is utilized by special ops teams to transport wounded and to identify and destroy enemy positions. It can be dropped into airfields to quickly survey the area. It has a radio and can carry up to two extra persons. (SOF)

RATT: Used during airfield seizures, RATT is a specialized medical vehicle that can carry up to 6 litter-borne patients (patients requiring stretchers) and three special ops personnel. (SOF)

★ ORDNANCE ★

Ordnance refers to all explosives, chemicals, pyrotechnics, and similar stores, e.g., bombs, guns and ammunition, flares, smoke, and napalm.

Dud: Explosive munition which has not been armed as intended or which has failed to explode after being armed.

Explosive ordnance: All munitions containing explosives, nuclear fission or fusion materials, and biological or chemical agents. Includes bombs, warheads, guided and ballistic missiles, artillery, mortars, rockets, small arms ammunition, mines, torpedoes, depth charges, demolition charges, pyrotechnics, clusters and dispensers, cartridge- and propellant-actuated devices, electro-explosive devices, clandestine and improvised explosive devices, and all similar or related items or components explosive in nature.

Matériel: From the French term for equipment or hardware, it refers to military equipment and supplies, either specifically or in general.

Bombs

AGM-62: Walleye. A smart, guided, free-fall bomb.

B28 Thermonuclear Bomb: A large, aerial thermonuclear bomb. Includes several variants as below:

B28EX: Carried externally by F-100, F-105, and F-4; no parachute.

B28IN: Carried internally by B-52 and F-105; no parachute.

B28RE: Carried externally; equipped with one 4-ft. pilot chute and one 28-ft. ribbon chute.

B28RI: Carried internally; equipped with one 4-ft. pilot parachute, one 16.5-ft. ribbon extraction chute, one 64-ft. solid chute, and one 30-in. stabilization chute.

B28FI: Carried internally; equipped with one 4-ft. pilot chute, one 16-ft. and one 24-ft. chute.

BLU-80/B: Bigeye. This was a safe-to-handle chemical weapon using VX agent as the warhead. It was designed to delay and disrupt airfields, troops, and logistical lifelines by forcing an enemy into a chemical protective posture.

Bomb: A bomb is an explosive filler material enclosed in a casing. They are classified according to the ratio of explosive material to total weight. The classes are general purpose (GP), fragmentation, penetration, and cluster bombs.

Cluster bombs: Cluster bombs are primarily fragmentation weapons. Cluster bombs, like GP bombs, can feature a variety of components to produce the desired effect.

DA: Delayed-action bomb.

Dumb bomb: Conventional bomb, dropped from above that relies on gravity; not laser-guided like "smart bombs."

Fragmentation bombs: Designed to fragment into pieces upon detonation. About 10 to 20 percent of a fragmentation bomb's weight is explosive material; the rest are specially scored cases that break into fragments, which travel at high velocities, and are the primary cause of damage.

GBU-10, GBU-12, GBU-15, GBU-16, GBU-25, GBU-27, and GBU-28: Paveway bombs, these are guided bomb units with capacity from 500 to 2,000 pounds munitions.

General purpose bomb: About half of the general purpose (GP) bomb's weight is explosive materials. These bombs usually weigh between 500 and 2,000 pounds and produce a combination of blast and fragmentation effects. The .5-inch-thick casing creates a fragmentation effect at the moment of detonation, and the explosive filler causes considerable damage from blast effect. The most common GP bombs are the MK-80 series.

Glide bomb: A bomb fitted with airfoils to provide lift and that is carried and released in the direction of a target by an airplane.

Incendiary: These munitions destroy by starting fires. They may contain a metallic incendiary material that burns at a very high temperature, or an incendiary gel ("napalm") that flows over a target as it burns.

JDAM: Joint direct attack munition is a guidance tail kit that converts unguided free-fall bombs into accurate, adverse-weather, "smart" bombs as a joint Air Force and Navy program. It is a guided air-to-surface weapon that uses either the 2,000-pound BLU-109/MK 84 or the 1,000-pound BLU-110/MK 83 warheads. With the JDAM, accurate air-to-surface weapons can be deployed against high-priority fixed and moving targets from fighter and bomber aircraft. (N, F)

LANTIRN: Low altitude navigation and targeting infrared for night, or LANTIRN, is a system for use on the Air Force's F-15E Eagle and F-16C/D Fighting Falcon, and the Navy's F-14 Tomcat. LANTIRN pods are used with Paveway bombs (N, M, F)

Laser-Guided Bombs, LGB: "Smart bombs" that utilize an infrared guidance system. All LGB weapons have a computer-control group (CCG), a warhead (bomb body with fuse), and an airfoil group.

Napalm: Incendiary gel. Napalm bombs contain gasoline mixed with a thickening agent to make the burning mix more viscous and sticky. Napalm derives its name from its original thickening agent, sodium palmitrate ("Na-palm"), but most modern napalm uses polystyrene beads as a thickener. Napalm bombs are normally stockpiled as empty tanks, and then "fueled" with napalm before use. During World War II, aircraft drop tanks fitted with fuzes were often used as napalm bombs.

Penetration bombs: These have between 25 and 30 percent explosive filler. The casings are designed to penetrate hardened targets, such as bunkers, before the explosives detonate. Penetration is achieved by either kinetic energy of the entire projectile or the effects of a shaped charge.

Smart bomb: Bombs with guidance system that makes them very accurate. These have been used since the end of the Vietnam War.

Thermite: A combination of powdered iron oxide and aluminum commonly used as an incendiary.

Grenades / Launchers / Flame Throwers

AN-M8: HC Smoke Hand Grenade. Weighing 25.5 oz., it contains 19 oz. of hexachloroethane which emits a dense smoke for up to 2.5 minutes. It has a two-second delay.

AN-M14: Incendiary (Thermite) hand grenade. It weighs 32 oz. and contains 26.5 oz. of TH3 Thermite mixture, and starts fires with forty seconds duration of 4,300 degrees Fahrenheit.

Arming pin: Safety device for grenades which prevents the unintentional action of the arming cycle, until it is removed. "Safety pin."

Frag: Fragmentation grenade. May be thrown or launched with grenade launcher.

M7A3 CS: Riot-control hand grenade. This 19-oz. weapon contains 9.5 oz. of CS gas that when ignited gives off a thick cloud of irritating agent for approximately sixty seconds.

M15: White phosphorous hand grenade replaced by the M34.

M18: Colored smoke hand grenade. Emits either red, green, or yellow smoke for up to one and a half minutes. Color is marked on the canister.

M25A2 CS: Riot-control hand grenade weighing 7.5 oz. with 3.5 oz. of CS gas with a unique arming system.

M26: Fragmentation hand grenade. Hand-thrown with a seven-second delay from arming to explosion.

M34: White phosphorous smoke hand grenade. This 27.2-oz. weapon contains 12 oz. of white phosphorous.

M67: Fragmentation hand grenade. The 14-oz. canister produces casualties within fifty feet (A, M).

M67A2: Flame-thrower tank with 260-gallon bottle of napalm, a coaxial mounted .30-caliber machine gun; it requires a crew of three. Its cruising range is 200 miles and weighs 50 tons when fully combat loaded.

M69: Training and practice grenades. The training version has all inert or expended parts; the only removable item is the pin. The practice grenade is the same as the training grenade except that it uses an active M228 fuse to indicate delay times and add realism to training.

M79: Shoulder-held, 40mm, single-shot grenade launcher with a range of 400 meters. Called a "blooper"

from the sound it makes when fired. (M)

M203: Lightweight, single-shot, breech-loaded, pump-action (sliding barrel), shoulder-fired weapon attached to an M16A2 5.56mm rifle. Effective range 100 ft. (A, M, SOF)

M228: Hand grenade fuse.

MK1: Illuminating hand grenade. The burning magnesium emits 55,000 candlepower for about twenty-five seconds.

MK19: 40mm machine gun, MOD3, air-cooled, blowback operated, belt-fed heavy grenade machine gun. The MK19 MOD3 40mm grenade machine gun is used in harsh environments with a firing rate of over 350 grenades per minute and it is effective to ranges of over 2200 meters. It was used effectively in the Middle East during Operation Desert Storm against enemy infantry. (A, N, M)

Stun grenade: Temporarily blinds as well as incapacitates. Also called a "flash-bang" or "crash-bang," for the sound it makes when fired.

WP: White phosphorus, also "Willie Peter," incendiary material that burns hot and is not extinguished with water. It was used in WP hand grenades and artillery rounds.

Mines

Acoustic mine: Mine with acoustic circuit that responds to the acoustic field of a ship or sweep.

Acoustic minehunting: Use of sonar to detect mines.

Active mine: A mine actuated by a target; live and ready to pop.

Antenna mine: Contact mine fitted with antennae that, when touched by a steel ship, sets up galvanic action to fire the mine.

Antisweep device: Any device incorporated in a mine or its mooring designed to impede the sweeping of that mine.

Antisweeper mine: Mine laid with the specific objective of damaging mine countermeasures vessels.

Antiwatching device: A device fitted in a moored mine that causes it to sink to prevent its position from being disclosed to the enemy.

Armed mine: Mine from which all safety devices have been withdrawn and arming devices have operated—ready to be actuated after receipt of target signal, influence or contact.

Armed sweep: Sweep fitted with cutters or other devices to enable it to cut mine moorings.

Attrition minefield: In naval mine warfare, a field intended primarily to cause damage to enemy ships.

Beach minefield: Minefield in shallow water nearing the shore at sites suited for amphibious landings.

Bottom mine: Mine with negative buoyancy, i.e., it sinks. Also, "ground mine."

Bouncing Betty: Shrapnel-filled mine that pops up a few feet into the air and then explodes; it hits at stomach level.

Bouquet mine: Naval mine in which several buoyant mines are attached to the same sinker, so that when one mine case is cut, another rises from the sinker like a bouquet of flowers.

Claymore: Directional antipersonnel mine with plastic explosive propelling ball bearings. Often used in perimeter defense.

Closure minefield: In naval mine warfare, a minefield which is planned to present such a threat that waterborne shipping is prevented from moving.

Coarse mine: In naval mine warfare, a relatively insensitive mine.

Combination influence mine: Mine designed to actuate only when two or more different influences (triggering mechanisms) are received, either at the same time or in a predetermined order.

Contact mine: A mine detonated by physical contact.

Controllable mine: A mine that can be controlled by the user to make it safe or live or fire it.

Countermine: To explode the main charge in a mine by the shock of a nearby explosion of another mine or independent explosive charge. The explosion of the main charge may be caused either by sympathetic detonation or through the explosive train and/ or firing mechanism of the mine.

Creeping mine: Buoyant mine that is weighted to be held below the surface but free to creep along the seabed by water currents.

Cutter: A device fitted to a sweep wire to cut or part the moorings of mines or obstructers.

Dead mine: Mine neutralized or rendered useless or safe.

Deep minefield: Antisubmarine minefield that is safe for surface ships to cross.

Defensive minefield: In naval mine warfare, a minefield laid in international waters or international straits with the declared intention of controlling shipping in defense of sea communications.

Delay release sinker: A sinker that holds a moored mine on the sea bed for a predetermined time after laying.

Depth charge: The oldest antisubmarine weapon, it has both explosive and fuse that explode at a predetermined depth. It is deployed by both ships and aircraft.

Disarmed mine: A mine for which the arming procedure has been reversed, rendering the mine inoperative. It is safe to handle and transport and can be rearmed by simple action.

Dormant: In mine warfare, the state of a mine during which a time delay feature in a mine prevents it from being actuated.

Drill mine: An inert filled mine or minelike body used in loading, laying, or discharge practice and trials.

Dummy minefield: In naval mine warfare, a minefield containing no live mines and presenting only a psychological threat.

Enabling mine countermeasures: Countermeasures (systems to prevent weapons from acquiring or destroying a target) designed to counter mines once they have been laid. This includes both passive and active mine countermeasures.

Explosive filled mine: In mine warfare, a mine containing an explosive charge but not necessarily the firing mechanism required to detonate it.

Fitted mine: In naval mine warfare, a mine containing an explosive charge, a primer, detonator, and firing system.

Floating mine: In naval mine warfare, a mine visible on the surface.

Free mine: In naval mine warfare, a moored mine whose mooring has parted or been cut.

Gap marker: In landmine warfare, markers used to indicate a minefield gap, where the area is free of mines.

Grapnel: In naval mine warfare, a device fitted to a mine mooring designed to grapple the sweep wire when the mooring is cut.

Gravel mines: Allied forces used these antipersonnel mines in Vietnam, sometimes disguised with animal feces. Smaller than a fist and dropped from low-flying aircraft in large numbers, they were dropped frozen; upon thawing, they self-armed and sent out a number of sensing arms for the purpose of maiming upon detonation.

Homing mine: In naval mine warfare, a mine fitted with propulsion equipment that homes on to a target.

Horn: In naval mine warfare, a projection from the mine shell of some contact mines that, when broken or bent by contact, causes the mine to fire.

Horizontal action mine: Mine designed to produce a destructive effect parallel to the ground.

Humanitarian demining: Department of Defense and Department of State program to assist other nations in protecting their populations from landmines and clearing land of the threat posed by landmines remaining after conflict has ended.

IED: Improvised explosive device. Any device improvised from destructive, lethal, noxious, pyrotechnic, or incendiary chemicals and designed to destroy, incapacitate, harass, or distract, usually from nonmilitary components.

Independent mine: A mine that is not controlled by the user after laying.

Inert mine: A mine or replica of a mine incapable of producing an explosion.

Kite: Weight used on sweepwire in minesweeping operation.

Land mine: Explosive devices designed to destroy or damage equipment or personnel. Equipment targets include ground vehicles, boats, and aircraft. A mine is detonated by the action of its target, the passage of time, or controlled means. There are two main types of land-based mines, antitank (AT) and antipersonnel (AP). *AT mines* are designed to immobilize or destroy vehicles and their occupants. An AT mine produces a mobility kill (M-Kill) or a catastrophic kill (K-Kill). An M-Kill destroys one or more of the vehicle's vital drive components (e.g., a tank's track) and immobilizes the target. An M-Kill does not always destroy the weapon system and the crew; they may continue to function. In a K-Kill, the weapon system and/or the crew are destroyed. *Ap mines* are designed to kill or incapacitate their victims. The mines commit medical resources, degrade unit morale, and damage nonarmored vehicles. Some types of AP mines may break or damage the track on armored vehicles.

Mine: In landmine warfare, an explosive material designed to destroy or damage ground vehicles, boats, aircraft, wound, kill, or maim personnel. Detonated by the action of its victim, by the passage of time, or by controlled means. In naval warfare, it refers to an explosive device laid in the water to damage or sink ships or deter ships from an area; the term does not include devices attached to the bottoms of ships by persons operating underwater, or devices that explode automatically after a predetermined time after laying.

Mine clearance: Process of removing all mines from an area.

Mine warfare: Use of mines and mine countermeasures. Laying of mines against the enemy or countering the enemy's mines.

Mined area: An area declared dangerous due to the presence, or suspected presence, of mines.

Minefield lane: A marked path through a minefield that is cleared of mines or unmined.

Minehunting: Using sensor and neutralization systems to locate and dispose of individual mines. Minehunting is conducted when minesweeping is not suitable or to verify an area free of mines.

Minesweeping: The technique of clearing mines using mechanical, explosive, or influence sweep equipment. *Mechanical means* removes, disturbs, or otherwise neutralizes the mines. A simple minesweeping operation may include dragging a heavy wire between two vessels to clear the water of mines. *Explosive minesweeping* either causes the mine to detonate or damages it, rendering it useless. *Influence sweeping* also detonates the mines via acoustic or magnetic means.

Service mine: A mine capable of a destructive explosion.

Sterilize: To permanently render a mine incapable of firing by means of a device (e. g., sterilizer) within the mine.

Warble: In naval mine warfare, the process of varying the frequency of sound produced by a narrow band noisemaker to ensure that the frequency to which the mine will respond is covered.

Wire: Trip wires (detonating portion) that set off booby traps or mines around a base.

Missiles / Mortars / Rockets / Rounds / Shells

AAI: Air-to-air interface; a missile shot from the air towards an airborne target.

AAM: Air-to-air guided missile, an air-launched guided missile for use against airborne targets.

ABM: Antiballistic missile, a missile used to counter ballistic missiles.

AGM: Air-to-ground missile; a missile shot from the air towards a ground target.

AGM-28B: Hound Dog. Turbojet-propelled, air-to-surface missile designed to be carried externally on the B-52. It's equipped with a nuclear warhead and can be launched for either high or low altitude attacks against enemy targets, supplementing the internally carried firepower of the B-52.

AGM-45: The Shrike, an air-launched antiradiation missile designed to home in on and destroy radar emitters.

AGM-65: The AGM-65 Maverick is a tactical, air-to-surface guided missile designed for close air support, interdiction, and defense suppression missions. It provides stand-off capability and high probability of strike against a wide range of tactical targets, including armor, air defenses, ships, transportation equipment, and fuel storage facilities. Mavericks were used during Operation Desert Storm and hit 85 percent of their targets. Mavericks can be launched from high altitudes to tree-top level and can hit targets ranging from a distance of a few thousand feet to 13 nautical miles at medium altitude. (N, F)

AGM-84: Harpoon SLAM, "Stand Off Land Attack Missile." This weapon system uses midcourse guidance with a radar seeker to attack surface ships. Its low-level, sea-skimming cruise trajectory, active radar guidance, and warhead design assure high survivability and effectiveness. The Harpoon missile was designed to sink warships at long ranges in an open-ocean environment. (N, F)

AGM-86 ALCM/CALCM: Air-to-ground conventional cruise missile intended for use on either the B-52G or B-52H bomber fleet as a strategic nuclear weapon against the former Soviet Union. Up to six missiles can be carried on external pylons and eight internally. The AGM-86A/B models utilize terrain-contour-matching navigation system for almost perfect accuracy. This system allows the missile to navigate based upon the terrain below by comparing built-in maps with radar-generated maps of the ground.

AGM-86BC: Air-to-ground cruise missile used on the B-52H bombers. It is powered by a turbofan jet engine that propels it at sustained subsonic speeds. After launch, the missile's folded wings, tail surfaces, and engine inlet deploy, and the missile can then fly complicated routes to a target via its terrain-contour-matching guidance system. Its strength lies in its small size and low-altitude flight capability (and thus is difficult to detect on radar), and in its numbers,

which would each have to be counterattacked.

AGM-88 HARM: The AGM-88 HARM (high-speed antiradiation missile) is an air-to-surface tactical missile designed to seek and destroy enemy radar-equipped air defense systems. It can detect, attack, and destroy a target with minimum aircrew input and is used on the F-16C. Its range is more than 30 miles at supersonic speed, and it was introduced in 1984. (N)

AGM-114: Hellfire. The Hellfire air-to-ground missile system (AGMS) is used for heavy antiarmor capability for attack helicopters. The first three variants us a laser seeker, and the fourth variant uses a radar frequency seeker. They are used as the main armament of the AH-64 and AH-1W Super Cobra helicopters. (A, N, M)

AIM-7: Sparrow. The AIM-7 Sparrow is a radar-guided, air-to-air missile with a high-explosive warhead. It's used by the Air Force for the F-15 Eagle. The ship-launched, surface-to-air version is called Sea Sparrow RIM-7. (N, F)

AIM-9: Sidewinder. A supersonic, heat-seeking, air-to-air missile carried by fighter aircraft with a high-explosive (non-nuclear) warhead and an infrared, heat-seeking guidance system. The Sidewinder was developed by the Navy for fleet air defense and was adapted by the Air Force for fighter aircraft use. The ground-to-air version is designated Chaparral MIM-72. (N, F)

AIM-54A: Phoenix. The AIM-54 Phoenix long-range air-to-air missile is carried in clusters of up to six missiles on the F-14 Tomcat. The Phoenix missile is the Navy's only long-range, air-to-air missile. It is an airborne weapons control system with multiple-target handling capabilities, used to kill multiple air targets with conventional warheads. The weapon system consists of an AIM-54 guided missile, interface system, and a launch aircraft with an AN/AWG-9 weapon control system. (N)

AIM-120 AMRAAM: Slammer. An advanced medium-range, air-to-air missile (AMRAAM) with an all-weather, beyond-visual-range capability. AMRAAM is a supersonic, air-launched, aerial-intercept guided missile employing active radar target tracking, proportional navigation guidance, and active radio frequency (RF) target detection. (N, F)

ALCM: Air-launched cruise missile.

ARM: Antiradiation missile, a conventional warhead missile that homes in passively on a radiation source.

ASROC: Antisubmarine rocket. A surface ship-launched, rocket-propelled, nuclear depth charge or homing torpedo used against submarines.

AT4: Antitank missile. (A)

Ballistic missile: Fire nuclear, chemical, biological or conventional warheads in a ballistic flight trajectory.

Ballistic missile early warning system: An electronic system providing for early warning of attack by enemy intercontinental ballistic missiles.

Ballistic trajectory: The trajectory traced after the propulsive force is terminated and the body is acted upon only by gravity and aerodynamic drag.

Bazooka: Rocket launcher. A World War II-period invention, it was the first of the modern rocket-launched weapons and was made in 2.75-inch (World War II, Korea) and 3.5-inch (Vietnam) versions. They were used against tanks, vehicles, and other profitable targets, but they were plagued by electrical problems. They were replaced by the M72 LAW.

BGM-71 TOW: Antitank missile still in use. (A, M)

BMD: Ballistic missile defense.

CALCM: Conventional air-launched cruise missile.

Chaparral: Short-range, low-altitude, surface-to-air Army air defense artillery system.

Creeping Jimmy: A high-velocity shell that gives no warning of its approach.

Cruise missile: A guided missile that usually has a jet propulsion system and carries a large conventional or nuclear warhead hundreds of miles with great accuracy. They often travel at high subsonic speeds, are self-navigating, and fly low to avoid radar detection.

Dum-dum: Soft round that expands upon impact.

Eight-charge: Eighty pounds of black powder, antiarmor howitzer package (M).

FGM-148: Javelin guided antitank missile, a man-portable, "fire-and-forget" missile fired by dismounted infantry. (A, M)

FIM-92A: Stinger missile, a lightweight, man-portable, shoulder-fired air defense artillery missile for low-altitude air defense of forward area combat troops. Used against low-altitude airborne targets, e.g., fixed-wing aircraft, helicopters, unmanned aerial vehicles, or cruise missiles. Launched from Bradley Stinger Fighting Vehicle, Bradley Linebacker, HMMWV, and helicopters as well as Man Portable Air Defense (MANPADS). (A, M)

Flare: Rocket fired at night from a pistol to light up enemy territory.

Free rocket: A rocket not subject to control by guidance or control in flight.

Guided missile: Unmanned vehicle moving along the surface of the Earth whose trajectory or path is capable of being altered by internal or external mechanism.

Gun: A cannon with a long barrel, operating with a long angle of fire, and having a high muzzle velocity. Guns provide flat-to-medium trajectories of longer range. Also includes cannons with tube lengths of .30 calibers or more.

Harpoon: All weather, antiship cruise missile capable of being deployed from surface ships (RGM-84), aircraft (AGM-84A), or submarines (UGM-84). The missile is turbojet powered and employs a low-level cruise trajectory. Terminal guidance is active radar. A 500-pound conventional warhead is employed.

Heavy antitank weapon: A weapon capable of operating from ground or vehicle, used to defeat armor and other material targets.

Homing: The technique whereby a mobile station directs itself, or is directed, towards a source of primary or reflected energy, or to a specified point.

Homing guidance: A system by which a missile or torpedo steers itself towards a target by means of a self-contained mechanism which is activated by some distinguishing characteristics of the target.

Howitzer: A cannon which combines characteristics of guns and mortars. It delivers projectiles with medium velocities, using medium-to-high trajectories. Normally, howitzers have tube length of .20–.30 calibers, but can exceed .30 calibers and still be considered a howitzer when the high angle fire zoning solution permits range overlap between charges.

Hummingbird: Artillery shell.

Incendiary: An artillery shell that burns upon impact, usually stuffed with white phosphorous.

Indirect fire: Means that the projectile does not follow the line of sight to the target.

LAAM: Light antiaircraft missile.

LAW: Light antitank weapon. It is contained in a collapsible, disposable fiberglass tube.

LGM-30G: Minuteman II, a silo-launched, surface-attack, guided, intercontinental ballistic missile (ICBM). Missiles are dispersed in hardened silos to protect against attack and connected to an underground launch control center through a system of hardened cables. There are approximately 500 Minuteman II missiles at bases in Wyoming, North Dakota, and Montana.

LGM-118A: Peacekeeper. This is America's newest intercontinental ballistic missile (ICBM), but is expected to be eliminated as part of the Strategic Arms Reduction Treaty II. It is a four-stage ICBM capable of carrying up to ten independently targetable reentry vehicles with greater accuracy than any other ballistic missile. Larger than Minuteman, it is over 70 feet long and weighs 198,000 pounds. The entire missile is encased in a canister in the silo to protect it against damage and to permit "cold launch." The Peacekeeper is ejected by pressurized gas some fifty feet into the air before first stage ignition.

M7: Larger, circular baseplate for the M224 mortar.

M8: Smaller, rectangular baseplate for the M224 mortar.

M-29: An 81mm mortar that is a smooth-bore, muzzle-loaded, high-angle, indirect-fire weapon. It consists of a barrel, sight, bipod, and base plate. The M-29 has a greater range, and its circular base plate allows for firing in any direction.

M47: Dragon missile. Man-portable, shoulder-fired, medium-range antitank weapon. A wire-guided (guidance of the missile to target is controlled by a thin wire), line-of-sight, antitank/assault missile weapon capable of defeating armored vehicles, fortified bunkers, concrete gun emplacements, and other hard targets. It is designed to be carried and fired by an individual gunner. (A, M)

M64: Sight (an optical device to help aim) for the M224 mortar.

M102: Light-towed howitzer. (A)

M103: Heavy gun tank with 120mm main cannon of extremely long range.

M109: Self-propelled howitzer. (A)

M120: 120mm mortar, replaced the M30 4.2 inch mortar in motorized infantry units. Transported on the M1100 trailer by HMMWV.

M136 AT4: The M136 AT4 is a recoilless rifle used primarily by infantry forces for engagement and defeat of light armor, as the Army's main light antitank weapon. It uses a 84mm high explosive anti-armor warhead, is man-portable, fired from the right shoulder only. The firer must be able to estimate the range (maximum of 250 meters) to the target. (A)

M170: Bipod for the M224 mortar.

M198: A howitzer that must be towed. (A)

M-220: Tube-launched, optically tracked, wire-guided (TOW) missile, antitank at a maximum range of more than 3,000 meters. Can be fired by infantrymen with a tripod or from vehicles and helicopters, launching three missiles in 90 seconds. Operates in all weather conditions and on the "dirty" battlefield. After firing the missile, the gunner must keep the cross hairs of the sight centered on the target to ensure a hit. First fielded in 1970, it is the most widely distributed antitank guided missile in the world with over 500,000 built and in service in the U.S. and elsewhere. Extensively used in Vietnam and the Middle East. (A, M)

M224: 60mm mortar consisting of the M225 cannon, the M170 bipod, and the M64 sight as well as two types of base plates, the circular M7 and the rectangular M8. Used to support airborne, air assault, mountain, ranger, special operations forces, and light-infantry units. The M224 can be drop fired (conventional mode) or trigger fired (conventional or hand-held mode). A lightweight auxiliary baseplate is used when firing the mortar in the hand-held mode. (A, M, SOF)

M225: Cannon for the M224 mortar.

M252: Medium-weight mortar. (A, M)

MGM-29A: Sergeant, a mobile, inertially guided, solid-propellant, surface-to-surface missile with nuclear warhead capability, designed to attack targets up to a range of 75 nautical miles.

MGM-51: Shillelagh, a missile system mounted on the main battle tank and assault reconnaissance vehicle for use against enemy armor, troops, and field fortifications.

MIM-23: Hawk, a mobile air defense artillery, surface-to-air missile system that provides non-nuclear, low- to medium-altitude air defense coverage for ground forces.

MIM-104: Patriot Missile, a long-range, all-altitude, all-weather, air defense system to combat tactical ballistic missiles, cruise missiles, and advanced aircraft. Used successfully in the Gulf War.

Mortar: Explosives that have high trajectories with short range. Used as indirect fire ordnance, they are projectiles with an explosive round at the bottom. Three primary types of mortar fires are as follows: *High explosive:* Used to suppress or kill enemy dismounted infantry, mortars, and other supporting weapons, and to interdict the movement of men, vehicles, and supplies in the enemy's forward area. *Obscuration:* Used to conceal friendly forces as forces maneuver or assault, and to blind enemy supporting weapons. *Illumination:* Used to reveal the location of enemy forces hidden by darkness.

Multi-Launched Rocket System: Conventional weapon capable of destroying an area the size of a dozen football fields, hence its nickname, "deadly dozen."

Polaris Missile: Submarine-launched, intercontinental ballistic missile (ICBM), nuclear capable. (N)

Poseidon missile: Early submarine-launched missile powered by a two-stage solid fuel rocket. It followed the Polaris missile in 1972, and was replaced by the Trident I in 1979. (N)

Quad 50s: An antiaircraft weapon employed by the Army during the Vietnam War. The Geneva Convention limits antipersonnel weapons to .30 calibers, so these four .50-caliber rifles could only be used on aircraft and other equipment. (A)

RGM-66D: Standard SSM (ARM), a surface-to-surface antiradiation missile equipped with conventional warheads.

Round: A cartridge containing a bullet, gunpowder, and primer in a single metallic case made to fit the firing chamber of a firearm. A cartridge without a bullet is called a *blank*.

Rubber heel: Any shell that gives no warning of its approach.

SCUD: Surface-to-surface missile system used by the Soviets during the Cold War and later by Iraqis during the Gulf War.

SLAM: Stand-off land attack missile, an all-weather, long range cruise missile developed from Harpoon missiles. (N)

SLBM: Submarine-launched ballistic missile, delivering nuclear weapons launched from submarines, e.g., Polaris, Poseidon, Trident.

SLCM: Submarine-launched cruise missile; cruise missiles delivering conventional weapons launched from submarines, e.g., Tomahawk.

SMAW: Shoulder-launched multipurpose assault weapon. A missile-firing weapon which fires an 83-millimeter encased rocket which detonates in either a fast mode against a hard (armored) target or a slow mode against a soft (unarmored) target. (A, M)

SRBM: Short-range ballistic missile. A ballistic missile with a range capability up to about 600 nautical miles, cheap and easy to obtain, but not very accurate.

TLAM: Tomahawk land-attack missile. (N, F)

TLAM/N: Tomahawk land-attack missile/nuclear. (N, F)

Tomahawk missile: Unmanned, rocket-launched, jet-propelled, ground-hugging cruise missile fired from land, ships, or B-52 bombers. Guided from onboard computer, it can hit a target 800 miles away from launch point. Land attack uses conventional or nuclear warhead; tactical antiship variant uses conventional warhead.

TOW: Tube-launched, optically-tracked, wire-guided missile. Variants are numbered beginning with the code BMG (refers to multiple-launch-environment surface-attack guided missile).

Tracer: Shell that leaves a trail of smoke to allow the shooter to check his aim; it also shows everyone else where the shots came from.

Trident Missile: *Trident I:* A three-stage, solid-propellant ballistic missile capable of being launched from a Trident submarine either surfaced or submerged. It is equipped with advanced guidance, nuclear warheads, and a maneuverable bus which can deploy these warheads to separate targets. It can carry a full payload for 4,000 nautical miles. *Trident II:* A solid-propellant ballistic missile capable of being launched from a Trident submarine, larger and more accurate than the Trident I. It will replace these in Ohio-class submarines. (N)

Very light: Particular flare fired by a Very pistol.

WM-44A: Submarine rocket, SUB-ROC, submerged, submarine-launched, surface-to-surface rocket with nuclear depth charge or homing payload, primarily antisubmarine.

Wooly bear: Type of shell that rolls and emits thick black smoke.

★ PERSONAL EQUIPMENT ★

ALICE: Acronym for "All purpose lightweight individual carrying equipment," a medium-sized framed backpack.

Body armor: Flack jacket.

ECU: "Environment control unit," otherwise known as tents. They often have pumps for air conditioning and heating. (F)

Extraction parachute: An auxiliary parachute designed to release, extract, and deploy cargo from aircraft in-flight and deploy cargo parachutes.

Flack jacket: Heavy fiberglass-filled vest worn for protection from shrapnel.

Foxtrot: Radio used in air traffic control, defense, or other secure communications. Lightweight with VHF-FM, VHF-AM and UHF-AM, and also equipped with integrated crypto functions.

Ghillie suit: Used by special operations forces and snipers, it is a camouflage suit that looks like shaggy leaves and brush. Made with jute burlap or synthetic leaves, it is durable and quick drying. (SOF)

GPS: Global positioning system, a handheld device to help navigate over any kind of terrain to within 3 meters. (SOF)

Green-eye: Starlight scope. Light-amplifying telescope, used to see at night.

Kestrel 4000: A handheld weather tracker.

LBE: Load-bearing equipment. Often "web gear" worn by infantry personnel to hold packs and tools, weapons, first aid kits, and whatever is worn by the person in the field.

LBV: Load-bearing vest. A vest that holds magazines of ammunition, grenades, and a cartridge belt to which other equipment are attached, such as a first aid kit, canteens, and a cup.

M40: Gas mask. (A)

M256: Chemical agent detector.

MOLLE: Modular lightweight load carrying equipment. A system which replaced the traditional harness, belt, and pack system to allow the infantryman to "wear" rather than "carry" equipment. (A, M)

P-38: The tool contained in every case of C-rations: a can opener, but which also functions as a screwdriver, rudimentary box opener, scraper, and more.

Pugil sticks: Padded training sticks used to simulate bayonet fighting.

Pup tent: A small, one-man tent used in World War I.

★ TECHNOLOGY ★

Balloon reflector: Used in electronic warfare, a balloon-supported confusion reflector to produce fake echoes.

Barrage jamming: Simultaneous electromagnetic jamming over a broad band of frequencies.

Chaff: Radar confusion reflectors; thin metallic strips of various lengths and frequency responses to reflect echoes for confusion purposes.

LVRS: Lightweight video reconnaissance system (LVRS). A lightweight video capture and transmit/receive system using standard battlefield communications. Used with other equipment by scouts to send near-real-time images of an engagement area or landing zone to aircraft already enroute.

NVG: Night-vision goggles. AN/PVS-5 night-vision goggles are a self-contained, passive, image-intensifying, night-vision-viewing system worn on the head with or without the standard battle helmet or aviator helmet. They provide night-vision viewing using available light from the night sky (starlight, moonlight). The built-in infrared light source provides added illumination for close-up work such as map reading. The PVS-5 is equipped with a headstrap to allow hands-free operation. They are used by vehicle drivers, riflemen, and unit leaders.

Stealth-equipped: Allows an aircraft to avoid radar detection. The equipment is protected from various types of electronic detection and includes a variety of technologies including radar wave absorbing paint to electronic jamming devices to specific body shapes.

★ TRENCH TERMINOLOGY ★

Dugout: Shelter hole dug by soldier.

Foxhole: Shelter hole dug by soldier. Also called *funkhole* or *fighting hole*.

Half-and-half trench: A trench whose depth is doubled by sandbags placed around the top; half dug, half sandbags.

In the Trenches: To be fighting, in the action. Refers to the excavations dug by infantry during World War I.

Nest: Dugout.

★ UNCONVENTIONAL WARFARE ★

Antimatériel agent: Living organism or chemical used to cause deterioration or damage to selected matériel.

Biological agent: A microorganism that causes disease in personnel, plants, or animals or causes matériel to deteriorate.

Blister agent: A chemical agent that burns the eyes and lungs or blisters the skin. "Vesicant agent."

Chemical agent: A chemical substance intended for use in military operations to kill, seriously injure, or incapacitate personnel through physiological effects. Excludes riot-control agents, herbicides, smoke, and flame.

HS: Mustard gas.

Lewisite: A chemical weapon that acts as a vesicant and lung irritant, and can be used in combination as mustard-lewisite. It is almost a hundred times more deadly than mustard gas.

Mustard gas: Gas that smells like mustard, makes the eyes water, and blisters skin.

Mustard imitator: Lewisite.

Napalm: Highly volatile gasoline in a jelly form used for burning out caves during World War II, Korea, and Vietnam. Also used by the Air Force to defoliate large areas of forests or jungles in Vietnam.

Nose cap: Gas mask.

Razor wire: Similar to barbed wire or concertina wire with a sharp edge on one side and spikes located about every inch.

★ WATERCRAFT ★

Boats are defined as watercraft less than 65 feet long. *Ships* are defined as large vessels equipped for deep-water operation. A *sailing vessel* is furnished with a bowsprit and three masts (a mainmast, a foremast, and a mizzenmast), each of which is composed of a lower mast, a topmast, and a topgallant mast, and square-rigged on all masts.

Aircraft Carriers

CV or CVN: Attack aircraft carrier. These are Navy warships used to support aircraft and attack targets afloat or on shore that engage in sustained operations in support of other forces.

The additional designation "N" means nuclear powered. All numbered carriers built since CV-67 are named for politicians; previous carriers were named for battles and famous Naval fighting ships. There are ten Nimitz-class (supercarrier) aircraft carriers, all nuclear powered: USS *Nimitz*, USS *Dwight D. Eisenhower*, USS *Carl Vinson*, USS *Theodore Roosevelt*, USS *Abraham Lincoln*, USS *George Washington*, USS *John C. Stennis*, USS *Harry S. Truman*, USS *Ronald Reagan*, USS *George H. W. Bush* (under construction). Each can support fifty or more aircraft. There are several additional aircraft carriers including USS *Kitty Hawk*, USS *Enterprise*, and USS *John F. Kennedy*. Carrier-based squadrons fly six different types of aircraft: F/A-18 Hornets, F-14 Tomcats, SH-60 Seahawks, S-3B Vikings, E-2C Hawkeyes, and EA-6B Prowlers. Missions range from reconnaissance and search and rescue to logistics and interdiction. (N)

Amphibious Assault Ships

Amphibious assault ships: Resemble small aircraft carriers and are generally named after World War II aircraft carriers. There are seven Wasp-class ships and four Tarawa-class ships still active. Amphibious operations are designed and conducted to move forward further combat operations; obtain a site for an advanced naval, land, or air base; deny use of an area or facilities to the enemy, and to fix enemy forces and attention, providing opportunities for other combat operations. (N)

Iwo Jima-class LPH-2: There were seven Iwo Jima-class amphibious assault ships built to transport more than 1,700 fully equipped Marine Assault Troops into combat areas and land them by helicopter at designated inland points. The ships can support a Marine battalion landing team, including armament, vehicles, equipment, and support personnel. The ships also support minesweeping operations and provide humanitarian assistance and noncombatant evacuations of American embassy personnel and citizens caught in civil-conflict overseas. Currently the USS *Guam* (LPH-9), homeported at Norfolk, Virginia, is the only remaining ship of this class in service. (M)

LHX-class: LHX-class amphibious assault ships are intended to replace the Tarawa-class ships with first planned launch in 2010; five are planned. (N, M)

Tarawa-class LHA-1: The Tarawa-class is used to land and sustain Marines on any shore during hostilities. The ships are designed to get a balanced force to the same place at the same time. One LHA can carry a complete Marine battalion, along with the supplies and equipment needed in an assault, and land them ashore by either helicopter or amphibious craft. This two-pronged capability, with emphasis on airborne landing of troops and equipment, enables the Navy and Marine Corps to fulfill their missions. Whether the landing force is involved in an armed conflict, acting as a deterrent force in an unfavorable political situation, or serving in a humanitarian mission, the class offers tactical versatility. It can operate independently or as a unit of a force, as a flagship, or individual ship unit in both air and/or surface assaults. Five Tarawa-class ships are in use. (N, M)

Wasp-class LHD-1: Wasp-class ships are the largest amphibious ships in the world. They were first to be designed to accommodate the AV-8B Harrier jump jet and the LCAC hovercraft, along with the full range of Navy and Marine helicopters, conventional landing craft, and amphibious assault vehicles to support a Marine expeditionary unit (MEU) of 2,000 Marines. The ships also carry sophisticated communications, command and control capabilities afloat, electronic systems, and defensive weaponry. They conduct prompt, sustained combat operations at sea and deliver command and support for all elements of a Marine landing force in an assault by air and amphibious craft. There are eight Wasp-class ships. (N, M)

Amphibious Transport Docks

Anchorage-class LSD-36: Anchorage-class dock landing ships (LSD) support amphibious operations, including landings via landing craft air cushion (LCAC), conventional landing craft, and helicopters, onto hostile shores. These ships transport and launch amphibious craft and vehicles with their crews and embarked personnel in amphibious assault operations. This is designed to operate as an integral part of a balanced, mobile, and modern amphibious strike force and features a well deck with a flight deck. Although designed to transport preloaded heavy landing craft to the shore and discharge them rapidly, the ship is also equipped with machine shops and facilities to provide dry docking and repairs to small boats. All five Anchorage-class LSD-36s will be retired from service by in the early 2000s. (N)

Austin-class LPD 4: The Austin-class of ship combines the functions of three different classes of ships: the landing ship (LSD), the tank landing ship (LST). All are planned for decommission by 2008. (N)

Charleston-class LKA-113: These amphibious cargo ships were designed to carry troops, heavy equipment, and supplies in support of amphibious assaults. Four of the five ships in the class were transferred to the reserve fleet by the early 1980s and were decommissioned in the early 1990s. (N)

Harpers Ferry-class LSD-49: The Harpers Ferry (Cargo Variant) ship docks, transports, and launches the Navy's landing craft, air cushion (LCA C) vessels and other amphibious craft and vehicles with crews and Marines into potential trouble spots around the world. The ship can also serve as primary control ship during an amphibious assault. Of twelve originally ordered, only four were built and were recently or will soon be decommissioned. (N, M)

Newport-class LST-1179: The Newport-class tank landing ships (LST) is larger and faster than earlier LSTs, and quite different; the traditional bow doors were replaced by a 40-ton bow ramp supported by two distinctive derrick arms. This feature enables it to operate with modern high-speed amphibious forces. A stern gate also makes possible off-loading amphibious vehicles directly into the water. Of twenty ships originally commissioned, only two remain and will soon be retired. (N)

Raleigh-class LPD-1: The Raleigh Amphibious Transport Dock (LPD)

ships transport and land Marines, their equipment, and supplies by embarked-landing craft or amphibious vehicles augmented by helicopters in amphibious assault. Both ships of this class were retired in the early 1990s. (N, M)

San Antonio-class LPD-17 (formerly LX Class): The San Antonio-class of amphibious transport dock ships is the first designed to execute operational maneuver from the sea (OMFTS) and ship to objective maneuver. It is designed to support embarking, transporting, and landing elements of a Marine landing force in an assault by helicopters, landing craft, and amphibious vehicles, in amphibious warfare missions. It is designated LPD-17-LPD-28; one has been commissioned thus far with the others in the pipeline. (N, M)

Whidbey Island-class LSD-41: These ships are configured as a flagship and provide extensive command, control, and communications facilities to support an amphibious task force commander and landing force commander. A secondary mission is evacuation and civilian disaster relief as well as mine countermeasures. Eight Whidbey Island-class ships have been built. (N)

Battleships

All the American battleships have been retired although two remain in "inactive" reserve. Nearly all were named for states.

Iowa-class: There were four BB-61 Iowa-class battleships tasked to conduct prompt and sustained-combat operations at sea, worldwide, in support of national interests. All were reactivated briefly to help the Navy correct a shortage in major fleet deployment capability during the 1970s and 1980s. These powerful, flexible capital ships increased the Navy's ability to provide an important new capability in maritime power, plus much-needed flexibility in carrier deployment schedules. No smaller ship can sustain a comparable level of offensive efforts in terms of volume, weight, and duration of firepower and in terms of both guns and cruise missiles, and survivability. Additionally, the cost to reactivate and modernize a battleship is about that of a modern guided-missile frigate. (N)

Coast Guard Cutters

Cutters are defined as any Coast Guard vessel 65 feet or longer with live-aboard facilities for their crew. A number of these have specific designations, as follows.

Coastal buoy tender, WLM: This class of cutter includes fourteen 175-foot long cutters that service coastal buoys.

High endurance cutter, WHEC: Twelve such cutters, with lengths of 378 feet along the waterline, are part of the Coast Guard. They are diesel powered and equipped with a helicopter flight deck. All are large ships that patrol the open seas.

Icebreaker, WAGB: There are three such Icebreakers, each 400–420 feet long, which are designed for open-water icebreaking with reinforced hulls.

Inland buoy tender, WLI: These cutters are 65–100 feet in length and are used to maintain buoys in inland rivers.

Inland construction tender, WLIC: These include cutters 160, 100, and 75 feet long that are used in harbor construction activities such as pile driving. The 75- and 100-foot WLICs are used to push construction barges from 68 to 84 feet long. The 160-foot WLICs are single units without barges.

Inland icebreaker, WLBB: Newly launched in April 2005, this class of cutter is used in icebreaking missions in the Great Lakes.

Large icebreaking tug, WTGB: These cutters are used for domestic ice breaking and are about 150 feet long. They are stationed in the Northeast and the Great Lakes.

Medium endurance cutter, WMEC: These include 210- and 270-foot, large, stable ships suited for the high seas whose missions include homeland security, search and rescue, and international and domestic fisheries enforcement.

Patrol boat, WPB: 110- or 123-foot long boats used for patrolling the coastal waters. About fifty are in use by the Coast Guard.

Patrol coastal, WPC: These 180-foot long cutters are used for homeland security, search and rescue and law enforcement in the Caribbean and Gulf of Mexico.

River buoy tender, WLR: These 65- to 75-foot long cutters push barges equipped with cranes which work aids to navigation (ATON). Some are equipped with "jetting" devices used to set buoys in rivers with sandy/muddy bottoms.

Seagoing buoy tender, WLB: There are sixteen Juniper-class buoy tenders. These boats maintain the aids to navigation (buoys) as well as carry out other missions.

Small harbor tug, WYTL: These are 65-foot tugboats used along the East Coast.

Training barque, WIX: The USCGEC *Eagle* is a three-masted sailing barque (ship) home ported in New London, Connecticut, originally taken as a war prize from Germany. It is the only active sailing vessel in the U.S. maritime services.

Coast Guard Boats Smaller Than Cutters

Aids to navigation boats, TANB/BUSL/ANB/ANB: These include a range of boats from 21–64 feet long that are used for inland navigation maintenance.

Deployable pursuit boat, DPB: Thirty-eight-foot high-speed boats used to intercept drug smuggling operations in fast boats.

Motor life boat, MLB: Designed for use as a first-response rescue resource in high seas, surf, and heavy weather, they are approximately 45 feet long and self-righting.

Rigid hull inflatable boat, RHI: Rigid inflatable boats have deep-V, glass-reinforced, plastic hulls with a special buoyancy tube inside. They are powered by either a gasoline outboard motor or an inboard/outboard diesel engine and are readily deployed from cutters. They are versatile and used in many missions.

Transportable port security boat, TPSB: This group includes 25-foot long boats used for inland water law enforcement and deployed in Operation Iraqi Freedom.

Utility boat, UTB: There are nearly two hundred of these 41-foot general-purpose "workhorse" boats used for a range of missions under moderate conditions and seas.

Cruisers

Guided missie cruisers are all designated CG. Modern cruisers are all named for battles, with previous cruisers named for cities (to CG-12), naval heroes (CG-15 to CG-35), or states (CG-36- to CG-42). (N)

Bainbridge-class: Designated CGN 25, the Bainbridge-class was the first nuclear frigate carrier, powered by two pressurized water reactors. It carried two twin Terrier missile launchers, two twin 3-inch .50-caliber radar controlled gun mounts, two torpedo mounts, and was equipped with state-of-the-art electronics and communications suites. Redesignated a cruiser; thus DLGN 25 became CGN 25. It was deactivated in 1996. (N)

Bellnap-class: CG 26, guided-missile cruisers used in a battle force role. Ships are multimission surface combatants capable of supporting carrier or battleship battle groups, amphibious forces, or of operating independently and as flagships of surface action groups. Due to their extensive combat capability, these ships have been designated as battle force capable (BFC) units. They are equipped with long range sonar, anti-submarine rockets, light airborne multi-purpose helicopters, and torpedoes as well as a single dual-purpose, rapid-fire, a 5-inch, .54 caliber gun for defense against air and surface attacks, two 20mm Gatling guns for close-in air defense, the Harpoon surface-to-surface missile system for use against enemy ships over the horizon, and a chaff deployment system for use as a decoy. Originally classified as guided missile destroyer leader (DLG) these ships were reclassified as guide missile cruisers in 1975. They were retired in the early 1990s after some thirty years of service. (N)

California-class: CGN 36, the California-class nuclear-powered guided-missile cruisers are used for offensive operations against air, surface, and subsurface threats. The nuclear-powered engineering plant allows the cruiser to conduct operations over extended periods of time anywhere in the world. This was the first class of nuclear-propelled surface warships intended for series production. These ships are a nuclear-propelled version of guided-missile designs proposed in the early 1960s. They are equipped with an array of weapons and sensors. Both ships were decommissioned in the late 1990s. (N)

Ticonderoga-class: All carry the Aegis combat system. Twenty-seven modern Navy guided-missile cruisers are used in a battle force role (battle force capable). Their main armament is the vertical-launching system with both Tomahawk cruise missile (long-range, surface-to-surface) and the standard surface-to-air missile. They are capable of sustained combat operations in any combination of antiair, antisubmarine, antisurface, and strike warfare environments and are used to support carrier battle groups, amphibious assault groups, as well as interdiction and escort missions. They were initially designated as guided-missile destroyers (DDG), but were redesignated as guided-missile cruisers (CG) in 1980. (N)

Virginia-class: There were four CGN-38 Virginia-class guided-missile cruisers used for multiple tasks in all warfare mission areas. They had the Tomahawk cruise missile system, the

Standard SM2 (MR) missile system, and air search radar. They were retired in 1997. (N)

Destroyers

Destroyers are given the designation DD, and are defined as high-speed warships designed for offensive operation with strike forces and in support of amphibious assault operations. They can also operate defensively against submarine, air and surface threats, and are usually armed with 3-inch and 5-inch guns and a range of antisubmarine warfare weapons. They have been all named for naval heroes since USS Bainbridge (DD-1). (N)

Arleigh Burke-class DDG-51: The Arleigh Burke-class guided-missile Aegis destroyers were first commissioned in 1991 with over fifty planned or in operation as the Navy's most capable and survivable surface combatant. It was the first Navy ship to utilize special techniques to reduce radar cross-section to reduce their detectability. It was designed to defend against Soviet aircraft, cruise missiles, and nuclear-attack submarines, but will be used in antiair, antisubmarine, antisurface, and strike operations. (N)

Charles F. Adams-class, DDG-2: The Charles F. Adams-class guided-missile destroyers were constructed in the

1950s–1960s and retired in the early 1990s. They were designated DDG-2 through DDG-24. (N)

Farragut-class DDG-37: The ten DDG-37 Farragut-class (also, "Coontz"-class) guided-missile destroyers were constructed in 1950s–1960s. They were significantly larger than previous destroyers, and the term *frigate* was reactivated to describe them. This class of ships was initially classified as destroyer leader (DL) and subsequently reclassified as guided missile frigate (DLG) in 1956. The ships were again reclassified in 1975, as guided missile destroyer (DDG), and given new hull numbers (e.g., DLG 10 *King* became DDG 41). Retired in the early 1990s, they were replaced by the Arleigh Burke-class (DDG 51). (N)

Kidd-class DDG-993: The Kidd-class destroyers are the most powerful multipurpose destroyers in the American fleet. They combine the combat systems capability of the former Virginia-class cruisers with the proven antisubmarine warfare qualities of a Spruance-class destroyer. The four Kidd-class guided-missile destroyers are similar to the Spruance-class destroyers, but have greater displacement and improved combat systems. Kidd-class armaments include the new threat upgrade (NTU) antiair warfare (AAW) system, as well

as two Mk 26 launchers for standard surface-to-air missiles, SQS-58 hull mounted active sonar, eight Harpoon surface-to-surface missiles, two 5-inch guns, and hangar facilities for one helicopter. Unique characteristics are its quiet operation (suitable for offensive use against submarines), sophisticated medium-range AAW systems, a reliable and responsive engineering plant, and a deadly surface-to-surface weapons capability. Thus it can operate offensively against simultaneous air, surface, and subsurface attacks. Four ships were built, all since decommissioned. (N)

Spruance-class, DD-963: These destroyers were developed for antisubmarine warfare, including operations as an integral part of attack carrier forces. More than twice as large as a World War II destroyer and as large as a World War II cruiser and using highly developed weapons systems, they are designed to hunt down and destroy high-speed submarines in all weather, but can also engage ships, aircraft, and shore targets, and are suited for surveillance operations. There have been thirty Spruance-class destroyers, seven of which have been decommissioned. (N)

Zumwalt-class: The DD-21 Zumwalt-class land-attack destroyer will replace the DD 963 and FFG 7 classes of destroyer and frigate beginning in 2008. The DD 21 is designed for advanced land attack in support of a ground campaign as a fleet destroyer, capable of wartime missions in land attack and undersea warfare, presence missions, noncombatant evacuations, escort, and diplomatic missions. Thirty-three are planned for production, designated DD-21 to DD-53. (N)

Frigates

Frigates are ships that perform antisubmarine warfare or serve as escorts for other ships. They are named for naval heroes. They are designated FF.

Bronstein-class FF 1037: These frigates were used as antisubmarine warfare combatants for amphibious expeditionary forces, underway replenishment groups, and merchant convoys; since retired. (N)

Knox-class FF 1052: Frigates used in antisubmarine warfare combatants for amphibious expeditionary forces, underway replenishment groups, and merchant convoys. About fifty ships were produced in the 1960s–1970s, all of which have been retired. (N)

Oliver Hazard Perry-class FFG-7: The Perry-class FFG is used in undersea warfare together with the Lamps-III helicopter on board. They have the Mk 13 Mod 4-missile launcher,

and are often referred to as "FFG-7." They are equipped to escort and protect carrier battle groups, amphibious landing groups, underway replenishment groups, and convoys, and are also used in counterdrug surveillance and maritime interception operations. Designated FFG-7 through FFG-51, about fifteen have been decommissioned. (N)

Gunboats

Boghammers: Small gunboats used in the Gulf War.

Gunboats: Any small boat carrying a gun, sometimes called patrol gunboats. In the Navy, these boats had the hull classification symbol PG. They usually displaced under 2,000 tons of water, were about 200 feet long, a 10–15 foot draft, and sometimes much less, and mounted several guns of caliber up to 5–6 inches.

Landing Craft

Landing craft, air cushion LCAC: The landing craft, air cushion (LCAC) transports weapons systems, equipment, cargo, and personnel of the assault elements of the Marine Air/Ground Task Force both from ship to shore and across the beach. The LCAC is a high-speed, over-the-beach, fully amphibious landing craft capable of carrying a 60- to 75- ton payload, including an M1 tank. (N, M)

Landing craft utility LCU: Landing craft are used by amphibious forces to transport equipment and troops to the shore. They can deliver tracked or wheeled vehicles and troops from amphibious assault ships to beachheads or piers. LCUs deliver personnel and equipment after the initial assault waves of an amphibious operation and have capability of sustained sea operations for approximately seven days. Each LCU has its own galley and berthing spaces. (N)

Mechanized landing craft LCM: The LCM-6 is designed for cargo and/or personnel transfer from ship to ship and ship to shore. The LCM-3 was replaced with the larger 70-ton LCM-8 in 1959. The LCM-8 requires a four-man crew and is constructed of steel and powered by two 12 V-71 diesel engines. The LCM-8 has twin screws and rudders that can be controlled from the pilothouse. It is built of welded steel with a nearly flat bottom. (N)

Submarines

Modern submarines are designated either ballistic or attack.

Attack submarines: May launch cruise missiles, sink ships and subs, and gather intelligence. Early attack submarines were named for fish. Land attack submarines are named for states, and include Virginia- and Ohio-class boats. Sea attack submarines are named for cities.

Ballistic submarines: These have one mission, to carry nuclear SLBMs (submarine-launched ballistic missiles). Early ballistic missile submarines were named for famous Americans. (N)

Benjamin Franklin-class SSBN-640: Similar to the SSBN-616 Lafayette-class, the twelve Benjamin Franklin-class (SSBN-640) submarines had a quieter machinery design. All were in service during the 1960s through the 1990s; one remains today. Two (the *Kamehameha* and the *James K. Polk*) were converted to SEAL-mission-capable attack submarines. In March of 1994, the USS *James K. Polk* (SSN 645) was converted from ballistic missile submarine to attack/special warfare submarine. The January 1999 inactivation of the *Polk* leaves the *Kamehameha* (SSN 642) as the Navy's only former ballistic missile submarine equipped with dry deck shelters (DDS's). (N)

Deep submergence rescue vehicle: The deep submergence rescue vehicles *Mystic* (DSRV 1) and *Avalon* (DSRV 2) of the Deep Submergence Unit were designed for submarine crew rescue. It is all-weather capable for rescue missions worldwide at a maximum operating depth of 5,000 feet. They can be transported by truck, aircraft, surface ship, or on a mother submarine and can dive, locate the disabled submarine, and attach themselves so that submarine personnel can enter directly into the DSRV. (N)

Ethan Allen-class SSBN-608: The USS *Ethan Allen* (SSBN-608), fired the only nuclear-armed Polaris nuclear missile ever launched (May 6, 1962) and remains to date, the only complete proof test of a U.S. strategic missile. With the ban on atmospheric testing, the chances of another similar test are remote. Five of this class were produced; all have since been decommissioned. (N)

George Washington-class SSBN-598: The world's first nuclear-powered ballistic missile submarine was a big factor in America's deterrence capability. Produced first in 1959, they had long-range strategic missiles. All five have been decommissioned. (N)

Lafayette-class SSBN-616: Used Polaris missiles. Nineteen subs of this class were produced and in service from the 1960s to the 1990s. (N)

Los Angeles-class SSN-688: The Los Angeles-class SSN was designed almost exclusively for carrier battlegroup escort; they were fast, quiet, and could launch MK48 and ADCAP torpedoes, Harpoon antiship missiles, and both land-attack and antiship Tomahawk cruise missiles. They were also used for escort duties and attacks. These are among the most advanced undersea vessels in the world. While antisubmarine warfare is still their primary mission, their stealth, mobility, and endurance are useful for missions of special operations forces deployment, minelaying, and precision-strike land attack. About sixty were constructed; some ten or twelve have been decommissioned. (N, SOF)

Narwhal-class SSN-671: The USS *Narwhal* was the quietest of submarines of its time, in use from 1969 to 1999. It was the only ship in its class. (N)

Ohio-class SSBN-726: Used for strategic deterrence since 1960s, the SSBN provides the nation's most survivable and enduring nuclear strike capability. The Ohio-class submarine replaced aging fleet ballistic missile submarines built in the 1960s and is far more capable. The Ohio-class submarines are specifically designed for extended deterrent patrols and to operate for more than fifteen years between overhauls. Each SSBN is at sea two-thirds of the time, including major overhaul periods of twelve months every nine years. One SSBN combat employment cycle includes a seventy-day patrol and twenty-five-day period of transfer of the submarine to the other crew, between-deployment maintenance and reloading of munitions. (N)

Permit-class SSN-594: The SSN-594 Permit-class was the first modern, quiet, deep-diving, fast-attack submarine, integrating a hydrodynamically shaped hull, a large, bow-mounted sonar array, advanced sound-silencing features, and an integrated control/ attack center with the proven S5W reactor plant. Originally designated the Thresher-class, but when the USS *Thresher* was lost in 1963, the designation was changed. Fourteen subs were produced. All have been retired (or lost, USS *Thresher*). (N)

Seawolf-class SSN-21: Seawolf-class submarines were designed to operate autonomously against the world's most capable submarine and surface threats. They were used to destroy Soviet ballistic missile subs before they could attack American targets. Three ships were built and remain op-erational, though twenty-nine were originally planned. (N)

Skipjack-class SSN-585: This class of submarine was the first attack submarine to combine nuclear power with a new hull design, and also had a single shaft. They operated from the early 1960s to the 1990s. (N)

Sturgeon-class SSN-637: Sturgeon-class submarines were built for anti-submarine warfare in the late 1960s and 1970s. Using the same propulsion system as their smaller predecessors of the SSN-585 Skipjack- and SSN-594 Permit-classes, the larger Sturgeons sacrificed speed for greater combat capabilities. They carry Harpoon and Tomahawk missiles, and the MK-48 and ADCAP torpedoes. The sail-mounted dive planes rotate to a vertical position for breaking through the ice when surfacing in Arctic regions. Designated SSN-637 to SSN-687, all have been decommissioned. (N)

Virginia-class SSN-774: The new attack submarine is the first U.S. submarine designed for battlespace dominance across a broad spectrum of missions. Covert strike by launching land attack missiles from vertical launchers and torpedo tubes; anti-submarine warfare with an advanced combat system and a flexible payload of torpedoes; antiship warfare, again, using the advanced combat system and torpedoes; battle group support with advanced electronic sensors and communications equipment; covert intelligence, surveillance, and reconnaissance, using sensors to collect critical intelligence and locate radar sites, missile batteries, and command sites as well as to monitor communications and track ship movements; covert minelaying against enemy shipping; and special operations, including search and rescue, reconnaissance, sabotage, diversionary attacks, and direction of fire support and strikes. (N, SOF)

USS *Constitution*

The Navy's three-masted frigate USS *Constitution*, better known as "Old Ironsides," is the world's oldest commissioned warship afloat. Congress called for the construction of six frigates, including the 44-gun frigates *Constitution, United States,* and *President* and the 36-gun frigates *Congress, Constellation,* and *Chesapeake.* They were constructed in Boston using live oak with copper spikes and sheathing hand-forged by Paul Revere. The *Constitution* was put to sea in July 1798. She served against the Barbary States of North Africa. In 1812, she destroyed the fast British frigate *Guerriere* in a few short minutes. The shot fired from the *Guerriere* seemed to bounce off the hull, leading to her nickname, "Old Ironsides." The battle gave American naval power great confidence and strength. The publication of Oliver Wendell Holmes's poem "Old Ironsides" kept it from being scrapped, although she was decommissioned in 1882. She was restored and recommissioned in 1931. Now the oldest U.S. warship still in commission, the *Constitution* remains a powerful reminder of the nation's earliest steps into dominance of the sea. She is docked at Charleston, Massachusetts.

Useful Resources for Understanding the U.S. Military

The military is easily contacted and researched via the Internet. Many offices provide their Internet address as the primary means to contact them. Following are a number of useful sources for obtaining further information on related topics.

ARMY

Army Web site: www.army.mil/

Public Affairs: Media Relations Division, Office of the Chief of Public Affairs, 1500 Army Pentagon, Washington, DC, 20310-1500, (703) 692-2000

Training and Doctrine Command (TRADOC): www-tradoc.army.mil/

U.S. Army Pacific Command: www.usarpac.army.mil/

U.S. Army Military District of Washington, D.C. (MDW): www.mdw.army.mil/

U.S. Army Matériel Command: www.amc.army.mil/

U.S. Army Intelligence and Security Command (INSCOM): www.inscom.army.mil/

U.S. Army Corps of Engineers (USACE): www.usace.army.mil/

U.S. Army Criminal Investigation Command (CID): www.belvoir.army.mil/cidc/

U.S. Army South (USARSO): www.usarso.army.mil/

U.S. Army Space and Missile Defense Command (SMDC): www.smdc.army.mil/

Surface Deployment and Distribution Command (SDDC): www.sddc.army.mil/

Army Forces Command (FORSCOM): www.forscom.army.mil/

Eighth U.S. Army Korea: www.8tharmy.korea.army.mil/pao/default.htm

U.S. Army Medical Command (MEDCOM): www.armymedicine.army.mil/

U.S. Ordnance Corps: www.goordnance.apg.army.mil

U.S. Army Quartermaster Corps: www.quartermaster.army.mil/

U.S. Army Signal Corps: www.gordon.army.mil/roa/history/reghist.htm

The Signal Corps Museum: www.gordon.army.mil/ocos/museum/,

Voice of Iron: The 143rd Signal Battalion: voiceofiron.com/

U.S. Army Transportation Corps: www.eustis.army.mil/overview.htm

U.S. Army Special Operations Command (USASOC): www.soc.mil/

Secretary of the Army, 101 Army Pentagon, Washington, DC 20310-0101

U.S. Military Academy (USMA): www.usma.edu West Point, NY 10996 (845) 938-4041

Golden Knights: www.usarec.army.mil/hq/GoldenKnights/Webpage2005_content.html

Confidence Course: goarmy.com/ProfileDetail.do?dir=/_res/xml/life/basic/&xml=week_list.xml&fw=basic&sn=week07.

Ordnance Corps History: www.goordnance.apg.army.mil/sitefiles/OrdnanceBriefHistory.htm

The United States Army and the Forging of a Nation, 1775–1917. Edited by Richard W. Stewart, 2005. Army Historical Series, American Military History, Vol. 1. Center of Military History, United States Army, Washington, D.C.

The Army Officer's Guide, 43rd ed. By Lt. Col. Lawrence P. Crocker. 1985. Stackpole Books: Harrisburg, PA. 565 pp.

Soldier's Manual of Common Tasks, Skill Level 1, 1985.
Dept. of the Army.

NAVY

Navy Web site: www.navy.mil/

Naval Open Source Intelligence (NOSI): www.nosi.org.

Public Affairs: Navy Public Affairs Center—Norfolk. Director, 9420 Third Avenue, Suite 200, Norfolk, VA 23511-2127. 757-444-8331 fax: 757-445-2085

Navy Public Affairs Center—San Diego. Director, 3985 Cummings Road, Suite 2, San Diego, CA 92136-5297. phone: 619-556-4907 fax: 619-556-5121

Secretary of the Navy, 1000 Navy Pentagon, Washington, D.C. 20350-1000

U.S. Naval Academy: www.usna.edu///homepage.php. U.S. Naval Academy, 121 Blake Road, Annapolis, MD 21402-5000.

Navy SEALs: Public Affairs Office, Naval Special Warfare Command, Naval Amphibious Base Coronado, San Diego, CA 92155-5037 (619) 437-3920

Blue Angels: Commanding Officer, Navy Flight Demonstration Squadron, Attn: PAO, Naval Air Station Pensacola, Pensacola, FL 32508-7801

The Navy. Edited by W. J. Holland, Jr. 2000. Barnes and Noble Books: NY.

MARINE CORPS

Marine Corps Web site: www.usmc.mil/

Marine Corps Recruiting: www.usmc.com

Commandant of the Marine Corps, 2 Navy Annex, Washington D.C. 20380-1775.

1st Marine Division, Camp Pendleton, CA 92055-5001 (760)725-4111

2nd Marine Division, Camp Lejeune, North Carolina.

3rd Marine Division, Camp Smedley Butler, Okinawa, Japan.

4th Marine Division, a reserve unit headquartered at New Orleans, Louisiana.

1st Marine Aircraft Wing, Marine Corps Air Station (MCAS) Futenma, Okinawa, Japan.

2nd Marine Aircraft Wing at MCAS Cherry Point, Norht Carolina.

3rd Marine Aircraft Wing at MCAS, Miramar, California: www.miramar.usmc.mil/

4th Marine Aircraft Wing, New Orleans, Louisiana (reserve unit).

1st Marine Logistics Group, Camp Pendleton, California 92055-5001, (760)725-4111

2nd Marine Logistics Group, Camp Lejeune, North Carolina.

3rd Marine Logistics Group, Camp Smedley Butler, Okinawa, Japan.

4th Marine Logistics Group, New Orleans, Louisiana (reserve unit).

Marine Corps Recruit Depot/Eastern Recruiting Region, 283 Blvd. de France, Parris Island, SC 29905 (843) 228-2111

Marine Drum and Bugle Corps: www.drumcorps.mbw.usmc.mil

United States Marine Band: www.marineband.usmc.mil/

myMarine: groups.yahoo.com/group/mymarine/ (a place for family and friends of Marine Corps recruits to ask questions and exchange information)

History of the U.S. Marines, rev. ed., by Jack Murphy, 2002. World Publications Group: North Dighton, MA.

The Marine Corps. 1998. Hugh Lauter Levin Associates, Inc.: Hong Kong.

The Marine Officer's Guide, 6th ed. By Kenneth W. Estes. 2000. Naval Institute Press: Annapolis MD.

The Navajo Code Talkers. By Doris A. Paul, 1973. Dorrance Publishing Co, Inc.: Pittsburgh.

United States Marines Guidebook of Essential Subjects. USMC Marine Corps Institute. 1983. Washington D.C.

AIR FORCE

Air Force Web site: www.af.mil

Air Combat Command, Public Affairs Office, 115 Thompson St, Ste 104, Langley AFB, VA 23665-1987. (757) 764-5014

Air Education and Training Command, Public Affairs Office, 100 H Street, Suite 4, Randolph Air Force Base, TX 78150-4330 (210) 652-3946

Air Force Matériel Command, Public Affairs Office, 4375 Chidlaw Road, Room N-152, Wright-Patterson AFB, OH 45433-5006 (327) 257-6308

Air Force Reserve Command, Office of Public Affairs, 255 Richard Ray Blvd., Robins AFB, GA 31098-1637 (478) 327-1751

Air Force Space Command, Public Affairs Office, 150 Vandenberg St., Suite 1105, Peterson AFB, CO 80914-4500 (719) 554-3731

Air Force Special Operations Command, Public Affairs Office, 229 Cody Avenue, Suite 103, Hurlburt Field, FL 32544-5273 (850) 884-5515

Air Mobility Command, Public Affairs Office, 503 Ward Drive Suite 217, Scott AFB, IL 62225-5335 (618) 229-7843

Pacific Air Forces, Public Affairs Office, 25E Street, Suite I-106, Hickam AFB, HI 96853-5496 (808) 449-9360

U.S. Air Forces in Europe, Public Affairs Office, Unit 3050, Box 120; APO AE 09094-0120 (011) 49-6371-47: usafe.pai@ramstein.am.mil

National Guard Bureau, Public Affairs, 1411 Jefferson Davis Highway, Suite 11200, Arlington, VA 22202-3231, (703) 607-3680

U.S. Air Force Academy, Public Affairs Office, 2304 Cadet Drive, Suite 320, USAFA, CO 80840-5016 (719) 333-2990; www.usafa.af.mil

Secretary of the Air Force, 1670 Air Force Pentagon, Washington, DC 20330-1670

Thunderbirds Demonstration Squadron (USAFADS): 4445 Tyndall Ave., Nellis AFB, NV 89191; Fax: (702) 652-6367, email at usaf.thunderbirds@nellis.af.mil

The United States Air Force Band, 201 McChord St., Bolling AFB DC 20032-0202

United States Air Force Academy Band, 520 Otis St., Peterson AFB CO 80914-1620

United States Air Force Band of Liberty, 25 Chennault St., Hanscom AFB MA 01731-1718

Air Force Recruiting: www.airforce.com

USAF History Support Office: www.airforcehistory.hg.af.mil

National Museum of the United States Air Force: www.wpafb.af.mil/museum/

U.S. military air bases: org: www.globalsecurity.org/military/facility/afb.htm

The Air Force. By James P. McCarthy and Drue L. DeBerry. 2002. Barnes and Noble Books: NY.

COAST GUARD

U.S. Coast Guard Web site: www.uscg.mil

Coast Guard Academy: U.S. Coast Guard Academy, 31 Mohegan Avenue, New London, CT 06320-8103, (860) 444-8444: www.uscga.edu

U.S. Coast Guard Semper Paratus Web site: www.uscg.mil/sounds/sempara.html

The Coast Guard. Edited by Tom Beard, Jose Hanson, and Paul C. Scotti. 2004. Hugh Lauter Levin Associates, Inc.: Hong Kong. 367 pp.

SLANG, TERMS, ACRONYMS

Dictionary of Military Defense Contractor and Troop Slang Acronyms. By Philip C. Gutzman. 1990. ABC-Clio, Inc.

A Dictionary of Military Slang. By Adrian Gilbert. 1992. Arrow Books: NY.

Dictionary of Military Terms (revised ed.). Joint Chiefs of Staff, US Department of Defense. 1999. Stackpole Books.

A Dictionary of the Modern United States Military: Over 15,000 Weapons, Agencies, Acronyms, Slang, Installations, Medical Terms and Other Lexical Units of Warfare. By Stephan F. Tomajczyk. 1996. McFarland & Company.

Eh, What's That You Said: Jargon of the Sea. By Don Marshall and Johna Marshall. 1998. Binford & Mort Publishing.

Military Jargon. By P. T. James, 1985. Beau Lac Publishers.

A Modern Military Dictionary: Ten Thousand Technical and Slang Terms of Military Usage (2nd ed.). By Max Bruce Garber. 1975. Gale Research Co.

Swear Like a Trooper: A Dictionary of Military Terms & Phrases. By William L. Priest. 2000. Howell Press Inc.

Swinging the Lead and Spiking His Gun: Military Expressions and Their Origins. By Anonymous. 2002. Castle Books.

An Unabridged, Unofficial Dictionary for Marines. Edited by Glenn B. Knight, Veteran Sergeant of Marines, Retired Air Force Master Sergeant. 4mermarine.com/USMC/dictionary.html

War Slang: American Fighting Words and Phrases Since the Civil War (2nd ed.). By Paul Dickson. 2003. Brassey's Inc.

War Slang: American Fighting Words and Phrases from the Civil War to the Gulf War. By Paul Dickson. 1995. Pocket Books.

Air Forces Customs and Courtesies: www.milterms.com/letter

Rod Powers, Web site: www.usmilitary.about.com/

PROTOCOL

The Army Officer's Guide, 43rd ed. By Lt. Col. Lawrence P. Crocker. 1985. Stackpole Books: Harrisburg, PA. 565 pp.

The American Legion Web site: www.legion.org

Veterans of Foreign Wars (VFW) Web site: www.vfw.org/

SPECIAL OPERATIONS FORCES

Delta Force: www.specialoperations.com/Army/Delta_Force/default.html

Special Operations.com: www.specialoperations.com/Army/Delta_Force/unit_profile.htm

Biological weapons (table): www.cnn.com/SPECIALS/1998/iraq/9802/weapons.effects/

Rangers: www.specialoperations.com/Army/Rangers/History.htm

Ultimate Special Forces. By Hugh McManners, 2003. DK Books: NY.

Special Operations.com: www.specialoperations.com/usspecops.html

EQUIPMENT

Any of the *Jane's Weaponry Books.* Jane's Publishing Co. Inc.: NY.

Attack and Interceptor Jets: 300 of the World's Greatest Aircraft. By Michael Sharpe. 1999. Friedman/Fairfax Publisher/Amber Books: London.

The Encyclopedia of U.S. Military Aircraft. By Martin W. Bowman. 1980. Bison Books, Ltd.: London.

Flying American Combat Aircraft: The Cold War. Edited by Robin Higham. 2005. Stackpole Books: Mechanicsburg, PA.

The Illustrated Directory of Modern American Weapons. Edited by David Miller. 2002. MBI Publishing Co: St. Paul, MN.

The Illustrated Encyclopedia of the World's Rockets and Missiles. By Bill Gunston. 1979. Leisure Books: London.

Military Small Arms of the 20th Century, 6th ed. By Ian V. Hogg and John Weeks. 1991. DBI Books Inc: Northbrook, IL.

Modern Military Aircraft Anatomy, Technical Drawings of 118 Aircraft 1945 to the Present Day. Edited by Paul Eden and Soph Moeng. 2002. Metro Books: NY.

Small Arms from the Civil War to the Present Day. By Martin J. Doughtery. 2005. Barnes & Noble Books: NY.

Submarines, War Beneath the Waves From 1776 to the Present Day. By Robert Hutchinson. 2005. Collins/Harper Collins Publishers: NY.

Twentieth-Century Artillery: 300 of the World's Greatest Artillery Pieces. By Ian Hogg. 2000. Friedman/Fairfax Publisher/Amber Books: London.

U.S. Military Vehicles. Field Guide. WWII–Present. By David Doyle. 2005. KP Books: Iola, WI.

Weapons, An International Encyclopedia from 5000 B.C. to 2000 A.D. Diagram Group. 1991. St. Martin's Press: NY.

GENEVA CONVENTIONS

The International Committee of the Red Cross: www.icrc.org (Full texts of the Geneva Conventions are posted, as well as signatory nations.)

Journalist's Guide to the Geneva Conventions. By Maria Trombly. 2000. Society of Professional Journalists: Indianapolis.

Summary of the Geneva Conventions. By Society of Professional Journalists. www.genevaconventions.org

International Journalism Committee page at the Society of Professional Journalists: www.spj.org

Human Rights Watch Web site: www.hrw.org

Doctors Without Borders (Medicins Sans Frontieres): www.msf.org

MILITARY ACADEMIES

See each branch for contact information for each academy.

MEDALS

Army Awards and Decorations Office, U.S. Total Army Personnel Command, ATTN: TAPC-PDA, 200 Stoval Street, Alexandria, VA 22332-0400, 703-325-8700. www.perscomonline.army.mil/tagd/awards/index.htm

Navy Awards and Special Projects, Office the Chief of Naval Operations, Pentagon, Room 4D453, Washington, DC 20350, 202-685-1763. awards.navy.mil/

Air Force Awards and Decorations Office, HQ Air Force Personnel Center, ATTN: DPPRA500 C Street, West, Suite 12, Randolph AFB, TX 78150-4714, 210-652-5880. www.afpc.randolph.af.mil/awards/

Marine Corps Awards and Decorations Office, Commandant, Marine Corps Medal, Claredon Square Building, CODE MHM-1, Arlington, VA 22214 , 703-784-9340. kuwait.manpower.usmc.mil/manpower/mm/mmma/awards.nsf

Coast Guard, Bureau of Naval Personnel, Liaison Office, Room 5409, 9700 Page Avenue, St. Louis, MO 63132-5100

Lost/Found Medals: Found items should be mailed along with a letter identifying the finder and the location where the item was found to the following address: The Secretary of Defense, Room 3E880, The Pentagon, Washington, DC 20301.

Congressional Medal of Honor Society Web site: www.cmohs.org/

UNIFORM CODE OF MILITARY JUSTICE

Uniform Code of Military Justice: www4.law.cornell.edu/uscode/10/stApIIch47.html

Manual for Courts-Martial: www.jag.navy.mil/documents/mcm2000.pdf

AMERICAN LEGION

The American Legion: www.legion.org

National Headquarters Indianapolis Office, 700 North Pennsylvania St., P.O. Box 1055, Indianapolis, IN 46206, (317) 630-1200, Fax: (317) 630-1223.

National Headquarters Washington Office, 1608 K Street, N.W., Washington, D.C. 20006; (202) 861-2700, Fax: (202) 861-2728.

Member Services Group (Member Benefits, Prescription Program, Annuity and Insurance programs, Financial Options) (317) 860-3013.

Public Relations (Press Releases, Media Advisories, Speeches, Editorials) (317) 630-1253 .

Family Support Network, (800) 504-4098.

Americanism, Children & Youth, (Baseball, Flag Education, Boys Nation, Boys State, Scholarships, Scouting, Jr. Shooting Sports, Oratorical Contest, Children's Welfare Foundation) (317) 630-1202.

Library, (Finding/locating people, Medals, History) (317) 630-1366.

Veterans Affairs and Rehabilitation, (Help with Claims and Benefits, Health Issues, Veterans Cemeteries) (202) 861-2700.

American Legion Baseball: www.baseball.legion.org/

VETERANS OF FOREIGN WARS (VFW)

Veterans of Foreign Wars (VFW) Web site: www.vfw.org/

Military Assistance Program (MAP): (816) 756-3390, ext. 211, Fax: (816) 968-1149 map@vfw.org

To order VFW's booklet **"Ten Short Flag Stories,"** send a self-addressed stamped envelope to the Citizenship Education Department, Veterans of Foreign Wars, 406 West 34th Street, Kansas City, MO, 64111.

VFW Tactical Assessment Center: A twenty-four-hour help line for veterans with questions or concerns about VA entitlements. (800) 839-1899.

UNITED SERVICE ORGANIZATION (USO)

USO World Headquarters, 2111 Wilson Boulevard, Suite 1200, Arlington, VA 22201: www.uso.org/

DEPARTMENT OF DEFENSE CURRENT CONTACT INFO

OFFICE OF THE SECRETARY OF DEFENSE:

Donald H. Rumsfeld, Secretary of Defense, 1000 Defense Pentagon, Washington, DC 20301-1000

Gordon R. England, Acting Deputy Secretary of Defense, 1010 Defense Pentagon, Washington, DC 20301-1010

Kenneth J. Krieg, Under Secretary of Defense, (Acquisition, Technology and Logistics), 3010 Defense Pentagon, Washington, DC 20301-3010

David S. C. Chu, Under Secretary of Defense , (Personnel and Readiness), 4000 Defense Pentagon, Washington, DC 20301-4000

Eric S. Edelman, Under Secretary of Defense, (Policy), 2000 Defense Pentagon, Washington, DC 20301-2000

Tina Jonas, Under Secretary of Defense, (Comptroller), 1100 Defense Pentagon, Washington, DC 20301-1100

The Chairman and Vice Chairman of the Joint Chiefs of Staff

Chairman of the Joint Chiefs of Staff, 9999 Joint Staff Pentagon, Washington, DC 20318-9999

Vice Chairman of the Joint Chiefs of Staff, 9999 Joint Staff Pentagon, Washington, DC 20318-9999

THE CHIEFS OF STAFF

Army Chief of Staff, 200 Army Pentagon, Washington, DC 20310-0200

Chief of Naval Operations, 2000 Navy Pentagon, Washington, DC 20350-2000

Air Force Chief of Staff, 1670 Air Force Pentagon, Washington, DC 20330-1670

Commandant of the Marine Corps, Headquarters USMC, 2 Navy Annex (CMC), Washington, DC 20380-1775

APPENDIX B

Rank, Pay Grades, and Insignia of the U.S. Military Branches

ARMY			
COMMISSIONED OFFICERS	**ABBR**	**PAY**	**INSIGNIA**
General of the Army (five star)	GOA	wartime only	
General (four star), Army Chief of Staff	GEN	O-10	
General (three star), Army Chief of Staff	LTG	O-9	
Major General (two star)	MG	O-8	
Brigadier General (one star)	BG	O-7	
Colonel	COL	O-6	
Lieutenant Colonel	LTC	O-5	silver
Major	MAJ	O-4	gold
Captain	CPT	O-3	silver

First Lieutenant	1LT	O-2	silver
Second Lieutenant	2LT	O-1	gold
WARRANT OFFICER			
Chief Warrant Officer 5	CW5	W-5	
Chief Warrant Officer 4	CW4	W-4	
Chief Warrant Officer 3	CW3	W-3	
Chief Warrant Officer 2	CW2	W-2	
Warrant Officer 1	WO1	W-1	
ENLISTED			
Sergeant Major of the Army	SMA	E-9	
Commander Sergeant Major	CSM	E-9	
Sergeant Major	SGM	E-9	
First Sergeant	1SG	E-8	
Master Sergeant	MSG	E-8	
Sergeant First Class	SFC	E-7	

Staff Sergeant	SSG	E-6	
Sergeant	SGT	E-5	
Corporal	CPL	E-4	
Specialist	SPC	E-4	
Private First Class	PFC	E-3	
Private	PV2	E-2	
Private	PVT	E-1	none

NAVY			
COMMISSIONED OFFICERS	**ABBR**	**PAY**	**INSIGNIA**
Fleet Admiral (five star)	FADM	wartime only	
Admiral (four star), Chief of Naval Operations	ADM	O-10	★★★★
Vice Admiral (three star)	VADM	O-9	★★★
Rear Admiral (Upper Half) (two star)	RADM (UH)	O-8	★★
Rear Admiral (Lower Half) (one star)	RADM (LH)	O-7	★
Captain	CAPT	O-6	

Commander	CDR	O-5	silver
Lieutenant Commander	LCDR	O-4	gold
Lieutenant	LT	O-3	silver
Lieutenant Junior Grade	LTJG	O-2	silver
Ensign	ENS	O-1	gold
WARRANT OFFICER			
Chief Warrant Officer 5	CWO5	W-5	
Chief Warrant Officer 4	CWO4	W-4	
Chief Warrant Officer 3	CWO3	W-3	
Chief Warrant Officer 2	CWO2	W-2	
Warrant Officer 1 (discontinued)	WO1	W-1	
ENLISTED			
Master Chief Petty Officer of the Navy	MCPON	E-9	
Fleet/Command Master Chief Petty Officer	CMCPO	E-9	
Master Chief Petty Officer	MCPO	E-9	

Senior Chief Petty Officer	SCPO	E-8	
Chief Petty Officer	CPO	E-7	
Petty Officer First Class	PO1	E-6	
Petty Officer Second Class	PO2	E-5	
Petty Officer Third Class	PO3	E-4	
Seaman	SN	E-3	
Seaman Apprentice	SA	E-2	
Seaman Recruit	SR	E-1	

MARINES			
COMMISSIONED OFFICERS	ABBR	PAY	INSIGNIA
General (four star), Commandant of the Marine Corps	Gen.	O-10	★★★★
Lieutenant General (three star)	Lt. Gen.	O-9	★★★
Major General (two star)	Maj. Gen.	O-8	★★
Brigadier General (one star)	Brig. Gen.	O-7	★
Colonel	Col.	O-6	

Lieutenant Colonel	Lt. Col.	O-5	silver
Major	Maj.	O-4	gold
Captain	Capt.	O-3	silver
First Lieutenant	1st Lt.	O-2	silver
Second Lieutenant	2nd Lt.	O-1	gold
WARRANT OFFICER			
Chief Warrant Officer	CWO5	W-5	
Chief Warrant Officer 4	CWO4	W-4	
Chief Warrant Officer 3	CWO3	W-3	
Chief Warrant Officer 2	CWO2	W-2	
Warrant Officer 1	WO1	W-1	
ENLISTED			
Sergeant Major of the Marine Corps	SgtMajMC	E-9	
Sergeant Major	SgtMaj	E-9	
Master Gunnery Sergeant	MGySgt	E-9	
First Sergeant	1stSgt	E-8	

Master Sergeant	MSgt	E-8	
Gunnery Sergeant	GySgt	E-7	
Staff Sergeant	SSgt	E-6	
Sergeant	Sgt	E-5	
Corporal	Cpl	E-4	
Lance Corporal	LCpl	E-3	
Private First Class	PFC	E-2	
Private	PVT	E-1	none

AIR FORCE			
COMMISSIONED OFFICERS	ABBR	PAY	INSIGNIA
General of the Air Force (five star)	GOAF	wartime only	
General (four star), Air Force Chief of Staff	Gen.	O-10	★★★★
Lieutenant General (three star)	Lt. Gen.	O-9	★★★
Major General (two star)	Maj. Gen.	O-8	★★
Brigadier General (one star)	Brig. Gen.	O-7	★
Colonel	Col.	O-6	

Lieutenant Colonel	Lt. Col.	O-5	silver
Major	Maj.	O-4	gold
Captain	Capt.	O-3	silver
First Lieutenant	1st Lt.	O-2	silver
Second Lieutenant	2nd Lt.	O-1	gold
ENLISTED			
Chief Master Sergeant of the Air Force	CMSAF	E-9	
Command Chief Master Sergeant	CCM	E-9	
First Sergeant	1stSgt	E-9	
Chief Master Sergeant	CMSgt	E-9	
First Sergeant	1stSgtT	E-8	
Senior Master Sergeant	SMSgt	E-8	
First Sergeant	1stSgt	E-7	
Master Sergeant	MSgt	E-7	
Technical Sergeant	TSgt	E-6	
Staff Sergeant	SSgt	E-5	

Senior Airman	SrA	E-4	
Airman First Class	A1C	E-3	
Airman Basic	Amn	E-2	
Airman Basic	AB	E-1	none

COAST GUARD			
COMMISSIONED OFFICERS	**ABBR**	**PAY**	**INSIGNIA**
Admiral (four star), Commandant of the Coast Guard	ADM	0-10	★★★★
Vice Admiral (three star)	VADM	0-9	★★★
Rear Admiral (Upper Half) (two star)	RADM (UH)	0-8	★★
Rear Admiral (Lower Half) (one star)	RADM (LH)	0-7	★
Captain	CAPT	0-6	
Commander	CDR	0-5	silver
Lieutenant Commander	LCDR	0-4	gold
Lieutenant	LT	0-3	silver
Lieutenant (Junior Grade)	LTJG	0-2	silver
Ensign	ENS	0-1	gold

WARRANT OFFICER			
Chief Warrant Officer 4	CWO4	W-4	
Chief Warrant Officer 3	CWO3	W-3	
Chief Warrant Officer 2	CWO2	W-2	
ENLISTED			
Master Chief Petty Officer of the Coast Guard	MCPOCG	E-9	
Fleet/Command Master Chief Petty Officer	CMCPO	E-9	
Master Chief Petty Officer	MCPO	E-9	
Senior Chief Petty Officer	SPCO	E-8	
Chief Petty Officer	CPO	E-7	
Petty Officer First Class	PO1	E-6	
Petty Officer Second Class	PO2	E-5	
Petty Officer Third Class	PO3	E-4	
Airman, Fireman, or Seaman	SN	E-3	
Airman, Fireman, or Seaman Apprentice	SA	E-2	
Airman, Fireman, or Seaman Recruit	SR	E-1	none

★
INDEX

A

Acronyms/abbreviations, U.S. military, 249-257

Advanced Individual Training, 54-56

Afghanistan War, 29, 45, 93, 112, 190

African Americans in U.S. military, 196, 199, 264

See also Buffalo Soldiers; Segregation, U.S. military; Tuskegee Airmen

Agent Orange, 189, 203, 209

Air Combat Command, 113-114, 125, 126

Air Education and Training Command, 114-115, 125

Air Force, U.S.

commissioned officers, 7, 8, 117, 128, 358-359

demonstration teams, 124-126

enlisted personnel, 117, 128, 359-360

history, 111-112, 202

insignias, 358-360

Medal of Honor recipients, 171

oath, 119

organization, 112-117

pay grades, 6, 358-360

personnel statistics, 112, 128

rank, 117, 358-360

responsibilities, 111

slang/expressions, 260, 262, 268

training, 118-121

uniforms, 118

useful resources, 344-345

vision, 111

See also Air Force Academy, U.S.; Air Force Basic Military Training; Air Force Basic Officer Training; Air Force Fighter Weapons School; Air Force Reserve; Air Force units; Air National Guard; Pacific Air Forces; Thunderbirds; Tuskegee Airmen; United States Air Forces in Europe; and specific Air Force commands

Air Force Academy, U.S., 20, 112, 121-124

academic program, 122

admissions, 123

athletics, 122-123

band, 126

cadet life, 124

character development, 121

Honor Oath, 121

military development, 122

number of cadets, 121

values, 121

Air Force Band, U.S., 126

Air Force Basic Military Training, 118-119

Air Force Basic Officer Training, 119

Air Force commands, major, 113-117

Air Force Cross, 172

Air Force Drum and Bugle Corps, 126

Air Force Fighter Weapons School, 120-121

Air Force Intelligence Service, 112

Air Force Matériel Command, 115

Air Force Reserve, 21, 112, 113, 114, 116, 126, 128

Air Force Reserve Command, 116

Army III Corps, 35, 37

Army Veterinary Corps, 42

Army warfighting elements, 34-36

Atlantic Fleet (Second Fleet), 64-65, 94

B

Bad Conduct Discharge, 167, 168

Ball, Bromley, 142

Basic Combat Training, 47-54

Blue Angels, 85-86

Boot Camp. *See basic training of specific U.S. military branches*

Bosnia War, 35, 93, 112, 160

Boswell, Bob, 127

Bronze Star, 173, 175

Buffalo Soldiers, 196

C

C-rations, 203, 275

Carstens, Mark, 142

Celebrity/famous veterans
  Air Force, 128
  Army, 61
  Coast Guard, 143
  Marines, 110
  Navy, 88-89

Chief of Naval Operations, 64

Civil War, 27, 36, 63, 92, 131, 149, 170, 182, 193-194

Coast Guard, Commandant of, 134

Coast Guard, U.S.
  civilian arrest/detention powers, 132
  commissioned officers, 7, 8, 136, 137, 138, 144, 360
  enlisted personnel, 138, 144, 361
  history, 131-132

insignias, 360-361

joining, 138

Medal of Honor recipients, 171

missions, 129-131

mottos, 131

as naval operating force, 63, 64

pay grades, 6, 360-361

personnel statistics, 144

rate, 136, 360-361

responsibilities, 129

slang/expressions, 258-260, 262, 264, 266-267, 269, 271, 273, 274

training, 138

uniforms, 137

useful resources, 346

vessel designations, 135-136

vessel terminology changes, 134-135

warrant officers, 361

See also Coast Guard Academy; Coast Guard Auxiliary; Coast Guard Basic Training; Coast Guard Chief Petty Officer Academy; Coast Guard districts; Coast Guard Officer Candidate School; Coast Guard organization; Coast Guard Reserve; Watercraft, military

Coast Guard Academy, U.S., 137, 138-142
  academic program, 139
  admission, 139
  athletics, 140
  cadet life, 140-142
  mission, 138
  organization by company, 140
  philosophy, 139
  physical program, 139
  values, 138-139

Coast Guard Auxiliary, 131, 137, 144

Coast Guard Basic Training, 138